Ronald Reagan and the 1980s

Perceptions, Policies, Legacies

Edited by

Cheryl Hudson
and
Gareth Davies

palgrave
macmillan

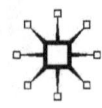

RONALD REAGAN AND THE 1980s
Copyright © Cheryl Hudson and Gareth Davies, 2008.

All rights reserved.

First published in 2008 by
PALGRAVE MACMILLAN®
in the United States—a division of St. Martin's Press LLC,
175 Fifth Avenue, New York, NY 10010.

Where this book is distributed in the UK, Europe and the rest of the world, this is by Palgrave Macmillan, a division of Macmillan Publishers Limited, registered in England, company number 785998, of Houndmills, Basingstoke, Hampshire RG21 6XS.

Palgrave Macmillan is the global academic imprint of the above companies and has companies and representatives throughout the world.

Palgrave® and Macmillan® are registered trademarks in the United States, the United Kingdom, Europe and other countries.

ISBN 978-1-349-37147-1   ISBN 978-0-230-61619-6 (eBook)
DOI 10.1057/9780230616196

Library of Congress Cataloging-in-Publication Data

Ronald Reagan and the 1980s : perceptions, policies, legacies / Cheryl Hudson and Gareth Davies [editors].
    p. cm.
Includes bibliographical references and index.

  1. Reagan, Ronald. 2. Reagan, Ronald—Political and social views.
3. Reagan, Ronald—Influence. 4. Presidents—United States—Biography.
5. United States—Politics and government—1981–1989. 6. Nineteen eighties. I. Hudson, Cheryl. II. Davies, Gareth Bryn.

E877.R6625 2008   [B]
973.927092—dc22   2008016176

A catalogue record of the book is available from the British Library.

Design by Newgen Imaging Systems (P) Ltd., Chennai, India.

First edition: November 2008

10 9 8 7 6 5 4 3 2 1

STUDIES OF THE AMERICAS
edited by
James Dunkerley
Institute for the Study of the Americas
University of London
School of Advanced Study

Titles in this series are multidisciplinary studies of aspects of the societies of the hemisphere, particularly in the areas of politics, economics, history, anthropology, sociology, and the environment. The series covers a comparative perspective across the Americas, including Canada and the Caribbean as well as the United States and Latin America.

Titles in this series published by Palgrave Macmillan:

Cuba's Military 1990–2005: Revolutionary Soldiers during Counter-Revolutionary Times
  By Hal Klepak

The Judicialization of Politics in Latin America
  Edited by Rachel Sieder, Line Schjolden, and Alan Angell

Latin America: A New Interpretation
  By Laurence Whitehead

Appropriation as Practice: Art and Identity in Argentina
  By Arnd Schneider

America and Enlightenment Constitutionalism
  Edited by Gary L. McDowell and Johnathan O'Neill

Vargas and Brazil: New Perspectives
  Edited by Jens R. Hentschke

When Was Latin America Modern?
  Edited by Nicola Miller and Stephen Hart

Debating Cuban Exceptionalism
  Edited by Laurence Whitehead and Bert Hoffman

Caribbean Land and Development Revisited
  Edited by Jean Besson and Janet Momsen

Cultures of the Lusophone Black Atlantic
  Edited by Nancy Naro, Roger Sansi-Roca and David Treece

Democratization, Development, and Legality: Chile, 1831–1973
  By Julio Faundez

The Hispanic World and American Intellectual Life, 1820–1880
  By Iván Jaksić

The Role of Mexico's Plural in Latin American Literary and Political Culture: From Tlatelolco to the "Philanthropic Ogre"
  By John King

Faith and Impiety in Revolutionary Mexico
   Edited by Matthew Butler

Reinventing Modernity in Latin America: Intellectuals Imagine the Future, 1900–1930
   By Nicola Miller

The Republican Party and Immigration Politics: From Proposition 187 to George W. Bush
   By Andrew Wroe

The Political Economy of Hemispheric Integration: Responding to Globalization in the Americas
   Edited by Kenneth C. Shadlen and Diego Sánchez-Ancochea

Ronald Reagan and the 1980s: Perceptions, Policies, Legacies
   Edited by Cheryl Hudson and Gareth Davies

Base Colonies in the Western Hemisphere, 1940–1967
   By Steven High

The Federal Nation: Perspectives on American Federalism
   Edited by Iwan W. Morgan and Philip J. Davies

Wellbeing and Development in Peru: Global and Local Views Confronted
   Edited by James Copestake

Beyond Neoliberalism in Latin America?: Societies and Politics at the Crossroads
   Edited by John Burdick, Philip Oxhorn, and Kenneth M. Roberts

Governance after Neoliberalism in Latin America
   Edited by Jean Grugel and Pia Riggirozzi

Fiction and Documentary Filmmaking in Latin America: Visual Synergies
   Edited by Miriam Haddu and Joanna Page

Youth Violence in Latin America: Gangs and Juvenile Justice in Perspective
   By Gareth A. Jones and Dennis Rodgers

Cuban Medical Internationalism: Origins, Evolution and Goals
   John Kirk and Michael Erisman

Law and Politics in Latin America: The Difficult Path towards Limited Government and Rights-Based Citizenship
   By Pilar Domingo

For Alan and Liz
—Cheryl Hudson and Gareth Davies

Contents

Acknowledgments ix

List of Contributors xi

Introduction: Reagan and the 1980s 1
Cheryl Hudson and Gareth Davies

Part I Perceptions

1 Ronald Reagan: Communicating the America Within 19
   Dan Rather

2 Only an Actor: Memories of a Reagan Biopic 29
   Godfrey Hodgson

3 "Just Say No": Drug Abuse Policy in the Reagan Administration 41
   Peter G. Bourne

4 Ronald Reagan and the End of the Cold War 57
   Jack F. Matlock, Jr.

Part II Politics and Policies

5 Reagan, Nuclear Weapons, and the End of the Cold War 81
   Simon Head

6 Reaganomics and its Legacy 101
   Iwan Morgan

7 African American Protest during the Reagan Years: Forging New Agendas, Defending Old Victories 119
   Stephen Tuck

8 Reagan's Religious Right: The Unlikely Alliance between Southern Evangelicals and a California Conservative 135
   Daniel K. Williams

9   Ronald Reagan and the Republican Party: Responses
    to Realignment   151
    Robert Mason

Part III   Legacies

10 The Baptist and the Messiah: Ronald Reagan and
    Margaret Thatcher   175
    Dominic Sandbrook

11 Transforming the Presidency: The Administration
    of Ronald Reagan   191
    Joel D. Aberbach

12 The Road to Mount Rushmore: The Conservative
    Commemoration Crusade for Ronald Reagan   209
    Niels Bjerre-Poulsen

13 Toward a Historiography of Reagan and the 1980s:
    Why Have We Done Such A Lousy Job?   229
    Gil Troy

Epilogue: Ronald Reagan and the Historians   249
M.J. Heale

Index   263

Acknowledgments

The progenitor for this volume is Hugh Davis Graham, who stimulated an interest in the public policy of the twentieth century in general, and the Reagan administration in particular for both of us, in different ways. We remember him fondly.

We would like to thank the director Paul Giles, the staff, and the benefactors of the Rothermere American Institute for making this book possible. Special thanks to Catherine Morley for originating the idea of a conference on Ronald Reagan and for all of her imaginative inputs. Thanks too to Andrea Beighton, Laura Lauer, and Ruth Parr for helping to execute it so successfully. Ruth's publishing expertise and her enthusiasm for this project encouraged us to make it happen.

The librarians at the Vere Harmsworth Library have been extraordinarily helpful. James T. Patterson's contribution to the conference from which this volume springs was enormous; his support is greatly appreciated by us. We are grateful to Iwan Morgan and James Dunkerley for their commitment to this volume from the outset. Everyone at Palgrave Macmillan has been supportive and extremely patient. We would especially like to thank Joanna Mericle and Luba Ostashevsky.

We owe a great debt to Michael Heale for all the time and energy he invested in the project and for access to his boundless knowledge of American political history.

Contributors

Joel D. Aberbach is Distinguished Professor of political science and public policy and director of the Center for American Politics and Public Policy at the University of California, Los Angeles. His latest book *Institutions of American Democracy: The Executive Branch* (Oxford University Press, 2005), coedited with Mark A. Peterson, won the 2006 Neustadt Award for the best reference work on the American presidency. He was elected a fellow of the National Academy of Public Administration in 2005. In 2006–2007 he was the John G. Winant visiting professor of American government at the University of Oxford and a fellow of Balliol College.

Niels Bjerre-Poulsen is an associate professor of American history and director of the Center for the Study of the Americas, Copenhagen Business School, Denmark. He has published widely in both Danish and English and his recent works include *Right Face: Organizing the Conservative Movement, 1945–65* (Museum Tusculanum Press, 2002) and *Bush's Amerika* (People's Press, 2006).

Peter G. Bourne is visiting scholar at Green College, Oxford University, and vice chancellor emeritus of St. George's University in Grenada, West Indies. Serving as special assistant to the president for health issues in Carter's White House, he simultaneously held the job of director of the Office of Drug Abuse Policy (ODAP), responsible for coordinating the law enforcement, treatment, and foreign policy aspects of America's drug policy. He has published extensively, including two political biographies—*Fidel: A Biography of Fidel Castro* (Dodd, Mead, 1986) and *Jimmy Carter: A Comprehensive Biography from Plains to Post Presidency* (Simon and Schuster/Scribner, 1996). His official website is www.petergbourne.co.uk.

Gareth Davies is a university lecturer in American history at St. Anne's College, Oxford University. He is the author of *From Opportunity to Entitlement: The Transformation and Decline of Great Society Liberalism* (Kansas, 1996), which won the Ellis Hawley Prize, and of *See Government Grow: Education Politics from Johnson to Reagan* (Kansas, 2007).

Simon Head is an associate fellow at the Rothermere American Institute, University of Oxford. He has been a contributor to the *New York Review of*

Books since 1973. His most recent book is *The New Ruthless Economy: Work and Power in the Digital Age* (Oxford, 2005).

M.J. Heale is emeritus professor of American History at Lancaster University and associate fellow of the Rothermere American Institute, University of Oxford. Among his many publications are *Twentieth-Century America: Politics and Power in the United States, 1900–2000* (Arnold, 2004); The *Sixties in America: History, Politics and Protest* (Edinburgh, 2001); and *McCarthy's Americans: Red Scare Politics in State and Nation, 1935–1965* (Macmillan, 1998).

Godfrey Hodgson is an associate fellow of the Rothermere American Institute and former director of the Reuter's Foundation Programme at Oxford University. Previously, he was the *Observer*'s correspondent in the United States, insight editor at the *Sunday Times*, presenter of Channel Four News, and foreign editor of the *Independent*. Among his books are *More Equal Than Others: America from Nixon to the New Century* (Princeton, 2004); *The World Turned Right Side Up: A History of the Conservative Ascendancy in America* (Houghton Mifflin, 1996); *The Gentleman from New York: Senator Daniel Patrick Moynihan* (Houghton Mifflin, 2000); and *America in Our Time* (Knopf, 1978).

Cheryl Hudson is a doctoral candidate in history at Vanderbilt University and an associate fellow at the Rothermere American Institute, University of Oxford. As the assistant director of academic programmes at the RAI, she coordinated the 2005 conference *Ronald Reagan and the 1980s*.

Robert Mason is a senior lecturer in history at the University of Edinburgh and the author of *Richard Nixon and the Quest for a New Majority* (University of North Carolina Press, 2004). He is currently working on a book about the history of the Republican Party during the twentieth century.

Jack F. Matlock, Jr. is former George F. Kennan professor at the Institute for Advanced Study in Princeton, New Jersey. He served as ambassador to the Soviet Union from 1987 to 1991, special assistant to the president for national security affairs and senior director for European and Soviet affairs on the National Security Council staff from 1983 to 1986, and ambassador to Czechoslovakia from 1981 to 1983. He is the author of numerous articles and books on Russian literature and history and U.S.–Russian relations, including *Autopsy on an Empire: The American Ambassador's Account of the Collapse of the Soviet Union* (Random House, 1995). His latest book is *Reagan and Gorbachev: How the Cold War Ended* (Random House, 2004).

Iwan Morgan is professor of U.S. studies and deputy director of the Institute for the Study of the Americas, University of London. His publications include *Nixon* (Oxford, 2002); *Eisenhower versus "the Spenders": The Eisenhower Administration, the Democrats and the Budget, 1953–60* (St Martin's Press, 1990); and *Beyond the Liberal Consensus: A Political History of the United*

States since 1965 (St. Martin's Press, 1994). He is currently writing a book on presidents and the budget deficit from Jimmy Carter to George Bush Jr.

Dan Rather is anchor and managing editor of Dan Rather Reports on HDNet. His many publications include *The American Dream* (Harper, 2002); *The Camera Never Blinks* (William Morrow & Co., 1977); and *The Camera Never Blinks Twice* (William Morrow & Co., 1994).

Dominic Sandbrook is a member of the Oxford University history faculty and a columnist for the *London Evening Standard*. Formerly a lecturer in history at Sheffield University, he is a prolific writer and broadcaster. His books include a biography of *Senator Eugene McCarthy* (Knopf, 2004), two bestselling histories of Britain in the 1950s and 1960s, *Never Had It So Good* (Little, Brown, 2005) and *White Heat* (Little, Brown, 2006), and a forthcoming history of the United States in the 1970s, *Spirit of '76* (Knopf, 2009).

Gil Troy is professor of history at McGill University in Canada. He specializes in modern U.S. political history and is the author of *Leading from the Center: Why Moderates Make the Best Presidents* (Basic Books, 2008); *Hillary Rodham Clinton: Polarizing First Lady* (Kansas, 2006); *Morning in America: How Ronald Reagan Invented the 1980's* (Princeton, 2005); *Mr. and Mrs. President: From the Trumans to the Clintons* (Kansas, 2000); and *See How They Ran: The Changing Role of the Presidential Candidate* (Harvard, rev. ed. 1996).

Stephen Tuck is university lecturer in American history at Pembroke College, University of Oxford. He has published on American race relations, racial protest, and white supremacy from the Civil War to the present, including *Beyond Atlanta: The Struggle for Racial Equality in Georgia, 1940–1980* (Athens, 2003). He is currently writing an overview of the struggle for racial equality in the United States from emancipation to Hurricane Katrina.

Daniel K. Williams received his PhD from Brown University and is an assistant professor of history at the University of West Georgia. His published articles examine the history of American evangelicalism and the rise of the contemporary conservative movement. His book *Republican Faith: The Making of America's Christian Right* will be published by Oxford University Press in 2009.

Introduction

Reagan and the 1980s

Cheryl Hudson and Gareth Davies

Decades and presidencies provide convenient ways of making rough sense of American historical time, of dividing it into manageable chunks and imparting to each chunk a distinct character, and a particular role in the broader sweep of the nation's development. A number of twentieth-century decades lend themselves to *both* approaches: Warren Harding and Calvin Coolidge nicely embody some dominant images of the Roaring Twenties; Franklin Roosevelt's leadership and response to the Great Depression are a key theme of the 1930s; Dwight Eisenhower is as good a symbol as any for the Cold War Consensus of the 1950s; and John F. Kennedy and Lyndon Johnson aptly convey the restlessness and reform ferment of the 1960s.

At first glance, Ronald Reagan's 1980s are another such decade. For one thing, as Michael Heale observes in the present volume, Reagan emerges in the literature as an unusually commanding figure—perhaps the most dominant president since FDR—and can easily be presented as that rare creature, a world historical figure, in his case the man who with Mikhail Gorbachev presided over the ending of a Cold War that had been the elemental geopolitical fact of the past half-century. At home, too, some have been tempted to see in Reagan's confident, optimistic presence and leadership a handy symbol for, perhaps also a source of, a renewal of national purpose and self-belief during the 1980s. The 1970s, according to this version of events, was a decade of demoralization and diminished expectations, presided over by three failed presidents (Richard Nixon, Gerald Ford, and Jimmy Carter), and defined by such distressing episodes as Kent State, Watergate, the communist takeover of Vietnam, and the energy crisis, and by such broader themes as rising crime rates, deindustrialization, anger at the courts, deteriorating educational standards, and galloping inflation and interest rates. The 1980s, by contrast, yielded a "Reagan revolution," featuring the start of the second long boom of the post–World War II era; a resurgence in entrepreneurial energy; a revival in the nation's global standing and military preparedness; an end to confiscatory taxation; and a definitive end to the misguided social theories of the Great Society era.[1]

On the other hand, liberal and left-leaning commentators have frequently presented the 1980s much less triumphantly, associating them with a very different kind of turning point.[2] According to them, the decisive political shift to the right entailed slashing attacks on the welfare state; the replacement of détente with saber-rattling rhetoric and a massive arms build-up; the abandonment of efforts to promote racial integration in schools; massive increases in socioeconomic inequality; the advent of a casino economy organized around the guiding ethic that "greed is good"; and callous official disregard in the face of the AIDS and crack cocaine epidemics.

For all their stark differences, characterizations such as these have shared the sense that the 1980 election was a critical turning point in American political history, and that Reagan was an unusually consequential president. How do those claims look from an early-twenty-first-century vantage point? By some measures, Reagan rides higher in the saddle than ever. On his death in 2004, it was not just conservative partisans who eulogized his leadership—so too did his Democratic successor-but-one as president, Bill Clinton, even though he had campaigned hard against Reagan's legacy in 1992. Meanwhile, the nation's current affairs and recent history bookshelves creak with hagiographic assessments of that legacy from conservatives, while rival Republican candidates for the 2008 presidential nomination vied with one another to enwrap themselves in Reagan's magical aura. Recent academic books too have been much more admiring of the fortieth president than one would have anticipated at the end of his tenure, finding him a rather less doctrinaire conservative than has previously been thought, being impressed too by his raw political skill, and according him a significant role in bringing the Soviet Union to the negotiating table, and ending the Cold War.[3]

In some other respects, however, subsequent events have served to complicate the portrait of Reagan as a world historical figure. On the one hand, the idea of a lasting Reagan revolution seemed to be vindicated by the subsequent electoral performance of the Republican Party GOP. Starting with Reagan in 1980, it won five out of seven presidential elections, broken only by the tenure of Clinton, whose conservative-leaning policies on welfare and crime, and rhetorical declaration that "the era of big government is over," only seemed to confirm the length of Reagan's shadow. And in 1994, the Republicans regained control of Congress for the first time in four decades, and many legislators who were swept to power in the Gingrich Revolution identified much more strongly with Reagan than had most congressional conservatives *during* his tenure.[4]

On the other hand, government continued to grow, especially—incongruously enough—during the presidency of George W. Bush, the one time during the two post-Reagan decades when the party dominated both ends of Pennsylvania Avenue. Some of Bush 43's domestic accomplishments—the No Child Left Behind Act of 2002, the expansion of Medicare to include prescription drugs in 2004—were hard to square with the antistatist conservatism of Ronald Reagan, and his presidency featured growing talk from disgruntled commentators on the Right about the phenomenon of big government conservatism."[5]

These developments illustrated anew the severe obstacles that the American system of government poses to politicians who seek not just to talk about cutting big government, but actually to do it. In their 2000 book *Presidential Greatness*, political scientists Marc Landy and Sidney Milkis contended that Reagan—recognizing this fact—had not in fact tried very hard. If that had contributed to his *popularity* as president, then it simultaneously diminished his claim to *greatness*, which "founder[ed] on his lack of programmatic ambition." Early on in his first term, they acknowledge, he appeared to be developing "an alternative public philosophy on which to base a party alignment." Ultimately, though, "he failed to propound it when it was most politically necessary for him to do so—during his reelection drive. At the critical moment, he returned to the conservative mould of his Republican predecessors, contenting himself with stalling the further expansion of the administrative state without challenging its fundamental tenets."[6]

Despite his commitment to conservative causes, Reagan's record measured in public policy terms is surprisingly scant. In areas such as welfare, social security, environmental reform, taxation, and civil rights, a significant policy legacy is detectable but not of sufficient stature to justify the contemporary notion of a Reagan revolution. Whereas early academic and journalistic critiques have explained the limits of Reaganism with reference to his disengagement from detail or his extremism, it might more positively be attributed to his pragmatism, and to his unwillingness to wage the kind of acutely divisive partisan warfare that Richard Nixon had contemplated a decade or so earlier.[7] In any case, it is doubtful that a more full-blooded commitment to a conservative counterrevolution would have resulted in a more far-reaching policy legacy, given the strong forces of inertia in American politics, and the continuing popularity of what Landy and Milkis call "the New Deal principle—the administrative state in the service of programmatic rights."[8]

The idea of Reagan's election in 1980 being a fundamental turning point is complicated further when we consider the events and developments of the previous decade. In important respects, the seeds of the post-1983 boom were sown during the 1970s, which was the decade of the personal computer, the fax, cordless phones, of the magnetic resonance imaging scan (MRI) and the first "test tube baby," of color photocopiers, videocassettes, and pocket calculators. And while the rustbelt suffered, presenting a seemingly obvious contrast to the economic boom times of the mid-1980s, it should be noted that American manufacturing did not completely collapse during the 1970s—rather the United States held its 25 percent share of global output. "America remained number one in the world," James Patterson notes, "in the manufacture and sale of aircraft, industrial and agricultural chemicals, engines, turbines, and office computing machines, and number two in the fields of plastics, drugs, and various forms of electrical machinery." Meanwhile, parts of the South and West—the Sunbelt—were absolutely humming with life, booming as never before.[9]

Reinforcing the idea that a simple 1970s/1980s dichotomy is problematic, a number of the conservative trends that we associate with the later decade can be seen to have roots in the Carter years, including supply-side economics, the ending of détente and the start of a new arms build-up, the trend to deregulation, conservative electoral gains (the midterm elections of 1978 were the starting point, not 1980), and the shift of the Republican party to the right.

What is more, distinctions between the two decades might be blurred in the other direction—some commentators argue that there were important continuities between the Carter and Reagan years as the crisis-ridden political sensibilities of the 1970s persisted into Reagan's first term.[10] One study that locates *this* sort of continuity is Philip Jenkins's *Decade of Nightmares* (2006), which is concerned with neither the 1970s nor the 1980s, but rather with a period beginning in 1975 and ending in 1986. Whereas other scholars have thought about the question of a revival in national morale in relation to politics of the 1980s, Jenkins focuses primarily on broader societal and cultural developments. And far from associating this period with any revival, he associates it with a broad, deep-rooted moral panic, born of a continuing reaction against perceived societal decadence and rampant criminality.[11]

However the grand themes of decline and resurgence look from an early twenty-first-century vantage point, what remains clear and unarguable is that America *seemed* to be in a very bad way at the end of the 1970s, that the world in which Americans lived had in important respects become more troubled, less secure during the past few years, that the economic, political, and international environments were highly disturbed.

What then were the central elements of the sense of crisis that suffused the presidential election campaign of 1980? Two were especially grave: the economic condition of the nation, and the deteriorating international environment. In the year of Reagan's election, interest rates peaked at an all-time high of 21.5 percent, inflation was in double figures for a second straight year (the first time that this had happened since World War I), unemployment reached 7.6 percent, domestic car sales plummeted by a quarter, and so did new housing starts. During the second quarter of 1980, real GNP fell at an annualized rate of 9.9 percent.[12] The state of the economy was overwhelmingly the biggest issue of the election. Polled by Gallup in September, an astonishing 60 percent said that inflation was the single biggest issue, while 16 percent chose unemployment (the second-ranked issue).[13]

As for foreign affairs, the promise of détente (which had contributed handsomely to Richard Nixon's luster in 1972) was no more, with the Soviet invasion of Afghanistan the most unsettling symbol of its collapse; the energy crises of 1973 and 1979 had provided frightening illustrations of national dependency on oil from an unstable Middle East; and the most agonizing product of that region's instability, the Iranian hostage crisis, suggested more starkly than ever that the United States had become the "pitiful, helpless giant" that Nixon had warned Americans about a decade earlier, unable to secure her will in the face of communist aggression, Islamic fundamentalism, or oil cartels.[14] Nothing in the recent literature that blurs the distinctions between the 1970s and 1980s has remotely disturbed the palpable sense of crisis, agony even, that this confluence of events created during the years of Jimmy Carter's desperately unhappy presidency.

A leitmotiv running through this litany of disaster was governmental failure. Having reached a high-point in 1964, popular faith in the integrity of politicians and in their capacity to solve public policy problems had collapsed in an almost unbroken line. The proportion of Americans who believed that they could "trust the government in Washington to do what is right" had plummeted during this period from 76 to 25 percent.[15] That development was rooted in part in the intrinsic complexity of the exogenous crises enumerated earlier, in further part in the particular characteristics of the men who had occupied the White House since the assassination of John F. Kennedy. Lyndon Johnson, Richard Nixon, Gerald Ford, and Jimmy Carter were all, in their way, talented men: Johnson had an unparalleled ability to get Congress to follow his will; Nixon had a rare capacity to think outside of the box, to wrestle with big ideas and grasp the big picture; Ford and Carter both exuded much-needed integrity and decency following Watergate. But their most obvious shared attribute was an almost complete inability to convey the kind of optimistic, can-do, larger-than-life persona, the infectious sense that America and its people had a bigger, better future, that had contributed so powerfully to the political success of Franklin Roosevelt during the dark days of the Depression.

No president since Hoover had sought reelection in such adverse circumstances as Carter did in 1980, and it is no surprise that his challenger, Reagan, should have won a commanding victory: 51 percent of the vote, compared to 41 percent for Carter, and 6 percent for John Anderson (a moderate Republican congressman from Illinois who stood as in independent). In the electoral college, meanwhile, Reagan's margin was greater still: he won by 489 votes to 49, outpolling Carter in all but six states.[16] Much more remarkable is the fact that the race had seemed to be neck-and-neck for much of the campaign, including during its final stages. According to Gallup's election-eve poll, Reagan led Carter by only 4 percent. Meanwhile, *Time* magazine had *Carter* ahead by 1.[17] All this despite the fact that Carter remained exceptionally unpopular throughout the campaign, with his approval rating going as low as 21 percent at one stage (half Lyndon Johnson's worst rating in 1968).[18]

Had voters made up their minds on primarily ideological grounds, Carter would have won, for only 31 percent of Americans in 1980 described themselves as being conservative. On the biggest issue, the economy, *Time* reported that Reagan had started the campaign with a handy lead over Carter, but that the incumbent now had the advantage, by a margin of 13 percentage points. Carter had already eliminated Reagan's initial advantage on foreign policy. Asked who they would "trust more not to overreact in times of crisis," 57 percent named Carter, while only 32 percent selected Reagan.[19] Particularly well disposed to Carter were his fellow evangelicals. Polled about their voting intentions in August (when Reagan had a strong lead overall), they preferred Carter to Reagan by a margin of 21 percent (46 percent of evangelicals approved of Carter's performance in office, compared to just 29 percent of non-evangelicals).[20]

So why did Reagan find the going so difficult during the 1980 campaign, despite Carter's weakness and the ghastly state of the economy? And why did he ultimately prevail, and by such an unexpectedly substantial margin? To start with the first question, his disadvantages were obvious, to the point that it is hard to think of other political circumstances in which he could have been elected. After all, he was well to the right of American public opinion on most of the key issues of the day, viewed askance by moderate Republicans such as Gerald Ford (who at one point contemplated coming out of retirement to save the GOP from extremism and defeat) and George Bush (who mocked his economic agenda). And he was also dogged by the age issue (were he elected, he would turn seventy in his first month in office), and, at least so many Democrats believed, by the damaging perception that he was ill-informed, casual, and disengaged. Shortly after the Republican convention, Vice President Walter Mondale was delighted at the GOP's choice of Reagan, predicting that "Reagan will fall like a crowbar ... awfully fast," undermined by his extremism ("his record on everything, domestic and foreign, is an abomination") and by the fact that "Reagan doesn't know anything about the Federal Government."[21] And as Reagan's initial post-convention lead duly disappeared, a Carter aide exulted: "That Reagan is doing our work for us."[22]

For all his subsequent political reputation, then, there is not much sense in news coverage of the 1980 campaign that Americans yet saw in Reagan a Moses-like figure who would carry them to the promised land, restore national strength, rekindle the American dream. Rather, his victory came about in substantial measure by default. His great achievement in 1980 was a negative one—he eventually persuaded sufficient numbers of independents, conservative and blue-collar Democrats, and moderate Republicans that he was not, in fact, either a wild man, or a mere geriatric, second-rate actor. Rather, he was a competent, mainstream, two-term governor of the largest and most modern state in the Union. The decisive moment in the campaign, and the explanation for the last-minute shift in voter sentiment, may have come with the television debate that Carter and Reagan conducted on the Friday before the election. Reagan came across as warm, witty, and confident about the nation's future, while Carter seemed testy and peevish.[23]

The political shift that occurred over the final weekend of the campaign was seismic and portentous, as voters moved decisively against both Carter and the Democratic party, each of which now, finally, found itself paying a high price for incumbency. Previously, perhaps, those voters had felt deeply gloomy, but feared worse under Reagan. Now, following the debate, they felt just as bad, but—says Patterson—saw in the challenger at least some echoes of the "jauntily optimistic FDR." When former LBJ aide Bill Moyers was asked what had gone wrong for the Democrats, he replied that "We didn't elect this guy because he knows how many barrels of oil are in Alaska. We elected him because we want to feel good."[24] Republicans generally benefited from this mood, winning control of the Senate for the first time in a third of a century, and making thirty-three gains in the House (which gave conservatives an ideological majority there, though the Democrats retained formal control).

Ronald Reagan, like Franklin Roosevelt, ushered in—perhaps even embodied—a new political mood. More than that, FDR was one of his political heroes. In Reagan's case, though, the upbeat tone was accompanied by a growing distrust of government, with the new president seeking to capitalize upon widespread political disillusionment, and the palpable sense of crisis in the political culture. Reagan famously joked that the nine scariest words in the English language are, "I'm from the government and I'm here to help."[25] Tapping into America's loss of trust in government and the discrediting of the ambitious liberal programs of the 1960s, he positioned himself as a traditional pre-big government conservative with little patience for government activism, save for forms of activism that promised to undo the "harm" that had been done to the body politic by the ruinous Great Society of the 1960s. His sense of humor and charm appealed to the electorate, softening what would otherwise have appeared a harsh, Goldwaterite message (with all the political risks that this would have entailed).[26]

Building on this point, a number of contributors to this volume have observed that Reagan's popularity rested as much upon his personal style and winning charisma as on his policy platform or commitment to particular issues. Indeed, his victory in 1980 might be attributed in greater measure to the antipolitical mood that he was able to capitalize on and (perhaps inadvertently) cultivate than on any specific, inspiring political vision that he placed before the American electorate. Despite his sometimes strong rhetoric, Reagan did not pursue and deliver on a full policy agenda and his strongest political "idea" was that of the futility and potentially disastrous unforeseen consequences of governmental action.

That said, during the early months of Reagan's presidency it seemed possible that 1980 might be a realignment year comparable to 1932 or 1896. The new president was immensely popular during his first few months in office, and used his popularity to force through the greatest spending cuts and the greatest tax cut in the history of the republic. Yielding to the strong mood in the country to give Reagan a chance, House Speaker Thomas P. "Tip" O'Neill declared that "Congress goes with the will of the people, and the will of the people is to go along with the President. I know when to fight and when not to fight."[27]

It was during this initial six months or so of the Reagan presidency that the impression of a Reagan revolution was created, and it is this period, together with the president's triumphant reelection in 1984, and the collapse of the Soviet empire at the end of the 1980s, that Reagan boosters most obviously have in mind when they elevate him to the pantheon of greatness. In part, they have in mind his tangible policy accomplishments.

To a greater extent, though, they are thinking of the less tangible impression of political command that he conveyed at his zenith, and it is that hard-to-measure sense of dominance, of having his opponents running scared, of inspiring a new generation of conservative activists to enter politics (sowing the seeds for the Gingrich Revolution of 1994) that makes it tempting to compare Reagan in his pomp to LBJ in 1964 and 1965, at the height of the Great Society, or to FDR in his first term, when the New Deal order was being constructed.

Yet the fact remains that President Reagan was not always a commanding, powerful political figure. There were two extended periods—for eighteen month following the sharp economic downturn in the fall of 1981, and for a year or so following the uncovering of the Iran–Contra scandal—when his opinion ratings dipped below 50 percent.[28] Because there were other times when he was very popular—during the first nine months of his first term, either side of his triumphant reelection in 1984, and right at the end of his tenure—the overall figures are good, higher than for any president since Kennedy. But they are lower than those for Bill Clinton. And, like Dwight Eisenhower, such popularity as he enjoyed did not invariably transmit to his party, not least because of his unwillingness to jeopardize his personal standing by waging all-out war on the New Deal–Great Society order. Compared to Nixon, or even to Eisenhower, he showed little enthusiasm for the task of creating a new Republican majority, and the overall partisan dynamic during the 1980s actually deteriorated by the most obvious measure, namely the GOP's position in Congress. In 1982, House Democrats clawed back most of the losses that they had sustained two years earlier, removing Reagan's ideological majority. And in 1986, the Democrats regained control of the Senate. Only for a fleeting period between the assassination attempt of March 1981 and the decline in his popularity in the fall of that same year can Reagan be said to have dominated Capitol Hill.

There is a clear danger, in other words, that present-day conservatives who view Reagan as the patron saint of their credo, and revisionist historians seeking to correct the sometimes caricatured impressions of disaster that characterized some early accounts of the 1980s, may exaggerate the importance of Reagan's legacy, the magnitude of his achievement. Perhaps his deification during the Bush 43 years tells us more about American political discourse during the early twenty-first century than it does about the 1980s? And perhaps his improving reputation in academic circles primarily reveals the intrinsic need of historians to overturn the judgments of their predecessors (it is hard to think of *any* recent president whose reputation has remained stable over the course of the past three decades). Perhaps, too, conservatives disillusioned with the record of Reagan's two GOP successors look back fondly on Reagan as someone who at least had something significant to say. Even as early as 1989 in an obvious dig at George Bush Sr., Ted Kennedy lauded Reagan as a great communicator, "not simply because of his personality or his TelePrompter, but mostly because he had something to communicate."[29]

While Reagan's sunny temperament and infectious optimism may have helped the nation find a way through the overwhelming sense of crisis and decline that drained its energies at the end of the 1970s, he was unable, perhaps unwilling, to completely restore faith in political institutions or actors. Although polls did show some increase in public confidence in the institutions of government during the decade, this renewed trust proved both superficial and temporary. As historian James Patterson has it, "they admired the star, not the play."[30] And polls taken since Reagan left office demonstrate that Americans remain suspicious and distrustful of government. Ironically perhaps, and following the trend established under Reagan, the American public have come to respond with more assurance to government and officials who promise to deliver *less* in policy terms—except, of course, in issues of national security following the 9/11 attacks.[31]

Recent historians have addressed the question of the Reagan legacy in a series of monographs, and two contributors to the present volume take a bird's-eye view of the broadly positive conclusions that they have reached. Another way to tackle the legacy question is to revisit particular aspects of Reagan's approach to leadership and public policy legacy, and consider the extent to which such analysis in depth reveals a picture that is compatible with these broad-brush strokes. When W. Elliott Brownlee and Hugh Davis Graham embarked on the project that resulted in the 2003 collection, *The Reagan Presidency: Pragmatic Conservatism and its Legacies*, they sought a "second generation" assessment, one that gained a measure of detachment because of the passage of time, and greater depth and refinement because of the recent opening of the holdings of the Reagan library in Simi Valley, California, and the recent publication of an enormously revealing set of Reagan's pre-presidential radio interviews. The result was a collection whose contributors generally challenged the polarized, bowdlerized versions of Reagan and his administration that had dominated early academic and journalistic treatments of those subjects. Five years on, the momentum of that effort to rehabilitate Reagan has significantly accelerated, with some serious academic authors, as well as a host of partisan cheerleaders, having embraced almost giddy assessments of the fortieth president's leadership and legacy. The time seems right for another, sober reanalysis of Reagan and the 1980s.

Contributors to this volume came together at a conference held at the Rothermere American Institute, University of Oxford, in November 2005. Given the nature of the subject matter, it seemed appropriate and important to include policymakers and contemporary commentators in the discussion alongside academics. This made for a lively and engaged exchange with a congregation of people from a variety of backgrounds and with assorted perspectives, allowing for a thorough sorting through of the current arguments about Reagan's administration and legacy. This volume reflects that diversity but is also united by a general sense that a new understanding of the politics of the 1980s is required; one that acknowledges the achievements of Reagan's two terms as well as frankly assessing their limitations.

The three sections of the book addressing the "perceptions," "policies," and "legacies" of the Reagan administration also separate the scholarly from the personal accounts. Opening the volume, journalists Dan Rather and Godfrey Hodgson reflect upon their own experience of reporting on Reagan's White House during the 1980s. Rather suggests that the difficulty of getting to grips with Reagan's legacy is that he is still so very much of our times. For Rather, the length of Reagan's shadow is so impressive because of his ability to personify the national experience at every stage of his career and most especially as President. Hodgson concurs that the success of Reagan's presidency was his ability to tap into the consciousness of the American people and to represent himself as one of the ordinary folk. Reagan's ability to communicate to the people their own fears and concerns is, Rather hints, perhaps partly compromised by questions about the balance of style and substance in his presentation. Interviewing Reagan, both Rather and Hodgson found him personally authentic, sincere, and extremely likeable. Perhaps these qualities have helped elevate Reagan's reputation today as twenty-first-century politicians seek ways to appear authentic and so make connections with the electorate.

The instructive accounts of two political insiders comprise the remainder of the first section. Peter Bourne presents a view from the trenches in the war on drugs during the 1980s. A former adviser on drugs policy in both Nixon's and Carter's White House, Bourne grew frustrated and angry at the increasing politicization of drugs and their use under Reagan but could see few workable solutions to a growing national problem. Sidelining health professionals who understood drug addiction, Reagan appointed a moral campaigner as his drugs policy adviser and ultimately undermined the independence and integrity of U.S. attorneys across the nation by making them foot soldiers in his war on drugs. Bourne's essay illuminates the political machinations behind Nancy Reagan's simple slogan, "Just Say No."

Serving on the National Security Council advising Reagan on arms negotiations and as Reagan's ambassador to the Soviet Union from 1987, Jack Matlock brings many personal insights to his account of Reagan's role in ending the Cold War. Neither the idiot nor the genius others have made him out to be in foreign affairs, Reagan was principled and determined during his dealings with the Soviet Union. His steadfastness and willingness to negotiate with Gorbachev rightly entitles Reagan to much of the credit for bringing the Cold War to an end. According to Matlock, a zero-sum game became a win-win situation under the guidance of the two leaders who were both willing to take risks in order to bring about world peace.

A rather different emphasis is given to the nuclear negotiations between Reagan and Gorbachev by Simon Head, whose essay begins the second section, which examines the politics and policies of the Reagan administration. Head suggests that while Reagan's approach to nuclear diplomacy might have been better informed, it was ultimately both visionary and productive. Passing through strategic stages of tough talk, weapons build-up, and the somewhat confused flaunting of the Strategic Defense Initiative

(SDI), Reagan was finally able to pursue his utopian vision of a nuclear-free world in negotiations with Gorbachev; negotiations that faltered initially but ultimately led to the ideological defeat of communism. Head concludes that Reagan's Cold War dealings may not have been pretty, but they got results.

Contemporary and more recent commentators have often hailed Reagan's foreign and economic policies as his greatest successes. Despite their different emphases, Matlock and Head share a mixed assessment of the success of Reagan's relationship with the Soviet Union. Iwan Morgan similarly takes up and modifies the generally positive perceptions of his inflation-busting, confidence-building economic program. Morgan points out that the management of inflation was due as much to the actions of the Carter-appointed head of the Federal Reserve as to Reagan, that tax cuts had a far greater political than economic impact, and that the United States became the world's largest debtor nation in the 1980s. Reaganomics did not achieve what it set out to but it did benefit from a number of positive economic developments during the decade, including more women in the workforce and increases in consumer spending (rather than saving). The full implications of the legacy of Reaganomics are yet to be revealed but unfortunately look increasingly ominous.

If nuclear diplomacy and economic policy were top priorities for Reagan, he has been consistently criticized for operating a policy of "benign neglect" in his approach to civil rights. Stephen Tuck's fresh look at race relations in the 1980s reveals that despite Reagan's lack of interest, civil rights movements advanced a number of new causes and defended old gains with great effect during the decade. Although the advent of hip hop might suggest that African American youth had succumbed to the same kind of individualism, commercialism, and political cynicism as much of the rest of Reagan's America, in fact in many localities and on many important issues, African Americans still worked together as a community of common interest. In the national arena, however, and in the face of conservative hostility to much of the civil rights agenda, definite cracks began to show.

Just as scrutiny of particular policies shines a light on Reagan's purpose and politics, so too does an examination of the type of support he was able to elicit and generate. Dan William's analysis of the relationship between Reagan and the religious right finds that despite Reagan's failure to deliver real policy results or even substantial political appointments, the religious right did benefit in a number of ways from their support for him. Gaining public exposure and political experience simply because of the credibility Reagan's rhetorical support for their pet causes (such as antiabortion and school prayer) provided, the religious right joined the national conversation as significant political players. Williams demonstrates how the loyalty of groups such as Falwell's Moral Majority was firm and actually motivated less by Reagan's action on their issues as on his moral patriotism and strong anticommunism. However, this type of political support for Reagan did not necessarily translate into committed support for his party.

In the final essay in this section, Robert Mason notes that one of Reagan's accomplishments was his ability to balance different segments of the Republican Party's support—including the religious right and yuppies—and to hold the whole together. He failed, however, to meet the Republicans hopes and expectations for a wholesale realignment. While there was a narrowing of the Democratic majority and finally an achievement of "parity status," the most interesting development was the continued process of political *dealignment*, as voter identification moved away from the parties and their platforms and toward individual candidates. Into the 1990s, the Republicans failed to capitalize on Reagan's legacy of personal popularity and hopes for a partisan realignment were buried with Gingrich's ironically divisive "Contract with America."

The third section of the book deals in more depth with elements of Reagan's legacy. The essays by Dominic Sandbrook and Joel Aberbach address two of the most striking aspects of the political restructuring that took place on Reagan's watch. In an examination of the "special relationship" between Reagan and Margaret Thatcher, Sandbrook demonstrates that on both sides of the Atlantic, the political compass shifted decisively as the two leaders worked in tandem to transform their respective polities. Although Sandbrook notes that both Reagan and Thatcher gained office due to the failures of liberal and leftist policies rather than as a result of a positive endorsement of their politics and that they both followed a middling, pragmatic course when in power, their impact on the future shape of politics was still significant. Their neoliberal legacy could not be rebuked but had to be embraced and adopted even by their political opponents.

Joel Aberbach's focus on Reagan's use of administrative strategies and techniques highlights another way that politics was transformed during the 1980s. By careful use of appointments and personnel management, regulatory decision-making and spending freezes, Reagan furthered the administrative presidency strategy initiated by Nixon. Moreover, his transformation of much of the cut-and-thrust of political negotiation into a process of managerial oversight gave some much needed credibility and legitimacy back to the office of the president after the debacles of the Nixon–Ford–Carter years. The legacy of this technocratic style is problematic since it represents, Aberbach hints, the beginning of the end for democratic politics. George W. Bush has thus far been the president to embrace the managerial style of governance most enthusiastically and he has succeeded in extending the powers of the president vis-à-vis Congress (and a largely Republican one at that) quite dramatically by doing so.

The final two essays in this section explore the legacy of Reagan in the public memory and the public record. Niels Bjerre-Poulsen and Gil Troy throw light on the extremely charged debates surrounding the issue of how Reagan is and will be remembered. Bjerre-Poulsen probes the mythology within which conservatives have enveloped Reagan and finds that in order to effectively memorialize him as a conservative icon, they must rewrite Reagan's actual record and ignore their own outrage about some of his decisions and policies at the time. Moreover, the more twenty-first-century conservatives succeed at making Reagan a national treasure, the more they empty him of his partisan value. Troy's essay takes up the evaluation of Reagan by historians and finds their attempts at impassive scholarship initially disappointing but is encouraged by recent contributions to the ongoing discussion. It is to be hoped that the present volume will improve further on our understanding of the impact and legacy of the fortieth president of the United States of America.

Notes

1. See Martin Anderson, *Revolution* (San Diego: Harcourt Brace Jovanovich, 1988); Dinesh D'Souza, *Ronald Reagan: How an Ordinary Man Became an Extraordinary Leader* (New York: Free Press, 1999); Lee Edwards, *The Essential Ronald Reagan: A Profile in Courage, Justice, and Wisdom* (Lanham, Md.: Rowman and Littlefield, 2005); and Jules Tygiel, *Ronald Reagan and the Triumph of American Conservatism* (New York: Longman, 2005).
2. See Haynes Johnson, *Sleepwalking Through History: America in the Reagan Years* (New York: Norton, 1992); Ronnie Dugger, *On Reagan: The Man and His Presidency* (New York: McGraw-Hill, 1983); Robert Dallek, *The Politics of Symbolism* (Cambridge, Mass.: Harvard University Press, 1984); Fred Block, Richard A. Cloward, Barbara Ehrenreich, and Frances Fox Piven, *The Mean Season: The Attack on the Welfare State* (New York: Pantheon, 1987); Barbara Ehrenreich, *The Worst Years of Our Lives: Irreverent Notes from a Decade of Greed* (New York; Pantheon, 1991).
3. See Gil Troy, *Morning in America: How Ronald Reagan Invented the 1980s* (Princeton, NJ: Princeton University Press, 2006); Robert M. Collins, *Transforming America: Politics and Culture in the Reagan Years* (New York: Columbia University Press, 2007); John Patrick Diggins, *Ronald Reagan: Fate, Freedom, and the Making of History* (New York: Norton, 2007); John Ehrman, *The Eighties: America in the Age of Reagan* (New Haven, Conn.: Yale University Press, 2005).
4. On the relationship between the Reagan years and the Gingrich Revolution, see Benjamin Shefter and Martin Shefter, *Politics by Other Means: Politicians, Prosecutors, and the Press from Watergate to Whitewater*, rev. ed. (New York: Norton, 1999).
5. See Michael Tanner, *Leviathan on the Right: How Big-Government Conservatism Brought Down the Republican Revolution* (Washington, D.C.: Cato Institute, 2007); Gene Healy, "The Era of Big Government Conservatism," February 1, 2004, article posted on the website of the Cato Institute (www.cato.org/dailys/02–01-04.html), downloaded on April 19, 2007; C. Bradley Thompson, "The Decline and Fall of American Conservatism," *The Objective Standard* vol. 1, no. 3 (Fall 2006), downloaded from www.theobjectivestandard.com on April 19, 2007; Kate O'Beirne, "A Congress Gone to Pot," *National Review*, May 22, 2006, downloaded from http://findarticles.com on April 19, 2007. See also "How the Right Went Wrong," the cover story of *Time* magazine, March 26, 2007. The cover depicted Ronald Reagan, with a tear running down his face.

6. Marc Landy and Sidney Milkis, *Presidential Greatness* (Lawrence: University Press of Kansas, 2000), 219, 200.
7. This argument animates many of the essays in W. Elliot Brownlee and Hugh Davis Graham, eds., *The Reagan Presidency: Pragmatic Conservatism and its Legacies* (Lawrence: University Press of Kansas, 2003).
8. Landy and Milkis, *Presidential Greatness*, 199.
9. James T. Patterson, *Restless Giant: The United States from Watergate to Bush v. Gore* (New York: Oxford University Press, 2005), 58–61.
10. Edward D. Berkowitz, *Something Happened: A Political and Cultural Overview of the Seventies* (New York: Columbia University Press, 2006); Bruce J. Schulman, *The Seventies: The Great Shift in American Culture, Society, and Politics* (New York: Free Press, 2001).
11. Philip Jenkins, *Decade of Nightmares: The End of the Sixties and the Making of Eighties America* (New York: Oxford University Press, 2006).
12. Figures taken from *Congress and the Nation, 1977–1980* (Washington, D.C.: Congressional Quarterly, 1981), 206–209, and *Historical Statistics of the United States—Millennial Edition*, online edition (New York: Cambridge University Press, 2006), Table Dc 531.
13. *Gallup Poll: 1980*, 199.
14. Richard Nixon, Speech on Invasion of Cambodia, April 30, 1970, text reproduced at http://vietnam.vassar.edu/doc15.html (accessed on September 24, 2007). Nixon said: "If, when the chips are down, the world's most powerful nation, the United States of America, acts like a pitiful, helpless giant, the forces of totalitarianism and anarchy will threaten free nations and free institutions throughout the world."
15. Seymour Martin Lipset and William Schneider, *The Confidence Gap: Business, Labor, and Government in the Public Mind* (New York: Free Press, 1983).
16. Carter won his home state of Georgia, plus Hawaii, Minnesota, West Virginia, Delaware, and Maryland.
17. *Gallup Poll: 1980*, 240; John F. Stacks, "Right Now: A Dead Heat," *Time*, November 3, 1980, downloaded from www.time.com, on September 9, 2007.
18. William Schneider, "The November 4 Vote for President: What did it Mean?," in Austin Ranney, ed., *The American Elections of 1980* (Washington, D.C.: American Enterprise Institute, 1981), 241.
19. *Time*, November 3, 1980.
20. *Gallup Poll: 1980*, 185–186.
21. "An Interview with Mondale," *Time*, August 25, 1980, downloaded from www.time.com on September 9, 2007.
22. Quoted by Ed Magnuson, "The Mood of the Voter," *Time*, September 15, 1980, downloaded from www.time.com on September 9, 2007.
23. On the debate, see Lou Cannon, *Reagan* (New York: Putnams, 1982), 295–298. For its political impact, see *Gallup Poll: 1980*, 242.
24. Patterson, *Restless Giant*, 150.
25. Downloaded from one of the many websites that collect and celebrate Reagan's humorous and/or rousing quips. See www.usa-patriotism.com/quotes.reagan.htm.
26. For a brilliant account of Reagan's sense of humor, and its political utility, see Lou Cannon, *President Reagan: The Role of a Lifetime* (New York: Simon and Schuster, 1991), 120–142.

27. Quoted in Gareth Davies, *See Government Grow: Education Politics from Johnson to Reagan* (Lawrence: University Press of Kansas, 2007), 253.
28. See polls cited in Gareth Davies, "The Welfare State," in Brownlee and Graham, eds., *Reagan Presidency*, 216.
29. Quoted in James T. Patterson, "Afterword: Legacies of the Reagan Years" in Brownlee and Graham, eds., *Reagan Presidency*, 361.
30. Ibid., 370.
31. Robert Samuelson, *The Good Life and Its Discontents, 1945–1995* (New York: Random House, 1997), 88–204, 263–264. See also "How Much Do Americans Trust Government" at http://mwhodges.home.att.net/trust.htm, which contains a very instructive graph. See also poll data at: http://www.abcnews.go.com/sections/politics/DailyNews/poll0120115.html.

Part I
Perceptions

Chapter 1

Ronald Reagan: Communicating the America Within

Dan Rather

When I was going over the program for the RAI conference to be held on November 11, 2005, one of the titles that caught my eye was the question raised by Gil Troy of McGill University: "Toward a historiography of Reagan and the 1980s ... why are we doing such a lousy job?" Now *that's* candor of a sort that is refreshing, and that is perhaps not seen enough in *my* business (or many others, for that matter).

As I think most of you probably know, I am not an historian—and those among you who don't know will, I promise you, be quite sure of it by the end of this essay. It is not for me to judge the quality of the historical work being done on Ronald Wilson Reagan, fortieth president of the United States of America. But *if* a "lousy job" is being done in this area, it occurs to me that one reason may very well be that, though nearly two decades have passed since President Reagan's second term ended, whatever dust may have gathered on the Reagan presidency has been given very little chance to settle.

Put another way, to engage many of the big *historical* questions concerning Ronald Reagan's legacy is to find oneself smack in the middle of the *political* debates that continue to transfix and, to varying degrees, divide America even today, twenty years after the height of Reaganism.

So for a practicing journalist, who strives to cover today's news and political events with impartiality, casting any sort of historical judgment on the Reagan years can be a tricky proposition—not unlike trying to change the fan belt on a moving Mercedes. This is true for Reagan in a way that it is not for, say, the Carter or the Ford, or the Nixon presidencies—presidencies where the consensus on their strengths and weaknesses has been much more firmly established, at least in popular, if not scholarly, conversation.

There are a number of reasons for this, not least of which is the fact that a period of two decades is—as a man of my age would like to think—simply not all that long a time and perhaps an inadequate vantage point for gaining a great deal of historical perspective. But the most obvious manifestation of—and cause for—this situation is the degree to which President

George W. Bush has, consciously and avowedly, embraced the Reagan presidency as a model. Some simplify this with the formula that George Herbert Walker Bush is George W. Bush's *biological* father, but Ronald Reagan is his *political* father.

But the implications go beyond symbolic questions of political patrimony to those of policy, where they resonate in debates ranging from those on tax policy to the wisdom or folly of deficit spending to approaches toward foreign policy.

And so, for example, the verdict one renders on the idea, put forth by some, that the U.S. boom years of the 1990s were really just a continuation of the Reagan economic expansion has real implications for whether one supported and continues to support President Bush's tax cuts and moves toward business deregulation.

And the degree to which one subscribes to the proposition that Ronald Reagan "won the Cold War" will also have ramifications for how one views President Bush's foreign policy, or at least its rhetorical tone—with its echoes of Reagan's "Evil Empire" in the present "Axis of Evil."

The influences, of course, run both ways. Just as champions of the Bush economic and foreign policies have their motives to champion the Reagan legacy, detractors of these policies are similarly motivated to try to debunk them.

And lately we have begun to see, to borrow a term from the Clinton era, "a third way" that the Reagan legacy is being put to use in news commentary and analysis: as President Bush's second-term troubles have mounted, the Reagan second term is increasingly being used as a point of comparison. Specifically, the measures taken by President Reagan to try to right his White House in the wake of the secret, missiles-to-Iran, secret money-for-war in Central America deals that became known as the Iran–Contra scandal and that tarnished and very nearly wrecked the Reagan second term—raising as they did questions of honesty, accountability, and constitutionality.

So, we've had, for example, former Reagan chief of staff Kenneth Duberstein counseling on the Op-Ed page of the *New York Times* that President Bush "might take a few lessons from the Reagan playbook"—to whit, bring "new blood" into the White House and stop "tilting at windmills." Duberstein suggested that Bush might, just as Reagan did over Iran–Contra, apologize for mistakes made in Iraq in order to repair his relationship with the public (and the press).[1] And we've also had presidential biographer Richard Reeves recalling Howard Baker's arrival in the spring of 1987 at the Reagan White House in a syndicated column in which he points out that Reagan not only had the assistance of new staff but Mikhael Gorbachev to help save his presidency. Moreover, Reeves continues,

> On Sept. 11, 2001, the Bush–Reagan analogy became much stronger, with the fear and loathing of terrorism replacing the fear and loathing of communism that drove Reagan's foreign policy. And now, after a series of blunders and stupidities, including rushing into a war he could not win, and the need

to start throwing friends overboard, Bush is where Reagan was in that spring of 1987, in deep trouble of his own making.

Not rating Bush's chance of recovery very high, Reeves ends with his stated opinion that "George W. Bush is no Ronald Reagan."[2]

These two citations bracket a range of such comparisons drawn by Reagan insiders and outsiders alike. And we can add to the list a number of particularly vehement lead editorials by the *New York Times* and, also, considerably more subdued and inferential remarks by U.S. senator and presidential candidate John McCain.[3]

But you can also find more subtle and indirect examples of this impulse to reach back to the Reagan presidency in assessing the current White House. A case in point could be found on the front page of *The Washington Post*'s November 2005 edition, where a piece of news analysis titled "Some in G.O.P. Regretting Pork-Stuffed Highway Bill" contains the following bit of background–foreground contrast, if you'll forgive me for quoting at some length:

> The highway bill has long been a reliable source of pork-barrel spending, and it has been used by Republican and Democratic leaders to reward or punish rank-and-file members. President Ronald Reagan once vetoed a highway bill because it contained 152 pet projects. Despite the pork inflation, Bush had no complaints about the current package when he signed it on August 10.[4]

Fair enough to use an episode from the Reagan administration to illustrate the point about how "Republican and Democratic leaders" have used the highway bill as a political club. But to cite this eighteen-year-old Reagan veto, without any additional or countervailing examples from Republican and Democratic administrations before or since or without prefacing it, even, with the words "for example" does, I think, beg the question of whether the paper or the writer of the piece is trying to set up a sort of "Et tu, Ronnie?" moment for President Bush. Out of context, Reagan's action appears to condemn Bush's but appearances are not everything. Especially, when one considers that Reagan's highway bill veto was seen as part of his administration's effort to reassert its political authority in the wake of the Iran–Contra mess.

These are just some of the ways in which the Reagan presidency breathes still, in today's news pages. So, as you see, in the case of Ronald Wilson Reagan, the words of William Faulkner ring especially true: "the past isn't dead ... it isn't even past."

* * *

If historians are having difficulty grappling with Reagan's legacy, it may be because those of us—journalists—who, as is sometimes said, write history's first draft have in this case gone way over deadline. Further, that first draft of journalists and editorialists cannot be properly put to bed until the politicians and their spokesmen and, indeed, the American public have finished with the subject. And, as of this late date, they have not. It's my opinion that they are not likely to for some time.

But, with apologies to Emerson, if I cannot give you history, I can give you some sense of biography, as seen and heard through these eyes and ears and with all the disclaimers that these limitations make necessary.

There may be considerably more consensus on the subject of Ronald Reagan, the man, and how that man occupied, inhabited, and indeed embodied the office of the presidency, than there is about the policies he generated in that role. Perhaps I can offer some small insight into how this consensus, which was in such abundant evidence upon President Reagan's death, came to be forged.

And though Ronald Reagan only left this earth in 2004, this was a decade or so after he wrote his own farewell, on the verge of, as he put it, "the journey that will lead me into the sunset of my life."[5]

The public life of Ronald Reagan ended near the close of the last century. And though the calendar tells us that that was not so long ago, experience can at times make it seem very far away indeed. I mention this by way of thinking of the term that the publisher Henry Luce coined for the twentieth century: with characteristic modesty, he called it The American Century—a conclusion he reached, mind you, in 1941.[6] If the twentieth century *was* the American century (and I would direct any of you with protests to take the matter up with Mr. Luce), then Ronald Reagan embodied its breadth and scope as well as any public figure America produced in that century.

One may agree or disagree with William Buckley on any number of things, but he was spot on—and early—with his assessment in 1967, as Ronald Reagan was finishing his first year as governor of California, that "Reagan is indisputably a part of America, and he may become a part of American history."[7] And though Bill Buckley did not make the connection explicit, at least not at that point, I think it can be said that the *first* part of that observation played a very big part in making the *second* part so.

Let's look for a moment at Ronald Reagan in the context of his times, at least as the popular imagination has come to frame them in hindsight:

- He was born and spent his early youth in Tampico, Illinois, a place that, even today, remains the quintessence of small-town, middle America with a population of 772.
- At a time when the iconic American young man was the collegiate football player, Reagan was a three-time varsity letterman at Eureka College.
- In the era we remember as "The Golden Age of Radio," Reagan was on the radio, as a sports announcer.
- In 1937, just in time for Hollywood's so-called Golden Age, Reagan took the screen test for Warner Brothers that led to his film career.
- While Franklin Roosevelt was president, Reagan considered himself an ardent New-Dealer; during World War II, Reagan served in the U.S. Army's Motion Picture Unit.

- When Washington, D.C.—and to a degree, America as a whole—was consumed with the question of Communist infiltration of Hollywood, Reagan, then president of the Screen Actor's Guild, testified as a friendly witness before the House Un-American Activities Committee.
- In the 1950s, Reagan resurrected his flagging acting career by becoming one of the first motion-picture actors to make the jump to television. In a time we have come to call, yes, "Television's Golden Age."
- When the modern American conservative movement was born with the presidential candidacy of Barry Goldwater, there was none other than Ronald Reagan, beginning his own political career in earnest with what would later become known, simply, as "The Speech."
- And finally, at a time when the state of California was both ground zero for American foment in the 1960s and primary incubator of the American counterculture—there was Governor Reagan, at the forefront of the "Establishment" opposition.

I hope you'll forgive me for reviewing here facts with which most of you are no doubt well acquainted. But I do so in this sort of compacted way to make a point. While I don't mean to suggest that Reagan was some sort of real-life Zelig, it *is* remarkable, I think, to note the degree to which he was involved—to which he involved *himself*—in so many of the defining movements and events of his times. Not always blowing with the prevailing winds, at least as they were perceived at the time; not always at the very epicenter of things, but *involved*, and in a way few people are, over such a prolonged stretch of time.

This goes far beyond the mere generational accident of his having lived through two World Wars and his having come of age during the Great Depression. His was a significant and, to a large degree, emblematic American life, and was so well before he was elected president.

* * *

I make this point by way of offering what thoughts I can on Ronald Reagan's powers of communication.

The well-worn title bestowed on Reagan as the "Great Communicator" sometimes grates on his partisans, who see in it either an effort to damn by faint praise or a reluctance to credit the Reagan ideology—or both. But the fact remains that he was an extraordinary spokesman for the beliefs that he held and that his fellow Republicans and conservatives shared and share still. And in a democratic—small "d"—republic, the ability of a leader to communicate his or her beliefs is no small thing. As president, Reagan always seemed to grasp that policy and politics need to be well-harnessed to the horse of persuasion.

Among the articles marking Reagan's passing was a perceptive piece in which Reagan biographer and *Washington Post* reporter Lou Cannon recast something that Walter Lippmann had once said of Charles de Gaulle: "The greatness of Reagan," Cannon wrote, "was not that he was in America, but that America was inside of him."[8] It's a statement that bears interesting echoes of the Buckley remark made nearly forty years before.

And at the time that Cannon wrote this, amid a sea of eulogies, it would have been easy to dismiss such a remark as a mere platitude. But that would have been a mistake, for I feel it gets to the very beating heart of why Reagan enjoyed and continues to enjoy such popularity among the American public: "America was inside of him."

Well, I've just recounted my list of just *what* of America—and to what dramatic extent—was "inside" of Reagan. And by the time Reagan was elected president, his understanding of his country and its major currents of thought and feeling must have been fundamental and innate. Even if one discounts all his considerable rhetorical and oratorical skill. President Reagan did not really have to reach—except within himself—in order to connect with his fellow Americans: if the times really do make the man, President Reagan was just about as American as they come. The small-town America about which President Reagan would often wax nostalgic, to go back to one example from his life, was not a rhetorical fabrication; it was the reality that young Ronald Reagan knew as a boy.

Much was, is, and continues to be made of the fact that Reagan was an actor. And I think it is easy to make too much of this, or at least to draw conclusions from it that are too easy. Whatever one may think of Reagan's politics and presidency, it is a matter of public record that his political views were long and deeply held, that they had evolved over time as a result of a certain amount of thought and introspection—and that they were, by any reasonable analysis, held sincerely.

Reagan certainly came across as sincere in my own limited encounters with him, first when he was governor and then again when he was president. The beginning of his presidency coincided with the start of my own tenure as CBS News anchor, and one of my first major assignments in that capacity was an hour-long, sit-down interview with President Reagan at the White House (and that was, to be perfectly honest, nearly the full extent of my personal and professional interaction with the man, aside from short, two-way television interviews conducted here and there throughout his presidency).

One hesitates to draw any kind of conclusions from such a small sample, but if I came away from that experience with anything of value, it is this: the celebrated Reagan traits of friendliness and warmth were not mere illusions of the television screen. If anything, he came across as friendlier and warmer in person. I recall that at one point in the interview session we took a break and one of his aides—I seem to remember that it was Michael Deaver, though I can't be positive on this point—approached me to do a bit of lobbying concerning an answer the president had given to one of my questions, an answer with which Deaver had not been completely satisfied.

Deaver had hardly had the chance to speak, though, before the president walked over and said, "You know, this is something I should talk to Dan about myself"—and he said, in essence, "I'm a little uncomfortable with that answer ... and certainly you will decide, but as I think about it I wasn't at my best, and if you could see your way clear to give me another crack at the question or revisit the subject, I'd certainly appreciate it."

Now, we journalists like to think of ourselves as hard-bitten types for whom such niceties do not make a difference. But the reality is that they often do. And by resisting any impulse toward imperiousness either by himself or by his staff, by instead being so genuine and sincere in his approach, he did himself a service in his relations with the press in general and this reporter in particular.

Again, one hesitates to make too much out of such a small thing, but if one can extrapolate from this episode to Reagan's dealing with other reporters during his presidency, one can see where his personality would have been a great boon to his cause.

And to return to the subject of Ronald Reagan, onetime actor, I think one might look upon his actor's training not as any kind of stand-in for substance and sincerity, or any kind of way to fake these things, but rather as a tool Reagan had in his arsenal that helped him to project what was already inside of him. And I'm sure, in the endless gantlet of personal appearances that the political professional must make—speeches, fundraisers, meet-and-greets, and on and on—the ability to *appear* "on" even when he did not necessarily *feel* on must have been a tremendous asset.

But this last bit is just guesswork. And without making any explicit or implicit judgment on the policies that Reagan, as president, espoused or enacted, or their degree of consistency with his stated ideological positions, what we can say with some certainty is that Ronald Reagan knew how to personify the American spirit of his times, and reflect it back to an American public that generally liked what it saw. This ability served his presidency very well, in the public's perception, and continues to do so.

It was also the view of many, at least in the United States, that President Reagan was able to reflect and project the American character with high effectiveness from his perch on the world stage. When CBS News covered the Reagan state funeral, we had with us official Reagan biographer Edmund Morris, who recalled that it had been said—once again—of de Gaulle that he had (roughly translated from the French) "a great sense of the state," and that President Reagan had also possessed this quality, in abundance, in Morris's view.

It's interesting to note the frequency with which de Gaulle's name crops up in comparisons with Reagan—and the comparison of Reagan with a French leader is one that might, in these times, confound some of Reagan's greatest admirers. But in de Gaulle we have a man whose name, in his time, had become virtually synonymous with that of his nation. In the 1980s, at the late height of the Cold War, Ronald Reagan achieved a similar level of identification with the United States of America—or at least, as I say, that was the view of many, from home.

Reagan spoke of and to an elevated sense of the American self and he did so convincingly, in language that carried neither a self-conscious populist pose nor the gloss of the policy shop. To recall President Reagan's public addresses—his first Inaugural, his memorializing of the *Challenger* crew, his Boys of Point du Hoc speech, the challenge he issued to Mikhail Gorbachev at the Brandenburg Gate—is to remember a time not so long ago when words still reached out to the American imagination.

President Reagan of course had his speechwriters but we can also see, in his papers, that the edits he made to these speeches were generally astute and performed with a professional sensitivity to the cadence and music of the spoken word. And, yes, his delivery was impeccable. But it may also be worth considering that, though we still have among us capable speechwriters and political speeches filled with finely wrought rhetoric, we live today in a very different media world than the one we inhabited during the Reagan years.

Today we are so inundated with information, not to mention a self-conscious awareness of the political process, that speeches—if we ever hear more of them than a few sound-bites (and even the sound-bites are shorter now)—seem inevitably to have lost a good deal of their power to truly move the public.

In the Reagan years, however, the current period of great change in media was only just getting underway. And this small bit of good timing combined well with professional gifts of communication to enable Reagan, as president, to convey externally the unique and large piece of the America psyche that resided within him. In this he succeeded to a remarkable degree, and in so doing he was able to achieve much according to the terms he had laid out for himself and for his administration.

What does all of this mean for us today? Again, putting aside questions of policy or ideology and focusing instead on his role as communicator, Ronald Reagan, without question, furthered and perhaps fundamentally changed our public understanding of what a president is and should be. And in terms of the *imagery* of the presidency, he continued the evolution of the television presidency that had first emerged with the telegenic Kennedy years.

Reagan's critics note this and, factoring in Reagan's tendency to delegate the minutiae of the executive office, depict a presidency in which style triumphed over substance or, in their darker depictions, where style masked a substance that—say the critics—voters might not have accepted so readily if it had not been presented with such skill.

Reagan's champions, meanwhile, either tend to discount the matter of communication—as I noted earlier—or remain reluctant to separate it from the substance they saw behind it. Their line is: Reagan was able to speak with such power in large part because the ideas he expressed *contained* such power.

You can be assured that I will not be joining *that* debate.

* * *

However, I would like to pose the question of what, if any, expectations the Reagan years left Americans for their future presidents, or indeed for their political leaders in general. Expectations of which some Americans may not, in fact, be fully aware. Ronald Reagan had the bona fides—a deeply felt ideology rooted in a full breadth of American experience. But, undeniably, he also, every inch, looked and sounded the part of president of the United States.

I wonder if this has in some sense closed the eyes of American voters to political candidates who might come along and who might not look the part to the degree that Reagan did. Who might have every bit as compelling an American experience in their respective biographies as Reagan did in his, but without the rugged good looks, the mellifluous voice, or the "presidential bearing."

And, to invert the question: Did the Reagan years also render American voters more open to candidates who might look and sound the part but who might otherwise lack the kind of experience and conviction held by President Reagan?

I used the word "evolution" earlier, and the Reagan presidency is not the first to raise these questions, either in hindsight or at the time. The questions of style against substance go back at least to John F. Kennedy's candidacy, and the notion of a "permanent campaign"—an important part of which is the imperative to consistently *project* presidential activity through imagery—has conscious and specific roots in the Carter presidency, as noted most recently by the commentator Joe Klein in a column for *TIME* magazine. Carter, advised by image consultants to conduct "a humble, informal presidency, cutting back 'imperial frills and perks,' giving fireside chats, wearing sweaters instead of suits" was, according to Klein, among the worst presidents as a "permanent campaigner." Reagan used his PR talents to the full and surely, the Clinton administration put their own high polish on these ideas, which have been further perfected by the Bush II administration.[9] There is a continuum and progression at work here, and the debate over campaigning versus governance, which is heating up once again on the opinion and op-ed pages, is not going away nor is it likely to with the next presidential administration or the one after that.

And to raise these questions is not to suggest in any way that I know the answers. My guess is that whatever answers there may be do not reside with pointing fingers at—or raising questions about—any one presidential administration, but rather make necessary a much more wide-ranging discussion of not only politicians, but also the role of the media, the expectations and civic responsibilities of voters, and the nexus at which all these forces intersect.

If I have drifted away, here at the end, from our main subject, I hope you won't hold it against me—but will take it, instead, as additional evidence of how Ronald Wilson Reagan, and the years on which he put his stamp, continue in the conversations and the work of those of us whose purview is the present, rather than the past.

Notes

With minor edits, this essay is as Dan Rather delivered it on November 11, 2005, as the keynote speaker at the RAI conference, "The United States in the 1980s: the Reagan Years."

1. Kenneth M. Duberstein, "Reagan's Second Half Comeback," *The New York Times,* November 2, 2005. Downloaded from http://www.nytimes.com/2005/11/02/opinion/02duberstein.html?scp=1&sq=Kenneth+M.+Duberstein+op-ed&st=nyt.
2. Richard Reeves, "George Bush: You're No Ronald Reagan," *U.Express.com* 28 October 2005. Downloaded from http://www.uexpress.com/richardreeves/?uc_full_date=20051028. See also Reeves, *President Reagan: The Triumph of Imagination* (New York: Simon & Schuster, 2005).
3. In mid-November 2005 when this essay was drafted, John McCain made two speeches. The first addressed the question of cruel and degrading treatment of prisoners, the second was a statement on the war in Iraq, in which McCain noted that "there is an undeniable sense that things are slipping—more violence on the ground, declining domestic support for the war, growing incantations among Americans that there is no end in sight" and called for a shift in policy. See John McCain's Senate website at http://mccain.senate.gov/public/index.cfm?FuseAction=Home.Home.
4. Shailagh Murray, "Some in G.O.P. Regretting Pork-Stuffed Highway Bill," *The Washington Post*, November 5, 2005, pA01.
5. Reagan announced his Alzheimer's disease to the American people in a farewell letter dated November 5, 1994. Available at http://www.americanpresidents.org/letters/39.asp.
6. Henry Luce, "The American Century," *Life Magazine,* February 7, 1941.
7. William F. Buckley, Jr., "A Relaxing View: On the Pros and Cons of a Would-Be President," *National Review*, November 28, 1967, available at http://www.nationalreview.com/flashback/buckley200407010912.asp.
8. Lou Cannon, "Why Reagan was 'the Great Communicator,'" *USA Today*, June 6, 2004, available at http://www.usatoday.com/news/opinion/editorials/2004-06-06-cannon_x.htm.
9. Joe Klein, "The Perils of the Permanent Campaign," *Time*, October 30, 2005, available at http://www.time.com/time/magazine/article/0,9171,1124332,00.html.

Chapter 2

Only an Actor: Memories of a Reagan Biopic

Godfrey Hodgson

"I thought it was a joke," said Pat Brown, the admired Democratic governor of California, when they told him that the Republicans were running an actor called Ronald Reagan against him. He was not even a Grade A actor, Brown pointed out. So he didn't regard Reagan as a strong candidate, though he was all too well aware of any liberal Democrat's vulnerability in the backlash climate of 1966. So at first he tried to ridicule the idea that a mere actor would run for governor of the most populous state in the Union. Passing two little African American boys, he said, "Who are you going to vote for?" And when the boys started at him in amazement, Brown said, "Well, remember, if you don't know, it was an actor who shot Lincoln."

When I interviewed him, Pat Brown readily acknowledged how foolishly he had underestimated Reagan. He said Reagan's acting experience was a "real plus" in his campaign, and attacking him as an actor had been a bad mistake, "absolutely fruitless," Reagan was "far superior" on television, and in the end he won "by a cool million votes."

* * *

When I set out to make a television biography of Reagan, near the end of his presidency, in 1987, I may have half-shared Pat Brown's opinion, or at least the opinion of those who thought poorly of Reagan's performance as president. But as I researched his record, as I followed the man and his history round the country, and as I interviewed more than one hundred people who had known him at every stage of his life, from colleagues in the radio station where he worked in Davenport, Iowa, to senior White House staff and cabinet members, his wife, one of his daughters, and some of his closest friends, I began to realize that the verdict might have to be more complicated.

By the time we started work, my view of the man and the president was a little more sophisticated than Pat Brown's. After all, twenty-two years had passed. I had watched Reagan at work during at least part of the 1968, 1976, and 1980 campaigns. And, from a distance, I had observed his performance in the presidency.

Yet I must admit that I still came to the task with the eyes of one who, if I had always tried to preserve professional objectivity, had strong sympathies with the New Frontier/Great Society approach and many friends among the survivors of those periods.

I had worked in Washington throughout most of the Kennedy and Johnson administrations.[1] I had covered the civil rights movement, from Oxford, Mississippi, to Selma. I had written, with two colleagues, an account of the 1968 presidential campaign.[2] I had published, in 1976, an ambitious attempt to tell the history of the 1960s and in particular to explain the crisis of the liberal consensus.[3] I had also written a book about presidency as an institution.[4] I was, in a word, thoroughly hooked on the—to me—mysterious paradoxes of the presidency, at once an apparently all-powerful and a persistently impotent institution.

I was not unfamiliar with the new conservatism, and not altogether unsympathetic to many of its ideas. I had covered the Goldwater campaign in 1964 and enjoyed the time I spent with Senator Goldwater in Arizona when I wrote a profile of him. I had always had a number of conservative friends and mentors, ever since I was a pupil of Robert Strausz-Hupé at the University of Pennsylvania. I knew well many people in the Nixon administration, including several in the Nixon White House.[5] But by the time Reagan became president I was no longer a resident correspondent, necessarily mixing with Republicans and conservatives on a daily basis. I had moved back to London, though I visited the United States frequently, at least four times a year for different lengths of time. I would claim that I never bought into the view that Reagan was a simpleton, a mere cowboy actor. I have always thought that journalists are too quick to assume that politicians are idiots, or at least to underestimate the sheer ability that is needed to get to the top of what Disraeli called "this exceedingly slippery tree." Still, I cannot deny that, as I began the round of interviews that ended with a long and friendly meeting with Reagan himself, I was no admirer. This is an attempt to record how and why my view of Ronald Reagan, as president and as a man, changed as a result of that exposure to him and to many of those who knew him best.

* * *

Reagan was in many ways, I still believe, a poor president. He could be casual. No doubt it is better to save some time for rest and relaxation than to work half the night checking boxes like Jimmy Carter or Richard Nixon. But Reagan gave too much latitude to a staff of mixed ability. At times—Iran-Contra is the supreme example—he was too laid back for his own good. It can be argued that, if it had not been for the recent trauma of Watergate, he might have been impeached over Iran-Contra. He was ideologically blinkered. He was remarkably ignorant, even contemptuous, of the world beyond America's borders. His management of the budget and the economy was open to severe criticism. His dreamy, feel-good attitude and his old-fashioned nationalist rhetoric could be infuriating, even to many Americans, and certainly to almost everyone else.

Yet in other respects it is hard to deny that he was highly effective. He had remarkable success in persuading many of his fellow-countrymen to share some of his core beliefs: his conviction that it should be possible to defuse the Cold War by speaking robustly to the Soviet leaders, and that there was a moral imperative to find an alternative to "mutual assured destruction"; his conviction that government was "part of the problem, not part of the solution"; above all his deep confidence in the ultimate wisdom and decency of the American people. More than any president since Franklin Roosevelt (whom incidentally he greatly admired) he was able to shift the center of gravity of the nation's entire political discourse his way. After almost two decades of division, bitterness, and a loss of confidence, inasmuch as a political leader can achieve such a transformation, Reagan restored the optimism and even the public vitality of the American people.

One of the most surprising things I came to understand was that at least part of his success was due to precisely those skills he had learned in his various experiences of show business in its different forms: as a live radio broadcaster, as a movie actor, and as a media propagandist for the General Electric Corporation. You could even say that the very facts about his career that led Pat Brown and many others to underestimate him so disastrously—that he was an actor, a radio sports reporter, and the host of General Electric Theater—were precisely the reasons for his success. His radio scripts, all written by him in pencil on yellow legal pad, are one illustration of that. We shall meet others. I had been led to believe that he was, if not near-illiterate, at least utterly dependent on his staff. Many of those who worked for him attested not just to his gifts as a communicator, but to his professionalism and skill as well.

His long years in show business equipped Reagan with many skills that an Eisenhower or a Jimmy Carter, or indeed a George W. Bush, could have used to advantage. What other president could have managed an exit as perfect as Reagan, head and hand high, pure theater? Who else could have brought off the vaudeville prat-kick with which he simultaneously showed off his affection for his wife and subtly put down the solemnity of the campaign film made for him in 1984? It is no good saying that these are low arts, unworthy of his great office. It is better to be able to succeed in them than to fail. Few other presidents, perhaps only FDR, John F. Kennedy, and on his day Bill Clinton, could take a speech as Reagan did, and "put it across."

There were, notoriously, also downsides. There were occasions, as in his destruction of the air traffic controllers' union or his demonization of student demonstrators at Berkeley, when he showed a side that was ruthless almost to the point of being nasty. Especially where weak or poor countries were concerned, in the cases of Lebanon, for example, or Libya or Grenada, he could act with an insensitivity that bordered on racist or at least unreconstructed behavior.

Sometimes, too, it almost seemed as though he had difficulty in distinguishing between show business and life, between the fictive and the real. It has often been pointed out that Reagan seemed to be able to persuade himself that experiences he had lived through only vicariously or on celluloid came to seem real to him. He seemed to believe that he had seen combat in World War II, when his war had been fought in the gilded safety of the back lot at Warner Brothers. In a more sinister instance, he spoke as if he had been an eyewitness to one of the most horrifying moments of the twentieth century. He actually told the prime minister of Israel that he had witnessed the liberation of the concentration camps and the revelation of the unimaginable horrors of the Holocaust, when he had been no closer to Dachau or Belsen than California, and had in fact, up to that time, never left the United States in his life.

For some, that was nothing more than abominable cynicism, plain lying. Others came up with psychological explanations, more or less plausible. I believe the film we shot, which included more than one hundred interviews, reveals complex implications of Reagan's ability, not just to confuse fact and fiction, but to turn that confusion to his advantage. But perhaps before we see Ronald Reagan, down-to-earth fantasist, in full flood, I should sketch some of the background of our project, which—I venture to suggest—brings some quite rich new supporting evidence to bear on the mystery of Reagan's strangely original but effective personality.

* * *

A BBC executive told me she could not commission a series on Reagan unless I had his promise to cooperate. After some months of lonely lobbying, I obtained his agreement, in writing and in his own hand: "Let's do it, RWR." But then the BBC changed her mind. As a freelance I found myself in a tricky, potentially ruinous situation. The president of the United States had agreed to grant me, with no financial or institutional backing, the very valuable prize of his cooperation. I would be more than somewhat discredited if I had to admit to him, or rather to his public relations people, that I couldn't deliver.

Then I had a stroke of luck. In my perplexity I found myself, at some television awards ceremony, sitting next to a former colleague, for whom I had, and have, the greatest respect, the late Phillip Whitehead. I explained my predicament to him. He agreed to help. To make television programs, you need two things: money and a slot. Channel Four in London promised us a slot, and that meant we could raise the money. Eventually the film was shown in more than twenty countries, including the United States.[6] Under the agreement we eventually negotiated with the Reagan White House, we were to have a formal, "sit-down" interview with the president; his approval of our approaching his staff, cabinet officials, political associates, friends, and family, including his wife; some access to him at work in the White House, and—something I stuck out for—permission to travel with him on at least one trip away from Washington. The interview was great fun. Reagan enjoyed it, and characteristically sent me a handwritten note to say so. He had offered half an hour, and stayed for an hour and a half.

The trip, however, offered a revelation. It was to the great Jesuit university, Notre Dame, in South Bend, Indiana, where Reagan was due to make a speech, a university forever associated with footballing prowess since the great team of the early 1920s, famous for four swift running backs known as the "Four Horsemen of the Apocalypse." What was revealed was something of Reagan's extraordinary personal magic.

He chose to link his visit to the Hollywood movie in which he had starred, almost fifty years earlier, as George Gipp, the Notre Dame footballer known as "the Gipper," one of the stars coached by the immortal Knute Rockne, known as the Rock. Reagan's big scene in the movie showed the Gipper dying of consumption, and bequeathing his philosophy of life and football to the coach. The sequence we shot began with eight thousand students in the university's basketball arena singing a full-throated version of Notre Dame's football anthem, the "Fight Song."

"Anywhere else," my commentary began, over the swelling of eight thousand young voices singing the Notre Dame football song, "he's the President of the United States. Here, he's the Gipper. The Fight Song welcomes him to Notre Dame. This is the shrine of the American Irish, of American football, and of the American cult of victory."

"One secret of Ronald Reagan's political magic," I said, "lies in his knack of mixing a potent cocktail of reality and myth. His gospel is national uplift. But he deftly mixes it with a movie role he played sanctifying the Notre Dame football star of the 1920s, George Gipp."

"Rock," said the youthful Reagan in the script, "some day when the team is up against it and the breaks are beating the boys, tell them to go out there with all they've got and win just one for the Gipper. I don't know where I'll be then, but I'll know about it and I'll be happy."

"As Americans, as free people," said the president, forty years on, "you must stand firm even when it is uncomfortable for you to do so. There will be moments of joy, of triumph. There will also be times of despair. Times when all of those around you are ready to give up. It is then I want you to remember our meeting today, and sometimes when the team is up against it and the breaks are beating the boys, tell the to go out and win one for the Gipper. I don't know ..."

"Not everyone is applauding," I commented, "but as he leaves the stage, Ronald Reagan has set the agenda for whoever comes after him." And we left him quoting his own youthful self, "I don't know where I'll be then but I know I'll know about it and I'll be happy."

Here even those who are convinced of his imbecility must surely agree that he is pulling off something quite extraordinary. At the risk of sounding pretentious, you could call it a postmodernist layering of great subtlety. Here is the president of the United States, playing his younger self, playing a long-dead football hero, and leaving scarcely a dry eye in an audience of eight thousand. Of course what he was really doing was using both his own film career and Notre Dame's own most cherished legend to inspire his audience and, by identifying with their aspirations and their pride, persuade them to identify with him. No one can say that this is not subtle, even if it was instinctive, rather than worked out in detail. And that was what he did, *mutatis mutandis*, wherever he went. As the historian Garry Wills said to us in an interview, "through hero worship, he becomes a hero." He is also, like any great orator, using fantasy to shape reality.

* * *

We followed his journey from where it began, in Huck Finn country, a few miles from the Mississippi river, the middle of Middle America. "I've often thought," Reagan told me, "that there's something out there, in small town America, ... where you know everyone and are known by everyone in the community, that is different than being anonymous in a large city, and being able to go down the street and no one knows who you are, or cares." His family, he pointed out, with more reason than most politicians, "were not well off, as a matter of fact, we were poor by any standard, but I never knew a time when my mother wasn't finding someone in the community who was worse off than we were, and she was helping them."

In an interview Garry Wills pointed out that the values Reagan picked up in the Middle West included religiosity, a sense of community, the myths of hard work and individualism. He has so typified what most Americans think of themselves, Wills—himself a Midwestern Catholic—argued, "that it's almost impossible for most Americans, for the ordinary American, to dislike Reagan. It's an astonishing thing, an amazing achievement." That is indeed an achievement, though it is not Reagan's alone. The Middle West has managed to suggest that it is the *Ur*-America, somehow more American than Georgia, or Massachusetts, or New York City, or Texas. It ain't necessarily so, but the rest of the country has been more or less grudgingly convinced, and Reagan was able to capitalize, without insincerity, on the myth of Midwestern authenticity.

In Depression America, my commentary went on, the hottest entertainment was professional sport, and the new medium was radio. Reagan crossed the Mississippi to Iowa and got a job as a sports announcer. It wasn't just any radio station. It was one of the most powerful in the Middle West. The boss, B.J. Palmer, one of the founders and promoters of chiropraxis, was in the great tradition of Middle Western supersalesmen; in his lifetime he gave two thousand lectures on the theme "Sell yourself!"

Garry Wills pointed out that "B.J." as he was known, was the perfect mentor for Reagan. He could take somebody who was not a rogue, as B.J. was, but a sincere authentic Middle Western boy, and add these touches of show biz, of skill, of technique, without the cynicism that B.J. himself had.

So Reagan, in Wills's phrase, "went to school in manipulation, without himself being inauthentic."

He certainly learned some dark arts of deception, as another Reagan biographer, Anne Edwards, explained. "When he covered the Chicago Cubs baseball games, he never went anywhere near the stadium. The wire operator would pass him the bare facts of what was happening, and he would make up all the detail." He would describe how a player had made second base, and the crowds were cheering, and a little boy in the bleachers had caught a fly ball. It was a powerful station, so the whole Midwest learned to know that voice. Reagan was a regional media hero before he even arrived in Hollywood.

In 1937 he had gone out to California to report the Chicago Cubs spring training. Friends fixed up an audition at Warner Brothers. The face fitted, and the studio gave him a contract. In one jump he had got where thousands of young men would have given their rights arms to be. At his tennis court in the Hollywood hills, I asked Charlton Heston to assess Reagan as an actor. He was dismissive. "He did not have an extraordinary career. He worked steadily but most of his films were action films made during the war, comedies, things of that kind."

Then, in the Beverly Hills hotel, I interviewed Olivia De Havilland, a girl-friend of Reagan's in his earliest Hollywood days, long settled in Paris. There was no hiding the tenderness in her recollection, or genuine respect. He had, she said, "the manners of an archduke." She told a telling anecdote.

> This charming young man, rather a celebrity, asked to meet me and I remember him as being full of good nature and affability and grace. When Ronnie and Errol Flynn and I were working on *Santa Fe Trail* we were asked to assemble in two rows for a production photograph. Ronald Reagan, the second male lead in *Santa Fe Trail*, found that his position was in the second row, instead of the first. Because the second row was positioned just below the ridge of the hill, all you could see of him was this [and she peeped over her hand] above Errol Flynn's shoulder. Very quietly, the future president of the United States began to kick the dirt with his feet into a little mound, and built the mound higher and higher, and finally when the photographer said, "All right, everybody, let's smile," the future president of the United States stepped up onto the mound and *towered* over Errol Flynn!

That was a good example, I thought, of Reagan's lasting ability to prevail in a nonaggressive way, indeed in a way that usually left no scars and little resentment. Olivia de Havilland's story about his put-down of Errol Flynn is a good example. Another is his gentle destruction of Jimmy Carter in the first televised debate: "There you go again!"

He had other strengths. I began my major interview with him by saying a number of people had told us that one of his strengths was that he had an agenda of just a few big things that he wanted to change. What were those goals? Here is his answer:

> I had always believed that there was a kind of hunger for a spiritual revival, if you could call it that, in our country. Not only a revival in those things of

morality and family and so forth, but in our nation as a whole. We set out to do that, and I hear from a great many people who say that they now have a restored belief in our country.

He put it even more succinctly, in the campaign film from which we used an extract. It was, he said, "morning in America." Reagan had the most remarkable gift, it seems to me, that a politician can have: the gift of firing off what the French call *les petits mots qui s'envolent*: "little words that take wing."

Later in the interview I asked Reagan, as I would ask any president, about the personal burden of the office in a nuclear age: Did he lose any sleep when he thought about his nuclear responsibilities? "Nope," he answered. "I sleep pretty well. After I've said my prayers." There you go again! "After I've said my prayers." What other twentieth-century statesman would be able to slip that line in so unobtrusively, so innocently, conveying something that could hardly be said in any other way: that his personal confidence, his courage, and his trustworthiness were rooted in Christian faith?

I asked Reagan about his experience as president of the Screen Actors Guild, and here he gave us the only actual news break in the whole series. He said he had been approached by the FBI and had given "some finding" on people he had dealt with. In other words, though he did not say so in as many words, he confirmed that he had been an agent for the FBI and, as he put it, "it did give me a real understanding of the Communist menace." Reagan's daughter Maureen told us that both her parents had been threatened with acid, a tactic of some of those in the gangster end of the unions in those days. She said they had a guard posted in their garage for a couple of months. I do not know whether the threat was made. I am sure that Maureen remembered being told that it had been made.

These various anecdotes, and the insights they and many others gave me into Reagan's value system, had one thing at least in common. They referred to values that the people I spent my time with, whether in the newsroom of the *Washington Post*, where I had a desk for some years, or in New York publishers' offices, or in the faculty club at Harvard or even Stanford, or in law offices across the country, held in disdain. Indeed, some of the chords Reagan touched—recollections of his mother's churchgoing or her amateur dramatic recitations, his exceptionalist patriotism, his claim to represent a more authentic, because Middle Western, ethos, his suspicion of communism and socialism, and much else—would have been dismissed by most of my friends as "corny," "phony," even "cheesy." I would go further. In the worlds of New York or Washington journalism, or Ivy League faculty, or Democratic politics, people would not entertain for a moment the idea that Reagan's belief system was genuine. His values, it was simply assumed, were faked, put on for effect, cynical.

I do not believe that was so. No doubt Reagan, like most people in politics, had learned what people wanted him to say, and what they wanted him to be. For example, Reagan, a divorced man who had spent years as an eligible bachelor in Hollywood, was not the puritan in his private life the "moral majority" would have liked him to be. His relations with his children were not always quite those advocated by "family values." No doubt in many other respects he "played the game." But I came to believe that it was precisely because many tens of millions of Americans actually shared much of what Reagan believed that they came to like him, even to love him, as they did.

Specifically, and I think this was crucial to his extraordinary and in some respects nonpolitical appeal, Reagan was able to articulate, because he actually felt, the reactions that made so many in the 1970s and 1980s reject "liberalism" with such anger. That anger, my experience of following Ronald Reagan and talking in depth to so many of his friends helped me to understand, did not really come from any ideological rejection of liberal or Leftist programs or proposals. It was not an outraged belief in the righteousness of the Vietnam War. It was not about health insurance, or welfare reform, or taxes. It was not even, at least not usually, about race, though Reagan did sometimes, discreditably, play the race card in the South. It was directed at those, in what seemed to be a liberal elite, who appeared to reject the basic conviction that Reagan upheld and was even seen as incarnating, of the decency, the superior decency, of America.

Never mind that the liberalism at which conservative commentators rant is a convenient construct. In particular, the idea, dear to those publicists, that liberals are all rich is as untrue as the idea that all the rich are liberals. Never mind, for the purpose of understanding Reagan's peculiar hold on the American imagination, that his personal vision of American exceptionalism is in many respects a shallow version of the American experience, and certainly one that does not honestly confront the darker places of American history. It is nonetheless a vision shared by many Americans, and his ability to articulate it, usually in a friendly, as opposed to a hot-eyed, way, was critical to his success.

In January 1974 in his famous speech at the first Conservative Political Action conference, Reagan garbled the circumstances in which John Winthrop preached his sermon about a "city set upon a hill."[7] He said much else that was sentimental, or tendentious, or plain untrue. But the idea that resonated was simple, and it made his political fortune. "We are not a sick society," he said. The implication was that his opponents, conveniently labeled liberals, were saying that America was a sick society. It was a skilful political device, because it lumped together all those critical of any specific aspect of inequality or injustice in American society with the marginal fringe who thought that America was a sick society, with those, for example, who liked to spell the word Amerika with a K.

Fifteen years later, as he left the political stage, he made a very similar speech, and at the end of it he came back again to John Winthrop and the phrase that had done so much to make his career. The city Winthrop had imagined, he said, was

> a tall proud city built on rocks stronger than oceans, wind-swept, God-blessed, and teeming with people of all kinds living in harmony and peace, a city with

free ports that hummed with commerce and creativity, and if there had to be city walls, the walls had doors and the doors were open to anyone with the will and the heart to get here. That's how I saw it and see it still.

There is an argument to be made, and I have made it elsewhere, that exceptionalist rhetoric in this vein can be dangerous. It has something in common with the eighteenth and nineteenth century chauvinism that led to so much imperialism and war. It marginalizes and frustrates those who point out that there have been dark sides to the American experience, and that inequality and injustice remain. By so doing it may well defend the interests of the privileged and the comfortable. It may even, as we have seen in the administration of George W. Bush, rationalize or encourage an unrealistic and ultimately an aggressive attitude to those who are not Americans. But it is important also, I think, to recognize that in Ronald Reagan's mind, and in the minds of his many listeners and admirers, it was neither an ungenerous nor a mean-spirited vision.

The point, when he came upon the political stage, was that many, many "ordinary" Americans were furious with those other Americans whom they saw as insulting their country. They especially hated it when those they saw as relatively privileged, and in particular students, appeared apparently ungrateful for the opportunities of America. Ronald Reagan expressed and embodied that anger, and was therefore able to turn it to political account.

After half a generation of doubt and division, from the assassination of President Kennedy, through the murders of his brother Robert and of Martin Luther King, after the turmoil and disorder of the civil rights struggle, through the humiliation of Vietnam and the confusion and sheer shame of Watergate, after the energy crisis and the failures and frustrations of the Carter years, Reagan was exactly the president many Americans wanted: a president who could restore what has always been one of the sovereign American virtues, self-belief.

And what did I think, after a year following Reagan, talking to his friends, his family, his critics, and his colleagues? Here, for what it is worth, is how I ended the three films.[8]

> He may be a figure of fun for sophisticates.
> His grip on reality may sometimes seem vague.
> His single-minded righteousness can be terrifying for those who are not American ... even fatal for some who have got in his way.
> He has political magic and its secret is very simple.
> He believes without question in the promise of America.
> He invites Americans to find inspiration, for a future many find troubling, in the heroic simplicities of the American past. Americans needed Reagan to tell them they were special. Perhaps it was Ronald Reagan who was special—even unique.

In what respects was Ronald Reagan truly unique? Nearly twenty years later, I still believe that Ronald Reagan, so far from being a buffoon, was an unusually skillful political operator. Part of his effectiveness came from the fact that he had decades of experience of what several branches of the commercial entertainment industry had to teach about how to influence and channel public opinion. Even more, he owed his political magic, for on his game he did have real magic, to two circumstances. He genuinely felt, and felt strongly, the things he said. And they matched, and expressed, what a broad swathe of other Americans felt.

Was that unique? Certainly neither of the two Bushes could claim anything like this degree of political empathy, though in foreign affairs at least the senior Bush was a more than competent president. Oddly, the recent president who perhaps came closest to sharing some of this same talent, or good fortune, was one whose instincts were very different, and whose appeal therefore was to a very different segment of the electorate: William Jefferson Clinton. Clinton did have, and still has, an instinctive empathy with what many Democrats feel.

The question arises: was Reagan unique in the sense that we are not likely to look upon his like again? How likely is it that the American political system will throw up other leaders with the same ability to articulate the deep undertows of national emotion? The administration of George W. Bush has lost the mandate of heaven. There is not yet any corresponding sense of where that mandate will alight. There has always been a strong recurrent pulse of alternation in American political history, even if the alternations are often slow and their duration hard to predict. When they do come, it is because the majority feels, not simply that it is time for a change, but that a political era has ended, and a political epoch has arrived.

Since the writings of V.O. Key[9] and Walter D. Burnham[10] a whole branch of America political science has grown up that examines "critical elections" and party realignment, and asks what circumstances lead to them. Reagan's election in 1980, even more than the Nixon victory in 1968, is generally felt to have been such an epoch. Perhaps what the Reagan experience really shows is that the shared empathy that makes it possible to change the terms of politics can only come after the trauma of acknowledged failure. If that is so, then Ronald Reagan's political secret had something in common with that of his early model, Franklin Roosevelt. We may still have to wait for clear evidence that the conservative ascendancy is generally acknowledged to have failed, and that, therefore, a new epoch is at hand. In the meantime, Ronald Reagan will remain an epochal figure.

Notes

1. I was the Washington correspondent of the London *Observer* from 1962 to 1965. In the mid-1960s I worked as a reporter for British independent television and from 1967 onward, for some years, I frequently wrote about the United States for the *Sunday Times* of London.
2. Lewis Chester, Godfrey Hodgson, and Bruce Page, *An American Melodrama* (New York: Viking, 1969).
3. Godfrey Hodgson, *America in Our Time* (New York: Doubleday, 1976).

4. Godfrey Hodgson, *All Things to All Men* (New York: Simon & Schuster, 1980).
5. Especially Daniel Patrick Moynihan, a close friend whose biography I later wrote: Godfrey Hodgson, *The Gentleman from New York* (New York: Houghton Mifflin, 2000).
6. In the United States, it was shown in a slightly reedited form with commentary by Garry Wills.
7. Reagan imagined that the sermon was preached off the coast of Massachusetts, when Winthrop actually gave it in Southampton, before he had ever left England. The ship was not the *Arabella*, as Reagan called it, but the *Arbella*. And Winthrop meant his colony to be a model for other colonies, not other nations.
8. This is taken from the draft in my files labeled "final draft." It may not be word for word identical to either the British or still less the American version of the broadcast.
9. V.O. Key, Jr., "A Theory of Critical Elections," *The Journal of Politics*, 17 (1965), 13–18.
10. Walter Dean Burnham, *Critical Elections and the Mainsprings of American Politics* (New York: W.W. Norton, 1970).

Chapter 3

"Just Say No": Drug Abuse Policy in the Reagan Administration

Peter G. Bourne

Introduction

I had served as an assistant director of the Special Action Office for Drug Abuse Prevention (SAODAP) under President Richard Nixon and had been one of the architects of the original federal strategy for dealing with the drug problem in the early 1970s. Later I became, in the Carter administration, director of the White House Office of Drug Abuse Policy (ODAP), an expanded version of SAODAP with authority over all treatment, law enforcement, and foreign policy aspects of drug abuse. Through three administrations, two Republican and one Democratic, a network of expertise had been built up both inside and outside the government. It was comprised of people who regarded themselves as career professionals in the field of addiction sciences. Mostly physicians, medical scientists, epidemiologists, social workers, and psychologists, and others in the helping professions, they created what amounted to the accumulated wisdom in the country with regard to drug addiction. Because of their professional backgrounds they tended to be politically liberal, but as long as they were producing significant results, as they did during the years when heroin was the major problem, political leaders of both parties were happy to defer to them. The fundamental principle in which these experts believed was that addiction was a disease and addicts were sick people who needed to be treated.

When Reagan came to power a dramatic change occurred that left the addiction experts, myself included, in deep dismay. This was on many counts. First, Reagan and his staff did not see drug abuse as a major priority, they did not accept the idea of the addict as a sick person, and they rejected the notion that reducing the harm caused by drug addiction (and especially reducing drug-related deaths) was a particular responsibility of the government. Focusing on marijuana use from which no one died and cutting funds for treatment programs for hard drugs was a fundamental repudiation of the entire basis of previous federal policy. If the policy was to be simply that all drugs are bad and any user will be punished not treated, you did not need to employ in the government people who were scientific experts in the field. Scientific measures of success or failure were similarly rejected. Numbers of arrests and convictions became the indicators that the new policies were working. What most of us, then, failed to perceive was the extent to which any government policy depends on the political context within which it exists. Politicians will support policies only as long as they are a popular with the constituency they represent. While a public health approach to drug addiction prevailed it was only because during that time it generated goodwill for those in the White House. The dramatic shift in policy under Reagan was more than anything a response to the pressures from constituencies in his party that wanted a completely different approach.

In June 2006 there was a day-long seminar in Washington to celebrate the thirty-fifth anniversary of the legislation that created the position of White House "drug czar." Nearly all the people who had held that job were in attendance (with the notable exception of Dr. Carlton Turner, the first person to hold that job under Reagan). There was a striking schism among the first four "drug czars," all of whom had treated addicts and had direct familiarity with the drug culture and those–in both parties—who served under Reagan or later presidents. When the former got up to speak they spoke in detail of the thought behind their strategies to reduce the mortality and morbidity due to drug use during their tenure. The latter group (including a general, and former secretaries of Commerce and of Education), lacking serious knowledge of the field, were largely reduced to telling anecdotes about their time in power as the drug czar.

Today, the level of drug use in the United States is not greatly different from what it was in the Reagan years and in particular during the antidrug frenzy of 1988, yet it commands very little attention from the media or from politicians. One can argue that due to the threat to the military and the demonstrable connection between drug use and street crime Nixon was right to see drugs as posing a serious threat to the country. His actions in creating SAODAP were then justified. However, the subsequent, greatly expanded law-enforcement approach has been counterproductive: drug addiction still contributes substantially to crime and gets little or no attention. It is clear that concern about drugs is first and foremost a matter of political expediency.

The Reagan Approach

Drug policy during the Reagan administration was a reflection of the broader ideology that the president and his supporters brought to the White House. The causes of social problems were no longer to be seen as the lack of opportunity, inequality, racism, or injustice, but rather as a matter of individual responsibility. The individual was to be held accountable for any lack of achievement or antisocial behavior rather than placing blame on society. This dovetailed with the commitment to reduce the size of government and its role in trying to solve social problems. At the time Reagan came to office, drug abuse by the objective standards of mortality and morbidity was not a major problem for the country, and was not seen as a significant priority by those around him. Very rapidly, however, grassroots pressure from a segment of the constituency that helped to elect him caused that to change. In the early years of the Reagan administration, therefore, the attention paid to the drug issue was strongly driven by political forces outside the government.

Reagan's drug policy represented a major philosophical departure from that of his three predecessors and can be understood only in the broader context of America's overall response to the drug issue in the second half of the twentieth century. After several decades of relative inattention, the illicit use of drugs was first identified as a significant social and political problem worthy of White House concern during the Nixon administration. After an initial abortive attempt through "Operation Intercept" to block the flow of marijuana across the Mexican border, the Nixon White House focused on heroin addiction as the primary problem. This was the result of two reports, the first showing a high correlation between heroin addiction and mushrooming street crime,[1] and the second revealing spiraling heroin use among U.S. troops in Vietnam.[2] While it would be correct to say, as with Reagan later, that there was a significant political component to Nixon's response, there was also a real national threat posed from reduced military effectiveness and soaring street crime. President Richard Nixon established the SAODAP, staffed primarily with professional experts in the field of addiction, regardless of their political affiliation. The philosophical and strategic underpinning of the program set up by the professionals was that drug addiction was a public health problem and that making treatment universally available, referred to as "demand reduction," combined with interdicting the supply, was the best way to counteract the problem. As health people with scientific educations, they generally measured their success in scientific terms, focusing on such indicators as overdose deaths, numbers of emergency room visits, and statistics for reduced street crime. They saw as their primary goal achieving a reduction in death and disability caused by illicit drug use and therefore their top priority was on the drug most responsible—heroin. They had relatively little interest in drug use merely because it was illegal if it did not result in serious health consequences.

The creation of SAODAP as an administrative entity within the Executive Office of the president, with its director confirmed by the Senate and subject to Congressional hearings, was highly unusual. It represented an unprecedented intrusion of the authority of the legislative branch into the executive branch. Traditionally, those working in the White House and reporting to the president were protected by executive privilege and exempted from being called to testify before the Congress. That SAODAP was allowed by Nixon to be such a striking exception reflected the strong bipartisan backing for the initiative and showed how important it was in his mind to demonstrate that he was taking an assertive proactive stance on the issue.

While Nixon and his political staff maintained a deeply moralistic attitude toward drug use and used it as one of the iconic weapons to disparage "their people" (blacks, the poor, hippies, antiwar activists, and liberals) as opposed to "our people" (whites, the privileged, war supporters, and conservatives), they desperately needed to show progress against the rising tide of crime in the cities and the embarrassing image of a sea of G.I. heroin addicts losing the war in Vietnam.[3] The fact that treating heroin addicts worked, especially on a large scale with methadone maintenance, made it clearly the most attractive option.[4] Led by physicians (mostly liberal Democrats) in SAODAP, the drug abuse professionals turned the program into a humanitarian venture aimed at reducing overdose deaths and rehabilitating addicts, defining them as patients and not criminals. This approach was expanded, refined, institutionalized, and made increasingly successful under President Gerald R. Ford, and more especially under President Jimmy Carter. The stated goal was that no addict should be able to say, "I want treatment but there is nowhere I can get it." By 1978, the overdose death rate from heroin had been reduced to roughly eight hundred annually (from a level of well over two thousand per year in the Nixon administration).[5] Effective strategies had to be tailored to different forms of drug use. The second largest cause of drug overdose deaths was from barbiturates (all originating from legitimate pharmaceutical sources). Under pressure from the Carter administration, the pharmaceutical industry agreed to a restriction on the prescribing of these drugs outside a hospital setting. Deaths in that category also went down.[6] The focus on reducing drug-related mortality and morbidity meant that marijuana use, from which no one died directly, was de-emphasized. It was clear that the overwhelming damage to people's lives from marijuana use resulted from draconian laws that led to long prison sentences for possession or sale. In a philosophical context emphasizing harm reduction, reform of those laws was the preferred strategy. By reducing marijuana possession to merely a finable offence, California saved during 1976–1985 an estimated $958,305,500.[7] During the same period there was no increase in marijuana use. At this point cocaine was still largely a recreational drug of the wealthy, causing less than ten deaths a year. Only later would the more lethal "crack cocaine" version of the drug appear.

The first four drug czars, as the directors of the White House drug office were known, were clearly committed to conceptualizing America's drug problem as a public health issue, and their strategies for control flowed from that. It is worth noting, however, that even on their terms drug addiction was, comparatively, a modest public health problem. In 1969, 1,601 individuals died from drug abuse, 2,641 choked to death on food, 1,824 died after falling down stairs, 29,866 died from cirrhosis of the liver (due to alcoholism), and more than 400,000 died from the effects of cigarette smoking.[8] For the majority of Americans drug abuse was, and to a large extent still is, more of a political, legal, economic, and moral issue than a health problem. The election of Ronald Reagan saw a dramatic shift back to that more traditional view and a rejection of the public health model. Public health, with its equal focus on the welfare of every member of society regardless of merit, not only hinted at "socialism," but was also incompatible with the Reagan philosophical focus on the primacy of the individual.

The Conservative Backlash

Despite the demonstrable success measured by lives saved and crime reduced, there was considerable criticism of the government's efforts during the last year or so of the Carter administration. It was based on several arguments deriving from an antithetical view of the government's role in addressing social problems, as espoused by conservative Republicans and championed by Ronald Reagan in the lead-up to the 1980 election. The attitude toward drugs was part of a larger philosophical shift espoused by the Republicans, which saw the cause of such problems as being not lack of opportunity, inequality, racism, or injustice, but rather the result of immoral acts by individuals failing to take responsibility for their own actions. The details of the Reagan drug program are well chronicled in the books *Smoke and Mirrors* (1996) by Daniel Baum[9] and *The Fix* (1998) by Michael Massing.[10] Several themes that they identified are noteworthy:

1. Drug addiction was not a health problem but a moral problem. Drug users were not patients, but sinners or criminals who should be punished not treated. The focus should not be on those who had become drug dependent, but on anyone who used an illicit drug, even once. Drug use, especially for recreational purposes, was seen as an important icon of a larger "culture war" in which Reagan and the conservatives had been engaged since the anti–Vietnam War movement or even earlier. The best way to stop addiction, they argued, was to prevent anyone from taking drugs in the first place, rather than focusing on the minority who had become addicted.
2. The government should not be involved in the provision of treatment services, which was the responsibility of the private sector. The overall Reagan philosophy called for government to be shrunk, and therefore tax dollars should not be used to support the hundreds of clinics around the country that were treating tens of thousands of addicts. While earlier administrations had focused on the health problem posed by those who became addicted, the Reagan administration was primarily concerned with stopping any form of illicit drug use.
3. The real drug problem in America was not heroin addiction, but marijuana use, which involved far larger numbers and (although unsupported by data), they felt, mainly affected white middle-class young people such as their own children. The ability of Reagan and his staff to de-emphasize the importance of heroin was, ironically, made possible by the very success of the strategy originally launched under Nixon, which they now derided. The public sense of alarm over heroin use had been successfully defused by Reagan's predecessors.

4. Government funding was pouring into black inner city communities, benefiting African American organizations that hired ex-addicts, community people, and welfare clients. It was seen as a form of political patronage that was predicated on heroin addiction being the top priority. Government contracts should, they believed, instead be going to consulting firms focusing on preventing ordinary teenagers in both rich and poor communities from ever trying drugs.

Those who espoused these beliefs had coalesced in the late 1970s into a nationwide network of "Parents' Groups." Maverick politician and multimillionaire Ross Perot hooked up with Dr. Carlton Turner, a pharmacological chemist, who conducted basic (but not clinical) research on marijuana at a government-funded facility at the University of Mississippi. In 1979 and 1980, supported by Perot's money, they toured together, mainly in the Bible Belt, warning of the horrors of marijuana and Washington's misplaced priorities.[11] Their message resonated well with parents whose greatest fear was that their own children were experimenting with drugs. These same parents related far less well to a public health model. Generated in Washington, the evidence-based public health model relied on statistical data to address overall health status in the country as a result of illegal drug use and was focused primarily on inner city populations with whom these parents felt little affinity. The Parents' Groups overlapped substantially with the supporters of the burgeoning Reagan presidential campaign.

When Reagan came to power, his attorney general, William French Smith, announced a tough new law-and-order policy, focusing, among other things, on America's drug users. Drug abuse was seen, initially, as one of several areas to be utilized in getting the public behind a drive to strengthen law enforcement and the judicial system. The Reagan Justice Department, pushed by Edwin Meese in the White House, also sought to centralize its power at the federal level. At the same time David Stockman, the budget director, and committed to Reagan's desire to shrink government, declared war on all domestic social programs with an evangelical zeal aimed at substantially cutting the overall federal budget. William French Smith was able to get the Justice Department exempted from any cuts by arguing to Reagan that his department was not a domestic agency, but "the internal arm of national defense." The federal funding of drug treatment slots was phased out in favor of giving "block grants" to states that they could spend in any way they wished. Few were inclined to spend the money on the treatment network that had taken ten years under three presidents to build and that had previously been almost entirely underwritten by the federal government. Drug abuse research at the federal level was immediately cut by 15 percent, but due to congressional opposition it still did better than child nutrition (down 34 percent), urban development grants (down 35 percent), education block grants (down 38 percent), school milk programs (down 78 percent), and energy conservation (down 83 percent).[12]

The Parents' Groups lobbied hard with the help of Ross Perot to have Dr. Carlton Turner appointed as the drug czar in the White House. When he was asked by Ed Meese, Reagan's domestic policy adviser, in the job interview, what his top priority would be, the chemist astutely replied, "strong law enforcement." Turner's appointment represented a sea change in defining America's drug problem and the manner of response. During the early part of the Reagan administration, however, he was made only an "adviser" on drug abuse to the president. Reagan's political staff did not want to appoint Turner as director of the White House drug office, because the required Senate confirmation would have stirred serious controversy in the Congress about his lack of qualifications for the job. Although Turner was a botanical chemist who was well trained and well respected as the leading scientific authority on the chemical components of the cannabis plant, he was not trained in, nor had he conducted research into, the effects of these chemicals on the human (or even on animal) bodies. He had no knowledge or background in the behavioral aspects of drug use, the treatment of drug abuse, law enforcement, or foreign policy aspects of drug abuse.

Reagan's policy advisers also knew that presenting marijuana as the number one drug problem could not withstand the scrutiny of a public scientific debate. Moreover, they wanted to reverse the Nixon precedent that had allowed a member of the president's staff to be called directly to testify before congressional committees. In 1982, when an Omnibus Crime Bill that the Congress had worked on for months reached Reagan's desk, he vetoed the entire legislation simply because it contained a provision calling on the president to nominate a drug czar to direct the White House Office of Drug Abuse Policy, who as a presidential appointee would be confirmed by the Senate.

The change of perspective was manifested in a number of ways. First, no longer was any distinction made between different drugs of abuse, or the strategy tailored to cope with each of them. All drugs were equally evil and, especially if treatment was no longer to be funded, there was no point in mentioning them individually. Ironically, under the Carter administration, whenever "drugs of abuse" were mentioned in a generic sense, the caveat "including alcohol and tobacco" was always added, but this was immediately dropped under Reagan. It was argued that the difference was that these substances were legal and therefore should be not be impugned by being lumped with "illegal drugs."[13] The fact that smoking was the cause of roughly three hundred–four hundred times the number of deaths each year as all illegal drugs added together, and alcohol a comparable figure, was of no concern. The agreement with the drug companies to limit barbiturate use was rescinded (even though it had been successful in reducing overdose deaths and the industry had been relatively happy with the arrangement). The shift away from a health orientation could not have been more clearly demonstrated.

Second, there was no longer an effort to find those who might be addicted and need treatment. Instead there was a fervent campaign to find any individual who was using, or had ever used, any illicit substance. Anyone could be forced to provide urine for a drug test on almost any pretext. All employees of the federal government and the military were required to be tested for drugs. President Reagan and Vice President George H. Bush even submitted urine samples—they passed (although once out of office, it emerged that Nancy and Ronald Reagan had used marijuana in their Hollywood days). Corporations became obsessed with a search for drug users among their employees, spawning a massively profitable industry to test urine for traces of the offending substances. By 1985, drug testing had become a hundred million dollars per year business. The association in the public mind of marijuana use with the adherence to liberal views led to the assertion by critics that urine assays were as much a political test as a drug test. With forty million Americans (mostly anti-Reagan) admitting to having used marijuana, a positive urine test could become a basis for conviction, a long prison term, or at least serious damage to a career. Under Reagan, prison populations soared, until the United States had a higher percentage of its population behind bars that any other nation. The majority were there on drug charges.[14]

With the new approach came a growing politicization in the role of U.S. attorneys, who had hitherto been insulated from politics. Although technically political appointees, they were mostly career professionals who frequently continued in their jobs through several changes in the presidency. Generally they had a low profile focusing on white-collar crimes, securities fraud, civil rights, and other major and complex federal crimes. State and local prosecutors dealt with the everyday crimes such as rape, murder, and armed robbery that generally caught the headlines. Rarely were drug crimes dealt with by U.S. attorneys unless the quantities were massive and significant conspiracies were involved. Under William French Smith in collaboration with Edwin Meese in the White House, that was all to change. The network of ninety-four U.S. attorneys across the country was seen as a vital instrument to extend the control and influence of the Reagan administration at the local level. While the rhetoric of conservative Republicans strongly advocated the devolution of power from Washington to the state governments, they were working feverishly in this area to achieve the reverse. Drugs were to become the stalking horse for a long-term strategy to terminate the independence of the prosecutors.

Smith hired Rudolf Giuliani, the former chief of the federal drug prosecution office in New York, and made him the number three person in the Justice Department. Through Giuliani, Smith ordered the U.S. attorneys to abandon their long-established emphasis on white-collar crime and focus instead primarily on drug violations. This was to be not just major traffickers but also street-level users and dealers. What mattered were numbers, so that the public could be shown clear evidence of what the Reagan administration was doing about drugs.[15] At a broader political level, the authority enjoyed by U.S. attorneys, unlike local prosecutors, to use wiretaps and convene secret grand juries from which no transcripts were made public was particularly attractive to Giuliani in enhancing local control by the administration.

The new directives from the Justice Department in Washington were met with disbelief and dismay. Several of the U.S. attorneys resigned in disgust.

It was not just that they resented the politicization of their jobs, but as serious senior professionals they felt demeaned when ordered to drop serious crime cases in favor of petty drug offences.[16]

This politicization of the once independent prosecutorial system that began under Reagan would have serious long-term consequences for the country. Subsequent administrations, both Democratic and Republican sought to use the federal prosecutorial system for the pursuit of political agendas. Instead of having a proud tradition of independence, the U.S. attorneys had become just another vehicle for trying to maintain permanent control by the party in power. The news media played along. Stories about heroin addiction vanished from the newspapers, to be replaced by dire warnings about the scourge of marijuana. Cocaine, rarely if ever mentioned in the first two years of the Reagan administration, received only the most cursory media coverage. Public service advertisements on television warned parents of the signs to look for in their children that might suggest they were using drugs, but without specifying what drugs, except to imply that marijuana was the probable problem. Many white middle-class teenagers were using marijuana, and their parents were then faced with the dilemma of what to do about it. A new industry began—the private rehabilitation (or "rehab") center. An attractive alternative to a prison term, these were of variable quality, but made large sums from affluent parents (four thousand dollars initially and one thousand dollars a week) who were terrified of what might be happening to their children. Dealing mostly with teenage rebellion (much of it normal), drug use was frequently an incidental manifestation of acting-out behavior and had nothing to do with addiction or serious health problems. To create the semblance of a treatment methodology, the term "tough love" was coined. It involved the creation of a rigid and often highly punitive environment combined with acceptance and approval for those who confessed their sins and accepted a new path to conformity. Some treatment facilities were justifiably criticized as brutal and cruel places. Others may have salvaged teenagers who were the victims of failed parenting. Yet they had little to do with any real threat to the country from drug abuse. These centers also needed to be distinguished from the several legitimate, private medical, facilities devoted to treating those with clinical addictions.

Such was the importance that the administration now attached to its new crusade against drugs that the First Lady got involved. Nancy Reagan's advisers wanted her to devote her time to cultural and artistic causes. She had already sought to draw a distinction between herself and her predecessor, Rosalynn S. Carter, by saying she would not be involved in any "policy issues." She and the president had taken an interest in those with an addiction problem they had encountered in the Hollywood community, however, and she insisted on talking about the subject. On July 4, 1984, Nancy Reagan was visiting Longfellow Elementary School in Oakland, California. Sitting in a semi-circle with a group of fourth-graders, she was asked by one child what he should do if his friends pressed him to smoke pot. She uttered the magic words, "Just say no." They were picked up by all the television networks on the evening news. The simple slogan was adopted across the country and became a rallying cry not merely against drug use but more subtly against "liberalism" generally. While it was derided by critics as being the equivalent of telling someone clinically depressed to "have a nice day," it had immense political appeal, because it simplistically cut through the complexities of understanding the effects of different drugs; the distinctions between use, abuse, and addiction, the benefits of different treatment modalities, and the legal versus medical arguments. For widely differing reasons, "Just say no" resonated across the political spectrum. To conservatives, eager to distil the complex down to the most succinct, it neatly summarized their philosophy on drug abuse; to liberals, it reflected the vacuousness they saw inherent in most of the administration's policies. Ineffectual, but relatively innocuous, the phrase has become the single most memorable legacy of Nancy Reagan's time in the White House.

In the middle of 1982, the prestigious National Academy of Sciences issued a report, commissioned earlier during the Carter administration, which reviewed the health and social aspects of marijuana. The scientific experts who conducted the study announced they had found "no convincing evidence" that marijuana permanently damages the brain or nervous system, or decreases fertility. They further noted that possession of small amounts of cannabis should not be a criminal offence, stating, "Alienation from the rule of law in a democratic society may be the most serious cost of the current marijuana laws."[17] Carlton Turner chose to ignore the findings of this distinguished panel as he did those of the Nixon Commission on the same topic. In so doing he alienated himself from the scientific community. He also discredited himself with his own professional colleagues. Previously accepted as a qualified researcher who knew as much as anyone about the chemistry of the substances contained in cannabis, Turner's rejection of the findings of the commission of experts raised eyebrows even among his immediate peers.

Similarly undeterred by scientific opinion, President Reagan on June 24, 1982, stood in the White House Rose Garden to announce his War on Drugs.[18] He decried the heavy focus of the Carter drug program on treatment as a policy of defeat. Reagan stated, "We're taking down the surrender flag...We're running up the battle flag." The only drug he mentioned specifically was marijuana. He called for the mobilization of parents, teachers, civic and religious leaders, and state and local officials. He stressed that law enforcement would be at the center of his program as well as an enhanced effort to stop the flow of drugs from outside the country. He made clear that the United States faced a dire threat and people should be appropriately frightened, but the specific nature of the threat was never spelled out, nor the precise strategy for dealing with it. It was a moral and political threat he was talking about, and the drug program was ill-equipped to cope with that problem. Reagan also used the speech as an opportunity to bring Carlton Turner out of the shadows as his drug adviser, finally making him director of a new Drug Abuse Policy Office.

Reagan quickly waived the 103-year-old Posse Comitatus Act that prohibited the U.S. military from performing law enforcement functions inside the country. Every Cabinet member was told to develop a drug program within their department. In five years, Pentagon funding for drug abuse programs went from $1 million to $196 million.

With the cutbacks in federal funding for treatment slots, some funds were made available for prevention programs. The latter were mostly unproven strategies with little or no scientific evidence that they had any real effect in discouraging drug use. They were aimed generally at the children of suburban families rather than inner city minorities, and the grants for their implementation went overwhelmingly to white middle-class organizations. The White House cited their implementation as evidence that Reagan was getting the "drug war back on the right track."[19]

Professional addiction experts, many of them highly trained physicians with years of experience in the field, became progressively dispirited. Several resigned from the federal government or the government-funded programs they had run. They were mostly replaced by young political appointees, most of whom had no training or experience in the addiction field, but were happy to adhere to the White House message that the drug problem could be solved if the country just accepted that any drug use was morally wrong. What had been a cadre of experts chosen over a number of years by virtue of their scientific competence and regardless of political affiliation was rapidly dissipated.

Figures compiled each month by the National Institute on Drug Abuse on the nationwide number of drug-related deaths (mostly overdoses) had for a decade been considered by professionals as the gold standard for a quick indication of whether a particular policy was working. Under Carter, this monthly figure had dropped to the lowest level since the early 1960s.[20] Within two months of Reagan taking office the number of deaths began to climb again, moving relentlessly higher month after month. After little more than a year the National Institute on Drug Abuse was ordered to stop releasing the figures. The explanation given was that the White House Office of Drug Abuse Policy had determined such figures "were no longer relevant to the War on Drugs."[21]

Ultimately one drug more than any other would be associated with the Reagan era, namely cocaine. Initially ignored by the Reagan administration, as it had been to large degree by earlier administrations, its use had steadily increased over the years especially in the entertainment industry. Overplayed by the media, its use became widely identified in the public mind with the free-wheeling capitalism of the Reagan era and the frenzied greed on Wall Street. Until the middle of the Reagan years, it caused a negligible number of deaths, partly because its cost limited its use, it was not widely available, and by-and-large those who partook of it tended to be relatively well-adjusted people using it for recreation, who were able to avoid addiction. A few, including celebrities, did develop severe dependency, and, particularly if they were public figures, their plight received widespread public attention, exaggerating the perception of the threat that particular drug, in its usual powdered form, posed.

In the middle of 1985, the National Institute on Drug Abuse began to get reports from California of a new form of cocaine. Cocaine paste cooked with baking soda formed small rocks that could be easily concealed, cheaply made, and sold on the streets in single dose amounts. It came to known as "crack." Easily concealed, it had an immediate appeal to the increasingly desperate population of America's inner cities.

The Reagan administration was suddenly confronted with an entirely new drug problem that no previous administration had to address. Suddenly they were paying the price for having driven out of government those with professional expertise and experience in the addiction sciences. Carlton Turner was not a physician and had never treated an addict. He had also thrown in his lot with the hard-line law enforcement contingent. No one in the federal government seemed capable of formulating a rational strategy to deal with this dramatic new development. Slogans alone could not stem the tide that crack had unleashed.

Experienced clinicians running clinics and therefore on the frontline interfacing with the drug culture had for some time been reporting a steady increase in cocaine use and first raised the alarm over crack. Turner refused to meet with any of these acknowledged experts, including the highly respected Dr. David Smith, director of the Haight–Ashbury Free Medical Clinic, and together with the Parents' Groups managed to prevent them from participating in any conference over which they had influence.[22] Turner refused to speak at any conference where professional treatment people were present. In so doing he insured that he insulated himself from the very people who might have been able to help him. Turner was hemorrhaging credibility. Eventually after visiting drug treatment facilities where he was told that "roughly 40 percent" of patients under eighteen had had homosexual experiences, he told a reporter from *Newsweek* that homosexuality was a sequel to marijuana use. Queried as to whether perhaps these men were gay first, he replied, "No, the drug came first." His remarks triggered a firestorm of criticism in the gay community, among drug treatment leaders, and even from more thoughtful Republicans.[23] Increasingly over his head in a job for which he was entirely unqualified he resigned shortly thereafter.

His replacement, Dr. Ian MacDonald, was a pleasant Florida pediatrician who had been drawn into the antidrug movement out of a sincere concern for the young marijuana users he had encountered. He had no background in the addiction field, but he had campaigned relentlessly across the country preaching against the evils of marijuana and had even put his own son in a treatment facility because of his use of cannabis. His unwavering loyalty to the Reagan ideology had earned him, despite his lack of administrative or policy experience, an appointment as the director of the Alcohol, Drug Abuse and Mental Health Administration. He was well-meaning and an eager learner. However, his appointment to the White House job put him into a political arena for which he was entirely ill-prepared.

Ed Meese, who had taken over as attorney general, saw the mushrooming drug issue as an irresistible opportunity to enhance his own power, influence, and visibility.[24] He chaired a Drug Enforcement Policy Board that met monthly to set policy. He removed the word "enforcement" from its name thereby establishing his committee as the pre-eminent policy body with authority across the board, notwithstanding MacDonald's role in the White House. Although invited to the meetings MacDonald found that he was marginalized and Meese orchestrated the agenda to insure that it focused almost entirely on draconian military and high-tech law enforcement approaches to the problem. Although situated in the White House, MacDonald, who almost never saw the president, lacked the full authority of that office behind him. As a physician, he sought to insert at least some consideration of treatment into the dialogue, but he was no match for Meese and others on the committee who had spent their careers in law enforcement and the ruthless world of Republican politics.[25]

It soon became clear that any rational dialogue to formulate a coherent and balanced strategy was being replaced by propaganda and fear, counseling and treatment by surveillance and punishment. Meese understood that the greater the fear he could engender in the public around the drug abuse issue the more unquestioned power and resources he would be given to deal with it and the less people would complain about the curtailment of civil liberties and constitutional rights. Meese pronounced the drug problem as a dire threat to national security that could only be dealt with by extreme measures. "Constitutional freedoms," Meese argued, "should not be used as a 'screen' to protect defendants who engaged in the evil of drugs." He implied that lawyers who defended drug cases were unpatriotic, and his Justice Department began using new subpoena powers to force defense lawyers to inform on their own drug clients. New laws allowing the confiscation of the assets of those facing drug indictments meant they were stripped of the resources they needed to hire a lawyer. Between 1986 and 1990, $1500 million in assets were seized by the Justice Department ($500 million in 1991 alone). Of those from whom property was confiscated by the police in 1991, 80 percent were never actually charged with a crime. Massive amounts of money ($35 million in 1987 and $63 million in 1989) were paid to drug informants, fueling the distrust and violence in the drug-using community.[26]

Between 1985 and 1987, 99 percent all drug trafficking defendants were African American.[27] In mid-1986, African Americans, who made up just 12 percent of the total population, passed the 50 percent mark in U.S. prisons. In 1989, 35 percent of all African American males aged sixteen and thirty-five were in prison, on parole, or facing drug charges. The drug war that early in the Reagan administration had been focused almost entirely on marijuana use by white suburban youth had evolved with the advent of crack into a preoccupation with the inner city black population. Fear of young black men bent on crime was widespread among the middle class. With few treatment options available for cocaine (as opposed to heroin) addiction, intensified law enforcement—to which the administration was already strongly inclined—seemed to offer the only alternative. Imprisonment sent a far clearer message than treatment clinics that on this front, at least, the war on drugs was being won. In some jurisdictions the jail sentence for possession of crack, the preferred form for blacks, was ten times the sentence for regular cocaine used mainly by whites. It dovetailed with the earlier broad Reagan administration message that the reasons your taxes are so high is because of government programs giving massive handouts to undeserving blacks—epitomized by Reagan's fantasized stories of "welfare queens" arriving in Cadillacs to pick up their welfare checks and other benefits. It not only resulted in a justification for wholesale arrests, but allowed the argument to be made that imprisonment of tens of thousands of young African Americans made the country safer.

Throughout the Reagan years the Congress was largely complicit in the draconian excesses associated with the administration's drug abuse policies. It was seen as being for all practical purposes an issue without political risk. Even liberal Democrats, such as Senator Joseph Biden, saw support for harsh penalties as a way of showing they were tough on crime. It was also a way of currying favor with the Reagan administration without losing votes in their home districts. In 1984 the Senate, by a vote of 91 to 1, abolished federal parole meaning that anyone convicted had to serve the full sentence they were given. Strict mandatory sentencing guidelines for drug offences were also put in place. The brother of then governor of Arkansas, Bill Clinton, was indicted in 1984 for selling cocaine and conspiracy. He received a sentence of two years of which he served sixteen months. Had he been convicted a couple of years later when the mandatory sentences went into effect he would have had to serve a full ten years.

A turning point occurred in June 1986 when a young college basketball star, Len Bias, died from a heart condition apparently precipitated by his use of cocaine. Anonymous young African Americans were dying everyday in the inner cities from drug overdoses, but when a clean cut star athlete succumbed it caught the nation's attention. In response to the public outrage over the death, Democrat Tip O'Neill, speaker of the house, was determined to get out ahead of the White House. He urged his committee chairmen to develop quickly legislation that would show Democrats could be as tough on drugs as Republicans. Dozens of hard-line bills were rapidly drafted usually with no hearings and rarely even the most cursory input from anyone knowledgeable about the drug problem. The central theme was to see who could be toughest on anyone associated with drug use. There were proposals to ban lawyers from representing drug defendants and anyone who did business of any kind with them. If a dry cleaner did business with a drug dealer they should be put in prison and their business seized, one congressman argued. Several advocated the death sentences for some trafficking offences. In four months twenty-nine new mandatory minimum sentences were approved, twenty-six of them being for drug crimes.

By the end of the Reagan years, there was near hysteria about drugs. During the Congressional session leading up to the election of 1988 a bidding war essentially took place to see who could propose legislation with the most horrendous penalties for sale or possession of drugs. No politician could lose by being "too tough on drugs." At the time Reagan came to power it was hard to see, by any measure, a drug problem that posed any real threat to America's welfare, especially compared with poor education in the public schools, inadequate healthcare, or a decline in family cohesion and parenting skills. Yet, there was an effort to portray the problem as a great moral struggle, to inflate the nature and magnitude of the threat way beyond what the objective evidence suggested, to demonize elements of the population (anyone who had ever used drugs and later crack cocaine users), and to use the inflamed public opinion to blunt criticism of a breaching of civil and constitutional rights and an ever increasing transfer of power to law enforcement agencies in Washington—the latter particularly tied to political control. Ironically, by politicizing the drug issue in the early years, driving out those with treatment expertise, and transforming the response into an entirely hard-line law enforcement approach they were quite unprepared when a real drug problem emerged. The development of the crack cocaine epidemic was an unanticipated event over which the Reagan administration had no control but their lack of preparedness in dealing with it led to a national panic that blew the problem completely out of proportion. As Reagan departed he left behind a hysterical fear about drugs that had serious and damaging implications for how the issue could be handled in the public arena. Once the drug abuse issue was "de-professionalized," politicians from both parties sought to play the issue for whatever political advantage they thought they could get. Reagan had opened a Pandora's box.

Notes

1. Nicholas Kozel, Robert DuPont, and B. Brown, "Narcotics and Crime: A Study of Narcotic Involvement in an Offender Population," *International Journal of the Addictions 7*: 3 (1972), 443–450. The data published in this chapter had earlier been made available to officials of the District of Columbia and the U.S. federal government in internal reports.
2. Robert Steele and Morgan Murphy (Members of Congress), *The World Heroin Problem: Report of Special Study Mission*, House Committee on Foreign Relations, 1971.
3. Daniel Baum, *Smoke and Mirrors* (Boston, Little Brown and Company, 1996), 10–11.
4. Peter G. Bourne, *Methadone: Benefits and Shortcomings* (Washington, D.C., Drug Abuse Council, 1975).
5. *Federal Strategy for Drug Abuse and Drug Traffic Prevention* (Washington, D.C., The Strategy Council on Drug Abuse, 1979), 10.
6. Ibid., n.p.
7. *Source Book of Criminal Justice Statistics* (Washington, D.C., U.S. Department of Justice, 1990).
8. Baum, *Smoke and Mirrors*, 28, 66.
9. Ibid.
10. Michael Massing, *The Fix* (New York, Simon and Schuster, 1998).

11. The notion of a "slippery slope" from marijuana use to an addiction to hard drugs is an argument unsupported by any credible scientific data. During the 1980s, forty-four million Americans said they had used marijuana and around 2 percent of that number had also used heroin (therefore 98 percent of marijuana users did not progress to heroin). A majority of heroin users had also used marijuana but virtually 100 percent smoked cigarettes. Correlation, of course, is not causation.
12. Baum, *Smoke and Mirrors*, 145.
13. Despite the defining of addiction as a crime not a disease, two top Reagan White House officials would later, when charged with criminal wrongdoing, argue in their defense that they suffered from alcohol addiction, "a disease," the first and only time that senior government officials have done so.
14. Baum, *Smoke and Mirrors*, 170.
15. Ibid., 149.
16. Ibid., 148.
17. *Marijuana and Health* (Washington, D.C., National Academy of Sciences, 1982).
18. *Public Papers of the Presidents of the United States, Ronald Reagan* (Washington, D.C., Government Printing Office, October 14, 1982), 1313.
19. Baum, *Smoke and Mirrors*, 166; Massing, *The Fix*, 146.
20. Peter G. Bourne, *Jimmy Carter: A Comprehensive Biography from Plains to the Post-Presidency* (New York, Simon and Schuster, 1995).
21. Personal communication from William Pollin, director, National Institute for Drug Abuse, with the author, Washington, D.C., November 15, 1981.
22. Massing, *The Fix*, 171.
23. *The Washington Post*, October 22, 1986.
24. Massing, *The Fix*, 161.
25. Much of the information in this paragraph comes from personal communication with MacDonald.
26. Baum, *Smoke and Mirrors*, 275.
27. Ibid., 249.

Chapter 4

Ronald Reagan and the End of the Cold War

Jack F. Matlock, Jr.

There are sharply conflicting assessments both of Ronald Reagan's performance as president of the United States and of the manner in which the Cold War ended. Critical views of Reagan abound, both in the United States and abroad: he was, it is said, an ill-informed and ideologically driven leader who pushed his country "in the wrong direction," raised international tensions to a dangerous level, and furthermore was an inattentive manager who, at crucial times, lost control of what his subordinates were doing.[1] There are, in contrast, supporters who assert that Reagan was a far-sighted statesman who "brought the country together again" and presided over a "Reagan Revolution," lowering taxes and freeing the economy of suffocating overregulation, while winning the Cold War and bringing down Communism.[2]

Perceptions of when the Cold War ended are equally divided: some picture it as ending with the collapse of the Communist system in Eastern Europe and the Soviet Union and the break-up of the Soviet Union itself; others believe it ended *before* Communist rule eroded in the USSR and that country fragmented into fifteen sovereign states. Nor is there consensus on *how* it ended: some—such as the Norwegian Parliament that awarded Mikhail Gorbachev the Nobel Peace Prize—give the Soviet leader the lion's share of the credit. Others assert that it was Reagan's military, political, and economic pressure on the Soviet Union that forced the change in Soviet policy.

As a diplomatic "insider" during much of the Cold War and President Reagan's adviser on Soviet affairs,[3] I believe that the opposing views of Reagan, both pro and con, miss the mark. I believe that Ronald Reagan's greatest achievement was his contribution to bringing the Cold War to an end. However, he did not do so alone, but in cooperation with Mikhail Gorbachev and others. As for the collapse of Communism and of the Soviet Union, these resulted from Gorbachev's decisions and the reaction of his subordinates to them, not from Reagan's policies.

Importance of the Cold War

It would be difficult to exaggerate the importance of the Cold War for both international relations and the domestic policy of the United States and its allies during much of the second half of the twentieth century. Once the Soviet Union built an extensive nuclear arsenal and the means of delivering weapons to any spot on earth, and had engaged the United States in an arms race resulting in tens of thousands of nuclear warheads in each country, a "hot war" between the two countries could have resulted not only in mutual suicide, but in the destruction of civilized life on earth. Never before in human history have the stakes of war and peace been so high.

The sense that only a Communist-ruled state could be a reliable ally had led Stalin to impose puppet governments on those areas of Eastern Europe occupied by the Soviet Army when World War II ended, and led his successors to support insurgencies throughout the "third world." The perceived need to resist the expansion of Communist rule led the United States and some of its allies into costly wars in Korea and Vietnam, and to offer military support to regimes confronted by Soviet-supported insurgencies, or to insurgencies against Soviet-backed regimes (as in Afghanistan in the 1980s).

The effects were also felt strongly in the domestic policy on both sides of the Iron Curtain. In the Soviet Union, the emphasis on military power required a funneling of enormous resources into the military–industrial sector, to the detriment of a civilian economy, which, in any case, was not as productive as the free-market economies of the West. In the United States, the military burden was also serious, though one more easily absorbed into a larger, more productive economy.

Not all the effects of Cold War competition were harmful to the United States. When the Soviet Union managed to place in orbit the first artificial earth satellite (the "Sputnik"), the United States was spurred to reform its teaching of mathematics and science, and to forge ahead in space, placing the first men on the moon and returning them to earth. But the competition distorted the economies of both countries and diverted resources that could have been put to more productive use.

While the impact of the Cold War was felt in virtually every aspect of life on both sides of the East–West divide, the competition in nuclear weapons was by far the most dangerous aspect of the Cold War; unless it could be contained it was difficult to see how the many other divisive issues could be addressed and solved.

Three Geopolitically Seismic Events

Between the late 1980s and the end of 1991, three events occurred, each of such geopolitical significance as to be comparable to the drift of continents over geologic time. The Cold War ended. Communist rule eroded, then collapsed, first in Eastern Europe, afterward in the Soviet Union. The Soviet Union itself broke apart into fifteen sovereign nations. The three events happened in such quick succession and were so poorly anticipated by the general public (and even by most officials) that many conflate the three and think of the Cold War as ending with the end of the Soviet Union as a state.[4]

This perception is a distorted view of what actually happened. The three "seismic events" were separate, with different causes, even though the second two could hardly have happened at that time if the Cold War had not ended.

These events were not predetermined, nor were they the result of impersonal forces acting without human guidance. Of course, a myriad of concrete facts and circumstances constrained the capacity of any person to influence events. Nevertheless, political decisions changed the nature of the East–West confrontation and made increasing cooperation, to the benefit of all, possible. The two key figures in the drama played out in the late 1980s were Ronald Reagan and Mikhail Gorbachev.

Let us first turn to Reagan and the situation he confronted when he became president in January, 1981.

The Standoff

In January 1981, U.S.–Soviet relations were at a nadir not matched since the Soviet-ordered Warsaw Pact invasion of Czechoslovakia in 1968. The heady optimism of the "détente" initiated by Richard Nixon and Leonid Brezhnev in 1972, when they signed the Anti-Ballistic-Missile Treaty (ABM), the agreement on limiting strategic weapons (SALT), and a Declaration of Principles, had gradually dissipated during the 1970s to expire totally when the Soviet Union invaded Afghanistan in late December 1979. In response to that invasion, President Jimmy Carter had withdrawn from Senate consideration the agreement to limit strategic arms that he and Brezhnev had signed in 1978 (SALT-II). Carter had also ordered a number of "sanctions" to punish the USSR for its transgression of international law, *inter alia* closing the U.S. consulate general in Kiev and ordering the Soviet Union to remove its consular representatives from New York, appealing to American athletes as well as those from allied countries not to participate in the 1980 Olympic Games in Moscow, and imposing a partial embargo on the sale of grain to the Soviet Union.[5] The Carter administration had also decided not to renew the U.S.–Soviet agreement on cultural and educational exchanges, which had been in force since the Eisenhower administration.

During his campaign for the presidency, Reagan had accused Carter of weakness in allowing American defenses to deteriorate and failing to respond adequately to Soviet aggression. However, he had criticized the boycott of the Olympic Games and the limited grain embargo on grounds that they penalized some segments of the American public for no good reason, since neither action was likely to induce the Soviet leaders to withdraw their troops from Afghanistan. He also considered the signed but unratified SALT-II treaty "fatally flawed," since in his view it failed to reduce the number of nuclear weapons substantially and lacked adequate verification provisions.

Reagan did not come to office with a fixed idea of how to tame the arms race and end the Cold War, and it was nearly three years before he presented to the public a comprehensive description of his policy toward the Soviet Union. Nevertheless, from the beginning of his presidency, he talked about the need to negotiate with the Soviet Union in order to reduce the high levels of arms, particularly nuclear weapons, and to do so with strict verification. He also made it clear that he believed that there were common interests between the United States and the Soviet Union, on which cooperation should be possible. But he accompanied these comments with sharp criticism of the Soviet system and of the operating style of Soviet leaders.

In his first press conference as president, he announced that he favored "an actual reduction in the numbers of nuclear weapons," and added that negotiations on arms should take into account "other things that are going on," and for this reason he believed in "linkage." During the same meeting, he was asked what he thought of "the long-range intentions of the Soviet Union," and whether "the Kremlin is bent on world domination" or whether "under other circumstances détente is possible." He replied at length, saying that the Soviet leaders had always proclaimed their support of "world revolution," and that to achieve that goal they considered it permissible "to commit any crime, to lie, to cheat," so that "when you do business with them, even at a détente, you keep that in mind."[6]

Understandably, the information media seized upon the vivid and pejorative description of the practices of the Soviet leaders and paid little attention to the context in which it was uttered. What Reagan thought he was suggesting was that he would be more careful in negotiating agreements with the Soviet leaders than his predecessors had been, not that he saw no point in negotiating. Yet, in much of the world, his criticisms of the Soviet Union drowned out the constructive goals he had set.

The impression that Reagan was bent on increasing tensions with the Soviet Union rather than easing them was reinforced by what seemed delays in reopening arms control negotiations. When Reagan took office, the Soviet government was refusing to negotiate on NATO's "dual track" decision—to deploy U.S. nuclear-armed missiles in Europe unless agreement could be reached with the USSR to remove the SS-20 missiles targeted on the NATO countries in Europe. The Soviet leaders were also continuing to insist that the United States ratify the SALT-II treaty before there could be further negotiations on nuclear arms.

The fact is that while Reagan was eager to reach an agreement that would reliably reduce nuclear arsenals, he was in no particular hurry to start the negotiations. He felt that U.S. defenses had deteriorated during the Carter administration and that he needed to build up U.S. military strength before he could negotiate effectively. Also, there were sharp divisions among his advisers regarding what acceptable arms control treaties would look like, and he needed time to sort through their views. Furthermore, he was convinced that time was on the U.S. side, given the growing economic difficulties the USSR faced. Therefore, his negotiating position would be stronger as time went by.

Negotiations on Intermediate-Range Nuclear Forces (INF) began in November 1981, and in June 1982, negotiations on strategic arms were resumed, this time under the acronym START (for Strategic Arms Reduction Talks, to contrast with the SALT acronym used in the 1970s, to emphasize that the goal was *reduction*, not merely limitation). However, the U.S. and Soviet positions were so far apart that prospects for progress were dim. The U.S. chief negotiator on INF, Paul Nitze, informally proposed a compromise agreement on INF, but his Soviet counterpart, Yuly Kvitsinsky, found that his government was unwilling to consider it when he described the idea to his superiors.[7]

By early 1983, Reagan decided that there was enough momentum in his defense program to allow him to negotiate effectively. Sweeping aside the objections of many on his staff, he began to seek a meeting with the Soviet leader.

Despite Reagan's desire, from early 1983, to meet the Soviet leader, circumstances made that impossible until he met Gorbachev two and a half years later. In the spring of 1983, Reagan announced his "Strategic Defense Initiative" (SDI), a research program to determine whether defenses against strategic missiles were technically possible.[8] The Soviet leadership jumped to the conclusion that this was part of an offensive strategy, either to develop space-based weapons to use against targets on earth, or to create an impenetrable defense that would permit the United States to launch a nuclear war and prevent retaliation. Neither of these suspicions was valid, but they continued to feed hostility to the program for years.

The tenuous health of the Soviet leaders made it unlikely that they would be able to meet Reagan even under favorable political circumstances. Yuri Andropov, Leonid Brezhnev's successor, was fatally ill with nephritis during most of his tenure, and his successor, Konstantin Chernenko, was in not much better health, with emphysema and other ailments. He lasted little more than a year in the top Soviet office.

In addition, things kept happening that made a meeting untimely. In September 1983, a Soviet fighter plane shot down a Korean passenger airliner that had accidentally strayed into Soviet airspace, killing 269 people, including an American congressman. At first the Soviet government denied that it knew what had happened, then accused the United States of sending the plane to spy—a patently false accusation.[9] As a result, the United States sponsored extensive sanctions against the Soviet airline and a meeting in Madrid between Secretary of State George Shultz and Foreign Minister Andrei Gromyko turned into a shouting match.

When the United States finally began deploying intermediate-range nuclear missiles in Europe in November 1983 to counter the Soviet SS-20s, Andropov withdrew Soviet negotiators from all arms control negotiations and issued an angry statement declaring that it was totally impossible to deal with the Reagan administration.[10] As we have since discovered, Andropov had already ordered the Soviet KGB to undertake clandestine activities to prevent Reagan's reelection in 1984.[11]

Reagan's Strategy

Faced with what appeared to be a sharp deterioration of relations, which many in the public felt could lead to actual hostilities—though neither side had threatened military action against the other—Reagan ordered his staff to redouble efforts to make his desire to negotiate differences with the Soviet Union clear, both to the public and to the Soviet leaders. In June of that year, Secretary of State George Shultz had told Congress the American approach to the Soviet Union would be based on "realism, strength, and dialogue," bywords that suggested the manner of American diplomacy but said little about the issues. The media and the public still seemed confused about American aims.

Reagan therefore asked his staff to draft a major address that would make clear his desire to reduce arms and find ways to cooperate with the Soviet Union. The speech, delivered in the East Room of the White House on January 16, 1984, was the most comprehensive exposition of goals for U.S.-Soviet relations Reagan had made.

While noting the various problems in the relationship, the speech's emphasis was on the need to cooperate to reduce arms, to withdraw from proxy conflict in third countries, to protect human rights, and to "improve the working relationship"—a euphemism for raising the Iron Curtain and allowing people and ideas to flow unimpeded across the East–West divide.[12]

While none of the specific goals cited in the speech was totally new to American foreign policy, several features of the speech distinguished it from previous statements, by Reagan and his predecessors. First, all of the goals were couched in terms of cooperation, not demands that the Soviet Union make unilateral concessions. While the substance of the issues would require the Soviet Union to make more changes in its practices than the United States, the approach was reciprocal, an appeal to work together to improve human rights protection, reduce arms, diminish regional conflict, and improve communication. Second, while it made no rigid linkage between one issue and others, it made clear that progress on any one of the goals would be influenced by progress or lack of progress on others; in other words, arms reduction—the principal Soviet interest—would not get very far until some of the other problems were on the way to solution.

Subsequently, Reagan elaborated in further detail each of the points in the January 1984 speech in public statements and private communications with the Soviet leaders, but that speech offered a capsule summary of his Soviet policy through the rest of his administration. His assumption was that the Soviet leaders were encountering increasing difficulties at home, particularly with the economy, and that Soviet commitments abroad to insurgencies and revolutionary regimes were sapping Soviet strength and creating dangers without tangible benefit. In short, much Soviet foreign policy was detrimental to the country's real interests. If the ailing Soviet leaders of 1983 and 1984 were unable to grasp that fundamental fact, perhaps a younger, more pragmatic leader would succeed them.

Soviet Policy before Gorbachev

In fact, Gorbachev's predecessors were incapable of understanding the predicament in which their country found itself. They were locked in the mentality of a "zero-sum game" in which contending sides "lose" proportionately every time there is a "gain" by the other side, and inflict a comparable "loss" on the other side for every "gain" on theirs. Their ideology divided the world into mutually exclusive, contending parties, between which there could be only temporary and very limited cooperation. There was no common interest, and though the nuclear age required avoidance of direct conflict, it did not end the international class struggle, to be conducted by any means not likely to result in a nuclear war.

The Soviet leaders before March 1985 were eager to tame the arms race, but they also wanted to retain a measure of military superiority, the right to intervene in neighboring Communist countries to "preserve socialism," and a free hand to use their arms wherever they chose in the "third world." Furthermore, they rejected any attempt by outsiders to influence their domestic practices, however barbaric. They had become so attached to traditional policies and attitudes that they could not discern the damage they were inflicting on the Soviet Union itself. While Yuri Andropov realized that there needed to be some reform of economic management, he was incapable of grasping that the Soviet system itself, and its class-struggle philosophy, lay behind the problems the Soviet Union was facing.

Reagan had tried to reach out to the Soviet leaders, even when he was criticizing them (as a group, not personally) in public. Shortly after taking office, he revoked Carter's partial embargo of grain sales without seeking anything in return.[13] While he was still recovering from an assassination attempt in April 1981, he penned a personal letter to Leonid Brezhnev. He sent it despite objections from his staff, but received only a cold, bureaucratic reply. Similar attempts were also rebuffed by Andropov and Chernenko.

Some might observe that the Soviet leaders could hardly be expected to respond favorably in the face of the sort of criticism Reagan made of their system. But they forget that Reagan was subjected to almost daily insults by the Soviet propaganda machine, and increasingly by the Soviet leaders themselves. He was called an imperialist warmonger, intent on launching a nuclear war. Reagan never replied in kind to that sort of invective: he was critical of the system and charged that Soviet leaders, as a group, held a philosophy that embraced different standards of public morality, but he never denounced individual leaders by name, and he never suggested that they wanted to go to war.

Former Soviet ambassador to the United States Anatoly Dobrynin wrote in his memoirs that the Soviet leaders were so accustomed to launching propagandistic attacks on Western leaders with impunity that they failed to see that Reagan was only giving them a dose of their own medicine.[14] In fact, it was not the public rhetoric that stood in the way of fruitful negotiations but the refusal of the Soviet leaders to reconsider entrenched positions.

Foreign Minister Andrei Gromyko was in undisputed control of Soviet foreign policy during the latter part of Brezhnev's rule and all of Andropov's and Chernenko's. Although some on his staff saw important new elements in Reagan's January 1984 speech and counseled a Soviet response, Gromyko rejected it, saying that the "music" had changed, but the substance was the same.[15] (Could he have really read the speech?) Therefore, the speech got no positive response from the Soviet leadership; the Soviet news agency TASS issued a laconic report that President Reagan had made a speech on relations with the Soviet Union that contained "no indication of any positive changes in the Reagan administration's approach."[16]

During most of 1984, the Soviet leaders avoided anything that might have facilitated Reagan's reelection. KGB efforts to ensure his defeat, which seem to have taken the form mainly of promoting, in susceptible media organs, the image of Reagan as a fanatic, bent on unleashing a nuclear war, had little effect on the American public. Soviet policies themselves—the continued occupation of Afghanistan, denial of responsibility for shooting down a civilian airliner, the withdrawal from arms control negotiations, the assaults on civil liberties within the Soviet Union—solidified support for Reagan's policies in the United States and helped him win the 1988 presidential election despite domestic economic difficulties.

As fall approached in 1984 and the opinion polls indicated that Reagan's reelection was assured, the Soviet leaders began to hedge their bets. Gromyko came to Washington in September and met with Reagan and Shultz. He had refused his usual annual visit during the UN General Assembly session the year before, so his meeting with Reagan was treated by the press as a sensational event. After Reagan won the 1984 election, Gromyko and Shultz met in Geneva in January 1985, and agreed to resume the negotiations on nuclear arms and strategic defense. Even before Gorbachev became general secretary, the Soviet leadership seems to have decided that they had no choice but to accept Reagan's invitation to negotiate.

Until Gorbachev reoriented Soviet policy however, it is hard to see how these negotiations could have made much progress. Gromyko had placed two rigid links on the Soviet negotiating position: there could be no agreement on INF, he said, until there was one on strategic arms (START). And there could be no agreement on either of these important topics until there was one on "space weapons"—in other words, until the United States abandoned its effort to develop defenses against ballistic missiles, a program dear to Reagan's heart. The American position was that it would negotiate on all three topics, but believed that if agreement could be reached in any of the three areas, it should be implemented without waiting for agreements in the other negotiating fora.

Gorbachev: Perestroika and "New Thinking"

Mikhail Gorbachev was elected general secretary of the Communist Party of the Soviet Union in March 1985, just after Chernenko died. President Reagan sent Vice President Bush to Moscow for the Chernenko funeral, and with him a letter to Gorbachev inviting him to come to Washington for a meeting. Shortly thereafter, Reagan was notified that Gorbachev agreed to a meeting in principle, but not in Washington; instead, he invited Reagan to come to Moscow. By June it was decided that the two would meet in Geneva in November of that year.

Eventually, Gorbachev was to reorient Soviet foreign policy, and then go on to alter the very fundamentals of Communist rule in the Soviet Union—to the point that the Communist Party was swept from power. Professor Archie Brown described the process in detail in his masterly *Seven Years That Changed the World: Perestroika in Perspective* (2007).[17] However, when Gorbachev came to power in March 1985, policymakers could not be sure what this representative of a new generation of Soviet leaders would do. He was obviously more capable than his predecessors and better educated, but some American officials felt that this could make him a more dangerous opponent. But many also hoped that he would turn out to be different, with fewer ideological blinders and a more pragmatic approach to the problems the Soviet Union was facing.

Most American officials, including President Reagan, understood that Gorbachev would need time to consolidate his power before he could begin to change Soviet policy—should that be his desire. Gorbachev's early statements pledging a continuation of past policies and a strengthening of Communist Party leadership were understood to be efforts of a new leader to reassure the Party elite. His immediate acceptance of an invitation to meet Reagan was considered a positive sign, and the favorable impression was reinforced in July when Eduard Shevardnadze, the leader of the Communist Party in Soviet Georgia, was named to replace Andrei Gromyko as foreign minister. Shevardnadze met George Shultz, the American secretary of state, in Helsinki a few weeks after Shevardnadze took office. Though Shevardnadze still defended the traditional Soviet positions on contentious issues, his manner was nothing like Gromyko's. Shevardnadze was personally considerate, showed a distinct sense of humor, and offered arguments calmly as topics for discussion and possible compromise. His negotiating style seemed the antithesis of Gromyko's penchant for presenting Soviet negotiating positions as revealed truth that only a dullard or implacable enemy could fail to accept. Having met Shevardnadze, Shultz and his staff felt that a new day had dawned on U.S.–Soviet relations, even though, at that point, there had been no substantive change in Soviet policy.

When the time and place for a meeting with the Soviet leader had been set, Reagan spent much of his time preparing for it. His staff arranged extensive briefings on the Soviet economy, military structure, foreign policy, and philosophy, and also prepared a series of papers that amounted to a university course on the Soviet Union. Reagan read books on Russian culture and history and discussed the Russian tradition with prominent historians. He was briefed in detail on the issues in the many negotiations that were underway. But what interested him most was the psychology of the Soviet leaders, and of Mikhail Gorbachev in particular. The CIA prepared a video presentation, using material taped from public broadcasts in Moscow and Paris, where Gorbachev had visited recently, to give Reagan a feel for his speaking style and manner.

While Reagan was being briefed on the Soviet Union and Gorbachev, diplomats worked to prepare for the meeting. The U.S. and Soviet Union were so far apart on arms control issues that there was no realistic hope that Reagan and Gorbachev could conclude an agreement in that area, but American officials proposed a number of cooperative projects—more extensive than any previously—and invited the Soviet Foreign Ministry to offer suggestions. The diplomats exchanged comments on the various ideas before the proposals were put in final form or publicized, thus setting a precedent that would be useful in the future. In the past, U.S.–Soviet negotiations had been hampered by the habit of both governments to make major proposals in public, in an effort to "one-up" the other side—obviously not a fruitful approach if agreement were the goal.

During these preparations, Reagan startled the diplomats by ordering that they not draft in advance a communiqué to be issued at the close of the meeting. This had been normal practice before other U.S.–Soviet summit meetings, and diplomats on both sides were outraged, suspecting that Reagan wished somehow to diminish the meeting's significance, or perhaps even to issue a statement at the close of the meeting that would not be acceptable to Gorbachev. Their suspicions were unfounded: Reagan gave the instruction because he did not want the meeting to be "pre-cooked." He felt that it was up to him and Gorbachev to decide what they would say after they had met, and that they should not be limited by language worked out in advance by subordinates.

This illustrates an important point about Reagan's view of summitry. He considered it a vehicle for negotiation, not simply a festive occasion to sign agreements reached previously. Earlier U.S.–Soviet summits, from the Nixon–Brezhnev meeting in 1972, had featured major arms control agreements, usually accompanied by a slew of other agreements, signed before television cameras as aides clinked champagne glasses. These scenes, used by both American and Soviet leaders for domestic political purposes, produced the impression with much of the public that summitry alone produced the agreements, and that a meeting of American and Soviet leaders that did not result in significant agreements would be a failure. Many on Reagan's staff were concerned that if Reagan met the Soviet leader when there was no major agreement ready for signature he would feel pressured to sign a bad agreement rather than risk the public perception of failure.

Reagan consistently thought otherwise. He believed that it was important to hold meetings with Soviet leaders without preconditions in order to discuss key differences and attempt to find ways around them. Ideally, in his view, meetings should be at regular intervals—say, annually—whether or not formal agreements were possible. Until Gorbachev accepted the idea of a "get acquainted" meeting, however, Soviet leaders, like some of Reagan's advisers, had objected to a summit meeting unless an important treaty was ready for signature.

Building Trust: Forms and Levels of Communication

A few days before Reagan and Gorbachev met in Geneva, in November 1985, Reagan wrote out by hand, on a yellow "legal pad" his thoughts regarding the upcoming meeting.[18] In it he anticipated that Gorbachev would be a tough negotiator who would try to split the United States from its allies in Europe, but that negotiation should be possible because of Gorbachev's need to tame the arms race. He considered protection of human rights extremely important, but something that should be pursued in private so as to facilitate Gorbachev's cooperation. He welcomed the anticipated agreement to expand contacts and cultural exchanges, but considered "security issues like arms control, the regional areas of conflict and the prevalent suspicion and hostility between us" the main topics with which he would be dealing.[19] He mused that he should let Gorbachev know in private that, if they could not reach "a solid, verifiable arms reduction agreement," an arms race would ensue that the Soviet Union was bound to lose. But he concluded his notes by writing: "Let there be no talk of winners and losers. Even if we think we won, to say so would set us back."

Before their meeting in Geneva, Reagan and Gorbachev had been in communication, both indirectly through diplomatic representatives and directly through personal correspondence.[20] These contacts, particularly those between George Shultz and Eduard Shevardnadze, not only continued but intensified following the Geneva summit meeting. Gradually, and not without occasional serious setbacks, a personal relationship of trust developed, not only between Reagan and Gorbachev, but also between Shultz and Shevardnadze and between many senior officials and negotiators on both sides.

Though most of the actual U.S.–Soviet negotiation occurred before and after summit meetings, much out of the public view, we can trace the transformation of relations between the Soviet and American governments by following the sequence of the meetings between Reagan and Gorbachev. It was they who set a pattern of regular summit meetings that was continued, following some hesitation, by Reagan's successor, George H.W. Bush.

Geneva Summit (November 1985)

Gorbachev and Reagan made some progress in regard to strategic nuclear weapons as Gorbachev agreed that arsenals in both countries could be cut by half. (In 1977, Brezhnev had summarily rejected Carter's proposal to reduce the number of these weapons by one-third.) Nevertheless, the U.S. and Soviet positions were still far apart concerning the way the reductions would be applied to the various components, on methods of verification, and several other difficult issues.

The more significant achievement was in other areas. The two leaders found that they could discuss difficult issues without personal acrimony, and they were able to agree on a significant statement that "a nuclear war cannot be won and must never be fought." They signed an agreement on cultural and educational exchanges that went far beyond previous agreements in the numbers of people that would be involved and the provision for younger people, such as undergraduates and secondary-school students, whom the Soviet authorities had excluded from earlier agreements. The two leaders also agreed that they would exchange visits over the next two years, with Gorbachev coming to the United Sates in 1986 and Reagan to the USSR in 1987. Thus, it seemed that there was an implicit agreement to place no preconditions on future meetings.

This turned out to be a faulty assumption on the American part. Gorbachev delayed setting a date for his visit to the United States, then commented that "one get-acquainted meeting was enough," and that the two should meet again only when they would be able to sign a significant agreement. In January 1986 he made a highly publicized proposal to eliminate nuclear weapons by the end of the century. American officials were skeptical: the goal seemed unrealistic, particularly given the inability of the two countries to agree on ways to reduce their strategic forces by 50 percent, and also because of the manner in which the proposal was made. Instead of discussing it in diplomatic channels and getting comment from Washington, Gorbachev publicized the proposal as soon as it was made.

Officials were skeptical, but the proposal caught Reagan's attention. Why? Because he had a visceral hatred of nuclear weapons and dreamed of finding a way, in his words, "to abolish them from the face of the earth."[21] He found the prevailing doctrine of "Mutual Assured Destruction" (MAD) abhorrent and worthy of its acronym. Unfriendly observers would gossip that he was incapable of understanding the reasoning behind the doctrine, but he understood it very well—and was appalled at its implications. "How can you tell me," I heard him say on a number of occasions "that the only way I have to defend the American people from a nuclear attack is to threaten destruction of millions of innocent people, and perhaps to start a war that would destroy civilization? That is unacceptable. There has to be a better way!"

Reagan's horror of nuclear weapons and their potential explains his attachment to his Strategic Defense Initiative, and also to his receptivity to Gorbachev's proposal to eliminate these weapons by the end of the twentieth century. Both Britain and France, the other Western powers with nuclear weapons, rejected the idea out of hand, as did China, but Reagan seized it. Although he judged that many elements in Gorbachev's proposal were unrealistic, he insisted that the U.S. reply endorse the idea that nuclear weapons should be eliminated eventually.

Nevertheless, the U.S.–Soviet nuclear arms negotiations did not prosper in early 1986. The United Sates was unwilling to accept Gorbachev's January proposal as a whole; it seemed both utopian and, given the Soviet positions at the negotiating tables, insincere. Soviet negotiators showed no flexibility in the ongoing negotiations, and Reagan saw no reason to modify the U.S. position unless it could lead to a reasonable compromise. Overall, Reagan felt he was being pressed by Gorbachev to make unwarranted concessions as the price for another meeting, and this put him in a stubborn mood. During the summer, he sent Gorbachev a letter with a confidential proposal to work toward the elimination of ballistic missiles, along with nuclear weapons.

Gorbachev did not reply to this proposal, but, in September, sent Reagan a confidential proposal to meet for one or two days in London or Iceland to agree on the terms of a treaty that could be signed when Gorbachev came to the United States. The letter arrived when the United States and Soviet Union were in the midst of a spy scandal. The United States had arrested a Soviet citizen employee of the United Nations (who, unlike diplomats in the Soviet Mission to the United Nations, had no diplomatic immunity) on charges of espionage. The Soviets retaliated by arresting Nicholas Daniloff, an American journalist who was not an espionage agent. This outraged President Reagan and the American public.

Nevertheless, Reagan accepted the proposal, with the explicit proviso that Daniloff be released promptly, and selected Reykjavík as the venue, thinking that the small city would provide greater privacy for the talks since available facilities would limit the size of delegations and the number of accompanying journalists. (More than three thousand journalists had gathered in Geneva to cover their first summit, which gave the setting, at times, the atmosphere of a sporting event, with thousands of journalists crowded in bleachers simply to watch the leaders arrive for their meetings.)

According to Gorbachev's foreign policy assistant Anatoly Chernyaev, Gorbachev rejected the first proposal drafted by the Ministry of Foreign Affairs and insisted on one that differed radically from previous Soviet positions. Gorbachev's intent was to "sweep Reagan off his feet" with proposals he could not refuse.[22]

Reykjavík Summit (October 1986)

More progress was made in resolving nuclear issues between the United States and the Soviet Union during the two days of talks in Iceland than had occurred (or was to occur) in any other meeting. Two years later, participants could look back and mark the meeting as the turning point in the relationship—not just between Reagan and Gorbachev, but between their governments as well. But it didn't seem so at the time.

Hopes had been raised that the leaders were on the verge of the most comprehensive arms-reduction agreement in history, only to find that they could not agree on what many considered a trivial matter. The meeting in Washington that the Reykjavík summit was supposed to prepare would not take place. Pictures of Reagan and Gorbachev emerging from Höfdi House, where they had been meeting, faces grim with disappointment, flashed around the world and conveyed without words the shock of dashed hopes.

Starting with somewhat more modest proposals, Gorbachev had agreed that both countries would reduce their strategic weapons by half in five years, and then would eliminate them in ten. Reagan had agreed to the 50 percent reduction in the first five years, and had proposed to eliminate all ballistic missiles in the second five years. At one point, he also agreed to eliminate all nuclear weapons (not just strategic ones) in the second five years, along with ballistic missiles (which could carry nonnuclear warheads). But Gorbachev refused to consider eliminating ballistic missiles and insisted that the United States keep its research on strategic defense in laboratories for at least ten years. Reagan was convinced that such a limitation would kill the program that he had vowed to pursue, and refused.

Reagan suggested that they have their negotiators draft a treaty to cover those points on which the two had agreed: the 50 percent reduction of strategic weapons over five years and the elimination of intermediate-range nuclear weapons in Europe. But Gorbachev refused to conclude any agreement without a commitment from the United States to keep SDI research in laboratories for ten years.

Shortly after Reagan and Gorbachev returned to their capitals, a scandal broke out in Washington when it was revealed that some American officials had arranged for the sale of defensive weapons to Iran, then resisting invasion by Iraq, and using the proceeds from these sales to fund the "Contras" in Nicaragua. (Congress had prohibited direct U.S. government funding of the Contras.) These events led to the resignation of National Security Adviser John Poindexter and the replacement of the senior staff on the National Security Council. The investigation and political recriminations dragged on for several months and preoccupied the senior members of the Reagan administration. For several months, the administration seemed paralyzed in respect to its Soviet policy.

The disagreement at Reykjavík poisoned relations between Reagan and Gorbachev for several weeks, but by early 1987 it became clear to Gorbachev that the Soviet Union had to make a deal. In February, he told the Politburo, "As difficult as it is to do business with the United States, we are doomed to do it. We have no choice."[23] He also seems to have grasped that dealing with the United States successfully would require more than making agreements to reduce arms. His assistant Anatoly Chernyaev observed at a conference in 1998: "Our policy did not change until Gorbachev understood that there would be no improvement and no serious arms control until we admitted and accepted human rights, free emigration, until glasnost became freedom of speech, until our society and perestroika changed deeply."[24] In other words, Gorbachev accepted implicitly the "four-part agenda" set forth by President Reagan three years earlier, recognizing that it would be impossible to tame the arms race unless there was progress in solving other key problems such as military support for insurgencies, protection of human rights, and lowering barriers to the movement of people, information, and ideas.

American diplomats noted that during 1987 Soviet officials accepted without demur a negotiating agenda based on Reagan's categories. American negotiators also observed Reagan's admonition not to "claim victory," particularly since, as of 1987, most Soviet policies had not changed greatly. And, indeed, there was no reason to consider Soviet acceptance of the agenda a "victory" since the four-part agenda had been designed not to put the Soviet Union at a disadvantage but to define those issues that gave rise to hostility and stood in the way of cooperation. Objectively, the Soviet government needed, in its own interest, to change policy and practice in the areas the agenda identified. Gorbachev came to understand that in 1987.

Gorbachev began to lecture the Politburo about the effect heavy military spending was having on the economy. He asserted that the United States and its Western allies were trying to force the Soviet Union into an arms race that would bankrupt them. The U.S. Pershing-II missiles stationed in Germany were "a pistol aimed at our head."[25] He ridiculed the demand that the Soviet Union retain SS-20s to "compensate" for British and French nuclear forces, pointing our that it was absurd to think that there could be a war with Britain or France. Perhaps by pre-arrangement, he allowed Andrei Gromyko, who had originally devised the "double linkage," and Yegor Ligachev, the second-ranking Party official who subsequently broke with Gorbachev over domestic reforms, to suggest that an agreement on INF be signed without reference to strategic weapons or strategic defense.[26]

Invitations were issued to British prime minister Margaret Thatcher and U.S. secretary of state George Shultz to visit Moscow in late March and April, and both were given extensive access to the Soviet information media. Both were forthright in their criticisms of Soviet policies, which the Soviet press reported, accurately for the most part, and accompanied with commentary refuting some of the criticisms. But for the Soviet public, the exposure of Western attitudes in the Soviet press was a novelty. Previously, they had been fed only the Soviet version of events.

George Shultz's visit to Moscow in April 1987 was the first important step to repair relations following the disappointment of the Reykjavík summit. His visit was controversial in the United States because the elements of an eavesdropping system had been found in the incomplete American Embassy building in Moscow and influential officials, including members of the U.S. Senate, demanded that Shultz not go to Moscow at that time for negotiations.[27] Both Shultz and Reagan rejected advice to limit direct communication with the Soviet leaders, and Shultz's visit in April set in motion the negotiations that, despite some last minute hitches, produced the treaty that Reagan and Gorbachev signed in December to eliminate INF.

Washington Summit (December 1987)

The INF Treaty was record-breaking in several respects: for the first time it provided for the elimination of a whole class of nuclear weapons, and, also for the first time, a U.S.–Soviet agreement set the rules for extensive on-site verification of compliance. The terms of the treaty matched the original

American proposal: to eliminate these weapons altogether instead of trying to limit their numbers—an arrangement that would have been technically difficult to verify with confidence. But even though it had been an American proposal, it was a solution in the Soviet interest from the time the Pershing-II and cruise missiles (GLCMs) were deployed in Europe. The arrangement Gorbachev had suggested at Reykjavík (and to which Reagan had reluctantly agreed)—to eliminate the missiles in Europe, but keep one hundred in Asia—would have been most difficult to verify (the missiles being mobile), and also would have hampered Gorbachev's goal of improving relations with both China and Japan.

It is ironic that many of the original supporters of the "zero/zero" INF proposal were reluctant to accept the agreement when it was reached—they proposed it originally assuming that the Soviet Union would never agree. Also, NATO military commanders had incorporated these weapons in a "ladder of deterrence" and worried about removing rungs in that ladder. Gorbachev had been advised by some of his staff—including Anatoly Dobrynin, the long-time Soviet ambassador to the United States—that the proposal was insincere and that the United States would find an excuse to reject it even if Gorbachev accepted it. But Reagan never hesitated. It was his proposal, it was fair (treating both sides alike), it was verifiable, and it *reduced* the number and type of nuclear weapons deployed rather than simply licensing a ceiling. It met all the criteria he had set, from his first days in office, for arms reduction agreements with the Soviet Union.

The INF Treaty provided a sturdy foundation on which to develop personal trust between the two leaders. It demonstrated to each that the other was not insisting on military superiority. Reagan's support of the treaty despite opposition at home showed Gorbachev that he was a serious negotiating partner. Gorbachev's agreement to tight on-site verification gave Reagan confidence that there would be no serious cheating. This was a different Soviet leadership than the one he had described in January 1981.

Although Reagan and Gorbachev were not able to reach agreement on the terms of a strategic arms agreement (SDI was still a barrier), their discussions in Washington opened the door to several subsequent agreements, including the one concluded a few months later for the withdrawal of Soviet forces from Afghanistan.

Gorbachev's first exposure to American society also had an effect. Crowds gathered to observe him, and when he stopped his motorcade to shake hands, he was cheered. At lunch following this experience, he told Reagan, "I will never again think of your country the way I did before."

When he returned to Moscow, he accelerated plans for internal reforms, but held the most radical proposals until just before Reagan's arrival in Moscow on a return visit. These proposals were issued officially as "Theses" for discussion and adoption at the CPSU Conference scheduled for the summer. They bore no trace of Marxist–Leninist ideology but incorporated the basic principles of democracy. When I briefed Reagan in Helsinki the day before his arrival in Moscow, I was able to tell him that if Gorbachev was sincere—and he had to be to present these ideas to a Communist Party Conference—the Soviet Union would never be the same.

Moscow Summit (May–June 1988)

The Reagan–Gorbachev summit meeting in Moscow produced no new groundbreaking agreements, though the leaders were able to exchange instruments of ratification of the INF Treaty they had signed in Washington. The treaty had been ratified by the American Senate despite five negative votes by Republican senators. If a Democratic president had presented the same treaty to the Senate, it is far from certain that it could have attracted the sixty-seven votes necessary for ratification.

A few weeks before Reagan arrived in Moscow, Shultz and Shevardnadze had worked out an agreement with the various interested parties to remove Soviet military forces in Afghanistan over the next twelve months. Thus, one of the most serious barriers to U.S.–Soviet cooperation had been removed.

Like the American public's reception of Gorbachev the previous December, the Soviet public cheered Reagan at his every appearance. His speeches to the students at Moscow University and to assembled writers and artists at the Soviet Writers Union received thunderous applause. He was treated as a national hero. And he was prepared to return the compliment.

During a stroll with Gorbachev on Red Square, a journalist inquired, "Is this still an evil empire?" He replied, "No, that was another time, another era." And then he was asked who was responsible and he said, "Mr. Gorbachev, of course. He is the leader of this country." Reagan's words were conveyed instantly to the far corners of the Soviet Union and Soviet citizens took note. The man who had called their country an evil empire and who had been vilified by previous Soviet leaders as a warmonger was in fact a man of peace. He wished them well, and thought that Gorbachev had put them on the right track. It was a powerful endorsement of *perestroika*.

Throughout 1988, contacts expanded and intensified between Americans (and other foreigners) and Soviet citizens. Private citizens came to Moscow and Leningrad in unprecedented numbers, and official contacts expanded rapidly, quickly progressing beyond wary formal meetings to nourish personal ties of respect and even friendship. When Frank Carlucci replaced Caspar Weinberger as American secretary of defense, visits and exchanges by senior military officers grew rapidly. Newly appointed editors to major Soviet publications turned stodgy, little-read propaganda organs into publications carrying a broad range of news and opinion. The Iron Curtain was becoming ever more permeable, as regulations permitting Soviet citizens to travel abroad were liberalized in July.

Though little noticed abroad, 1988 also witnessed a fateful debate over Marxist ideology.[28] In July, Foreign Minister Shevardnadze told a conference of Soviet diplomats that "peaceful coexistence" was *not* "a special form of the class struggle." A few days later, Yegor Ligachev, who then was second only to

Gorbachev in the Communist Party hierarchy, gave a speech asserting the opposite. Then, Alexander Yakovlev, at the time the central committee secretary for ideology, delivered a speech in Vilnius asserting that the "common interests of mankind" were superior to class interests.

December 1988: Ideological End of the Cold War?

Gorbachev came to New York in December 1988 to address the UN General Assembly and to meet with Reagan and Vice President George H.W. Bush, who had been elected in November to succeed Reagan. His UN address was a sensation, since he announced that the Soviet Union would unilaterally reduce its armed forces by half a million men. But he also implicitly discarded the "class struggle" hypothesis when he observed that there could be no limitation on the freedom of choice nations have in international relations (i.e., that there was no basis for the "Brezhnev doctrine").

In East–West negotiations, the traditional Cold-War "zero-sum" mentality had already begun to be replaced by a "win-win" attitude, an effort to find a way to solve problems in a manner acceptable to both sides. As Reagan noted in his diary after his December meeting with Gorbachev in New York, "Gorbachev sounded as if he saw us as partners making a better world."[29] From the time Gorbachev delivered his UN speech, the trend of thinking in cooperative terms accelerated, extending deep into the bureaucracy. Many serious problems remained, but these were seen as obstacles to be removed rather than contests to be won or lost.

After Reagan: End of Cold War Confirmed

Although the "Cold War" spirit had largely disappeared from Soviet diplomacy in early 1989 when George H.W. Bush replaced Reagan, Europe was still divided, a treaty to reduce strategic arms and one on conventional forces still eluded negotiators, travel and emigration by Soviet citizens were still severely limited, and insurgent groups in several countries still received Soviet support.

Nevertheless, Gorbachev held to the principles he enunciated at the United Nations. He allowed the Communist regimes in East and Central Europe to fall and be replaced by non-Communist elected governments; in 1990, he allowed the Federal Republic of Germany to absorb the German Democratic Republic and stay in NATO; he concluded a treaty to reduce conventional weapons; when Iraq invaded Kuwait, he joined the Western powers in condemning the Iraqi attempt to annex Kuwait.

When Gorbachev and Bush met at Malta in December 1989, they agreed that they would no longer consider their countries enemies. The "ideological" end of the Cold War had been confirmed by events. The Cold War was over—purely, simply, and completely.

A War without Losers

Neither Gorbachev nor Reagan thought of the end of the Cold War as the victory of one country over another. Gorbachev has insisted that "all the peoples of the world benefited from the end of the Cold War,"[30] while Reagan observed in his memoirs that it was a victory of one system of government, one ideology, over another, not of one country over another.[31] Both are correct in their assessments; in fact, every agreement Gorbachev made to end the Cold War was in the interest of the Soviet Union. By ending the arms race, opening his country to the world, and introducing practices of democratic governance, Gorbachev created the possibility of reforming a failing system. These reforms turned out to be only partially successful—and eventually the forces they unleashed destroyed the Soviet state that had been created and held together by force. When Gorbachev undermined the instruments of compulsion, inherent contradictions in the state, above all nationalist tendencies suppressed under Communism, brought it down.

Reagan's Achievement

To anyone familiar with the factual record, it is absurd to claim (as some have) that Ronald Reagan "defeated communism" and "brought down" the Soviet Union. It is true that he considered communism an exploitative, aggressive system, but he understood that he had no power to bring it down, and if he tried, his attempts were likely only to strengthen the system's resistance.

The most important achievement of Reagan's presidency was his contribution to ending the Cold War. He did not do it alone and could not have done it alone. Mikhail Gorbachev's contribution was essential. Each needed the other to create a window of opportunity that had not been available to their predecessors.

Reagan brought several relevant qualities to his dealing with other political leaders. While he was not an intellectual who mastered a lot of facts, he knew what he didn't know and was eager to learn. He concentrated attention on a few key questions, including, notably, relations with the Soviet Union and the threat that nuclear weapons pose for mankind. Unlike many on his staff, he believed that Soviet policies could be changed, in part by persuasion, but persuasion bolstered by policies that discouraged continuation of typical Cold War practices. For example, he made it clear that if the Soviet government decided to continue the arms race, he would make sure the Soviet Union lost the race. At the same time, he avoided demanding the impossible—such as, for example, calling for "regime change." He had an instinctive understanding of how far a political leader could go without fatally undermining his support, and the need any leader has not to be seen by his own people as weak. Thus, he never claimed "victory," or took credit if, for example, political prisoners in the Soviet Union were released as a result of American representations.

These qualities allowed Reagan to devise policy and tactics, none of them totally new, likely to be effective in convincing a pragmatic Soviet leader that it was not only safe, but indeed necessary, to end the arms race and open up his country to the outside world. They also enabled him to recognize change in Soviet policy and to reward it in ways available to him. Finally, his reputation for firm anticommunism helped him convince a skeptical American public that it was safe to cooperate with the Soviet Union.

Both Reagan and Gorbachev needed help in their efforts, and they received it from George Shultz, Eduard Shevardnadze, and their staffs. But it was Reagan and Gorbachev who appointed them, listened to them, defended them from critics, and ultimately took responsibility for their decisions.

I believe that the Cold War would not have ended, when and as it did, and as peacefully and completely as it did, if Ronald Reagan and Mikhail Gorbachev had not been in office in their respective countries at the time they were. We are all, as Gorbachev has suggested, the beneficiaries of their ability to understand what needed to be done, and to get it done.

Notes

1. For example, Haynes Johnson, *Sleepwalking Through History: America in the Reagan Years* (New York: Anchor Books, 1992); and the chapter on Reagan in Stephen Graubard, *Command of Office: How War, Secrecy and Deception Transformed the Presidency from Theodore Roosevelt to George W. Bush* (New York: Basic Books, 2004), 441–472.
2. For example, Peggy Noonan, *When Character Was King* (New York: Viking, 2001); and Peter Schweitzer, *Victory: The Reagan Administration's Secret Strategy That Hastened the Collapse of the Soviet Union* (New York: Atlantic Monthly Press, 1994).
3. I served in the American Foreign Service from 1956 until 1991, much of that time dealing directly with the Soviet Union either from Washington (as director of Soviet Affairs in the Department of State from 1971 to 1974 and as senior director for European and Soviet affairs on the National Security Council from 1983 to 1986), or from the American Embassy in Moscow, where I spent a total of eleven years between 1961 and 1991, the final four years as American ambassador. My interpretation of events is presented in greater detail in *Reagan and Gorbachev: How the Cold War Ended* (New York: Random House, 2004); and *Autopsy on an Empire: The American Ambassador's Account of the Collapse of the Soviet Union* (New York: Random House, 1995).
4. This was the contention of the multipart television series on the Cold War produced by Sir Jeremy Isaacs.
5. This was not a total embargo, since the U.S.–Soviet Long-Term Grain Agreement gave the USSR the right to purchase up to eight million tons of wheat without the approval of the U.S. government. The agreement, however, required the advance approval of the U.S. government for purchases in excess of eight million tons, and the USSR had been purchasing more than twenty million tons a year since 1972. The "embargo" therefore, was a refusal to sanction the export of more than eight million tons a year.
6. The full text of the press conference can be found in the *Weekly Compilation of Presidential Documents* (Vol. 17, No. 5, 66–67), published by the White House.

7. Both negotiators have described the compromise proposal in their memoirs. See Paul H. Nitze, *From Hiroshima to Glasnost: At the Center of Decision—A Memoir* (New York: Grove Weidenfeld, 1999); and Julij A. Kwitzinski, *Vor dem Sturm: Erinnerungen eines Diplomaten* (Berlin: Siedler Verlag, 1993).
8. Critics consistently referred to the program as "Star Wars," after a popular movie.
9. Murray Sayle, "Closing the File on Flight 007," *The New Yorker*, December 13, 1993, 90–101.
10. Published in *Pravda* and *Izvestiya*, September 29, 1983, English translation in the *Current Digest of the Soviet Press*, October 26, 1983 (Vol. 35, No. 39).
11. According to Oleg Gordiyevsky, instructions were sent to KGB residencies in the United States in February 1983 to plan "active measures" to prevent Reagan's reelection in November 1984. See Christopher Andrew and Oleg Gordiyevsky, *KGB: The Inside Story* (London: Hodder and Stoughton, 1990), 494.
12. The full text was published in the *Weekly Compilation of Presidential Documents* (Vol. 20, No. 3, 40–45), and by the Department of State as *Current Policy*, No. 537, "The U.S.–Soviet Relationship." For a scholarly analysis, see Beth A. Fischer, "Toeing the Hard Line? The Reagan Administration and the Ending of the Cold War," *Political Science Quarterly*, Vol. 112, No. 3, 1997, 477–496.
13. This was done against the advice of Secretary of State Alexander Haig. Reagan explained that he was only fulfilling a campaign promise, but Soviet leaders should have understood that despite his criticism of their system, he was no advocate of economic warfare.
14. Anatoly Dobrynin, *In Confidence: Moscow's Ambassador to America's Six Cold War Presidents (1962–1986)* (New York: Random House, 1995), 527.
15. Statement by Oleg Grinevsky at a conference on understanding the end of the Cold War at Brown University, May 7–10, 1998 (see Matlock, *Reagan and Gorbachev*, 86).
16. "Vystuplenie R. Reygana," *Izvestiya*, January 17, 1984.
17. Archie Brown, *Seven Years That Changed the World: Perestroika in Perspective* (Oxford: Oxford University Press, 2007).
18. In my book *Reagan and Gorbachev*, I reported that Reagan had "dictated" this note to his secretary (150–153). That was my understanding at the time, when I was shown a typewritten copy, corrected in his hand. However, since then I have learned that in fact he wrote the memorandum by hand, had his secretary type it, then made a significant correction. The handwritten memorandum, without the correction, was quoted in Edmund Morris, *Dutch: A Memoir of Ronald Reagan* (New York: Random House, 1999), 545–546.
19. Lest these three priorities seem obvious, even anodyne, to the contemporary reader, it should be recalled that the Soviet position was that an arms control agreement (on Soviet terms) was necessary before anything else in the relationship could be improved, that conflict in the "third world" was not a proper subject for negotiation, or even discussion, since it was only the inevitable march of history, and that distrust and suspicion were also unavoidable between countries that represented the interests of opposing economic classes (proletariat versus bourgeoisie, in Marxist terms).
20. Reagan quoted liberally from the exchange of correspondence and from the transcripts of his meetings in his autobiography, *An American Life* (New York: Simon & Schuster, 1990), Part VI, 545–723.

21. See Paul Lettow, *Ronald Reagan and His Quest to Abolish Nuclear Weapons* (New York: Random House, 2005); and Frances Fitzgerald, *Way Out There in the Blue: Reagan, Star Wars, and the End of the Cold War* (New York: Simon & Schuster, 2000).
22. Anatoly Chernyaev, *My Six Years with Gorbachev* (University Park Pennsylvania: Pennsylvania State University Press, 2000), 82–83.
23. Notes on Politburo sessions on February 23 and 26, 1987, archive of the Gorbachev Foundation, Moscow.
24. Statement at a conference on understanding the end of the Cold War, Brown University, May 7–10, 1998.
25. The Pershing IIs had been designed with a range just short of Moscow from the bases in Germany, since the United States did not want to leave the impression that it had the capability to eliminate the Soviet leadership in a sudden nuclear strike. However, the Soviet leaders assumed that the range was, in fact, sufficient to reach Moscow, and thus feared that the Pershing-IIs could be used in a decapitating first strike.
26. Matlock, *Reagan and Gorbachev*, 251–252.
27. I described this issue, which attracted extensive media coverage, in detail in *Reagan and Gorbachev*, 254–259.
28. I describe this debate in detail in Matlock, *Autopsy on an Empire*, 142–148.
29. Reagan, *An American Life*, 720.
30. Mikhail Gorbachev, *My Country and the World* (New York: Columbia University Press, 2000), 53.
31. Reagan, *An American Life*, 715.

Part II
Politics and Policies

Chapter 5

Reagan, Nuclear Weapons, and the End of the Cold War

Simon Head

During the twenty years of close, sometimes fraught, and eventually constructive diplomacy between the United States and the Soviet Union lasting from the early 1970s to the early 1990s, the state of the nuclear balance between them was never far from the center of their attention. During the Cold War era conflicts between the United States and the Soviet Union took on a heightened significance because of the possibility, however remote, that such crises might escalate to the level of all-out thermonuclear war. Even in the absence of crises, supposed imbalances between the nuclear forces of the two superpowers, especially if linked to an alleged operational superiority possessed by one side or the other, could themselves become sources of enmity as the inferior side sought to eradicate its disadvantage with a build up of its own nuclear arsenal.

In the eight years of his presidency Ronald Reagan played a role in the U.S. diplomacy and strategy of the nuclear balance for which there was little precedent in the administrations of any of his seven predecessors of the Cold War era, beginning with the Truman administration in the 1940s. Judged by the exacting standards of the Nixon–Kissinger era, Reagan's practice of nuclear statesmanship was haphazard and amateurish. Notoriously, he never mastered the small print of arms control[1]; he was reluctant to mediate the disputes between leading figures in his own administration, nor did he delegate this power to any of his five national security advisers.

He could also be embarrassingly ignorant of some of the most basic facts about nuclear weapons. One of his White House advisers General Brent Scowcroft was amazed to find in 1983 that Reagan did not know that long-range bombers were carriers of nuclear weapons. Other gaps in Reagan's knowledge were that he did not know that ballistic missiles, once launched from submarines, could not be recalled; or that the Soviet strategic nuclear arsenals relied much more heavily upon land-based ballistic missiles than did the American. So he did not realize that his own administration's proposals to reduce warheads on ballistic missiles by equal percentages were heavily biased in the United States' favor.

Yet there were two occasions during his presidency when Reagan rose up like some twentieth-century Gulliver and, casting aside the constraints of politics, diplomacy, and of his own ignorance, forced upon his administration and indeed the whole world a vision of the future of nuclear weapons that was uniquely his and that was deeply at odds with the policies of his administration, of his European allies, and indeed of his predecessors of the Cold War era. In his Star Wars Speech of March 1983 Reagan turned his back on the doctrine of Mutually Assured Destruction (MAD), which had governed the strategic relationship between the superpowers since the 1950s, whereby each of the superpowers deterred the first use of nuclear weapons by the other by the threat of massive retaliation with its surviving nuclear forces.[2] In place of MAD Reagan committed his administration to the research, development, and eventual deployment of a system of defense against ballistic missiles that he believed would protect the territory and population of the United States from incoming Soviet missiles and that would also enable the United States to defend itself against a Soviet attack without having to retaliate in kind and so trigger a catastrophic nuclear exchange.

Then, at the Reykjavik Summit three and a half years later, Reagan took the logical next step in this world where the defense would prevail over the offence: the elimination by both the United States and the USSR of all ballistic missiles, followed by the elimination of all strategic nuclear weapons. If ballistic missiles could no longer threaten the enemy's territory with a first strike, and if they were no longer needed to respond to an enemy's first strike, then they served no useful purpose and could be negotiated away.

In the intrigues of the Reagan White House it was a common for one set of Reagan advisers to call upon the other to "let Reagan be Reagan." The president's official biographer Edmund Morris became so confused about the identity of the real Reagan that he resorted to the desperate measure of inventing fictional encounters between Reagan and himself in the hope that the true Reagan might somehow emerge. But on the issues of nuclear war and peace, who indeed was the real Ronald Reagan? How to reconcile the utopianism of his Star Wars Speech and of the Reykjavik Summit with the grim, bellicose orthodoxy of his first three years in office when he did little more than inflate the U.S. defense budget and denounce the Soviet Union as the "evil empire."

How also to reconcile his strong, even passionate views on the seminal issues of nuclear war and peace, with his ignorance of actual nuclear weapons, his carelessness about the small print of arms control, and his detachment from the day-to-day negotiations that make arms control possible? So it was typical of Reagan that once he had shaken the foundations of deterrence with his Star War Speech, he reverted to his customary lethargy and failed to set in motion a policy review that could begin the daunting task of reconciling the president's new vision with existing administration policies.

Faut de mieux the task devolved on his warring subordinates, which simply added another dimension to their quarrels.[3]

In this quest for Reagan the events of his first three years of office, 1981–1983, may provide some clue because they followed a clear and recognizable pattern. For Soviet–American relations these were years of almost continuous stress, unrelieved by diplomacy. The origins of this revived Cold War lie at least partly in the belief of conservatives, including Reagan himself, that the SALT I treaty signed by President Nixon and General Secretary Brezhnev in 1972 had allowed the Soviet Union to achieve nuclear superiority over the United States. By the time Reagan took office in January 1981, this Soviet superiority was, in the conservative view, at hand.

In the early 1970s the leading conservative opponent of Nixon and Kissinger's détente with the Soviet Union, and of the SALT I Treaty, was Senator Henry Jackson, a Democratic defense hawk from the state of Washington. Jackson's expertise on the minutiae of the nuclear balance was largely due to the talents of a then-obscure aide who will become one of the central figures in this whole narrative, Richard Perle. Jackson and Perle saw the SALT I treaty as fatally flawed, because it contained loopholes in the clauses governing the deployment of land-based, intercontinental ballistic missiles, or ICBMs. They believed that SALT I permitted the USSR to achieve nuclear superiority over the United States in the form of a disarming, first strike capability against the United States' own land-based ICBMs. This Jackson–Perle vision of the nuclear balance is of considerable importance because it is the view that Ronald Reagan had adopted, pretty much in its entirety, by the time he assumed the presidency in January 1981.

This chapter will not describe the elaborate scenarios of nuclear doom weaved during these years by Richard Perle, complemented in the mid- and late 1970s by the equally gloomy vision of the veteran arms control negotiator and nuclear theologian Paul Nitze, their views often put out under the auspices of the Committee on the present Danger. But there is a need to give some sense of this nuclear theology because it exerted such a strong influence on the defense policies of Reagan's first years in office.

Neither Richard Perle nor Paul Nitze ever actually stated that the Soviet Union, emboldened by its possession of nuclear superiority, would, out of the blue, launch a first strike against the United States. But both certainly believed, and frequently stated, that because the Soviet Union would in fact emerge the victor in a nuclear exchange with the United States, an awareness of this Soviet superiority would decisively influence the conduct of both superpowers in the context of a major confrontation between them. So, to cite a very pertinent example, if the nuclear balance of the late 1970s had existed in the early 1960s, then the outcome of the Cuban missile crisis could have been different, with President Kennedy having to accept the presence of Soviet missiles in Cuba.

Paul Nitze's account of what the superpower diplomacy of an administration espousing his and Perle's views would look like throws much light on

White House thinking in the early 1980s.[4] Essentially, it can be boiled down to three principles. The first priority of any incoming administration would be to eliminate the Soviet Union's margin of nuclear superiority with an immediate build up and modernization of U.S. strategic nuclear forces. Second, while this build up was underway, it was not in the U.S. interest to enter into arms control negotiations with the Soviet side. Such negotiations should be postponed until strategic parity between the superpowers was restored. And finally, in this period of build up, the United States was obliged to compensate for its continuing nuclear inferiority by demonstrating strength and resolution in other spheres of its relationship with the USSR. This, as we shall see, was not the strategy advocated by this same Paul Nitze when he himself joined the Reagan administration in 1981.

But it was certainly the strategy followed by the Reagan administration during, at least, its first three years in office. From 1981 onward the U.S. defense budget increased in annual increments of 20 percent. The administration committed to building one hundred MX missiles, three thousand air-launched crises missiles, and a hundred B-1 bombers, as well as new Trident submarines carrying Trident 2 missiles, each armed with ten multiple warheads. During this period the Reagan administration showed little interest in the continuation of the SALT process, and those disarmament proposals that did see the light of day in Washington were so biased in the United States' favor as to provide no basis for negotiations with the Soviet side.[5]

Reagan also launched what he saw as an ideological offensive against the Russians, designated the USSR as the evil empire, and defined the obscure civil war in El Salvador as a global test of American resolve. In his introduction to Strobe Talbot's book *The Russians and Reagan* (1984) the former secretary of state Cyrus Vance wrote that during those early Reagan years Soviet–American relations were "close to an all-time low."[6] Vance was perhaps exaggerating. In those first years Reagan was certainly spoiling for a fight, but it took two to fight the Cold War, and on the Soviet side those were the final years of what Mikhail Gorbachev called "the era of stagnation"; the death throes, literally, of the generation that had ruled the Soviet Union since the death of Stalin in 1953.

Events might have turned out differently if a latter-day Khrushchev had been in charge in 1981–1983, but as it happened those years coincided with the final, twilight months of Leonid Brezhnev's long rein. There then followed the brief interregnum, clouded from the start by ill health, of Yuri Andropov; followed by the even briefer interregnum of the now forgotten Konstantin Chernenko. Ronald Reagan used to say that during those years he had no one to negotiate with, his Soviet counterparts kept dying on him. But one can also say that he had no one to cross swords with either.

* * *

Historian Beth Fischer argues that the Reagan administration "abandoned its hard line policy" in January 1984, but that implies a coherence and decisiveness in Washington that at the time was strikingly absent.[7] In early 1984, and for at least two years thereafter, there was not so much a definitive abandonment of hard-line policies by the Reagan administration, but rather the pursuit of a fractious mélange of policies old and new, which created confusion and *immobilisme* in Washington. On January 16, 1984, in a radio address to the nation, Reagan did indeed say that "1984 finds the United States in the strongest position in years to establish a constructive and realistic working relationship with the Soviet Union" so that "together we can strengthen peace, reduce the level of arms, and know in doing so know that we have helped fulfil the hopes and dreams of those we represent, and indeed, of people everywhere."[8]

In fact there were those within the Reagan administration who had been trying to establish a dialogue with the Soviet side during the previous eighteen months, though with little success. Here the resignation of Alexander Haig as secretary of state in July 1982 and his replacement by George Shultz had been a significant event. Shultz was a skilled and determined manager of U.S.–Soviet relationship in the tradition of Henry Kissinger. He believed in finding areas of common interest with the Soviet side, even in the face of objectionable Soviet conduct.

But whereas Kissinger had made much of "linkage," the practice of making agreements with the Russians in one sphere contingent on Soviet good conduct in another, Shultz distanced himself from linkage and argued that the United States should be ready to seek agreements with the Russians when it was in the U.S. interest to do so, and even in the face of hostile Soviet behavior. Shultz followed this course after the shooting down of the Korean Airlines Flight 007 by the Russians in September 1983.[9]

Shultz also took on the wearying task of improving relations between the Reagan administration and the Soviet leadership. In February 1983 he literally smuggled the veteran Soviet ambassador to the United States, Anatoly Dobrynin, into the White House to see Reagan, and in September 1984 he arranged for the even longer serving Soviet foreign minister, Andrei Gromyko, to come to Washington for talks with Reagan. In July 1983 he encouraged Reagan to send a personal, handwritten letter to Yuri Andropov, Brezhnev's successor as general secretary of the CPSU, in which Reagan wrote

> You and I share an enormous responsibility for the preservation of stability in the world. I believe we can fulfil that mandate but to do so will require a more active level of exchange than we have heretofore been able to establish. We have much to talk about with regard to the situation in Eastern Europe, South Asia, and particularly this hemisphere, as well as in such areas of arms control, trade between our two countries, and others ways in which we can expand east-west contacts.[10]

However, the event that dominated the nuclear diplomacy of the superpowers during Reagan's first term was his Star Wars Speech of March 23, 1983. Reagan was already two years into his first term when he delivered the speech, and the pattern of his working life at the White House was by then well established, with the president relying heavily on his staff to inform him about decisions that needed to be taken, and reluctant to take decisions unless there was a consensus among his staff about what should be done. In his biography of Reagan Lou Cannon makes the remarkable claim that "as far as I have been able to determine in scores of interviews, Reagan never once asked his national security advisers about the progress of arms control negotiations or other foreign policy initiatives. The closest he ever came to this, and it is an important exception, was inquiring about the feasibility of missile defence."[11]

This was indeed the exception and in the days preceding the Star Wars Speech Reagan behaved like a man possessed, and here George Shultz's account of these days in his memoirs is revealing.[12] Once Reagan had heard from the joint chiefs of staff and his own scientific adviser Jay Keyworth that breakthroughs in the relevant technologies had improved the prospects of a defense against ballistic missiles, he insisted on making this known to the American people without delay. In his rush to the microphones Reagan did not consult with either Shultz or Defense Secretary Weinberger. Shultz himself only heard about the speech on March 21, 1983, two days before it was due to be delivered.

After being briefed on its content by one of his deputies Lawrence Eagleburger, Shultz felt that a disaster was in the offing. He was particularly concerned about the speech's closing paragraph in which Reagan told his audience "my fellow Americans tonight we're launching an effort which holds the promise of changing the course of human history."[13] Shultz believed, correctly as it turned out, that Keyworth and the joint chiefs had much exaggerated the advances in the technologies of missile defense, which anyway they were not properly qualified to evaluate. Shultz also found that the joint chiefs had failed to explain to Reagan that the defensive shield of what came to be known as the Strategic Defense Initiative (SDI) would protect the U.S. population, if at all, only against ballistic missiles, and not against non-ballistic cruise missiles and bombers. Shultz felt that the president's rhetoric "must be consistent with what is and is not being covered," but was not. Shultz also wanted the speech to be amended so as to make clear the limits of Reagan's protective shield, and also to tone down the speech's closing rhetoric about "changing the course of human history." Neither change was made.

Since the Star Wars Speech, in Shultz's words, changed "the whole strategic view and doctrine of the United States," the impact of the speech on Soviet–American relations was profound and, for three years at least, almost entirely negative. This becomes clear if we look at the impact of the speech from the perspective of the four main groups of actors involved. First, George Shultz, Paul Nitze, and the "pragmatists" at the State Department; second, Caspar Weinberger, Richard Perle, William Casey, and the "hardliners" at the Pentagon and the CIA; third, the Soviet leaders in Moscow; and fourth, Ronald Reagan in the White House.

After recovering from his initial post-speech shock, Shultz and the newly pragmatic Paul Nitze tried to reconcile Reagan's support for missile defense with proposals for arms control that would have some chance of being accepted by the Soviet side. Their approach was to conceive of SDI as a bargaining chip that could be deployed on a much reduced scale if the two sides agreed to reduce their inventories of ballistic missiles. As Shultz repeatedly told Reagan "we have to be willing to give up something in SDI. An agreement for massive reductions on strategic missiles can use SDI research and potential deployment of strategic defense as a means to win Soviet compliance on continuing reductions."[14]

After *his* initial post-speech shock, focused on Reagan's apparent abandonment of the doctrine of MAD, Secretary of Defense Weinberger also regrouped and soon became a strong supporter of SDI. Weinberger resisted any attempt by Shultz and Nitze to dilute the "president's vision" in the interests of pursuing arms negotiations with the Soviet side. As Weinberger explains in his memoirs, *Fighting for Peace* (1990), his sole concern was what he saw as the parlous state of the military balance between the United States and the USSR.[15] He was strongly opposed to the United States' continued observance of the still unratified SALT II Treaty, the successor to SALT I, which had in his view allowed the Russians to push ahead with the build up of their strategic nuclear forces to the point where these forces could now threaten U.S. land-based ICBMs with a disarming first strike. From this strictly military perspective SDI deployment was desirable because it could protect U.S. ICBMs, though not the U.S. population, from a Soviet first strike. Also, because the USSR was far behind the United States in the technologies of missile defense, it was unlikely that the Soviets could match the United States in protecting their land-based ICMBs from a U.S. attack. The SDI therefore had the potential to shift the strategic balance decisively in the United States' favor.

It was precisely for this reason that the reaction of the Soviet leadership to the Star Wars Speech was negative in the extreme. Ambassador Dobrynin warned Shultz that with the Star Wars Speech the United States was opening a new phase in the arms race.[16] Andropov found Reagan's vision "irresponsible" and "insane" and accused Reagan of "attempting to disarm the Soviet Union in the face of the US nuclear threat." For the following four years the Soviets made any further agreement on the limitation of strategic nuclear weapons conditional upon the United States conducting research on SDI strictly within the guidelines laid out in the ABM Treaty of 1972, which limited the deployment of defenses against ballistic missiles and which, in the Soviet view, excluded any testing or development of SDI outside the laboratory.

So where does that leave Ronald Reagan? For ten years at least he had shared Weinberger's alarmist view of the state of the military balance between the United States and the USSR, and also Weinberger's criticisms of the SALT I and SALT II Treaties. He had been Weinberger's staunch ally in the build up of U.S. nuclear and conventional forces, which had gotten underway the moment Reagan became president in January 1981. Just two weeks before making the Star Wars speech Reagan had appeared before the National

Association of Evangelicals in Florida and made his famous Evil Empire speech. He warned the Evangelicals against ignoring "the facts of history and the aggressive impulses of an evil empire: to simply call the arms race a giant misunderstanding and thereby remove yourself from the struggle between right and wrong and good and evil."[17]

Although Reagan's engagement in the day-to-day business of arms control was haphazard, his commitment to SDI and his unwillingness to place any restrictions on its testing and development made him an ally of Weinberger and Perle in the infighting on arms control between the State Department and the Pentagon, which was carried on virtually without interruption for the three years following the Star Wars Speech.[18] Thus Reagan rejected Shultz's advice to allow SDI to be used as a bargaining chip to achieve a reduction of force levels in the Strategic Arms Reduction Talks (START), the successor to SALT II, with the Russians. He supported Weinberger and Perle's moves to "reinterpret" the ABM Treaty so as to permit the testing and development of SDI outside the laboratory. He was also tolerant of Weinberger's efforts to end compliance with the terms of the unratified SALT II Treaty.

Yet to portray Reagan simply as a hard-line ally of Weinberger who stood in the way of arms control and was intent on using SDI to achieve strategic superiority over the Soviet Union is misleading. There was also the utopian Reagan who had arisen with the Star Wars Speech, and was to do so again at the Reykjavik Summit with Gorbachev in October 1986, where Reagan and Gorbachev were within reach of getting rid not just of ballistic missiles but of all strategic nuclear weapons. How to reconcile this Reagan with the militant cold warrior of the late 1970s and early 1980s is the kind of mystery that has so baffled Reagan's official biographer.

The simplest explanation is perhaps the most plausible. Reagan himself believed, as he said in his January 1984 speech, that "the United States had come a long way since the decade of the seventies...when the US seemed filled with doubt and neglected its defences" so that "in 1984 the United States finds itself in the strongest position in years to establish a constructive and realistic working relationship with the Soviet Union."[19] One does not have to accept Reagan's self-serving view of the evolving military balance to see that this perspective gave him confidence to negotiate with the Soviet side.

Reagan was also feeling the pressures of domestic politics. In 1980 he had run against Jimmy Carter as a nuclear re-armer who would close the missile gap with the Soviet Union. Up for reelection in 1984 he was obliged to say, and did say, that he had indeed closed the gap, and that American strength was restored. "America is Back" as he himself put it during the 1984 campaign. Americans were also beginning to tire of Reagan's bellicosity and expected him to use the nation's newfound strength in constructive ways. In February 1984 a Gallup poll found that only 38 percent approved of Reagan's handling of foreign policy, and Gallup commented that "Americans' concern over the threat of war has grown to its highest point since the Viet Nam war."[20] There was also the important role played by Mrs. Nancy Reagan in moving the president in a less bellicose direction.

But once Reagan started moving in this direction ambitions and beliefs came into play that took him far away from Weinberger and the hardliners and brought him much closer to Shultz, despite Reagan's refusal to allow SDI to be a bargaining chip in the arms control negotiations that continued under the acronym START—Strategic Arms Reduction Talks. So although Reagan and Weinberger both supported SDI, they did so for fundamentally different reasons; Weinberger as a means of reinforcing the foundations of MAD, Reagan for getting beyond them. In his own words

> MAD was the craziest thing I ever heard of: Simply put, it called for each side to keep enough nuclear weapons to obliterate the other, so that if one attacked, the second had enough bombs left to annihilate its adversary in a matter of minutes...we were placing our entire faith in a weapon whose fundamental target was the civilian population.[21]

Once in the White House Reagan wondered if it might be possible to develop a defense against missiles other than the fatalistic acceptance of annihilation that was implicit under the MAD policy: "We couldn't continue this nervous standoff forever."[22] This was the origins of Reagan's maximalist concept of SDI as a shield protecting the population and territory of the United States from attack. But Reagan's critique of MAD and his vision of SDI were linked to another powerful conviction of his, the need to move as quickly as possible to a world without nuclear weapons.

In his memoirs Reagan writes frequently of this ambition and of how it separated him from the Pentagon hardliners:

> My dream became a world free of nuclear weapons. Some of my advisers, including a number at the Pentagon did not share this dream...they tossed around macabre jargon about "throw weights" and "kill ratios" as if they were talking about baseball scores...But for the eight years as president I never let my dream of a nuclear free world fade from my mind.[23]

At the time Reagan's talk of a world without nuclear weapons was largely written off as a fantasy having no bearing on current policies. But Shultz and Cannon provide a wealth of evidence that, from the start of his presidency, Reagan didn't at all regard his ambition as a fantasy, and wanted it to be seriously discussed both within his administration and with the Russians. Once Gorbachev was in firm control by the spring of 1986, it certainly was.

According to Reagan's first secretary of state, Alexander Haig, as early as April 1981 the president wanted to write to Leonid Brezhnev "about a world without nuclear weapons." Haig persuaded Reagan to leave out these words because "they might perhaps be confusing to the Soviet leaders."[24] In July 1983 Reagan's then national security adviser William Clark had to persuade the president not to include in a letter to Andropov a passage that read: "If we can agree on mutual, verifiable reductions in the number of nuclear weapons we both hold, could this not be a first step towards elimination of all such weapons? What a blessing this would be for the people we both represent." Shultz notes that "Reagan was consistently committed to his personal vision of a world without nuclear weapons; his advisers were determined to turn him away from that course."[25]

Shultz found himself more and more having to explain to senior members of the administration that Reagan's commitment to a nonnuclear world had to be taken seriously. In January 1984 he told Assistant Secretary of State Rick Burt that "every meeting I go to the president talks about abolishing nuclear weapons. I cannot get it through your heads that the man is serious. We either have to convince him he is barking up the wrong tree or reply to his interests with some specific suggestions."[26] Responding in January 1986 to comments by Richard Perle and other senior officials that "the President's dream of a world without nuclear weapons was a disaster," Shultz told Perle, perhaps with a touch of *Schadenfreude,* "You've got a problem. The president thinks it is a good idea...we need to work on what a world without nuclear weapons would mean to us."[27]

The Reykjavik Summit of October 11–12, 1986, is usually thought of as the moment when both Reagan and Gorbachev got caught up with the heretical ideas about nuclear strategy and arms control that so horrified more orthodox figures such as Henry Kissinger and Mrs. Thatcher, who described the summit as an "earthquake." But in fact it was Gorbachev who broke the diplomatic stalemate wide open in January 1986 when he proposed to Reagan that together they should work toward a world without nuclear weapons, which of course was Reagan's goal. Thus began a year of diplomatic high drama of which Reykjavik was the culmination, and not the single, isolated act.

Gorbachev's January proposal was that the United States and the USSR should eliminate all strategic nuclear weapons—ballistic missiles, cruise missiles, bombers—over a ten-year period, with 50 percent of the weapons eliminated in the first five years, the remaining 50 percent in the second, which was, in Shultz's words, "a staged program toward zero."[28] Most arms control specialists in the State Department and the Pentagon wrote off Gorbachev's proposals as propaganda but this was not the president's view: "Why wait until the end of the century for a world without nuclear weapons?" he told Shultz. The next time Shultz discussed nuclear issues with Reagan he "could see that anyone trying to talk (Reagan) out of his vision of a world free of nuclear weapons was wasting his breath."[29]

Although Shultz himself shared neither Reagan's vision of a nuclear free world nor his commitment to SDI, he felt an obligation as Reagan's secretary of state to find ways of embedding the president's vision in current policies, and it was largely thanks to him that Gorbachev's January proposals set off an intense dialogue on arms control within the administration and between the United States and the USSR, which culminated in the Reykjavik Summit. The administration's first response to Gorbachev, drafted in the State Department, was therefore positive. It reiterated the president's "vision of a world without nuclear weapons" and stressed that the first phase in any reduction in strategic weapons was a path to such a world.[30]

It was indicative of the way the wind was blowing in Washington that in June 1986 Caspar Weinberger, of all people, suggested that the United States should include a proposal to eliminate all ballistic missiles in its response to Gorbachev. Reagan and Shultz "left the meeting on the note that Cap's idea should be studied carefully but quietly to see how we might make it a part of our reply to the latest Soviet offer."[31] Weinberger's idea did become part of Reagan's response to Gorbachev, and as a result the United States' negotiating package for the Reykjavik Summit already contained the proposal that so horrified Mrs. Thatcher; a readiness to eliminate all ballistic missiles.

In his response to Gorbachev's January 1986 initiative Reagan followed him in proposing that reductions in strategic arsenals should take place in two phases of five years each.[32] The elimination of ballistic missiles would take place in the second phase and was linked to a deployment of SDI on both sides and with a U.S. willingness to share SDI technology with the Russians. In Reagan's words,

> if the tests (of SDI) demonstrated that the system was effective, and once we had scrapped fifty percent of our missiles, each of us would destroy the balance of our missiles and both countries would share all SDI technology. At the ten year point, when all ballistic missiles were eliminated, each of us would deploy the SDI systems simultaneously.

The willingness of the United States even to consider the elimination of the most powerful, accurate, and, in the case of ICBM's launched from submarines, survivable components of its strategic forces shows how far Reagan and Gorbachev had already opened up the subject matter of arms control in the run up to the Reykjavik Summit.

This chronology sets the scene for Reykjavik itself, and particularly for the notorious negotiating session between Reagan and Gorbachev that took place on the afternoon of Sunday, October 12, 1986, when Reagan accepted Gorbachev's proposal to eliminate *all* strategic nuclear weapons during the second half of the ten-year period, which had featured in Gorbachev's original January 1986 letter to Reagan. The scope and pace of the negotiations during the session was breathtaking, but that was not because Reagan and Gorbachev, unprepared and unbriefed, had freed themselves from their advisers and were winging it. It was because they were dealing in ideas that had been around since the beginning of the year and in Reagan's case, much longer.

Thanks to the U.S. Freedom of Information Act and the diligence of the National Security Archive at George Washington University (GWU) in Washington D.C., we now have access to both the U.S. and Soviet transcripts of the Sunday afternoon negotiations.[33] As the GWU commentary notes, the two versions are "remarkably congruent...with no direct contradictions." But the Soviet transcript is verbatim and gives a much fuller account of the exchanges between Reagan, Gorbachev, and Shultz than does the American one. Exchanges that are briefly described in the U.S. version are reproduced in full in the Russian. The critical exchanges focus on the reductions in the strategic nuclear arsenals of both sides that would take place during the ten-year period in which the ABM Treaty would continue to be observed.[34]

The session opened with Gorbachev reiterating his January proposals that the two sides should eliminate 50 percent of their strategic forces during the first five years of the ten-year period, and then eliminate all remaining strategic weapons during the second five years. Reagan follows by reiterating the United States' July proposal that the 50 percent reductions of the first five years should be followed only by the elimination of ballistic missiles during the second five years. Gorbachev then pressed Reagan to accept the elimination of *all* strategic nuclear weapons, bombers and cruise missiles included, during the second five-year period, and Reagan readily concedes: "Evidently we have simply misunderstood you. But if that's what you want, all right."[35]

Shultz then intervenes to say "we need to be careful here," but his warning isn't about the very significant concession on strategic weapons that Reagan has just made, but about the secondary issue of short-range ballistic missiles in Europe. In fact the record shows that at Reykjavik Shultz strongly supported Reagan on the elimination of all strategic nuclear weapons during the second five-year period, something that Shultz does not make entirely clear in his memoirs. So having delivered his "warning," Shultz then looks for a formula that would capture what Reagan and Gorbachev have just agreed to: "Perhaps we could formulate it this way: by the end of 1996 all strategic offensive weapons and offensive ballistic missiles of the USSR and the US will be eliminated." And again a few minutes later: "I propose that we write that by 1996 all strategic weapons and all offensive missiles are to be eliminated."

The exchanges continue with Reagan proposing that the two sides get rid of every kind of nuclear weapon, everywhere:

> *Reagan*: Let me ask this: Do we have in mind—and I think it would be very good—that by the end of the two five year periods all nuclear explosive devices would be eliminated, including bombs, battlefield systems, cruise missiles, submarine weapons, intermediate-range systems, and so on?
> *Gorbachev*: We could say that, list all those weapons.
> *Shultz*: Then let's do it.

These remarkable exchanges did not produce an agreement to eliminate, or drastically reduce, each side's strategic nuclear arsenals because the two sides could not agree on SDI and its relation to the ABM Treaty of 1972. Gorbachev insisted on an interpretation of the treaty that would confine research on SDI to the laboratory. Reagan insisted on an interpretation that permitted research, testing, and development of SDI beyond the laboratory. The two sides also disagreed about what would happen with SDI at the end of the ten-year period covered by a prospective treaty. Gorbachev proposed that there should be further negotiations about SDI, Reagan that the two sides should at that moment be free to deploy the system.

But the Soviet position was not set in concrete, which is why Reykjavik remains one of the great "what ifs" of recent history. The transcript of the CPSU Politburo's meeting of October 30, 1986, held just eighteen days after Reykjavik, shows Gorbachev and Shevardnadze, the Soviet foreign minister, struggling with their definition of "laboratory" so as to accommodate the U.S. position on SDI. So Gorbachev: "Our new positions are the following: Testing is allowed in the air, on the test sites on the ground, but not in space." Then Shevardnadze: "If we see that Shultz is in a serious mood, then we should open our position on what we mean by laboratories."[36]

In the early months of 1987 the Soviet position on SDI underwent further significant change. In one of the great ironies of Soviet history it was Andrei Sakharov, the world renowned physicist, inventor of the Soviet H-bomb, Nobel-prize winner, and the regime's most formidable critic who, on his return to Moscow from exile in Gorki at the end of 1986, took the lead in persuading Gorbachev that his fear of SDI was much exaggerated and that he should reverse the position taken at Reykjavik and decouple the INF (Intermediate Range Nuclear Forces) and START negotiations from SDI. At a conference on disarmament held in Moscow in mid-February, and attended by Gorbachev, Sakharov argued that SDI would never be militarily effective against a well-armed opponent; rather it would be "a Maginot Line in space."[37]

"I believe" Sakharov said, "that a significant cut in ICBM's and medium range missiles and battlefield missiles and other agreements on disarmament should be negotiated as soon as possible, independent of SDI... compromise on SDI can be reached later." In the case of intermediate-range missiles in Europe (INF) Gorbachev followed Sakharov's advice and in February 1987 the Russians decoupled the INF negotiations with the United States from SDI, which then paved the way for the signing of the INF Treaty by Reagan and Gorbachev at the Washington Summit in December 1987.

However in the case of strategic nuclear weapons the backlash in Washington and in Europe to what happened at Reykjavik was so great that the Reagan administration did not respond to these signals from the Soviet side that the chief obstacle to the Reykjavik agreements was now crumbling. In November 1986 Margaret Thatcher descended on Washington like an avenging angel and read the riot act to Reagan on the indispensability of ballistic missiles and the sanctity of MAD. Admiral William Crowe, chairman of the joint chiefs of staff, also told Reagan that the chiefs were alarmed at the idea of giving up ballistic missiles. Henry Kissinger characteristically warned that the Europeans, "unable to rely on an instant US nuclear response" would "make their political accommodation with the Soviet Union."[38] At the beginning of November the Reagan administration was further blown off course by the breaking of the Iran–Contra scandal, which in a single month reduced Reagan's approval ratings in a *New York Times*–CBS poll by 21 percentage points, the largest one-month decline in a president's rating ever recorded.[39]

Eventually the START negotiations were decoupled from SDI, but not until George H.W. Bush had succeeded Reagan in the White House, and a more orthodox view of arms control prevailed in the White House. The spectacular reductions in strategic nuclear armaments envisaged by Reagan and Shultz at Reykjavik were no longer on offer. The START I Treaty, signed by Gorbachev and President George H.W. Bush in July 1991, permitted each side to deploy up to 6,000 nuclear warheads on ICBMs, submarines, and bombers. In 2007, the United States had 5,866 deployed warheads, and Russia 4,162. Under the Strategic Offensive Reduction Treaty (SORT) signed by George W. Bush and Vladimir Putin in July 2002, the two sides agreed to reduce their deployed warheads to 1,700–2,200 by 2012.[40]

* * *

However Reykjavik was not the end of the story, or rather it was the end of one story and the beginning of another. Reykjavik was a Janus-faced event that pointed backward to a whole series of superpower summits that began at Geneva in 1955. But Reykjavik also pointed forward to the extraordinary events that were soon to follow. From a backward perspective Reykjavik was, for a veteran Cold War manager like Kissinger, an act of folly with Reagan gambling fecklessly with the security of the United States and the world. But looking forward, Reykjavik was a portent of things to come. At Reykjavik Reagan was not the only nuclear utopian present. In the rush to a nonnuclear world he was matched every inch of the way by Gorbachev.

It might be argued that the events of Reagan's last two years in office do not belong to our history because negotiations on strategic arms reduction (START) took a backseat to the great drama of the Gorbachev revolution in the USSR, although the superpowers did during this period conclude the agreement on INF in Europe. But I would dispute this. The transformation of Soviet–American relations during those two years, which owes much to Ronald Reagan, paved the way for the administration of George H.W. Bush to wind up the Cold War and to negotiate a reduction in the strategic nuclear arsenals of both sides, with SDI pushed to the sidelines.

I have already referred to a variety of beliefs that influenced Ronald Reagan's approach to the Soviet Union, including his belief in a world free of nuclear weapons. I now have to add two more. Ronald Reagan took the ideological struggle between the communist and capitalist worlds seriously. This led to much rhetorical posturing during his first term, but it also meant that Reagan did not take the survival of the Soviet Union for granted. In the early 1980s he rightly saw that the USSR was vulnerable to the crisis of communist legitimacy in Poland and indeed throughout Eastern Europe.

In a prescient speech delivered in London in 1982, Reagan argued that the USSR was

> undergoing a crisis...where the demands of the economic order are conflicting directly with those of the political order...a political structure that no

longer corresponds to its economic base, a society where productive forces are hampered by political ones...Either a small ruling elite attempts to ease domestic unrest though greater repression or it chooses a wiser course. It allows its people a voice in their destiny.[41]

Not a bad description of the USSR at the very end of "the era of stagnation," with the death of Brezhnev only months away. So when a Soviet leader emerged who did acknowledge that the USSR was in crisis, and who did begin to embrace democratic values, Reagan was ready for him in a way that more orthodox figures such as Kissinger were not.

Reagan, the Great Communicator, also believed fervently that he could break through the ideological barriers standing between him and his Soviet counterparts, and find common ground in a bedrock of shared values. This confidence in his powers of communication and persuasion accounts for his handwritten letters to Brezhnev and Andropov, sent at a time when Soviet–American relations were at a very low ebb. Henry Kissinger in particular has ridiculed the belief of successive American presidents that they could, through personal contact, overcome the ideological divide with their Soviet counterparts. FDR, Truman, and Eisenhower had all been targets of Kissinger's withering scorn. But in the case of Gorbachev, Ronald Reagan was right, and Kissinger was wrong. Gorbachev's long years in the Soviet provinces as party secretary of the Stavropol Region, a consequence of senior citizen hegemony in Moscow, gave him a privileged view of the system's decay. His travels in Western Europe as a young *apparatchik* also gave him a sense of how things might be done differently at home.

So there *was* a bedrock of shared values between Reagan and Gorbachev, and there was an awareness of this on both sides that grew with each of their four Summits: Geneva in 1985, Reykjavik in 1986, Washington in 1987, and Moscow in 1988. Equally important was the compelling political theater of the Moscow and Washington Summits when Reagan presented Gorbachev to the American people as only he could, and as someone with whom the United States could do business.

These events marked the beginning of the end of the Cold War, and Ronald Reagan will be rightly celebrated and remembered as the man who, with Mikhail Gorbachev, presided over the Cold War's demise. Yet historians face a formidable task in working out exactly how the complex and contradictory elements of the public Ronald Reagan came together to bring off this spectacular achievement—something that hardly anyone had foreseen during Reagan's first term. There was Reagan's combination of re-arming bellicosity and of nuclear-free utopianism; of political willfulness and of sloth in dealing with the bureaucracy; of ideological rigidity at the outset of his presidency, and of creative open-mindedness toward the end.

The history of the Soviet–American relationship passed through three broad phases during the Reagan years, and this chronology provides a valuable framework in trying to sort out Reagan's conduct and motives. There was the opening period of ideological and military bellicosity that dominated the first three years of his presidency; then a middle period of stasis and confusion, lasting for most of 1984 and 1985, when the forces of confrontation and conciliation within the administration fought it out; and finally there was the breaking of the diplomatic logjam with the Russians from 1986 onward.

The evolution from the first of these periods to the second is perhaps easier to account for than the evolution from the second to the third. By 1984, and in the run up to the presidential election of that year, Reagan was, as we have seen, under strong public pressure to curb his bellicosity and to negotiate with the Soviet side, and Reagan himself clearly felt that the military build-up of the preceding years had strengthened his hand in dealing with the Russians. But there then followed Reagan's middle years of confusion and drift, and Frances FitzGerald is surely right in arguing that the coming of SDI was the event that more than any other shaped this period.

FitzGerald's is the preeminent scholarly account of how, during the period, Reagan's shortcomings were an obstacle to achieving progress on arms control, and indeed in Soviet–American relations generally: his propensity for wishful thinking; his neglect and ignorance of diplomatic detail; his unwillingness or inability to keep his subordinates in line.[42] Thus Reagan severely underestimated the extent to which SDI would be perceived as threatening by the Soviet side; he failed to see how SDI would vastly complicate the task of securing reductions in strategic nuclear arsenals; and he allowed hardliners such as Caspar Weinberger and Richard Perle to paralyze the administration's policymaking by manipulating the small print of SDI and SALT.

Yet the logjam *was* broken and during the last years of Reagan's presidency the Cold War moved spectacularly toward its end. Future historians of the end of the Cold War will have to reckon with the powerful and nuanced account of this period by Melvyn Leffler in his book *For the Soul of Mankind* (2007).[43] The strength of Leffler's work is that his analysis of key turning points in Cold War history keeps in play the full range of forces that influenced U.S. and Soviet conduct; ideological, territorial, military, and political.

Leffler argues that it was the boldness and, in a Soviet context, originality of Gorbachev's ideological revisionism during the late 1980s that contributed most to the end of the Cold War, and at a time when Gorbachev was still buoyed domestically by the popularity of *glasnost* and *perestroika* and so had the power to frame policies that embodied his revisionism. Neither the passage of time, nor the failure of Gorbachev's domestic economic reforms, nor his decline and fall in 1990–1991 should blind us to the truly revolutionary boldness of his revisionism, which amounted to a renunciation of the critical political and ideological supports of Soviet rule since the October Revolution.

There were the theses of the CPSU Party Conference of 1988 that called for the abandonment of Leninist "democratic centralism" and its replacement with a government based on the rule of law; there was the renunciation of the "class war" and the "capitalist encirclement" as the foundations of Soviet foreign policy, which opened up an unlimited space for collaboration between the capitalist and socialist worlds; and there was Gorbachev's "revolution in military affairs" according to which the security of the Soviet state, massively assured by its nuclear and conventional forces, no longer needed to depend either on the imperial glacis in Eastern Europe, or on a nuclear arsenal thousands of warheads strong. Taken together, Gorbachev's diplomatic and military revisionism led him to conclude that the Soviet Union could allow its Eastern European satellites to go their own way, the development that perhaps more than any other marked the end of the Cold War.

Reagan responded positively to Gorbachev's revisionism and, as we have seen, was led to do so both by his belief that the Soviet Union faced a political and economic crisis that might produce a reformist leader to find a way out, and by his confidence that his own powers of communication and persuasion could create trust across the ideological divide. Melvyn Leffler is also surely right to argue that Reagan's understanding of the Soviet Union and its leaders deepened during his second term. But there were also those weaknesses, amply documented by Frances FitzGerald, Lou Cannon, and indeed by George Shultz, that produced confusion and drift in Reagan's middle years. There is I believe a third aspect to Reagan that resolves this paradox and helps account for his role in ending the Cold War.

His intellectual laziness and his passivity in dealing with the day-to-day affairs of government notwithstanding, Reagan was on occasion capable of spectacular acts of presidential will that could break asunder the bonds weaved by the Lilliputians and transform the military or diplomatic *conjoncture* literally overnight. The most remarkable example of this was Reagan's Star Wars Speech of March 1983, which, put together with minimal consultation within the administration, superseded at a stroke the strategic nuclear doctrines of both the United States and NATO. The Reykjavik negotiation was another example of presidential unilateralism, when Reagan and Gorbachev were within sight of a nonnuclear world.

Its clear that from 1986 onward internal conviction and external events came together in such a way that Ronald Reagan saw the way forward to a transformed and more peaceful world, and that once this happened, Reagan went into high gear and there was no stopping him. Gorbachev's revisionism was the catalyst for this transformation and the evidence of the middle years shows that, without Gorbachev's lead, Reagan would have been hard pressed to put forward a coherent vision of how to end the Cold War, let alone impose this vision on his fractious administration. So Gorbachev was, as Leffler argues, the chief architect of the Cold War's end, but Reagan was Gorbachev's enthusiastic and indispensable partner, and for that we are in his debt.

Notes

1. For Reagan's ignorance about nuclear weapons and arms control, see Lou Cannon, *President Reagan: The Role of a Lifetime* (New York: Simon and Schuster, 1991), 291.

2. For Reagan's Star Wars Speech, see "Address to the Nation on Defense and National Security," March 23, 1983. Available online at CNN Perspectives Series,www.cnn.com/SPECIALS/cold.war/episodes/22/documents/starwars.speech.
3. For chapter and verse on Reagan's lethargy, see Cannon, *President Reagan*, chapter 10, "Passive President," 172–205; see also Hedrik Hertzberg, *Politics: Observations and Alignments, 1966–2004* (New York and London: Penguin Books, 2005), Part 2, "The Child Monarch: Ronald Reagan's Surprising Presidency," 70–93.
4. This account is taken from my own notes of telephone interviews with Paul Nitze in the late 1970s.
5. For an analysis of these proposals, and a listing of the details of Reagan's military build up, see Frances FitzGerald *Way Out There in the Blue: Reagan, Star Wars And The End Of The Cold War* (New York: Simon and Schuster, 2000), 151–152, 181–185.
6. Strobe Talbott, *The Russians and Reagan*, Foreword by Cyrus R. Vance (New York: Council on Foreign Relations, 1984), ix.
7. Beth A. Fischer, "Reagan and the Soviets: Winning the Cold War" in W. Elliot Brownlee and Hugh Davis Graham (eds.), *The Reagan Presidency: Pragmatic Conservatism and Its Legacies* (Lawrence, Kansas: University Press of Kansas, 2003), 117.
8. The Public Papers of Ronald Reagan, January 1984, available online at www.reagan.utexas.edu/archives/speeches/1984/84jan.htm.
9. For Shultz's views on linkage, see George P. Shultz, *Turmoil and Triumph, My Years As Secretary of State* (New York: Charles Scribner's Sons, 1993), 488–489.
10. Ibid., 458–460.
11. Cannon, *President Reagan*, 304.
12. See particularly Shultz, *Turmoil and Triumph*, chapter 17, "The Strategic Defense Initiative."
13. Ronald Reagan, "Address to the Nation," 7.
14. Schultz, *Turmoil and Triumph*, 716.
15. Caspar Weinberger, *Fighting for Peace: Seven Critical Years at the Pentagon* (London: Michael Joseph, 1990), chapter 10, "The Strategic Defense Initiative," 204–232.
16. Shultz, *Turmoil and Triumph*, 256.
17. Cannon, *President Reagan*, 317–318.
18. For a detailed account of these disputes, see FitzGerald, *Way Out There in the Blue*, chapter 7, "Hardliners vs. Pragmatists," 265–313.
19. "The Public Papers or Ronald Reagan, January 1984," for online reference, see footnote 8.
20. Cannon, *President Reagan*, 510.
21. Ronald Reagan, *An American Life* (London: Hutchinson, 1990), 13, 549.
22. Ibid., 258.
23. Ibid., 550.
24. Cannon, *President Reagan*, 301.
25. Shultz, *Turmoil and Triumph*, 360.
26. Ibid., 466.
27. Ibid., 701.
28. Ibid., 700.

29. Ibid., 705.
30. Ibid., 706.
31. Ibid., 719–720.
32. Ibid., 716–717, 722–723, 758; Reagan, *An American Life*, 676.
33. George Washington University, The National Security Archive, "The Reykjavik File: Previously Secret Documents from U.S. and Soviet Archives," edited by Thomas Blanton and Svetlana Savranskaya. Available at www.gwu.edu/~nsarchiv/NSAEBB203/index.htm.
34. For the U.S. and Soviet transcripts of the Sunday afternoon session, see GWU, National Security Archive: Document 15, "US Memorandum of Conversation, Reagan–Gorbachev Final Meeting, 12 October 1986, 3.25 pm–4.30 pm and 5.30 pm–6.50 pm." Also Document 16, Russian transcript (in translation) of "Reagan–Gorbachev Summit in Reykjavik, 12 October 1986 (afternoon)" published in FBIS-USR 93-121, September 20, 1993.
35. This account of the exchanges between Reagan, Gorbachev, and Shultz is drawn from the Russian transcript of the Sunday meeting.
36. GWU, National Security Archive, Document 23, "USSR CC CPSU Politburo Session. Reykjavik Assessment and Instructions for Soviet Delegation for Negotiations in Geneva, 30 October 1986," 2.
37. For a discussion of Sakharov's role, see Frances FitzGerald *Way Out There in the Blue*, 410–411.
38. Shultz, *Triumph and Turmoil*, 776–777; FitzGerald, *Way Out There in the Blue*, 368–369.
39. FitzGerald, *Way Out There in the Blue*, 384.
40. Warhead details from Federation of American Scientists (FAS) website, www.fas.org/main/home.jsp.
41. For text of the speech, see "Public Papers of Ronald Reagan, June 1982: Address to Members of the British Parliament," available online at www.reagan.utexas.edu/archives/speeches/1982/82jun.htm.
42. See particularly FitzGerald, *Way Out There in the Blue*, chapters 5–8.
43. Melvyn Leffler, *For the Soul of Mankind: The United States, the Soviet Union, and the Cold War* (New York: Hill and Wang, 2007).

Chapter 6

Reaganomics and its Legacy

Iwan Morgan

In his memoirs, Ronald Reagan underlined the primary significance of economic policy to his presidential agenda. As he put it, "Nothing was possible unless we made the economy sound again."[1] From the late 1960s to the early 1980s the United States had experienced its worst economic problems since the 1930s. The development of stagflation—concurrent inflation and stagnation—had produced three recessions and unprecedented price instability. Matters appeared to reach crisis point by late 1980. Productivity growth had ground to a virtual halt and the misery index—the combined rate of inflation (13 percent) and unemployment (7 percent)—stood at 20 percent. In the quarter-century since 1983, by contrast, the American economy has been a vibrant engine of almost continuous growth, high employment, and low inflation. In this period there have only been two shallow recessions (at time of writing), an average of one every twelve years. Never before has the United States enjoyed a period of such prolonged expansion and little contraction. Between 1949 (the date of the first postwar recession) and 1980 the average duration of each expansion cycle was barely 4.5 years. During the era of what some economists call "the great expansion," the United States consolidated its position as the number one economic power in the world, a status it had looked to be in danger of losing by the end of the 1970s.

Ronald Reagan promised the most dramatic changes in economic policy since the New Deal to tackle the worst economic crisis since the Great Depression. He blamed America's woes on postwar liberal statism that burdened the economy with high taxes to support big spending government. As president he looked to develop a market-oriented political economy that freed the productive potential of individuals from the dead hand of government.[2] Unsurprisingly conservatives have attributed the great expansion to the ongoing influence and legacy of Reaganomics. In 2000, conservative economist and former Federal Reserve governor Lawrence Lindsay declared that the years since 1983 were best seen "as a single expansion, with its roots in the policy changes of the late 1970s and early 1980s."[3] In 2004, Stephen

Moore, president of the Club for Growth—a Washington-based group that lobbies for lower taxes—declared that George W. Bush had completed the transformation of the GOP into a supply-side party. "It has evolved over the past forty years," he avowed, "from being a party of Eisenhower balanced-budget Republicans into a party of Reaganite pro-growth advocates."[4]

The record of the economy since the early 1980s did not fulfill the gloomy foreboding of Reagan-era liberals that their nemesis was destroying its well-being. Typifying their disdain, Keynesian doyen James Tobin of Yale, one of the founding fathers of the 1960s "new economics" as a member of the Kennedy CEA, charged that Reaganomics was "a fraud from the beginning." In his view it simply proved that "a nation pays a heavy price when it entrusts its government and economy to simplistic ideologues."[5]

In a not uncritical study of Reagan and his era, historian Robert Collins offers a more balanced and persuasive assessment. Reagan's achievements, he suggests, should be counted in terms of the alternatives he forestalled. Without his free-market approach, the U.S. response to stagflation and an increasingly competitive international economy would have probably moved in the direction of statist programs of industrial policy and strategic trade exemplified by the then successful model of Japan's Ministry of International Trade and Industry. However, the subsequent stagnation of the Japanese economy revealed the limitations of a political economy that gave government greater responsibility than the market for resource allocation. At the same time Collins warns against attributing too much influence to Reagan for the economic success that continued long after he left office because policies and circumstances changed significantly.[6]

It is worth recalling that the New Deal hardly had a stellar economic record but its significance in launching the Keynesian political economy of the postwar era is not in dispute. With this in mind, this essay assesses Reaganomics as a mixture of success and failure in terms of its management of the economy and offers a brief evaluation of its legacy for the post-Reagan era. It focuses on three issues: the fiscal–monetary mix in economic management; the significance of Reagan's tax program; and America's transformation in the 1980s from being the world's largest creditor nation to being its largest debtor nation.

The Monetary–Fiscal Mix of Reaganomics

The new political economy that emerged in the 1980s was different in critical respects from Reagan's blueprint. This was most evident in its operation of massive budget deficits instead of the balanced budgets originally promised. To his critics, Reagan replaced a "tax-and-spend" economic policy with a "spend-and-borrow" one. Equally significant was the development of a monetary–fiscal mix of demand management to promote economic growth in place of the supply-side strategy initially heralded as the means to this end.

The original manifesto of Reagan's economic ideas was *Economic Policy Memorandum Number 1*, drawn up in 1979 by aide Martin Anderson in readiness for the presidential campaign. The *Program for Economic Recovery* [*PER*] that the new president sent to Congress in February 1980 embodied its principles. As enunciated in these two statements, Reaganomics had a fiscal core of tax reduction and domestic spending restraint. Its emphasis on tax cuts as the agency of economic growth reflected new supply-side economic ideas that high marginal tax rates weakened the incentive of individuals to work, save, and invest. Its commitment to balance the budget by the end of Reagan's first presidential term reflected conventional conservative belief that big government spending was a drag on the economy. The role of monetary policy in this schema was a supporting one of keeping inflation under control through moderate restraint while fiscal measures worked their magic to revitalize productivity growth as the ultimate guarantor of price stability.[7]

However Federal Reserve chairman Paul Volcker was reading from a different script that cast him as commander-in-chief in an all-out war on inflation. His appointment in the summer of 1979 was an act of desperation by Jimmy Carter in the face of double-digit inflation. Volcker had won the confidence of Wall Street as an inflation hawk in his former post as head of the regional New York Federal Reserve. Hitherto postwar Democratic and Republican administrations had largely prioritized fiscal policy in managing the economy in accordance with the Keynesian formula for growth and high employment. With the emphasis changed to fighting inflation through monetary policy in the late 1970s, the Fed chair became the chief manager of prosperity, a role that the Employment Act of 1946 had implicitly conferred on the president. The political economy of the 1980s only served to confirm his status in this regard.

Volcker considered the central bank complicit in fueling inflation through its easy money policies in the 1970s. He drew three lessons from this era. First, policymakers' pursuit of a "Phillips curve" trade-off that targeted appropriate rates of employment growth for inflation growth had only made things worse. Second, the conquest of inflation at whatever temporary cost to unemployment was the precondition for economic revival. Finally, inflation-wary lenders would not commit sufficient investment funds to promote economic growth unless the Federal Reserve had credibility as an inflation-fighter.[8]

Under Volcker, the Fed immediately pursued a money-targeting strategy to control the money supply that helped push the economy into a brief but sharp recession in mid-1980. Despite temporary relaxation to assist recovery, the consequence of Fed policies in the form of higher borrowing costs and rising unemployment proved unhelpful to Jimmy Carter's hopes of reelection. Volcker did not change course with a new president in the White House. In the second quarter of 1981 the Fed stepped up the restrictive strategy that it had pursued almost continuously since late 1979 in a bid to wring inflation out of the economy once and for all. This precipitated the worst recession since the 1930s. The downturn began in August 1981 and lasted through 1982. At the trough, unemployment stood at 10.8 percent of the workforce, compared with the average of 7.1 percent at the same stage of previous postwar recessions, and factory utilization was only 68 percent of capacity, the lowest since records were first compiled in 1948. Although recovery began in early 1983, unemployment rose to a peak of 11.5 million in January.[9]

The recession had grave consequences for the fiscal calculations of Reaganomics. It destroyed the harvest of new revenues that economic growth was supposed to deliver with the tax-cut fertilizer. By FY1985 federal receipts had only recovered to 86 percent of the level projected by PER. By undermining Reagan's popularity, the downturn also helped stiffen the resolve of the Democrat-controlled House of Representatives to resist further domestic retrenchment to help pay for the other elements of his fiscal program. Reagan's blitzkrieg of tax cuts, defense expansion, and a first installment of domestic retrenchment had stormed the legislature during his first year in office but budgetary politics became bogged down in the stalemate of trench warfare for the remainder of his presidency. This combination of circumstances drove the deficit into the stratosphere with the consequence that the national debt held by the public rose from $711.9 billion at the end of 1980 to $2.1 trillion eight years later.[10]

The huge deficits threatened to derail Reagan's promises of economic growth because financial markets conventionally regarded them as harbingers of inflation. Reagan adviser Alan Greenspan warned that the Fed would likely keep its foot on the monetary brakes to assuage market psychology as long as federal finances continued to hemorrhage red ink. Contrary to expectations, Volcker relaxed monetary policy in July 1982 shortly before enactment of the Tax Equity and Fiscal Responsibility Act (TEFRA) that purported to raise $98 billion over three years mainly through closure of tax loopholes. There was no clear evidence that Reagan's deficit-control concession on new taxes had brought about the Fed's change of course, but the president was convinced that it had. Further monetary relaxation over the next three months allowed the M1 money supply (currency in circulation and checking accounts) to grow by 15 percent, which did much to generate economic recovery in early 1983.[11]

Projections that the deficit would remain around $200 billion for years to come made the president nervous that Volcker might once again rain on his parade. A distraught Reagan reportedly exclaimed to the Budget Review Board on January 3, 1983, "How can we come out with that string of figures without driving interest rates right back up?"[12] However, the Fed stayed its hand because inflation did not revive in the face of the huge deficits. Double-digit inflation had vanished in the recession. The consumer price index rose by a yearly average of only 3.5 percent during the remainder of Reagan's presidency. Accordingly, monetary aggregates grew on average quite rapidly from mid-1982 to early 1987 at a rate that would have been deemed inflationary in the late 1970s. Only when mild inflationary pressures resurfaced in 1987–1988 did the Fed engage in a modest tightening of monetary policy.[13]

The monetary castor oil of 1979–1982 had purged massive inflation from the economy. A combination of other factors worked against its renewal.

American manufacturers grew leaner and more efficient but at a cost to jobs in the context of an increasingly competitive international economy. Manufacturing productivity rose by 4.1 percent from 1980 through 1987, well above the postwar norm, which allowed for the maintenance of production levels with fewer workers. By the end of 1987, only 19.3 million Americans worked in manufacturing compared with 21 million in 1979. A global oil glut in the mid-1980s ensured no repeat of the supply shocks that had been a major source of inflation in the previous decade. Finally, the unprecedented numbers of women and baby-boomers that had entered the labor force in the 1970s became more productive with greater experience.[14]

The conquest of inflation, which had troubled the American economy for more than a decade, was the greatest economic policy success of the 1980s. The institutional actor primarily responsible for this was the Federal Reserve under Paul Volcker's leadership. In the latter's estimate, Reagan's most important contribution to the battle was defeating the air traffic controllers' strike in 1981 because this helped temper labor militancy and preempt a new round of inflationary wage increases. He also appreciated that Reagan's steadfast public support shielded him against the open criticism of many politicians from both parties in Congress, even though administration officials lobbied him behind the scenes in the spring and summer of 1982 for monetary relaxation.[15]

The tight money policy that had blown the Reagan administration's optimistic economic projections off course ultimately proved the salvation of its tax program. Once reassured that $200 billion deficits were not going to drive up interest rates again, the president could dig in his heels against any retreat on personal income tax reductions for the sake of deficit control.[16] In the 1984 presidential election, Democratic candidate Walter Mondale ran on a platform calling for deficit-reducing tax increases to avert another economic catastrophe like that of 1981–1982. With the recovery now gaining momentum, Reagan was able to turn the contest into a referendum on his tax program. He defined the election as a choice between growth based on the fundamental values of individual freedom represented by his personal income tax cuts and stagnation resulting from Mondale's statist agenda of tax increases.[17]

The renewal of economic growth hardly represented the triumph of supply-side economics. The management of prosperity in the Reagan era relied on a flexible monetary policy that varied between being very tight and relatively relaxed and an expansionary fiscal policy, a combination that operated through the demand side of the economy. This proved far from a perfect mix, however. As discussed later in this chapter, the expansionary budget deficits contributed to a collapse in national saving. Compensating for this, even though the Federal Reserve relaxed monetary policy from mid-1982 onward, it kept real interest rates (the actual interest rate minus the rate of inflation) above their postwar norm to attract investment in the United States by foreign savers. The consequences were a strong dollar and a growing trade deficit that produced a slower decline in unemployment than in previous recovery cycles. Joblessness did not fall below the 1980 recession-year level of 7 percent until 1986.

In the opinion of conservative economist Herbert Stein, the 1980s demonstrated two realities for economic policymakers. First, the supply-side approach provided neither explanation nor solution for inflation. Second, the power of government to influence the supply-side of the economy was much smaller than its capacity to manage demand.[18] The Fed's conquest of inflation was proof of the former. The limited benefits of the Reagan tax program for productivity growth of output per employee was proof of the latter. The strong gains in manufacturing productivity were the exception rather than the rule in the 1980s. Total non-farm productivity growth averaged only 1.3 percent annually under Reagan compared with 2.8 percent between 1945 and 1973. Economic growth, which averaged 4.1 percent from 1983 through 1988, was largely due to aggregate demand catching up with potential GNP after a serious recession. Whatever else it achieved, Reaganomics did little to boost capital formation, the prerequisite for productivity improvement. Private investment in 1980–1992 was only 17.4 percent of GDP compared with 18.6 percent in the economically troubled 1970s.[19]

The Reagan Tax Program

Tax reduction was the defining element of Reaganomics but its economic significance was more ambiguous than its political importance. Reagan's tax cuts gave the Republicans the banner issue that was fundamental to their electoral success in the late twentieth century and beyond. As it eventually developed, however, his tax program was a manifestation of his populist conservatism rather than of supply-side economics.

Enactment of the Economic Recovery Tax Act (ERTA) of 1981, the largest tax reduction in U.S. history, was Reagan's greatest success in his first year as president. This cut the top individual income tax rate from 70 percent to 50 percent on January 1, 1982, and reduced rates for all other taxpayers in three annual stages of 5, 10, and 10 percent (aggregate reduction 23 percent). Congressional add-ons significantly expanded the measure beyond the terms of the administration's original bill. In particular, the automatic indexation of personal income tax to inflation from FY1985 onward eliminated the "bracket creep" phenomenon that had enlarged individual tax burdens and federal receipts in the 1970s. In addition ERTA was turned into a Christmas tree of deductions and benefits to business, including faster write-offs for capital expenditures, an increase in the investment tax credit, and benefits for oil producers.

Reagan consistently supported the ERTA personal tax cuts for the remainder of his presidency even as he made concessions on other forms of taxation. In his eyes, high personal taxes threatened the liberty of American citizens by confiscating the wealth they created to feed a rapacious big government.[20] The president's priorities were at variance with those of first-term Office of

Management and Budget director David Stockman. Originally a true believer in Reaganomics and in many respects the engineer charged with turning its blueprint into reality, Stockman quickly lost faith when the consequences for the deficit became apparent in the second half of 1981. In late September the budget director vainly advocated a one-year deferment of the second and third installments of the ERTA personal tax cuts to mitigate deficit growth. In unguarded remarks to journalist William Greider, he described the across-the-board income tax cuts as a "Trojan horse." From his perspective, their sole purpose was to provide a political smokescreen for ERTA's tax breaks for business and the immediate cut in the top rate of personal income tax that would be the real drivers of economic expansion because of their benefits for investment. Stockman's influence in the White House went into decline following publication of these comments.[21] He had failed to understand that his boss regarded across-the-board personal tax reduction as the core of his economic program rather than the trimmings.

Far from accepting that ERTA had inflated the deficit, Reagan clung to the belief that the economic growth it generated would produce a compensatory revenue reflow.[22] This conviction was based on the theory of supply-sider Arthur Laffer that there was a point on the tax rate curve between 0 and 100 percent beyond which higher taxes yielded fewer revenues than a lower tax rate. The "Laffer curve" never plotted the point at which the change occurred, acknowledged that a higher tax rate would still yield more revenue than a lower rate below this apex, and did not claim that tax cuts would pay for themselves.[23] However, Reagan's simplistic distortion of this theory reinforced his conviction that income tax cuts generated additional revenue for government and income tax increases had the opposite effect.[24]

The experience of the 1980s offered conclusive proof that the reverse was true. Allowing for the effects of recession, ERTA cost $643 billion in revenue in its first five years of operation. In contrast, corporate income tax increases levied by TEFRA and the Deficit Reduction Act of 1984, a smaller loophole closing measure enacted to blunt deficit concerns in an election year, benefited federal coffers. In combination with the social security tax increases of 1983, these measures offset the revenue loss from ERTA by about a third.[25]

If Reagan's misappropriation of the Laffer curve theory fortified his belief in tax reduction, it is difficult to find other consistent threads of supply-side principle in his administration's tax program. The president's 1982 *Economic Report* promised that the ERTA incentives would significantly encourage new investment.[26] Belying this, TEFRA eliminated a number of the business tax breaks that Congress had appended to the 1981 tax cut. Supply-siders regarded the change of course as a self-defeating betrayal of their faith on Reagan's part. In their eyes, TEFRA crowded productive dollars out of the economy at a time of recession, thereby hindering economic expansion that was the most effective instrument of deficit reduction. To the relief of pragmatic White House aides such as chief of staff James Baker, a number of supply-siders—notably Treasury officials Paul Craig Roberts and Norman

Ture—quit the administration in 1982 as Reagan moved toward approving the tax increase.[27]

Worse was to follow from the supply-siders' perspective as Reagan turned into a tax reformer in his second term.[28] The original inspiration for this was to counter anticipated Democratic charges in the 1984 election that his tax program was biased to the rich. Donald Regan and James Baker, who exchanged their first term posts as Treasury secretary and chief of staff, promoted development of what became the Tax Reform Act of 1986. This simplified the fourteen-bracket tax code into two of 15 percent and 28 percent (with a complicated surtax that put some upper middle class families in a "bubble" bracket of 33 percent). An estimated 80 percent of American taxpayers came within the 15 percent bracket. Meanwhile the top tax bracket, which had been 70 percent in 1981, was now lower than the bottom marginal tax rate in some Western European countries. Thanks to enhanced exemptions for taxpayers with dependents, TRA also removed six million poor Americans from the tax rolls. At the same time it eliminated or reduced deductions and other benefits that favored high-income taxpayers. Accordingly, the measure produced lower taxes for about 60 percent of taxpayers, higher ones for 15 percent—mainly the wealthy, and left them the same for 25 percent.[29]

To ensure that this largess did not inflate the deficit, TRA paid for its personal tax cuts by shifting a tax burden of $120 billion from individuals to corporations in its first five years of life. Even though it cut the basic rate of corporate taxes, it significantly broadened the corporate tax base through elimination of the investment tax credit, much slower depreciation allowances, and a stiff alternative minimum tax for corporations. ERTA's strategy of creating tax expenditures to encourage saving and investment was reversed by the TRA's elimination of seventy-two of these benefits for business and individuals in the cause of tax fairness. According to one estimate, TRA raised the effective tax rate on new business investment in equipment of all kinds by some 20 percent. No dispensation was made for research and scientific equipment, so the measure arguably had adverse consequences for America's efforts to compete in new technology and related industries.[30]

If Reagan's tax program did not live up to supply-siders' hopes of boosting investment, some analysts still considered it instrumental in improving living standards for many Americans in the 1980s. Historian John Diggins argued that impressions of the Reagan era as "a time when the rich exploited the poor must be revised if history is to be faithful to statistics." In the two years after TRA's enactment, the top 5 percent of taxpayers paid 45.5 percent of all personal income taxes compared to 41.8 percent in 1986, while the bottom 50 percent of taxpayers moved in the opposite direction from 6.6 percent to 5.7 percent. Income distribution data also suggested that the economic recovery that ERTA helped to generate was a rising tide that lifted all boats not just the yachts of the wealthy. By 1986, the bottom income quintile accounted for 28 percent of the total personal income gain since 1977 compared with 11 percent for the top quintile.[31]

Whether lower income groups did become significantly better off in the 1980s is open to question. The regressive social security tax increases enacted in 1983 to safeguard program trust fund solvency canceled out the benefit of the Reagan income tax cuts for many Americans in the bottom half of the income distribution. Moreover the standard of living of single-income families stagnated in the 1980s. In 1983 the average U.S. worker earned $281 per week, but only $271 as measured in 1983 dollars by the end of 1989. In the Reagan era, most families in the lower half of the income distribution only increased their income by having two adult earners rather than one. By 1987, 49 percent of all married couples were working couples. Even two-income families found that higher costs for housing, health care, and education offset a goodly portion of their growing income.[32]

If the debate on the distributional benefits of Reaganomics remains unresolved, what is not in doubt is that there was no investment revolution in the 1980s. Net business capital formation annually averaged 3.5 percent of total income during the 1960s and 3.3 percent in the 1970s but only 2.3 percent from 1981 through 1987. Between 1980 and 1987 the rate at which the capital intensity of America's production rose declined by half. In contrast the demand side of the economy underwent some expansion in the Reagan era. Per capita consumer spending rose 2.2 percent a year in this period, comparable with the pre-1973 level but well above that of 1.4 percent for 1973–1980.[33]

As noted earlier, the growth of two-income families offers some explanation for the expansion of consumer spending. Additionally, Reagan fiscal policy worked to the benefit of family budgets in an unexpected way. In 1979 the share of individuals' income that went on tax payments was 18.2 percent, while the share of their income provided through government transfer payments to individuals (such as social security, veterans' benefits, welfare assistance) was 12.4 percent. The 5.8 percent differential was not far out of line with the approximately 6 percent differential that pertained in the 1950s and 1960s. By 1986, the total tax payment of individuals was still 18.2 percent because the social security tax increases counterbalanced the effects of ERTA, but transfer payments had risen to 13.4 percent of individual income. This produced a differential of 4.8 percent, making an extra 1 percent of income available for consumer spending compared with 1979. The third factor that financed real consumption growth without real earnings growth was the reduction that took place in individual saving. Americans saved 7.2 percent of their after-tax income on average from the 1950s to the 1970s. This rate declined to 6.5 percent on average from 1981 to 1984 but then fell steadily to 3.7 percent by 1987. In other words the Reagan economic recovery was fueled in part by a decline in saving, which Reaganomics had originally promised to boost.[34]

Debtor Nation

One of the most significant economic consequences of huge budget deficits in the Reagan era was their impact on national saving. Until 1980 private saving by individuals and business, though never historically strong in comparison with other nations, more than offset the relatively small deficits that the federal government ran almost continuously since 1945. However the growth of federal "dissaving" in the shape of mammoth deficits compounded the problem of the decline in private saving in the 1980s. The overall rate of national saving (private savings minus government borrowing) underwent a precipitous decline from a yearly average of 7.7 percent in the 1970s to 3 percent in the late 1980s.[35] Left to rely on its own resources, the United States would have experienced a comparable decline in private investment as a result of the collapse of national savings, but it made up the deficiency through attracting a massive inflow of foreign capital.

Thanks to the collapse of national saving, the United States was transformed from a creditor with net foreign assets of $141 billion to a debtor with net foreign liabilities of $111 billion in 1985, a swing of $250 billion in just four years. Foreign capital was attracted to the United States by interest rates that were some 2 percent above those of Western European countries and Japan in the mid-1980s. On average the real short-term interest rate in the United States was 4.9 percent in the 1980s compared with 0.79 percent from the 1950s through the 1970s. The difference reflected America's need to borrow from abroad in the later period and the adequacy of its domestic savings in the earlier era. At one juncture in 1983 Paul Volcker had criticized as excessive a Fed staff projection that the net inflow would need to reach $75 billion a year to cover America's needs. In the peak year of 1985, however, it went as high as $103 billion.[36]

Higher interest rates resulted in a strong dollar that led in turn to a growing trade deficit. Between October 1979 and February 1985 the dollar rose in value by over 80 percent against a basket of eleven major currencies. America's annual merchandize trade deficit rose in conjunction from $26 billion in 1980 to a record high of $159 billion in 1987 before the effects of currency revaluation that had been going on for two years brought about a steady decline to $108 billion by 1990. Benefiting from the favorable exchange rates of the early 1980s, manufactured goods from East Asia and Western Europe undercut American products not only in domestic but also in foreign markets. Foreign competition was blamed for the loss of jobs and the slow recovery of employment from the recession. Japan, with whom the United States operated a $56 billion bilateral deficit in 1987, was singled out for particular criticism for taking supposedly unfair advantage of the situation. The inevitable consequence was the rise of protectionist sentiment in Congress, particularly among Democrats who represented blue-collar constituencies.[37]

The Reagan administration preached the virtues of free trade as part of its free market mantra, but found excuses in its first term to do the opposite in practice. In 1981, for example, it secured Japanese agreement for "voluntary" restrictions on their automobile imports in the United States in order to head off the danger of import quota legislation.[38] Seizing on renewed congressional demands for protectionist measures, Treasury Secretary James Baker negotiated with Volcker's assistance the so-called Plaza Accord with their G-5 (France, Japan, United Kingdom, and West Germany) counterparts in September 1985. This entailed a joint commitment to intervene in financial markets by means of selling dollars and buying other currencies in order to depress the value of the greenback. The dollar went into a rapid and prolonged decline that saw it fall from a peak exchange rate of 263.5 against the Japanese yen in February 1985 to 153.5 two years later. Volcker characterized this as "the most aggressive and persistent effort" to manipulate exchange rates on a global scale since the end of the Bretton Woods system of dollar-based fixed exchange rates in the early 1970s.[39]

The Louvre Accord of February 1987 sought to extend the process of international economic coordination among G-7 nations (Canada and Italy had now been allowed to the table) by agreeing Baker's proposal for dollar stabilization in return for America's trading partners stimulating their economies to boost imports. However, this only revealed the limitations rather than the possibilities of global cooperation. It proved impossible to connect exchange rate realignment with macroeconomic adjustment. The United States would not raise interest rates to pump up the dollar's value for fear of precipitating another recession and Japan and West Germany would not lower their interest rates for fear of generating inflation. The huge differences between America's huge external account deficit and the large surpluses operated by some high-saving G-7 nations, notably Japan, also made coordination difficult.[40]

An official report later suggested that fears of a foreign dollar strike in response to the declining value of America's currency was a factor in bringing about the stock market crash of October 19, 1987. Whether justified or not, this bespoke of growing concern at the erosion of America's economic sovereignty in a new era of global interdependence.[41] Prompt action by the Federal Reserve to guarantee banks necessary liquidity ensured that the crash did not precipitate a new recession. Nevertheless, the stock market collapse prompted political compromise between the Reagan administration and the congressional Democrats over the Omnibus Trade and Competitiveness Act of 1988. This was the first comprehensive trade bill since the protectionist Smoot–Hawley Act of 1930 that was widely blamed for precipitating global depression. It originally contained a Democratic proposal for imposition of quotas on countries running a large bilateral surplus with the United States. Fears of provoking a trade war at a particularly critical moment for the global economy led to its substitution with a provision authorizing negotiations with countries that operated unfair trade barriers and retaliation only if talks failed.[42]

In meeting the unexpected challenges posed by America's new status as a debtor nation, the Reagan administration's efforts to promote international coordination of exchanges rates and macroeconomic policies arguably constituted its clearest deviation from the free market ethos proclaimed by Reaganomics. This intervention did nothing to cure the fundamental problem of America's external imbalance that underlay its changed position in the international economy. The solution required an increase in national saving, which was best achieved by reducing the deficit not by manipulating currency rates.

The Legacy of Reaganomics

Since Reaganomics was not true to its own self in many respects, it is hardly surprising that its legacy has been ambiguous. The New Deal had pursued an inconsistent and shifting macroeconomic strategy before settling belatedly on a form of Keynesianism, but it had never started with a coherent blueprint in the manner of Reaganomics. It was World War II that provided the laboratory for the successful testing of Keynesian policies whose efficacy remained in question at the end of the 1930s. Reaganomics did not experience a comparable consolidation in the 1990s. Instead, what became known as Clintonomics offered a highly successful variant to the macroeconomic policies of the 1980s.

Bill Clinton's economic policy incurred liberal criticism for being Reaganomics Mark II, but it was distinctive in important regards.[43] Most significantly, it developed a different fiscal–monetary combination in economic management. This featured monetary relaxation and fiscal tightness, the reverse of the Reagan-era pattern. The transition from Reaganomics actually began during George H.W. Bush's presidency. The bipartisan deficit reduction agreement of 1990, which cost Bush his no-new-taxes election pledge and split the GOP, initiated the drive for fiscal restraint that was the dominant feature of budgetary policy in the final decade of the twentieth century. Clinton's 1993 deficit reduction plan and the bipartisan budget agreement of 1997 built upon this foundation. Under Volcker's successor, Alan Greenspan, the Federal Reserve in 1990 reversed the tight money regime instituted in 1987 and hewed to a course of monetary relaxation until 1999, when it moved to douse stock market inflation. The only significant exception to this trend was a twelve-month period in 1994–1995 when Greenspan plotted a soft landing for a fast growing economy.[44]

Aided by a benign monetary regime, the United States entered a remarkable period of economic growth that benefited from an investment revolution absent in the 1980s. Between 1996 and 2000, the unemployment rate fell from 5.6 percent to 4 percent, well below the 1984–1988 average of 6.6 percent, inflation kept on its lowest track since the 1950s, and productivity growth almost doubled to 2.7 percent. Broader changes in the economy—the advent of new technology, globalization, and well-functioning venture capital markets—underlay this success, but economic management played its part. Two Democratic economists, Alan Blinder of Yale and Janet Yellen of Berkeley, whom Clinton appointed to serve on the Federal Reserve Board of Governors, argued that the experience of the 1990s offered different lessons to those of the 1980s. First, tight budgets and easy money created a pro-investment macroeconomic climate by holding down real interest rates. Second, "contractionary" fiscal policy did not harm economic growth because the resultant decline in inflationary expectations encouraged the bond market to relax long-term interest rates and the decline of government borrowing had supply-side benefits of freeing up loan finance for private use. Finally, Greenspan's successful manipulation of interest rates disproved Paul Volcker's contention that fine-tuning to achieve an appropriate trade-off between inflation and unemployment was impossible.[45]

Economic growth in combination with deficit reduction measures brought about a balanced budget much sooner than expected. The federal government operated four consecutive surplus budgets from FY1998 to FY2001 for the first time since the 1920s. This was achieved through a reversal of Reagan's budgetary priorities. The end of the Cold War facilitated a significant reduction of defense spending from 5.6 percent GDP in FY1989 to 3 percent in FY2000. The Democrats, moreover, won the central political battle of the 1990s to balance the budget at a high rate of revenue that protected domestic program outlays over Republican preferences to do so at a low level of revenues that would require domestic retrenchment. In the balanced budgets of FY1998–2001 receipts averaged 20.2 percent GDP, a level unmatched since the peak tax years of World War II in FY1944–1945 (average 20.7 percent GDP).[46]

George W. Bush's attempt to renew Reaganomics only appeared to squander the legacy of Clintonomics. The Bush tax cuts embodied in the Economic Growth and Tax Relief Reconciliation Act of 2001 and the Jobs and Growth Tax Relief Reconciliation Act of 2003 sought to revive an economy that had been plunged into a brief but sharp recession by the dotcom collapse and the 9/11 attacks in 2001. The combination of recession, tax cuts, and increased security expenditures to fund the war on terror at home and abroad transformed the decade of surpluses that seemed possible at the dawn of the twenty-first century into a new age of deficits. Between FY2000 and FY2004 the budget moved from a surplus of 2.4 percent GDP to a deficit of 3.6 percent GDP. This fiscal deterioration of 6 percent GDP was almost comparable to the Depression-era deterioration of 6.7 percent GDP from FY1930 to FY1934.[47]

Bush proved a stouter supply-sider than Reagan had been. The bulk of his tax cuts benefited upper-income groups and business to boost investment growth. The richest 1 percent of taxpayers received 45 percent of the benefits of the 2001 tax reduction, while the poorest 60 percent received just 13 percent. Among other inducements, the 2003 measure reduced the maximum tax rate on capital gains and dividends. Nevertheless, Bush's promise that his tax cuts would pay for themselves through economic growth was as empty as his predecessor's. In 2007, U.S. Treasury data suggested that they had recouped just 7 percent of their $1.1 trillion costs.[48]

The tax cuts indicated that the Bush political economy had moved in the Reaganite direction of fiscal expansion. In contrast to the 1980s, monetary policy also moved in the same direction. Ongoing productivity gains from the new technology and the capital-equipment investment boom of the 1990s countered the renewal of inflationary pressures. Moreover, the depressing effect of renewed budget deficits on national saving did not necessitate a return of high real interest rates to attract foreign capital. The American consumer market had become the engine of global economic growth.

The export-driven economies of East Asia, led by the People's Republic of China, built up dollar reserves in the form of Treasury securities and other investments to maintain currency exchange rates that ensured competitive price levels for their products in the United States. America's current-account deficit (mainly comprising its trade deficit, net interest liabilities on its international investment balance) consequently grew to $856 billion in 2006, equal to 6.5 percent GDP and far in excess of the Reagan-era peak of 3.5 percent GDP in 1987. Many analysts questioned the sustainability of this external imbalance and worried about the vulnerability of a foreign dollar strike.[49] More immediately, the availability of cheap credit inflated the housing market and created a mountain of individual debt. Concerns about this eventually produced U.S. stock market turbulence in 2007 that had ripple effects throughout the world.[50]

Conclusion

In defense of Reaganomics, its supporters can justifiably argue that it conquered inflation, revived confidence in the American economy's capacity for growth, and freed the market from the unproductive aspects of big government. In this regard, it arguably laid the foundations for the successes of the 1990s. However, its long-term policy influence was more open to doubt. Clintonomics offered a significantly different variant and Bush's recalibration of Reaganomics has served to revive concerns about the problems associated with the original. Keynesianism enjoyed a heyday of some forty years before its failure to conquer stagflation discredited it. The problem that Reaganomics exacerbated and that might ultimately cast a shadow over its claim to a positive historic legacy is its effect on national saving, the seed corn for America's economic future.

The national savings rate has never truly recovered from the decline of the 1980s. Even Clintonomics failed in this regard. Its reversal of public dissaving was more than offset by a rapid decline of private saving in the late 1990s as Americans cashed in on the consumer and stock market booms.[51] By 2006 the United States was consuming nearly four-fifths of the savings that the rest of the world did not invest at home, equivalent to more than $2 billion a day. The growing reliance on foreign savers to make up the shortfall in domestic savings has created an unprecedented imbalance in America's external accounts that logic suggests is unsustainable. The day of reckoning that contemporary skeptics warned would be the consequence of Reagan's economic policies never came in the 1980s but the United States may yet have to face it if the fundamental problem bequeathed by Reaganomics remains unsolved.

Notes

1. Ronald Reagan, *An American Life* (London: Hutchison, 1990), 333.
2. For Reagan's statements of his economic philosophy, see two collections edited by Kiron K. Skinner, Annelise Anderson, and Martin Anderson, *Reagan: A Life in Letters (RLIL)* (New York: Free Press, 2003), esp. 292–326; and *Reagan's Path to Victory: The Shaping of Ronald Reagan's Vision: Selected Writings* (New York: Free Press, 2004).
3. U.S. Congress, Joint Economic Committee, *The Great Expansion: How it was Achieved and How it Can be Sustained, Growth and Prosperity Series*, Vol. 4, 106th Congress, Second Session, April 2000, 5. See also Lawrence Lindsay, "The Seventeen-Year Boom," *Wall Street Journal*, January 27, 2000.
4. Quoted in John Cassidy, "Tax Code," *New Yorker*, June 9, 2004, 9.
5. James Tobin, "Reaganomics in Retrospect," in B.B. Kymlicka and Jean V. Matthews, eds., *The Reagan Revolution?* (Chicago: Dorsey Press, 1988), 103. See, also, e.g., Benjamin Friedman, *Day of Reckoning: The Consequences of American Economic Policy under Reagan and after* (New York: Random House: 1988); Robert Lekachman, *Visions and Nightmares: America after Reagan* (New York: Macmillan, 1987); and Haynes Johnson, *Sleepwalking through History* (New York: Norton, 1990).
6. Robert M. Collins, *Transforming America: Politics and Culture during the Reagan Years* (New York: Columbia University Press, 2007), 87–91.
7. These statements of Reaganomics are reproduced in: Martin Anderson, *Revolution* (San Diego: Harcourt Brace Jovanovich, 1988), 114–121; and James Tobin and Murray Weidenbaum, eds., *Two Revolutions in Economic Policy: The First Economic Reports of Presidents Kennedy and Reagan* (Cambridge: MIT Press, 1988), 291–317.
8. Paul Volcker, "The Role of Monetary Targets in an Age of Inflation," *Journal of Monetary Economics* 4, No. 4 (1978): 329–339; W. Carl Biven, *Jimmy Carter's Economy: Policy in an Age of Limits* (Chapel Hill: University of North Carolina Press, 2002), 237–252. For a journalistic account of Volcker's Fed, see William Greider, *Secrets of the Temple: How the Federal Reserve Runs the Country* (New York: Simon & Schuster, 1987).
9. Michael Mussa, "U.S. Monetary Policy in the 1980s," in Martin Feldstein, ed., *American Economic Policy in the 1980s* (Chicago: University of Chicago Press, 1994), 86–114; Friedman, *Day of Reckoning*, 147–149; John W. Sloan, *The Reagan Effect: Economics and Presidential Leadership* (Lawrence: University Press of Kansas, 1999), 225–229.
10. Aaron Wildavsky and Joseph White, *The Deficit and the Public Interest: The Search for Responsible Budgeting in the 1980s* (Berkeley: University of California Press, 1989), esp. chapters 9–11, 13.
11. Alan Greenspan, untitled enclosure, "Briefing Book for Long-Range Planning Meeting," Camp David, February 5, 1982, Box 1, Richard Darman Files, Ronald Reagan Library (RRL); *Public Papers of the President of the United States: Ronald Reagan 1982* (henceforth PP: *Reagan*), 1030, 1052.
12. Richard Darman, *Who's in Charge: Polar Politics and the Sensible Center* (New York: Simon & Schuster, 1996), 118–119.
13. Mussa, "U.S. Monetary Policy in the 1980s," 115–131.
14. See, in particular, Sloan, *The Reagan Effect*, 229–235, 237–244; and Friedman, *Day of Reckoning*, 206–207.

15. See Volcker's comments in "Monetary Policy," in Feldstein, *American Economic Policy in the 1980s*, 145–151, 157–164 (esp. 162).
16. Reagan to Martin Feldstein, July 21, 1983, and to Arthur Burns, February 22, 1984, in *RLIL*, 317, 319. For Council of Economic Adviser chair Feldstein's advocacy of deficit reduction, see his memoranda to Reagan, "Tax Increases and Economic Recovery," October 18, 1983, and "Deficits and Inflation," January 8, 1984, Martin Feldstein Files, OA9815, RRL.
17. James Savage, *Balanced Budgets and American Politics* (Ithaca, N.Y.: Cornell University Press, 1988), 229–231; Amos Kiewe and Davis W. Houck, *A Shining City on a Hill: Ronald Reagan's Economic Rhetoric, 1951–1989* (New York: Praeger, 1991), 165–173.
18. Herbert Stein, *Presidential Economics: The Making of Economic Policy from Roosevelt to Clinton*, third, revised ed. (Washington D.C.: AEI Press, 1994), 326–330.
19. Friedman, *Day of Reckoning*, 194–198, 206–208; Paul Krugman, *Peddling Prosperity: Economic Sense and Nonsense in the Age of Diminished Expectations* (New York: Norton, 1994), 126–127.
20. *PP: Reagan 1981*, 139, 178, 200, 468, 510, 557–558, 567; David Stockman, *The Triumph of Politics: Why the Reagan Revolution Failed* (New York: Harper & Row, 1986), 272.
21. Stockman, *The Triumph of Politics*, 306–321; William Greider, "The education of David Stockman," *Atlantic Monthly* (December 1981): 27–54.
22. For early expressions of this belief, see Speech to the Phoenix, Arizona, Chamber of Commerce, March 30, 1961, *A Time for Choosing: The Speeches of Ronald Reagan, 1961–1982* (Chicago: Regnery Gateway, 1983); "Inaugural Address as Governor of California," January 5, 1967, http://www.cnn.com/SPECIALS/2004/reagan/stories/speech.archive/cal.inaug.html.
23. For contrasting views of this theory, see Stein, *Presidential Economics*, 245–247, and Robert Bartley, *The Seven Fat Years and How to Do it Again* (New York: Free Press, 1992), 57–59, 169–173.
24. Reagan once horrified Council of Economic Advisers chair Martin Feldstein by claiming that no tax increase in U.S. history had generated increased revenues but every tax cut since World War I had done so. The latter responded with a memorandum demonstrating every tax increase since 1917 had increased revenues. See Stockman, *The Triumph of Politics*, 374; Feldstein to Reagan, "Tax Rates and Tax Revenue," January 10, 1984, Martin Feldstein Files, OA9815, RRL. He restated his belief in the revenue benefits of tax cuts in *An American Life*, 232–233.
25. Based on calculations in Dennis S. Ippolito, *Uncertain Legacies: Federal Budget Policy from Roosevelt through Reagan* (Charlottesville: University Press of Virginia, 1990), 65.
26. Council of Economic Advisers, *Economic Report of the President, January 1982* (Washington D.C.: GPO, 1982), 122.
27. Paul Craig Roberts, *The Supply-Side Revolution: An Insider's Account of Policymaking in Washington* (Cambridge: Harvard University Press, 1984); Wendell Gunn to James Baker, "... The Last Remaining Supply-Siders," March 8, 1983, James Baker Files, Box 5, RRL.
28. For this evolution, see W. Elliot Brownlee and C. Eugene Steuerle, "Taxation," in W. Elliot Brownlee and Hugh Davis Graham, eds., *The*

Reagan Presidency: Pragmatic Conservatism and Its Legacies (Lawrence: University Press of Kansas, 2003), 155–181.
29. Michael J. Boskin, *Reagan and the Economy: The Success, Failures, and Unfinished Agenda* (San Francisco: Institute for Contemporary Studies, 1987), 158–159. See also Ronald F. King, "Introduction: Tax Reform and American Politics," *American Politics Quarterly* 19 (October 19, 1991): 417–425.
30. Friedman, *Day of Reckoning*, 291; Norman Ture, "The Tax Reform Act of 1986: Revolution or Counterrevolution" in David Boaz, ed., *Assessing the Reagan Years* (Washington D.C.: Cato Institute, 1988), 30, 39.
31. John Patrick Diggins, *Ronald Reagan: Fate, Freedom and the Making of History* (New York: Norton, 2007), 338–339.
32. Wallace C. Peterson, "The Silent Depression," *Challenge* (July–August 1991): 29–34. For a more detailed exposition, see the same author's *Silent Depression: The Fate of the American Dream* (New York: Norton, 1994).
33. These data are drawn from National Income and Product Accounts. In a demonstration as to how statistics can be manipulated, if 1979 is taken as the point of comparison—because consumption was affected by recession in 1980—then the after-inflation gain in per capita spending was 1.8 percent a year, that is, 0.1 percent less than in 1973–1979.
34. This discussion is largely based on Friedman, *Day of Reckoning*, 150–158.
35. Krugman, *Peddling Prosperity*, 126.
36. Paul Volcker and Toyoa Gyohten, *Changing Fortunes: The World's Money and the Threat to America's Leadership* (New York: Random House, 1992), 178–179, 248. For cogent discussion of the implications of America's external indebtedness in the 1980s, see Sloan, *The Reagan Effect*, 194–224.
37. Stephen Grubagh and Scott Summers, "Monetary Policy and the U.S. Trade Deficit," in Joseph Hogan, ed., *The Reagan Years* (Manchester: Manchester University Press, 1990); Jeffrey Frankel, "The Making of Exchange Rate Policy in the 1980s," in Feldstein, *American Economic Policy in the 1980s*, esp. 295–302.
38. Stockman, *The Triumph of Politics*, 155–58; I.M. Destler, *American Trade Politics*, 2nd ed. (Washington D.C.: Institute for International Economics, 1992), 178.
39. Volcker and Gyohten, *Changing Fortunes*, 229. See also Yoichi Funabishi, *Managing the Dollar: From the Plaza to the Louvre*, 2nd ed. (Washington D.C.: Institute for International Economics, 1989). For James Baker's recollections, see his memoir (with Steve Fiffer) *Work Hard, Study... and Keep Out of Politics: Adventures and Lessons from an Unexpected Life* (New York: Putnam, 2006), 426–442.
40. Volcker and Gyohten, *Changing Fortunes*, 266–268; "The Making of Exchange Rate Policy in the 1980s," 306–309.
41. R. Taggart Murphy, "Power without Purpose: The Problem of Japan's Economic Dominance," *Harvard Business Review* 67 (March–April 1989): 72–74.
42. Bob Woodward, *Maestro: Greenspan's Fed and the American Boom* (New York: Simon & Schuster, 2000), 36–47; Destler, *American Trade Politics*, 95.
43. For a critique, see Michael Meeropol, *Surrender: How the Clinton Administration Completed the Reagan Revolution* (Ann Arbor: University of Michigan Press, 1998).

44. Alan S. Blinder and Janet L. Yellen, *The Fabulous Decade: Macroeconomic Lessons from the 1990s* (New York: The Century Foundation Press, 2001), 5–33; Iwan Morgan, "Jimmy Carter, Bill Clinton and the New Democratic Economics," *Historical Journal*, 17 (December 2004): 1015–1039.
45. Blinder and Yellen, *The Fabulous Decade*, 83–86. See also Gregory Mankiw, "U.S. Monetary Policy in the 1990s" and Douglas Elmendorf, Jeffrey Liebman, and David Wilcox, "Fiscal Policy and Social Security in the 1990s," in Jeffrey Frankel and Peter Orszag, eds., *American Economic Policy in the 1990s* (Cambridge: MIT Press, 2002), 19–43, 61–119, respectively.
46. Dennis S. Ippolito, *Why Budgets Matter: Budget Policy and American Politics* (University Park: Penn State Press, 2003), 258–289.
47. Richard Kogan and Robert Greenstein, "President Portrays Social Security Shortfall as Enormous, but his Tax Cuts and Drug Benefit Will Cost Five Times as Much," *Center on Budget and Policy Priorities*, March 11, 2006. For analysis of budgetary change, see Iwan Morgan, "The Bush Administration and the Budget Deficit," in Iwan Morgan and Philip Davies eds., *Right On? Political Change and Continuity in George W. Bush's America* (London: Institute for the Study of the Americas, 2006), 111–130.
48. David Rosenbaum, "Doing the Math on Bush's Tax Cut," *New York Times*, February 15, 2001, A12; James Horney, "A Smoking Gun: President's Claims that Tax Cuts Pay for Themselves Refuted by New Treasury Analysis," *Center on Budget Policy and Priorities*, July 27, 2006.
49. Larry Summers, "America Overdrawn," *Foreign Policy* (July/August 2004): 47–49; Brad Setser and Nouriel Roubini, "How Scary is the Deficit: Our Money, Our Debt, Our Problem," *Foreign Affairs* (July/August 2005): 194–200.
50. Andrew Clark and Larry Elliott, "Market Turmoil Grows as Leading U.S. Lender Seeks Emergency Aid," *The Guardian*, August 17, 2007, 26; Daniel Gross, "The New Money Pit: Why the Housing Market Will Only Get Worse," *Newsweek*, September 10, 2007, 36–37.
51. Elmendorf, Liebman, and Wilcox, "Fiscal Policy and Social Security in the 1990s," 76.

Chapter 7

African American Protest during the Reagan Years: Forging New Agendas, Defending Old Victories

Stephen Tuck

In November 1979, *Rapper's Delight* by the Sugarhill Gang entered Billboard's R&B chart. That same month, in a conference room in the New York Hilton, former California governor Ronald Reagan launched his third bid for the Republican nomination for president. He promised to pursue the principle of "responsible liberty for every individual so that we will become that shining city on a hill."

The rap from the Sugarhill Gang, and Reagan's talk of the shining city on a hill, seemed to mark the beginning of new eras in popular culture and national politics. *Rapper's Delight* was the first hip hop hit. By the end of the century, hip hop dominated the music industry in terms of sales, awards, and advertising. As for Reagan, he won the election and (after a landslide victory in 1984) a second term. Reagan's victory heralded the resurgence of conservative Republicans in national politics. He was succeeded by his vice president, George H. W. Bush. Although Democrat Bill Clinton won the presidential election of 1992, he distanced himself from Great Society liberalism. Two years later, under the aggressive leadership of staunch conservative Rep. Newt Gingrich, Republicans won a Congressional majority for the first time in forty years.

On the face of it, hip hop and modern conservatism were two entirely unrelated movements. Reagan's optimistic campaign theme of "Morning in America" chimed with the affluence and aspirations of middle class suburbanites. By contrast, hip hop emerged as the voice of African American inner city poor. Grandmaster Flash's "The Message," one of the first major hip hop records, could hardly have been more different from "Morning in America"; "Broken glass everywhere/People pissing on the stairs...Got no money to move out...You'll grow in the ghetto, living second rate/And your eyes will sing a song of deep hate."

Yet hip hop and conservatism had more in common than just the coincidental timing of their launch. Both benefited from a loss of faith in the old styles. By the summer of 1979, Democrat president Jimmy Carter faced an economic crisis at home and a hostage crisis abroad. That same summer, teenagers held disco record demolition parties. Both had already gained grassroots strength before the breakthrough. In the West and South, conservatives such as Barry Goldwater and George Wallace railed against the Great Society, high taxes, and forced racial integration. In the South Bronx, DJs such as Grandmaster Flash and Afrika Bambaataa developed hip hop at house parties.[1] Both movements integrated a wide range of adherents. The conservative coalition included the religious right, social libertarians, and fiscal conservatives. Hip hop began as a mixture of graffiti artists, break dancing, MCing, and rapping.

Above all, both conservatism and hip hop had important implications for the struggle for racial equality at the end of century. To take the rise of conservatism first: after Reagan's victory, civil rights leaders saw the federal government as foe rather than friend.[2] Their complaints were legion: Reagan's administration pursued a policy of constructive engagement with South Africa's apartheid regime; Reagan appointed conservative judges to the federal bench; he promoted black conservatives who opposed affirmative action; and his Justice Department proved reluctant to protect minority rights. African American leaders were also angry at the racial slights. Reagan famously failed to recognize Charles Pierce, the sole African American member of his cabinet, at a meeting of black mayors. Perhaps most important of all, Reagan's mantra was "government is not the solution to our problems; government *is* the problem." By contrast, civil leaders had long seen big government as key to solving the problem of persistent inequality.[3]

Mainstream civil rights leaders challenged the new conservative politics. Rev. Jesse Jackson led the way. Born in South Carolina in 1941, by the 1980s Jackson was based in Chicago working to improve the conditions of nonwhite poor people. Talented and telegenic, Jackson seemed the closest thing to Martin Luther King that the Reagan era had to offer. It was an image he cultivated carefully. Jackson had worked with King, he often quoted King, and he claimed to have cradled King as he lay dying on a Memphis motel balcony. Jackson ran for the Democratic nomination twice, in 1984 and 1988. Indeed in 1988, Jackson was the frontrunner for a time, winning fifteen primaries and caucuses. Just one generation after the Voting Rights Act, the emergence of a credible African American contender for the Democratic nomination was an impressive development. Yet for all his strengths, Jackson could not craft a winning coalition. Even the Democratic Party was reluctant to embrace his policies or staff personnel.

Thus it was ironic that at the very moment of the so-called Reagan revolution, African American artists reoriented national popular culture. African American public intellectual Cornel West observed the "Afro-Americanization of white youth."[4] White youths embraced hip hop culture. They idolized black sports stars. Yet few seemed interested in the problems of the ghetto. One *Newsweek* columnist reckoned "All this fascination with hip-hop is just a cultural safari for white people."[5] Indeed, images of aggressive jewelry-laden black men hardly made the case for state funding for the deserving poor.

Some African American leaders blamed hip hop stars for turning young people away from tackling issues of racial injustice. Adrienne Shropshire, a thirty-one-year-old community organizer in Los Angeles, complained "Oftentimes the music reinforces the very things that we are struggling against... How do we work around issues of economic justice if the music is about 'getting mine'?"[6] By the end of the century, some of the pioneer artists agreed that hip hop had done more harm than good. Afrika Bambaataa bemoaned, "a lot of brothers and sisters... they're losing respect of the 'us syndrome' and getting into the 'I syndrome.' You can't build a nation with an 'I' you got to build a nation with an 'us.'"[7]

A further irony was that for a time in the 1980s, it seemed as though rappers might replace civil rights leaders as representatives of the race. When Public Enemy—the leading hip hop band of its day—paraded in open cars through Philadelphia in 1988, the band's publicist Bill Stephney was astonished by the response. "You're seeing these graying forty-something Black men, tears in their eyes, throwing the Black power salute like the revolution has come back." Lead rapper Chuck D complained that the media "treat me like *I'm* Jesse Jackson." Yet it soon became clear that few hip hop artists wanted to stand in the gap for political leaders. Stephney reckoned "hip-hop was not just a 'Fuck you' to white society, it was a 'Fuck you' to the previous Black generation as well."[8] Especially after the rise of gangsta rap in the late 1980s, rap songs seemed increasingly self-centered, self-harming, and self-defeating in equal measure.

For the traditional civil rights leadership, the rise of Reagan and rap spelled double trouble—an assault on the movement from without and within. Benjamin Hooks, executive director of the National Association for the Advancement of Colored People (NAACP), complained, "The age of the volunteer is coming to an end."[9] By the end of the 1980s, NAACP membership had plummeted from half a million to barely a hundred thousand. The contrast with the 1960s was stark: majority support for nonviolent, progressive students had been replaced by majority condemnation of violent, idle young black men. The commemoration of the civil rights movement during the 1980s—through museums, marches, and the introduction of an annual Martin Luther King holiday (signed into law by Reagan)—made the contrast all the more starker. Little wonder, then, that many traditional leaders and journalists hankered after the good old days of "the movement."

Scholars of the civil rights movement have tended to follow suit. Invariably, histories of the civil rights movement describe the Reagan years (if they take the story that far forward) as years of atrophy and decline. The downturn in fortune experienced by many African Americans during these years seems to confirm the gloomy picture. The inequality gap in wages and employment that had been closing since World War II held steady from mid-1970s through the mid-1990s, and in some aspects the gap widened. Inner city poverty, family breakdown, and gang violence were seemingly entrenched. The arrival of crack cocaine in the mid-1980s compounded the problem. New get-tough crime measures led to an astonishing rise in numbers of young black men in prison. During the 1980s, sociologists popularized the term "underclass"—a group with no prospect of breaking out of poverty. Little wonder then that many polls showed increasing pessimism among African Americans that the racial equality would be achieved within a lifetime.

Yet the despondency of the old guard leadership, and the popular narrative of decline, only tells part of the story. In the first place—as Reagan scholars have demonstrated—the "Reagan revolution" had its limits, especially in terms of its policy legacy. Reagan's election did not mark the overthrow of the old guard in the American state. In electoral terms, Democrats shared control of Congress (and won sole control in 1986). In the judiciary, a number of federal appeals court circuits remained strongly liberal, and the Supreme Court only swung to a conservative majority after Reagan left office. Moreover, some contemporary critics from the American right castigated Reagan for not even seeking a conservative (or conservative enough) revolution in the first place.[10]

Meanwhile, rap did not signal the end of African American protest. Much of the criticism of rap lyrics missed the point. At house parties, people wanted a sound, a beat, not a political commentary. As Chuck D remembered, "You could throw in one line or two, like 'Reagan is bullshit.' Motherfuckers be like, 'Yeah, okay' [but] you better rock the fucking crowd."[11] Many listeners understood that some of rap's boasting was a remake of the traditional street wordplay "the dozens," an outlandish trade of insults.[12] As rapper Ice T put it "Rap is really funny, man. But if you don't see that it's funny, it will scare the shit out of you." In any case, to quote the National Black Police Association soon after Reagan left office, "There are no statistics to support the argument that a song can incite someone to violence." Rather, hip hop was a reflection of existing tensions. Chuck D's famous description of rap as "the Black CNN" had some merit. "Rap gives you the news on all phases of life, good and bad, pretty and ugly: drugs, sex, education, love, money, war, peace—you name it."[13]

In fact, a representative Black CNN would also have broadcast news of a continued, vibrant struggle for black equality. During the Reagan years and beyond, thousands of individuals and hundreds of organizations sought to advance the position of African Americans. Indeed, in some ways, the conservative assault spurred rival groups to work together. The sheer scale of activity was on a par with the celebrated 1960s. Some activists continued to tackle old issues—the search for a decent wage and housing, a voice in local politics, a positive image, freedom from police brutality. Many activists addressed new issues too—such as South African apartheid, environmental problems, AIDS, drugs, and black imprisonment.

The importance of conservatism was that it framed this continued protest. Gone were the days of a national movement, with the wind at its back, boldly seeking to advance the rights of African Americans—hence the nostalgia for times past. Rather, at the national level, civil rights groups spent much of their time resisting the conservative challenges to civil rights legislation. But such protest was no less important because it was defensive. Civil rights groups had some success too, such as their defense of affirmative action legislation. And at times, on specific single issues—notably the campaign against South African apartheid—activists were able to push a new agenda in national politics.

In general, though, the conservative resurgence in national politics meant that many of the most significant campaigns developed at the grassroots. Some of the themes raised in rap—unemployment, poor housing, prison, and the police—were very much the issues raised by campaigners on the ground. Meanwhile some of the tensions exposed in rap—sexism, homophobia, attacks on bourgeois African Americans—pointed to conflicts within black communities. African American women, homosexuals, and other marginalized groups fought to broaden the definition of racial equality to encompass a wide range of human rights. Inevitably, this grassroots protest was often hidden from public view. But in an age rightly associated with conservative rhetoric and inner city decline, it is striking how much progress many local groups were able to achieve. And in a generation of ironies, perhaps the biggest irony of all was that at a time when the media focused on young black men as never before, many of the most effective local leaders were elderly women.

The Perfect Combination: Lifting Mandela's Spirits and Attacking Reagan

On November 6, 1984, Reagan won a landslide reelection victory. On Capitol Hill, members of the Congressional Black Caucus feared four years on the sidelines. The prospect of an emboldened conservative Republican in the White House was one thing. Worse still, despite Jackson's strong showing in the primary, the Democrats had played down civil rights issues. Rep. Ron Dellums of California felt, "it was as if we had leprosy." African American leaders met together. According to Rep. John Conyers of Michigan, "we were...looking for a strategy to begin our second term of office under this president."[14] They chose a strategy that tackled Reagan on an issue that was eight thousand miles away—South African apartheid.

On Thanksgiving Eve, four African American leaders met with the South African ambassador at the embassy. During the meeting, one of the four slipped out to alert the press that the other three would "sit-in" at the office demanding the end of apartheid. Thus the TV cameras were in perfect position to capture the unfolding drama. The police escorted the three dignified, handcuffed protesters to the police cars and then on to a night in the cells. The Free South Africa Movement (FSAM) was born.

During the next two years, some six thousand demonstrators would be arrested.[15] In 1986, Congress passed legislation imposing sanctions on South Africa—inflicting on Reagan his most serious foreign policy setback. By this time, more than half of the American firms and numerous states and colleges had divested from South Africa. African American journalist Juan Williams exulted: "After years of looking for lightning to strike—the right issue at the right time to revive the moribund civil rights movement—black Americans have found the issue in apartheid."[16]

In fact, black Americans found apartheid long before 1984. Martin Luther King and Chief Albert J. Lutuli of the African National Congress jointly issued a call for sanctions against South Africa. During the 1970s, the CBC and other groups formed TransAfrica—the organization that launched FSAM. Jesse Jackson made apartheid one of his top campaign issues. But the reason that "lightning struck" late in 1984 was because of the deteriorating situation in South Africa. In September, the South African government responded to a resurgence of demonstrations with shocking brutality. The South African newspaper *Sechaba* reported, "Afro-Americans who understandably identify with the struggles of the African people, regard an attack on the African continent as an attack on them."[17]

As the CBC deliberations showed, though, the reason that this was "the right issue at the right time" had a good deal to do with U.S. politics too. *Newsweek* rightly observed that FSAM mobilized "against South African racism—and against Ronald Reagan's approach to dealing with it."[18] Along with Britain's prime minister Margaret Thatcher, Reagan vetoed UN attempts to impose sanctions. Archbishop Desmond Tutu, Cape Town's Nobel-Prize-winning antiapartheid campaigner, called Reagan's preferred policy of "constructive engagement" "evil and totally un-Christian."[19] In 1985 he met with Reagan to try and win him over. Reagan was impressed by Tutu. But he would not agree to sanctions. Tutu was outraged. "I think I should say now [Reagan] is a racist pure and simple"[20] African American campaigners even blamed Reagan for the South African government's assault on demonstrators. Randall Robinson, the director of TransAfrica, believed that the recent "oppression...was almost pegged to the re-election."[21]

Moreover, the campaign against apartheid was not just a campaign against Reagan's foreign policy, but a chance to express anger against the Reagan presidency in general. Therein lay its popularity. At a time when civil rights leaders felt on the defensive, this was one national policy where they could go on the attack. In previous generations, mainstream African American leaders had played down their criticism of U.S. foreign policy so as not to alienate the government and jeopardize potential domestic gains. (Indeed, they had pressed the case for domestic reform as one way to help repel Communist propaganda abroad.) But ironically under Reagan, they felt they had nothing to lose. Reagan had refused to meet with the Congressional Black Caucus (even Nixon had extended that courtesy). Meanwhile only one of the state department's top hundred officials was an African American.

The Free South African Movement evoked memories of the civil rights movement. This was quite deliberate. Many FSAM leaders had first tasted direct-action during the 1960s. The choice of four people confronting the U.S. ambassador was a carbon copy of the first student sit-in. As in the civil rights movement, the focus was not on persuading the oppressors to relent but on forcing the U.S. federal government to do something about the problem. And as in the civil rights movement, the demonstrations were media savvy. A typical day outside the U.S. Embassy would see a fairly quiet march. Then, when the news cameras appeared in mid-afternoon, the chanting would increase for a few minutes, a celebrity would get arrested, the TV cameras would leave, and the protesters were free to return home and enjoy the clip on the evening news.

The reasons for the success of FSAM mirrored that of the civil rights movement of the 1960s too. FSAM enjoyed a groundswell of grassroots support, in the churches, on campus, and among unions. The apartheid issue united anti-racists and anti-imperialists, leftists, and liberals. The primary reason for FSAM's success, though, was that apartheid had few defenders left in the United States. The issue seemed clear cut, not least once the South African government—as white Southerners had done two decades previously—resorted to brutal repression. As one black leader put it, "There is no question which side is the good side."[22] Reagan condemned apartheid even as he argued that constructive engagement was the better approach. Thus protesters did not have to change people's minds, just persuade them to act. Polls suggested that three-quarters of white Americans who knew about the protests supported them.[23]

Although the CBC felt marginalized, the course of the apartheid campaign suggested that the Caucus potentially had more clout than African Americans had ever had before in Congress. Dellums introduced a sanctions bill during each session of Congress in the 1980s, which gained support year on year. Reagan tried to stall the movement by promoting a weak sanctions bill, but bipartisan support forced through a tougher bill. On October 3, 1986, the Senate voted 78–21 to override Reagan's veto. CBC member Rep. Mickey Leland of Texas was exultant, "This is probably the greatest victory we have ever experienced."[24] It was certainly the first time in U.S. history that African Americans had decisively shaped American foreign policy.

It is hard to measure the impact of the campaign on South Africa. No doubt apartheid would have crumbled at some stage without U.S. pressure. But the loss of American support clearly deprived the South African government of outside resources at just the moment when it faced its greatest challenges at home. Tutu was delighted. The American position is "not anti-South Africa," he declared, "it is...anti-apartheid."[25] The South African Rand plummeted. South African president F.W. de Klerk saw the writing on the wall. In 1990 he committed his government to move toward ending apartheid, and released some political prisoners. The most famous prisoner was Nelson Mandela. In one of his first interviews after his release, Mandela praised the FSAM. My "spirits were lifted," he said. "It was an impressive role for Black Americans to choose arrest."[26] His words were a reminder that struggles for racial justice were not bounded by national boundaries, not even by prison walls.

FSAM leaders hoped the victory would spawn a wider revival of the civil rights movement. To some extent, it did. In the San Francisco Bay Area, hundreds of students from U.C. Berkeley and other campuses picketed in support of Longshore workers who refused to unload South African cargo.

Activists used the campaign to spotlight other issues. For example, in 1985, twenty-two NAACP members completed the "longest civil rights march in history" (from coast-to-coast) to support sanctions and to encourage voter registration.[27] The antiapartheid campaign also gave African American politicians the authority to speak out on other African and Caribbean issues. In 1985, Rep. Leland spearheaded the campaign that led to the passage of the Africa Famine Relief and Recovery Act that provided $800 million for famine victims in Ethiopia. As in the 1960s, other activist groups borrowed movement tactics for their own causes too. Shortly before Christmas 1984, three demonstrators were arrested at the British embassy singing (to the tune of a well-know civil rights anthem), "Ireland will be free one day."[28]

On June 20, 1990, Nelson and Winnie Mandela arrived in America to a heroes' welcome. Nearly a million New Yorkers cheered them along Broadway. Yankee Stadium was packed. Ever the showman, Nelson donned a Yankees cap. For many African Americans, it was an exhilarating moment of triumph. Yet the Mandela visit proved to be bittersweet. It signaled the unraveling of the antiapartheid coalition. As in the 1960s, the unraveling was bitter at times. African American campaigners were appalled at the "Wall Street corporate approach" of the tour—and many accused white liberals and democrats of hijacking the antiapartheid movement. Black campaigners resented, too, the public outcry against a problem across the ocean but the lack of concern with race problems at home. On college campuses, black students demanded control of the antiapartheid struggle. As Barbara Ransby, a leader of the Columbia divestment campaign, put it, "We argued that the antiapartheid movement should be an extension of the Black freedom movement here, and that as a result Black students should be in the leadership."[29]

The Mandela tour also marked the end of FSAM's ability to pressure the American government into action. Mandela urged Congress to retain sanctions until South Africa promised open elections. But his arrival gave the impression that victory was already won. Bush lifted sanctions soon after he left. The CBC's repeated attempts to pass tougher legislation (even with the backing of a national day of fasting in the black churches) did not make it past the Senate.[30] Meanwhile the U.S. media focus on black "tribal" violence in South African townships—which fit well with the portrayal of hip hop gang violence in the United States—muddled the issue (as it turned out, the South African government was responsible for fomenting much of the violence). As one Africa analyst put it, "the days of 'ANC good, apartheid bad' are over."[31] The days of FSAM and the hopes for rekindling an old-style civil rights movement were over too.

Fighting Old Battles: Seeking Equality in the Workplace

In 1963, in the city of Birmingham, Alabama, police faced down young civil rights campaigners with dogs and fire hoses. It was one of the confrontations—perhaps *the* confrontation—that defined the civil rights movement. Two decades later, the same city was the scene of another important (albeit less publicized), confrontation. During the 1970s, the city had signed a Consent Decree, promising to hire at least one minority applicant for every two white applicants (the city also agreed to a minimum quota of women). In 1984, ten white men, who failed to get into the services, filed suit, claiming "discrimination against whites and males." Reagan's Justice Department eagerly joined the plaintiffs. Birmingham's first African American mayor, Richard Arrington, who had helped negotiate the Consent Decree, was exasperated. The Decree "could have healed a 100-year-old wound," said Arrington wistfully. "Now we will have to fight old battles."[32]

Fighting old battles was the order of the day at the end of the century. To be sure, the antiapartheid campaign showed that African Americans fought new battles when the opportunities arose. But for the most part, the main battle in national politics was trying to defend the gains of the 1960s and 1970s. From the question of access to higher education to the drawing of election districts, civil rights leaders lobbied politicians, battled in court, and appealed to public opinion. Each battle was contentious and important, none more so than the battle over affirmative action in employment.

There would be no repeat of snarling dogs. But the conservative rhetorical assault on hard-won compensatory legislation was ferocious, and enjoyed much broader support than had the defenders of Jim Crow.[33] In the battle for hearts and minds, some conservative publicists labeled affirmative action as reverse discrimination and spoke of quotas rather than targets. Prominent black conservatives (who received wide publicity despite being few in number) argued that affirmative action stigmatized African Americans and stopped the fulfillment of Martin Luther King's dream of a color-blind society. The administration's bite did not match the bark of conservative rhetoric (not least because support for affirmative action was embedded in some government bureaucracies). Even so, the Reagan administration proposed a significant change in government policy. His administration sought to overturn Executive Order 11246, signed by Lyndon Johnson, which required federal contractors to implement affirmative action policies. As the Birmingham case showed, the Reagan administration also tried to win cases in court to stop private employers from pursuing affirmative action.

Civil rights activists tried to push back. The battle over Executive Order 11246, said one civil rights veteran, aroused "the largest coalition ever on a civil rights issue."[34] The NAACP poured resources into defending affirmative action in court. Civil rights spokesmen and women fought for hearts and minds too. They released compelling evidence of continued discrimination at the workplace, in housing, and in mortgage lending.

Although affirmative action advocates were on the defensive, they still had some power. As with the antiapartheid campaign, civil rights groups joined with significant allies—particularly among democrats and unions. Campaigners found some support from the courts, too. Although the courts ruled against general affirmative programs,[35] in cases such as *Local 128 of the Sheet Metal Workers' International Association v. EEOC* (1986), the Court upheld affirmative action targets when there was specific evidence of intentional discrimination or severe under representation. As for public opinion, polls showed that although a majority opposed quotas, a majority (including many Republican voters) still supported affirmative action.[36] Or to put it another way, a majority opposed compensatory action but supported diversity.

In the final analysis, the battle over affirmative action added up to a stalemate in theory and something of a reversal in practice. Even a powerful conservative administration could not muster sufficient support to overturn Executive Order 11246. Republican senate majority leader Bob Dole advised Reagan to "leave it as it is." A decade later Clinton pursued much the same line on affirmative action, promising to "mend it not end it." But Reagan's administration starved enforcement agencies of resources to leave them limp and ineffective. Both Reagan and Bush appointed conservatives to the Equal Employment Opportunities Commission. Clarence Thomas, the most controversial appointee of all, reckoned that to work with white conservatives "you must be against affirmative action." One economist commented in 1986, "If the tax laws of the United States were enforced as slackly as the antidiscrimination laws currently are...very few people would pay taxes."[37]

One of the problems of having to fight old battles was that it meant there was little chance of pushing for new, more ambitious solutions. Well before the battle over Executive Order 11246, African American economists worried that affirmative action programs could not resolve entrenched racial inequality. Or as National Urban League (NUL) president John Jacob put it soon after Reagan came to power, "whatever statistics you use the end result is the same...there is a severe economic penalty attached to being black in America."[38] Some made bold suggestions. In 1990, Jacob renewed the NUL's call for a domestic Marshall Plan—transferring $50 billion from the military budget to create full employment and provide training for nonwhite workers. In a widely reprinted series of articles, the African American journalist Ron Daniels backed the Plan with a call for action. "African Americans need to revive the strategy and tactics of civil disobedience...Are we prepared to tie up Congress, surround the White House...and go to jail in MASSIVE numbers?"[39]

The short answer was no. But such talk of reviving the civil rights movement to disrupt the federal government missed the point. In the Reagan (and Bush) era, it was clear that national protests could expect little return. After all, African Americans had only once been able to face down the government over the issue of jobs alone—and that was at the outset of World War II, when the government was at its most vulnerable and when the lilywhite nature of federal defense employment made the issue clear cut. In any case, issues such as Executive Order 11246 did not capture the imagination of African Americans at the grassroots. Lobbying in Washington was done by professional civil rights organizations, such as the NUL, rather than mass marches. What such calls also missed was the fact that mass mobilization was already taking place, just not as a single, top down movement.

The Grassroots Movement: "Building by Building, Block by Block"

From time to time, local civil rights demonstrations rekindled memories of the 1960s. In 1987 in Forsyth County Georgia, civil rights leaders led a nonviolent confrontation like old rockers on a comeback tour. In 1912, white residents had expelled all African American residents from the county. Three-quarters of a century later, the county was still lily-white. Some twenty thousand people—led by King's former colleagues—joined a "March against racial intimidation." A *Washington Post* editorial reckoned that local white supremacists recreated "the worst of the '60s scenes—fools in Klan outfits shouting obscenities."[40] Pulitzer-prize winning African American columnist William Raspberry was not especially impressed. "A 1960s-style march...no matter how much it looks like something King might have done, strikes me as a waste of courage, a purposeless exercise in nostalgia."[41] It didn't begin to tackle bigger problems in America—it didn't even begin to tackle underlying problems in Forsyth County. A decade after the march, the county remained the whitest of the United States' six hundred largest counties, with only thirty-nine black people.[42]

For the most part, however, grassroots campaigns at the end of the century were less concerned with set-piece confrontations over access to public space and more with longer-term efforts to improve the lives of African Americans. Such efforts were often based on traditional community institutions—the church, campuses, labor groups, women's groups, and tenants' organizations—and linked together through new social justice organizations. One campus activist explained, "students are much more interested in volunteerism than in political action...What they've told us is, 'Our service work is not an alternative to politics—it is alternative politics.'"[43] What was true for students was true more generally. In an era ostensibly bedeviled by materialism and defeatism in equal measure, the struggle for racial equality was to be found in the age-old politics of building the community. And nowhere more so than in the ghetto.

Take the example of Genevieve Brooks, the driving force behind the Mid-Bronx Desperadoes Community Housing Corporation. Aged seventeen, Brooks left South Carolina for New York City. By the 1970s, the small, energetic accountant, now in her forties and recently widowed, moved to a handsome integrated apartment in the mid-Bronx. But soon the white tenants started moving out. Before long, the landlord stopped cleaning the apartment block. When Brooks complained, the landlord suggested she move away. After all, by this time the neighborhood was fast degenerating into a wasteland of boarded and burnt out homes. Many of the apartment blocks were burnt by landlords trying to pick up a final insurance check, or by tenants seeking priority on the city's placement list for new housing projects.

What Brooks faced was the classic problem of urban decay. By the 1980s, the Bronx had become a byword for ghetto despair. In 1977, the New York Yankees hosted the Los Angeles Dodgers in the second game of the World Series. During the game, the overhead helicopter cameras panned out from

Yankee stadium to a fire in a nearby school. TV commentator Howard Cosell famously told sixty million viewers, "There it is, ladies and gentlemen, the Bronx is burning." In 1981, Hollywood released *Fort Apache: The Bronx*, a tale of violent crime and police corruption. Both Carter and Reagan visited the Bronx. Carter called it the worst slum in America. Reagan compared it to London after the blitz. There had been no war, of course, but the combined effects of urban renewal and suburban flight were just as devastating.

Reagan used the example of the Bronx to justify his attack on big government programs. Or as he put it, "The government fought a war on poverty, and poverty won." His administration cut spending on affordable housing by two-thirds. Local government followed suit. According to Brooks, city officials "thought that because this was a predominantly minority area it was just junkies and welfare folks." Within the city, African American political power—and thus the power to pull in government funding—was based in Harlem. The only thing of note to come out of the Bronx was hip hop—and this hardly suggested a progressive political response. In the meantime, many of those that could afford to leave the Bronx did so.[44]

But Brooks decided to stay. With the help of neighbors and members of her church, she formed a tenants' association. "We started sweeping our own streets; we went into the backyards and pulled the garbage out." By the start of the 1980s, hers was the only inhabited block in the neighborhood. Brooks' group linked with other tenants groups in the Mid-Bronx. Their aim was simple—to create a safe and healthy neighborhood, "building by building, block by block." Because they were so desperate, someone suggested they call themselves the Desperadoes. The name stuck.

Brooks left her job to work full time for the desperadoes. With her trademark gardenia in her hair, she spent time—in her words—"skinnin' and grinnin'" with local officials. Using tax shelters and state subsidies for low-income housing projects, the Desperadoes worked with developers and financiers to rehabilitate four abandoned apartment blocks. Brooks hired local gangs to protect the new buildings. The Desperadoes screened applicants and arranged childcare facilities for new residents. As the Desperadoes proved their worth, the city government channeled millions of dollars into redevelopment. By the end of the century, the Desperadoes and similar groups in the Bronx had helped rebuild hundreds of apartments and homes for low-income families. In 1997, President Clinton made the now customary presidential pilgrimage to the Bronx. But this time it was a celebration. "If you can do it, everybody can," said Clinton.[45] The only disappointed people were Japanese holidaymakers on Fort Apache bus tours.

Three presidential visits and one Hollywood movie were unique for a ghetto. Few communities saw quite the change around in housing conditions either. Yet in many ways, Brooks' experience was emblematic of grassroots activism around the country. Older women often took the lead. The work focused on the most pressing community problems. The Desperadoes primary concern was housing. Around the country, local organizations sprung up for a wide range of issues: to fight drugs, to improve schools and hospitals, to demand childcare, to reform prisons, to change college curricula, to win compensation for displaced black farmers, to improve the environment, to protest negative black images in the media, or to gain fair access to mortgages. It was often painstakingly slow work. But the work of the Desperadoes showed that in the post–civil rights generation, there were still plenty of activists seeking a better life for people of color. Even in the Bronx.

From Race Rights to Human Rights: The Black Gay and Lesbian Movement

The struggle for racial equality in the Reagan years was not just diverse—it was divided. During the heyday of the civil rights movement, the leading black spokesmen (and they were mostly men) had campaigned for race rights. By the 1980s (in part because of the successes of the civil rights movement) many African Americans groups sought to broaden the struggle for equality to encompass a wide range of human rights. As black women, welfare workers, and other previously marginalized groups found their voice, they also challenged the right of the traditional civil rights leadership to speak on their behalf. This was particularly true in the struggle of lesbian and gay African Americans for acceptance and respect. By highlighting the question of sexuality, they also threatened the traditional civil rights leadership's long-cherished commitment to Christianity, the nuclear family, and sexual respectability.

During the civil rights movement of the 1960s, African American homosexuality had remained hidden from public view. Martin Luther King's colleague Bayard Rustin, Mississippi freedom fighter Aaron Henry, and many other civil rights figures were openly gay. But they had subordinated the issue of gay rights to the quest for civil rights. In any case, civil rights leaders were keen to keep the issue quiet. White supremacists tried to tarnish the civil rights movement with charges of homosexuality and promiscuity. James Forman, president of the Congress on Racial Equality (CORE), had made sure none of the freedom riders were gay.[46]

During the late 1980s, however, gay activists brought the issue to prominence. In part it was because black gay networks had more money than before (not least because black homosexuals were less likely to have dependents). In part it was because both the African American and gay rights movements had put the issues of race and sexuality in the public domain. Yet at the same time, neither of these movements sought to empower African American homosexuals. If anything, the end of the century saw a resurgence of homophobia from some influential African Americans. And rap artists declared gay men unmanly. Or as Ice Cube put it "Real niggers ain't faggots."

Above all, the horror of AIDS meant the issue was no longer one of recognition and respect, but of life and death. The first media reports of AIDS in the 1980s focused exclusively on white gay men. But the African American lesbian gay community soon realized that AIDS was very much a black disease. By the end of the century, one in two HIV-positive men was an African

American. It wasn't just a male disease either. Two in every three female victims were black. In response, black gay and victim support groups started lobbying for action, holding the first "National Conference on AIDS in the Black Community" in 1986.[47] At the local level, AIDS support centers sprung up, often in church offices, almost always run by women volunteers (women staffed most church programs, and many volunteers were related to AIDS sufferers). When basketball star Earvin "Magic" Johnson announced he had HIV in November 1991, the movement gained national publicity too.[48]

This grassroots campaign sought to influence two social movements. The white lesbian gay movement began to share some resources with African Americans. Meanwhile mainstream civil rights leaders belatedly began to address the issue. Yet at the close of the century, gay activists still felt they had a long way to go. In 2000, the campaigning journalist Earl Ofari Hutchinson wrote, "The national gay and lesbian publication, BLK, might as well gather dust in the Smithsonian Museum for all that most Blacks know or care to know of it."[49] Religious groups joined the fight against AIDS while refusing to accept the gay lifestyle—or as church leaders put it, they loved the sinner but not the sin. At the end of the century, polls showed a majority of African Americans still opposed gay marriage. Gil Gerald, executive director of the National Coalition of Black Lesbians and Gays, even questioned the integrity of mainstream civil rights leaders' support for AIDS relief. At a meeting in 1987 at the Office of Minority Health, Gerald became "convinced they were all a homophobic bunch of people who had come to the table for money." She cried out "Which one of you has ever held a person with AIDS in your hands, in your arms?" There was silence.[50]

* * *

In many ways, African American protest during the Reagan years stood in stark contrast to the civil rights movement. Well-known black Americans were more likely to be controversial artists than upstanding activists. Protest at the national level was mostly about defending earlier gains, rather than making advances; across the country there were many different voices rather than a single leader or agenda; and local struggles were incremental campaigns rather than set-piece confrontations. But this contrast was with the popular memory of the civil rights movement, rather than with the actual history of the long African American struggle for equality.[51] In fact, African American protest had been ever thus—in diverse ways and in diverse places in U.S. history, Africans Americans had sought to build a better life, and resist those who interfered. And during the Reagan years, they continued to do so.

Indeed, African American protest during the Reagan years was marked by proliferation as much as fragmentation. Community groups continued the fight to make rights real, and hitherto marginalized African American groups were able to assert their own agendas. (They would continue to do so in new ways into the 1990s and beyond—from the Million Man March, to the campaign against environmental racism, to the reparations movement.) In the end, the so-called Reagan revolution turned out to be anything but on the question of race—the Reagan administration did not consistently seek to reverse the legislative gains of the 1960s and 1970s, and where it did, it often found it lacked the power to do so.

Notes

1. They in turn drew on musical traditions from America and around the world. Flash was from the Caribbean, Bambaataa was inspired by Zulu history.
2. This was not the first time. In his last months, Martin Luther King complained bitterly about the Johnson administration, and in 1970, Bishop Stephen G. Spottswood, chairman of the NAACP board, accused Richard Nixon of adopting a "calculated policy to work against the needs and aspirations of the largest minority of its citizens."
3. Since the 1960s, the state had taken an active role in tackling discrimination and funding antipoverty measures. Most job gains, especially for black women, were in state sector work.
4. Bakari Kitwana, *Why White Kids Love Hip-Hop* (New York: Basic Books, 2005), 10.
5. Ibid., 53.
6. Angela Ards, "Organizing the Hip-Hop Generation," in Murray Forman and Mark Anthony Neal, eds., *That's the Joint! The Hip-Hop Studies Reader* (New York: Routledge, 2004), 315.
7. Pero Dagbovie, "Of All Our Studies, History is Best Qualified to Reward Our Research: Black History's Relevance to the Hip Hop Generation," *Journal of African American History*, Vol. 90 (June 2005), 299–323.
8. Jeff Chang, *Can't Stop, Won't Stop: A History of the Hip-Hop Generation* (London: Ebury Press, 2005), 210, 276.
9. Nancy Maclean, *Freedom is Not Enough: The Opening of the American Workplace* (Cambridge: Harvard University Press, 2007), 291.
10. See, e.g., Hugh Davis Graham and W. Elliot Brownlee, *The Reagan Presidency: Pragmatic Conservatism and its Legacies* (Lawrence: University Press of Kansas, 2003); John Skrentny, *The Minority Rights Revolution* (Cambridge: Harvard University Press, 2004).
11. Chang, *Can't Stop*, 247.
12. In 1990, Henry Louis Gates used this argument in various articles defending 2 Live Crew after the band's single, "Me So Horny," was blocked on charges of obscenity.
13. Ibid., 251, 397.
14. *Washington Post*, December 12, 1984.
15. *Washington Post*, November 27 1985; Evalyn Tennant, "Dismantling U.S.-Style Apartheid," *Colorlines*, Volume 7, Issue 1, April 30 2004, 10.
16. *Washington Post*, December 12, 1984.
17. http://www.ecu.edu/african/sersas/Papers/JohnsonTeklaAliSpring 2004 htm
18. Newsweek quotation in Evalyn Tennant, "Dismantling U.S.-Style Apartheid," *Colorlines* (Spring, 2004) downloaded from http://www.colorlines.com/article.php?ID=57&p=3.

19. Francis Njubi Nesbitt, *Race for Sanctions: African Americans against Apartheid, 1946–1994* (Bloomington: Indiana University Press, 2004), 127.
20. *Washington Post*, September 10, 1985.
21. *Washington Post*, November 29, 1984; December 3 1984.
22. *Washington Post*, December 12, 1984.
23. *Washington Post*, January 27, 1985.
24. Nesbitt, *Race for Sanctions*, 143.
25. Ibid., 143.
26. D. Michael Cheers "NELSON MANDELA: A Special Message to Black Americans," *Ebony*, May, 1990.
27. *Tri-State Defender*, Volume 35, Issue 21, June 18, 1986, 1.
28. *Washington Post*, December 23, 1984.
29. Nicolas Alexander, "Whatever Happened to the Free South Africa Movement?" *Third Force, Volume 1, Issue 1*, April 30, 1993, 9.
30. Nesbitt, *Race for Sanctions*, 151.
31. Alexander, "Whatever," 9.
32. *Time*, March 19, 1984.
33. Martin Luther King III reckoned "we're still dealing with the same old dog. The dog looks friendlier, but it's the same old dog." *Los Angeles Sentinel*, May 12, 1999.
34. Maclean, *Freedom*, 302.
35. Such as in *City of Richmond v. J.A. Croson Co.* (1989), 488 U.S. 469.
36. See, e.g., Robert M. Collins, *Transforming America: Politics and Culture during the Reagan Years* (New York: Columbia University Press, 2006).
37. Maclean, *Freedom*, 302, 308, 313.
38. John Jacob, *Columbus Times*, February 2, 1983.
39. Ron Daniels, *Michigan Citizen*, January 27, 1990.
40. *Washington Post*, January 28, 1987.
41. *Washington Post*, January 23, 1987.
42. *New York Times*, April 8, 1999.
43. Kendra Hamilton, "Activists for the New Millennium," *Black Issues in Higher Education*, Volume 20, Issue 5, April 24, 2003, 16
44. Alexander von Hoffman, *House by House, Block by Block: The Rebirth of America's Urban Neighborhoods* (New York: Oxford University Press, 2003), 31–62.
45. *New York Times*, July 25, 1986.
46. John Howard, *Men Like That: A Southern Queer History* (Chicago: University of Chicago Press, 1999).
47. Cathy Cohen, *The Boundaries of Blackness: AIDS and the Breakdown of Black Politics* (Chicago: University of Chicago Press, 1999), 96.
48. *USA Today*, June 11, 2001.
49. *New Pittsburgh Courier*, August 9, 2000.
50. Cohen, *The Boundaries*, 262.
51. See, e.g., John Dittmer, *Local People: The Struggle for Civil Rights in Mississippi* (Urbana: University of Illinois Press, 1995); and Stephen Tuck, *Beyond Atlanta: The Struggle for Racial Equality in Georgia, 1940–80* (Athens: University of Georgia Press, 2003).

Chapter 8

Reagan's Religious Right: The Unlikely Alliance between Southern Evangelicals and a California Conservative

Daniel K. Williams

When leaders of an emerging Christian Right began campaigning for Republican presidential candidate Ronald Reagan in 1980, some evangelicals expressed dismay at this seemingly incongruous alliance. Reagan, after all, was a divorced Hollywood actor who, as governor of California, had signed into law one of the nation's most liberal abortion bills only thirteen years earlier. Why would evangelicals who wanted to bring America back to "traditional values" campaign for a candidate whose cultural and political background reflected the influence of the secular forces that they denounced? "It would disturb me if there was a wedding between the religious fundamentalists and the political right," evangelist Billy Graham told *Parade* magazine in February 1981. "The hard right has no interest in religion except to manipulate it."[1]

Nevertheless, despite Graham's premonition, evangelicals' alliance with Ronald Reagan proved to be enduring. In 1980, 67 percent of white evangelical voters supported Reagan, and when he ran for reelection in 1984, that figure increased to 76 percent. By the time that Reagan left the White House, Christian Right leaders proclaimed him one of the nation's greatest presidents. "Ronald Reagan saved the country," Moral Majority founder Jerry Falwell told the press in 1988.[2]

Why did Falwell sing the praises of a man who seemingly had done so little for the Christian Right's cause? Had evangelicals who voted for Reagan in 1980 and 1984 been misled into supporting a secular conservative who was using religious rhetoric to manipulate their vote? Or were they instead voting for a man who provided a crucial catalyst to the Christian Right? Even if Reagan failed to deliver on social conservatives' legislative agenda, the Christian Right achieved political prominence during his presidency, and it did so partly because of his actions.[3] While some may have thought it incongruous for conservative evangelicals to ally themselves so closely with a non-evangelical president whose political priorities were largely secular, the relationship between Reagan and the Christian Right was based on a broader array of shared values than most people realized, and it benefited conservative Christians as much as it did the president.

But although Reagan eventually became a hero to the Christian Right, he did not begin his political career by kowtowing to social conservatives. As governor of California from 1967 to 1975, he combined rhetorical attacks on "big government" with a moderately libertarian approach to some issues of sexual morality. In 1967, he ignored the antiabortion protestations of Catholic clergy and signed into law an abortion liberalization measure that allowed women to obtain abortions for health-related reasons. Similarly, in 1978, after he left the governorship, Reagan again offended social conservatives by publicly repudiating an antigay rights state referendum that would have made it illegal for homosexuals to teach in California's public schools. Jerry Falwell, who had traveled to California to campaign for the referendum, said that because Reagan seemed to favor gay rights, he would "have to face the music from Christian voters two years from now" in his bid for the White House.[4]

Nevertheless, despite Reagan's moderately libertarian positions on abortion and gay rights—the two issues that later became the Christian Right's chief concerns—some of his other policy proposals won him support from social conservatives. Many of the nation's white evangelical leaders lauded Reagan's stance on racial issues, tax policy, and social welfare spending. In addition, they welcomed the rare occasions when the California conservative explicitly endorsed their pet causes, such as classroom prayer in public schools. Although his church attendance was somewhat sporadic and was confined entirely to mainline Protestant, rather than evangelical, denominations, Reagan occasionally discussed his religious faith with the press. In 1967, he convened a prayer breakfast at which he told the assembled pastors that "trusting in God for guidance will be an integral part of my [gubernatorial] administration."[5]

When Reagan challenged President Gerald Ford for the Republican presidential nomination in 1976, he relied heavily on the support of conservative evangelicals who were disappointed with Ford's lackluster record on social issues. First Lady Betty Ford had outraged many social conservatives in 1975 by announcing that she would not find it disconcerting if her children smoked marijuana or had premarital sex. In contrast, Reagan, who realized the appeal that a socially conservative message had for many Americans, used an interview with an evangelical talk show host in the summer of 1976 to proclaim his devotion to traditional morality. Marijuana, he said, should remain illegal. Likewise, state governments should resist the trend to repeal laws against homosexuality, because sexual "immorality" contradicted God's "higher natural law." And even though he had signed an abortion rights bill nine years earlier, he assured potential supporters that he was now firmly pro-life. "You cannot interrupt a pregnancy without taking a human life," he said.[6]

Reagan's support for traditional moral values appealed to Republican social conservatives who had already volunteered for his presidential campaign because of their interest in his broader conservative platform. His delegates at the 1976 Republican National Convention included several fundamentalists from Bob Jones University, as well as leading evangelicals such as Christian singer Pat Boone, head of California Christians Active Politically. "God is working in the political process here," Boone told his fellow Republican delegates at the convention.[7]

After Reagan's successful appeal to evangelicals in 1976, he tried a similar strategy in 1980. Reagan's advisors made an effort to retain evangelical support, because they feared that without a high turnout from the Christian Right, their candidate would have difficulty winning a national election, even in a contest against the unpopular Democratic incumbent president, Jimmy Carter. The Republican Party was in difficult straits. Although Republicans had picked up seats in Congress in the midterm elections of 1978, the GOP had not controlled either the House or the Senate in more than twenty years. The Watergate scandal had tarred the Republican Party as the party of corruption, and the last Republican president, Gerald Ford, had lost his bid for reelection. At a time when the GOP seemed to be hemorrhaging at its base, Republican strategists were delighted to learn that several conservative Protestant preachers were moving into Reagan's camp, though the deputy director of the Republican National Committee conceded in July 1980 that the party's newly created alliance with southern evangelicals was "not yet a marriage made in heaven." But as one Republican senator said, "When you're as distinct a minority as we are, you welcome anything short of the National Order of Child Molesters."[8]

If Reagan needed evangelical support to carry the South and defeat Carter, evangelicals had an even greater need of Reagan. For the previous four years, conservative evangelical leaders had felt alienated from the federal government. Many of them had hoped that Carter would restore a socially conservative vision to the nation, but instead, they had watched in dismay as the federal government did nothing to stop the nation's rising abortion rate and the flood of municipal gay rights ordinances. Despite Carter's Southern Baptist faith, he showed little interest in endorsing public school prayer, appointing evangelicals to administrative positions, or speaking out against abortion, pornography, and gay rights. As a result, evangelicals began looking for a candidate who would champion their vision of America and give them a voice in Washington.[9]

Evangelicals were delighted to find that Reagan shared their view of America as a divinely chosen nation destined for greatness. Conservative evangelical leaders believed that the solution to all of America's national problems of the late 1970s—the "malaise" of stagflation, high oil prices, the Iran hostage crisis, and the nation's foreign policy failures—was national moral revival coupled with faith in God and country. In an age of increasing national cynicism, conservative evangelicals remained fiercely patriotic. For four years prior to the presidential election of 1980, Falwell had taken a group of Christian college singers on tour to conduct patriotic "I Love America" rallies on the steps of state capitol buildings. He proudly wore pins bearing the image of the American flag, and he frequently spoke of his hope that America could once again become a great nation because of its Christian heritage. "Unlike any other nation, America is a nation under God," Falwell said.[10]

Reagan shared evangelicals' belief that the nation had experienced a moral crisis and was now ready for revival. "There has been a wave of humanism and hedonism in the land..." the former governor said in 1976. "However, I am optimistic because I sense in this land a great revolution against that...The people of this country are not beyond redemption. They are good people and believe this nation has a destiny as yet unfulfilled."[11] Reagan was fond of quoting Puritan forebear John Winthrop's claim that America was a "shining city upon a hill" with a unique mission to be a "beacon" of liberty in a world wracked by tyranny. "Can we doubt that only a Divine Providence placed this land, this island of freedom, here as a refuge for all those people in the world who yearn to breathe freely?" Reagan asked in his acceptance speech at the Republican National Convention.[12] When Reagan's campaign popularized the slogan "Let's Make America Great Again," evangelicals were ready to give a hearty amen.

Reagan and his evangelical allies believed that national "redemption" would require a stronger military in order to defend against "godless" Communism. When Reagan told the National Association of Evangelicals in 1983 that the Soviet Union was an "evil empire," he echoed what Billy Graham had been saying since 1949, when the preacher had called Communism an "anti-God colossus."[13] In contrast to his recent predecessors in the White House, Reagan had long viewed America's conflict with the Soviet Union as a battle between good and evil. In October 1964, the same month in which a nationally syndicated, fundamentalist radio preacher was telling his supporters that the nation could either choose to "save freedom" or give in to "Satanic Communism," Reagan had told Americans that they faced a choice between giving in to the Soviet Union and facing "a thousand years of darkness" or preserving "for our children this, the last best hope of man on Earth."[14] In his speech at the Republican National Convention in 1976, he had echoed the same theme, and had said that America faced the choice between surrendering to Communist totalitarianism or standing up for freedom with the help of a strong military. Three years later, as he launched his presidential campaign, he again spoke of the need to stand up to the USSR. "Negotiation with the Soviet Union must never become appeasement," he warned.[15]

Reagan's promise to take a hard line against the Soviet Union was especially appealing to conservative evangelicals when he ran for president in 1980, because they had spent the previous year lobbying against President Carter's Strategic Arms Limitation Treaty (SALT II), which they claimed was biased in favor of the Soviets. Christian Voice, a California-based Religious Right organization, warned in late 1979 that "SALT compromises

America in favor of Communists," while Jerry Falwell, who founded the Moral Majority only months before the Senate was scheduled to vote on SALT II, said that if the treaty were ratified, "one day the Russians may pick up the telephone and call Washington, D.C., and dictate the terms of our surrender to them."[16] Falwell was still making alleged appeasement of the Soviet Union a central theme in his preaching in the spring of 1980, when Reagan was trying to reach out to the evangelical constituency in his quest to win the Republican presidential nomination. "The Soviets only understand one language, and that's a loaded gun," the Baptist pastor told a crowd in Tallahassee, Florida, in early March 1980, one week before the state's presidential primary.[17] Reagan's rhetoric against the Soviet Union was not as baldly militaristic as Falwell's, but it expressed the same sentiments. During the same month in which Falwell spoke in Tallahassee, Reagan gave speeches castigating the Carter administration for its foreign policy of "vacillation, appeasement, and aimlessness," and reiterated his promise to increase defense spending if elected.[18]

Reagan realized the appeal that his views on defense policy had among conservative Protestants, which was why he reserved some of his strongest rhetoric against the Soviet Union for southern evangelical audiences. When he spoke at Bob Jones University in January 1980, in preparation for the South Carolina primary, he devoted much of his speech to a denunciation of SALT II and a proposal for an escalation in military spending in order to defend against the "godless tyranny of communism."[19] Reagan's attempt to appeal to conservative Protestants by casting the Cold War in religious terms did not begin with his well-known evil empire speech at the National Association of Evangelicals' annual meeting in 1983; it started on the campaign trail.

Many evangelicals also appreciated Reagan's support for limits on federal power, because they, like the California conservative, distrusted the government. Their experiences with federal authority during the Carter administration had been mostly negative. In 1977, they rallied against the International Women's Year Conferences, which had received federal funding and the endorsement of the Carter White House. In 1978, Christian school advocates led a lobbying campaign against a proposed policy of the Internal Revenue Service that would have denied tax exemptions to private schools failing to meet federal standards for racial integration. In 1979, conservative evangelicals rallied to the defense of a Texas Baptist preacher who had his preaching program cancelled by a Dallas television station because of concerns that its antigay content violated the Federal Communications Commission's equal time policy. Reagan echoed the sentiments of disaffected evangelicals when he accused the government of trying "to inject itself between parent and child." "Over the last two or three decades the Federal Government seems to have forgotten both 'that old time religion' and that old time Constitution," Reagan told religious conservatives in August 1980. As president, he promised to "keep government out of the school and the neighborhood; and above all—the home."[20]

Although he did not make social issues his main platform, Reagan endorsed conservative evangelicals' moral views, just as he had in 1976. In the late 1970s, many conservative evangelicals had become active in single-issue campaigns against abortion, the Equal Rights Amendment (ERA), gay rights, and pornography, but to their dismay, President Carter appeared to be on the "wrong" side of every one of these issues. Reagan, on the other hand, campaigned as a pro-life candidate, and his campaign aides directed the Republican National Committee to rescind the party's traditional support for the ERA. While Reagan had occasionally taken libertarian stances on social issues in the past, he made it a point to meet with pro-life activists in New Hampshire in January 1980 in order to assure conservative Republican primary voters that he was now a true believer in their cause. Conservative evangelicals believed him when he promised to toe the conservative line on such issues in the future, and they told their supporters that Reagan was a Christian Right candidate who would enact the moral legislation that they demanded. "I want a President who will give us prayer in the schools," one evangelical who volunteered for the Reagan campaign told a reporter while handing out "Reagan for President" leaflets in San Antonio. "I want a President who opposes drafting women, homosexual rights, the equal rights amendment, abortion. I want to get back to the original concepts on which this country was founded."[21]

Despite Reagan's willingness to embrace social conservatism, some of his campaign aides insisted that their candidate did not have any special affinity for the Christian Right. "It's a group of people that Reagan's not going to ignore, but they're certainly not going to dictate to him," policy advisor Martin Anderson told the press in April 1980.[22] Yet as the campaign continued, it became harder to insist that Reagan had only minimal ties to his evangelical supporters. In August 1980, he appeared with Jerry Falwell, Southern Baptist Convention president Bailey Smith, and other leading pastors and religious broadcasters at a Christian Right rally in Dallas, where he told the fifteen thousand evangelicals who had assembled to hear him, "I know you can't endorse me. But I want you to know that I endorse you and what you are doing."[23] The pastors loved it. Ed McAteer, the Southern Baptist conservative activist who had organized the rally, told the press the following month, "This movement will put Ronald Reagan in office."[24]

As Election Day approached, the relationship between Reagan and the Christian Right became even closer. In October, Reagan spoke at a meeting of the National Association of Religious Broadcasters and visited Falwell's Liberty Baptist College in Lynchburg, Virginia. Earlier in the year, he had confined his remarks at meetings with evangelicals mainly to his views on defense policy and school prayer, areas in which he was able to find common ground with religious conservatives. But by the last two months of the campaign, he was ready to go beyond these issues in an effort to emphasize his affinity for the Christian Right. He surprised the press by questioning Darwinian evolution, which he claimed was "theory only," and said that if public school teachers taught their students about evolution, then "the biblical theory of creation...should also be taught." Reagan assured his evangelical supporters that he welcomed religious influence in public affairs. "I would use...the bully pulpit, for whatever good it could do in establishing or maintaining the basic values upon which I think our civilization and this country are based," he promised. "I believe deeply that this is a nation under God."[25]

Reagan's public depiction of his personal faith seemed to become more evangelical as his presidential campaign continued. For much of his adult life, his religious beliefs had included a faith in the power of prayer and an interest in end-times theology, but he was not overtly pious, and he gave less than 2 percent of his annual income to charity. Thus, it came as no surprise early in the campaign when Reagan stumbled over a reporter's question about whether he had been "born-again," and argued that his adolescent baptism in the mainline Protestant Disciples of Christ denomination could be equated with an evangelical conversion experience. Yet by the end of the summer, Reagan seemed eager to trumpet the credos of conservative Protestantism. Like evangelicals, he claimed that the Bible offered solutions to every problem. "It is an incontrovertible fact that all the complex and horrendous questions confronting us at home and worldwide have their answers in that single book," he told a group of Christian conservatives in August 1980.[26]

Evangelicals seized on Reagan's religious statements and portrayed the candidate as a born-again, true believer. The Christian Right organization Christians for Reagan sent copies of the book *Reagan: A Man of Faith* to evangelicals throughout the country. When D. James Kennedy, a member of Moral Majority's executive board, introduced Reagan at an evangelical gathering, he focused his remarks on Reagan's faith. "Here is a man who believes that Word, who trusts in the living God and his Son Jesus Christ," Kennedy said.[27]

As a strong admirer of Reagan, Falwell was so concerned about the outcome of the presidential election of 1980 that in addition to engineering a voter registration effort that he claimed resulted in several million new evangelical voters, he issued a national appeal for a day of fasting and prayer for God to give America "the president He wants us to have."[28] When Reagan won the election, Falwell was sure that the prayer had been answered. Christian Right leaders heralded the Republican candidate's victory as a triumph for religious conservatives and an opportunity for the Moral Majority to effect its political agenda. Calling Reagan's election "the greatest day for the cause of conservatism and American morality in my adult life," Falwell promised that "the '80s is the decade in which this country is going to have a moral rebirth."[29]

But in spite of Falwell's hope for a Reagan-led moral revival, the president showed little interest in the Christian Right's social legislative proposals during his first year in office, and instead focused his attention on tax cuts and fiscal policy. Senate majority leader Howard Baker told Christian Right leaders that their favorite issues, such as school prayer and abortion legislation, would have to wait until 1982.[30] When New Right activist Paul Weyrich, who had been instrumental in helping Falwell launch the Moral Majority, warned George Bush that he personally needed to endorse the Christian Right's view on abortion and school prayer if the administration wanted to count on the support of social conservatives, Bush brusquely dismissed the admonition, "I am not intimidated by those who suggest I better hew the line," he said. "Hell with them."[31]

In contrast to his vice president, Reagan at least claimed to listen to evangelicals' concerns. He gave conservative evangelicals a few appointments in his administration, including one position in the Cabinet when he selected the devout charismatic Christian James Watt as his secretary of the interior. Robert Billings, the executive director of the Moral Majority, became assistant to the secretary of education, while C. Everett Koop, a Presbyterian elder who had become a hero in the evangelical world for co-producing the pro-life film *Whatever Happened to the Human Race?* was Reagan's choice for surgeon general. At lower levels of the administration, pro-life leaders such as Marjory Mecklenburg, and future Christian Right activists such as Gary Bauer, also found policymaking or advisory positions. This represented a larger share of presidential appointments than conservative evangelicals had had in the Carter or Ford administrations, but some members of the Christian Right felt cheated when they learned that secular conservatives and "old guard" Republicans would receive all of the top positions in the Cabinet. Rather than celebrating his co-religionists' newfound access to the White House, Billings found himself having to reassure evangelicals in early 1981 that the Reagan administration had not forgotten them. "There are a lot of good people being put into positions, not at the Cabinet level but behind the scenes—the kind of people who love our ways," he told the National Association of Religious Broadcasters in January 1981.[32]

Billings's exhortation to evangelicals to maintain their faith in the Reagan administration reflected the view of most Christian Right leaders, especially Falwell, who supported the president even when it appeared that he was acting contrary to the wishes of religious conservatives. Reagan's nomination of Sandra Day O'Connor to a seat on the Supreme Court in the summer of 1981 tested the alliance between the president and social conservatives, but in spite of Falwell's misgivings about the nomination, he was unwilling to break with the president on the issue. Although he at first expressed doubts about O'Connor's position on abortion and called her nomination a "disaster" that would offend "good Christians," he fell into line behind the president as soon as he received a call from Reagan assuring him of the wisdom of the choice. While the Senate debated her confirmation, Falwell remained neutral on the question, and reiterated his support for the president. Reagan, the Baptist televangelist said, was "the greatest President we've had in my lifetime and history may say the greatest President ever."[33]

On the two issues that were of greatest concern to Falwell—abortion and school prayer—he was willing to settle for rhetorical support from Reagan, rather than substantive leadership. In 1982, Reagan endorsed congressional proposals that would have enshrined the right to school prayer in the Constitution and rescinded *Roe v. Wade* by prohibiting most abortions. That same year, he dispatched Vice President Bush to the Southern Baptist Convention to assure evangelicals of the administration's support for their political program. As Southern Baptists passed resolutions supporting constitutional amendment proposals pertaining to school prayer and abortion—votes that were timed to coincide with the president's socially conservative legislative proposals on those issues—Bush stood beside Billy Graham on the platform at the New Orleans Superdome and told the Baptists that the Christian Right movement was "an essentially healthy development."[34] Christian conservatives could perhaps be forgiven for assuming at that point that the president was fully committed to their agenda. Yet rather than risk his own reputation to secure such legislation, Reagan encouraged the Christian Right to lobby for the bills on his behalf, thus preserving his own political capital for initiatives that he considered of greater importance while simultaneously securing the loyalty of conservative evangelicals who were now using his name in their advertising. Falwell acquiesced to this arrangement, because he was delighted to be able to tell his supporters that the White House was on his side. "The President himself has asked our immediate help," Falwell told his supporters in an election-year fund-raising letter that highlighted Reagan's support for the school prayer initiative. "Of course, we cannot fail our President—and we certainly cannot fail our children and our children's children... This may very well be the *last* opportunity we will *ever* have to return the freedom of speech and freedom of religion to our little children."[35]

When Christian conservatives realized that Reagan had done little to shepherd the proposed school prayer and antiabortion constitutional amendments through Congress and had instead been content to let the bills languish in committee, they grumbled about his lack of effort on behalf of moral legislation, but they continued to insist that they were "deeply appreciative" of their president. During Reagan's reelection campaign of 1984, they avoided mentioning their dissatisfaction with the lack of attention that he had given their causes, and instead trumpeted the symbolic gestures that he had made toward their movement. They celebrated the fact that Reagan had allowed a religious publisher to issue the pro-life book *Abortion and the Conscience of a Nation*, in 1984, and they were also delighted when his secretary of health and human services, Richard Schweiker, addressed the March for Life on the Washington Mall. Social conservatives could take comfort in the knowledge that if Reagan's actions on behalf of their causes seemed tepid, he was at least willing to give abortion restriction and school prayer more rhetorical support than they had received from previous presidents. He spoke at national evangelical conventions at several points during his presidency, and each time, he gave Christian conservatives reason to believe that he supported their view of the place of religion in the nation's public life. And occasionally, he gave conservative evangelicals small legislative victories, such as budget cuts for family planning initiatives or passage of the Adolescent Family Life Act, which provided federal funding for abstinence-based sex education programs. The Reagan administration's drug war also earned strong commendations from leaders in the Christian Right, because it epitomized their quest for a social moral order.[36]

But ultimately, Reagan retained the support of Christian conservatives not because of his stances on social issues, but because of his view of America's place in the world. Reagan's views on foreign policy had formed the central component of some of his earliest, most successful speeches to members of the emerging Christian Right during his presidential campaign in 1980, and he continued to highlight those themes in public addresses during his first term in office. In 1980, he had attracted the support of Falwell and other Christian Right leaders because he opposed SALT II; in 1983, he retained their support by opposing a nuclear freeze. While liberal Protestant and Catholic clergy favored restrictions on the development of nuclear weapons, many conservative evangelical pastors feared that any arms reductions would make the nation more vulnerable to communist takeover. Thus, when Reagan promised to maintain his hard-line policy toward the Soviet Union and oppose a suggested freeze on nuclear weapons development, Christian Right leaders enthusiastically supported his stance. Falwell embarked on a public campaign against the "freezeniks," and argued that defense policy, an area in which he wholeheartedly supported Reagan, was more vital to the nation's well-being than the social issues that had been the centerpiece of the Moral Majority's earlier political efforts. "The debates over school prayer, abortion, and homosexuality are not as important as one issue that has recently loomed before us," Falwell said in 1983. "If our country is militarily overshadowed by the Soviet Union, I believe that we will not have the opportunity for free and open debate about these or any other issues for long."[37]

Predicting that the nuclear freeze would be the most important political issue in the election of 1984, Falwell prepared to do whatever was necessary to assure Reagan's reelection. He organized voter registration drives, advised the Republican Party's platform committee, and warned his supporters about the alleged dangers of electing Democrats to high office. "As it now stands, the Democratic party is basically controlled by the radical ideas of a dangerous minority—homosexuals, militant feminists, socialists, freezeniks, and others of the ilk," Falwell said, in the midst of the election.[38]

Falwell was not the only evangelical who felt this way. Reagan's actions during his first term in office prompted a realignment in party identification among the nation's conservative evangelicals, especially in the South. While only 29 percent of Southern Baptist pastors were registered Republicans in 1980, by 1984, 66 percent of them were.[39] But Falwell hoped that that percentage would increase still further. As Reagan prepared for his reelection campaign, he and his fellow Christian Right leader Tim LaHaye launched a voter registration drive that they hoped would bring more than one million new voters into the Reagan camp. "This President has done more to advance traditional moral values and to return our nation to those values than any President in my lifetime," LaHaye said in justifying his unprecedented partisan endorsement of Reagan.[40] Other evangelicals concurred. Reagan was "probably the most evangelical president we have had since the founding fathers," Pat Robertson declared two months before the election of 1984.[41]

Realizing that the Christian Right's influence depended partly on its relationship with the president, Falwell frequently highlighted his close association with Reagan in his televised sermons and fund-raising appeals. Once, in the midst of a typical discussion about the need to lobby the president for a particular piece of legislation that the Christian Right favored, Falwell pointed out that his connection to the executive office guaranteed his supporters an influence on the president that they would have been unable to gain on their own. "If you send this kind of a letter in the mail to the White House, it is usually answered by a member of the staff; and the President may never even know that it has arrived," Falwell wrote in a direct mail appeal. "But I believe that, if I personally deliver your letter and the letters of other Moral Majority friends, it will get President Reagan's undivided attention."[42] In 1985, after Falwell had already lost his fights for constitutional amendments on abortion and school prayer, he continued to reassure his supporters that the president was listening to his concerns. "Over the last four years I have met with Ronald Reagan many times," Falwell said. "And I have found that he and I share a deep commitment to bringing moral values back into public life."[43]

During Reagan's second term, the Christian Right's support for the president grew stronger, even during the politically contentious Iran–Contra scandal. When congressional Democrats held hearings to investigate the actions of Lt. Col. Oliver North, the Marine commander accused of illegally aiding Nicaraguan contras on behalf of the Reagan administration, Falwell solicited contributions for a defense fund on his behalf and collected two million petitions from his supporters to demand that Congress clear the lieutenant colonel of all charges. To conservative evangelicals, North was a "brave American hero," because he had aided the "freedom fighters" in Nicaragua who were allegedly defending their nation against communism.[44]

Christian Right activists idolized Reagan as a hard-line anticommunist, but faced a dilemma during Reagan's second term when he engaged in arms control talks with Soviet president Mikhail Gorbachev. Although conservative evangelicals abhorred the idea of signing arms limitation treaties with the Soviet Union, they did not want to criticize a president whom they viewed as a strong ally. Thus, even though they questioned Reagan's judgment in meeting with Gorbachev and condemned the Intermediate-Range Nuclear Forces (INF) Treaty that he signed, they directed their criticism not toward Reagan, but toward Democrats in the Senate who had voted to ratify the treaty; their admiration for their president remained as strong as ever.[45] A few months after the treaty's ratification, conservative evangelicals such as Falwell devoted another election cycle to campaigning for Republican candidates. In November 1988, 81 percent of white evangelical voters cast their ballots for George Bush, an action that reflected their continued loyalty to the Reagan administration despite their lack of enthusiasm for Bush himself.[46]

As some non-evangelical conservatives surveyed this situation, they concluded that Reagan had hoodwinked the Christian Right, and that evangelicals who had allied with Reagan had received nothing in exchange for their support. "The religious right was sweet-talked in 1981," New Right activist Paul Weyrich said in 1984. "The Reagan Administration told us that we should wait our turn because saving the economy was more important than saving babies. The religious right bought that line and let the issues go on the back burners." New Right fundraiser Richard Viguerie concurred. "They have bought the symbolism," he said. "But they can get more, and they have a right to more."[47]

But perhaps in reality, the Christian Right had received what it had wanted from Reagan. By supporting Reagan even when he failed to deliver on the evangelical agenda, conservative Christian activists proved their loyalty to the Republican Party and acquired the political experience necessary to obtain greater control over the GOP. By the time that Reagan left the White House, Christian Right leaders had gained enough political stature through their association with the president that they were able to begin shaping their party's platform and running for office themselves. Deputy Undersecretary of Education Gary Bauer left his position in the Reagan administration to direct the Family Research Council, which became one of the nation's leading Christian Right organizations in the 1990s and early twenty-first century. James Dobson, the founder of Focus on the Family and one of the most influential Christian Right leaders at the beginning of the twenty-first century, gained some of his earliest political experience on an anti-pornography panel appointed by Attorney General Edwin Meese.[48] Even before Reagan left office, the Christian Right was already deriving benefits from the media exposure that it received as a result of its association with the president. Religious broadcaster Pat Robertson's campaign for the Republican presidential nomination in 1988, and his ability to finish second in the Iowa caucuses and win delegates in several other states, would have been inconceivable without the institutional relationship that conservative evangelicals developed with the Republican Party during the Reagan years. Nor could Ralph Reed have engineered such an effective takeover of several state Republican parties during the early 1990s if conservative evangelicals had not already embraced Reagan as a political hero.

In Reagan, Christian Right activists found a president who proclaimed their vision of an anticommunist, Christian nation. Though his actions did not always accord with the sentiments he expressed in his speeches, the rhetoric alone was enough to attract media attention to their cause and give them the institutional support that they needed to acquire a wider influence in the nation's public life. When Falwell called Reagan the "finest president since Lincoln," he was not engaging in flattery or naïve adulation, but was instead acknowledging his sincere appreciation of a man who had been partly responsible for the Christian Right's prominence in the Republican Party.[49] Perhaps, in the end, conservative evangelicals' decision to ally with Reagan was a shrewder move than it had initially seemed.

Notes

1. Marguerite Michaels, "America is not God's Only Kingdom," *Parade*, February 1, 1981, 6.
2. Corwin Smidt, "Evangelicals and the 1984 Election: Continuity or Change?" *American Politics Quarterly*, 15 (1987): 431; Mike Anderson, "Falwell's Retirement from Politics is Short," *Lynchburg News and Daily Advance*, August 18, 1988. Some polls estimated that 81 percent of white evangelical voters cast their ballots for Reagan in 1984 (Erling Jorstad, *The New Christian Right, 1981–1988: Prospects for the Post-Reagan Decade* [Lewiston, NY: Edwin Mellen, 1987], 144).
3. Several historians and biographers, including James Patterson, John Ehrman, and Lou Cannon, have correctly pointed out Reagan's lack of attention to the Christian Right's legislative program. See James T. Patterson, *Restless Giant: The United States from Watergate to Bush v. Gore* (New York: Oxford University Press, 2005), 177; John Ehrman, *The Eighties: America in the Age of Reagan* (New Haven, CT: Yale University Press, 2005), 178; and Lou Cannon, *President Reagan: The Role of a Lifetime* (New York: Simon and Schuster, 1991), 812–813.
4. "Bishops Fight Changes in State Abortion Law," *San Francisco Chronicle*, December 8, 1966; "Right to Life League: Abortion Foes Open Campaign Here," *San Francisco Chronicle*, April 20, 1967; Michael D. Lopez, "Evangelist Helps Raise a Hope, a Prayer and Money for Prop. 6," *San Diego Union*, October 31, 1978. For information on Reagan's decision to sign an abortion reform bill in 1967, see Lou Cannon, *Governor Reagan: His Rise to Power* (New York: Public Affairs, 2003), 213.
5. Donald H. Gill, "Will the Bible Get Back into School?" *Eternity*, May 1964, 10; Bill Rose, "Reagan Charts Course," *Oakland (CA) Tribune*, March 25, 1967.
6. UPI, "Betty Ford Would Accept 'An Affair' by Daughter," *New York Times*, August 11, 1975; O.B. Baker, "White House Evil," *Baptist Examiner*, September 27, 1975, 1, "Abortion" folder, G. Archer Weniger Files, J.S. Mack Library, Bob Jones University, Greenville, SC; "Reagan on God and Morality," *Christianity Today*, July 2, 1976, 39–40.
7. Tim Miller and Tonda Rush, "God and the GOP in Kansas City," *Christianity Today*, September 10, 1976, 59.
8. Lisa Myers, "The Christian Right: New Wave in Politics," *Washington Star*, July 7, 1980; Bruce Nesmith, *The New Republican Coalition: The Reagan Campaigns and White Evangelicals* (New York: Peter Lang, 1994), 40.
9. James Mann, "Preachers in Politics: Decisive Force in '80?" *U.S. News and World Report*, September 15, 1980, 24.
10. Rosemary Thomson, "Jerry Falwell: 'Let's Love America,'" *Christian Life*, September 1980, 37.
11. "Reagan on God and Morality," 39.
12. Ronald Reagan, "We Will be a City Upon a Hill," Conservative Political Action Conference, January 25, 1974 (http://www.american-partisan.com/cols/reagan1974.htm); Ronald Reagan, "Farewell Address," January 11, 1989 (http://www.reaganlegacy.org/speeches/); John F. Stacks, *Watershed: The Campaign for the Presidency, 1980* (New York: Times Books, 1981), 194.
13. Ronald Reagan, Address to the Annual Meeting of the National Association of Evangelicals, March 8, 1983 (www.americanrhetoric.com/speeches/

ronaldreaganevilempire.htm); Sara Diamond, *Roads to Dominion: Right-Wing Movements and Political Power in the United States* (New York: Guilford Press, 1995), 100.

14. Billy James Hargis, "A Communist World: Must it Be?" *Christian Crusade*, October 1964, 34; Ronald Reagan, "A Time for Choosing," October 27, 1964 (http://www.reaganlegacy.org/speeches/).
15. Ronald Reagan, "Intent to Run for President," New York, November 13, 1979 (http://www.reaganfoundation.org/reagan/speeches/speech.asp?spid=4).
16. Jerry Falwell, Moral Majority Direct Mailing (1979), "Moral Majority" folder, Weniger Files, BJU; Robert Lindsey, "Fundamentalist Christian Unity in Politics Sought," *New York Times*, September 20, 1979.
17. David Finkel, "Hundreds Praise Preacher's Prayer," *Tallahassee Democrat*, March 4, 1980.
18. Steven V. Roberts, "Reagan, in Chicago Speech, Urges Big Increases in Military Spending," *New York Times*, March 18, 1980.
19. Sally Saunders, "Reagan Agrees to Debate in State," *Greenville News*, January 31, 1980.
20. William Martin, *With God on our Side: The Rise of the Religious Right in America* (New York: Broadway Books, 1996), 168–199; David E. Rosenbaum, "Conservatives Embrace Reagan on Social Issues," *New York Times*, April 21, 1980; Howell Raines, "Reagan Backs Evangelicals in their Political Activities," *New York Times*, August 23, 1980; Helen Parmley, "Religious Conservatives Launch Bid to Influence Presidential Politics," Religious News Service, August 25, 1980, "Moral Majority" folder, Weniger Files, BJU.
21. Rosemary Thomson, *Withstanding Humanism's Challenge to Families: Anatomy of a White House Conference* (Morton, IL: Traditional Publications, 1981), 139, 141; Rosenbaum, "Conservatives Embrace Reagan."
22. Rosenbaum, "Conservatives Embrace Reagan."
23. Bruce Buursma, "Evangelicals Give Reagan a 'Non-partisan' Stump," *Christianity Today*, September 19, 1980, 50.
24. James Mann, "Preachers in Politics: Decisive Force in '80?" *U.S. News and World Report*, September 15, 1980, 24.
25. Anthony Lewis, "Religion and Politics," *New York Times*, September 18, 1980; Rosenbaum, "Conservatives Embrace Reagan."
26. Gary Scott Smith, *Faith and the Presidency: From George Washington to George W. Bush* (New York: Oxford University Press, 2006), 331–336; Phil Gailey, "Charitably Speaking," *New York Times*, January 22, 1982; Raines, "Reagan Backs Evangelicals."
27. Buursma, "Evangelicals Give Reagan," 50.
28. Transcript of Jerry Falwell, Old Time Gospel Hour Broadcast, September 21, 1980, OTGH 418, FM 3–5, Liberty University Archives, Lynchburg, VA.
29. Kenneth A. Briggs, "Dispute on Religion Raised by Campaign," *New York Times*, November 9, 1980; Marjorie Hyer, "'Christian Right' Optimistic: Seeking a Born-Again America," *San Francisco Chronicle*, January 31, 1981. See also, "Moral Majority: Here to Stay," *Evangelical Review* (April 1981), 4, for evidence that the Christian Right interpreted Reagan's election as a divine blessing.
30. Matthew C. Moen, *The Christian Right and Congress* (Tuscaloosa: University of Alabama Press, 1989), 100.

31. Edwin Warner, "New Resolve by the New Right," *Time*, December 8, 1980, 27.
32. Smith, *Faith and the Presidency*, 339; Michelle McKeegan, *Abortion Politics: Mutiny in the Ranks of the Right* (New York: Free Press, 1992), 66–67; Marjorie Hyer, "'Christian Right' Optimistic: Seeking a Born-Again America," *San Francisco Chronicle*, January 31, 1981.
33. Jon Margolis, "The American Conservatives' Two Faces," *Chicago Tribune*, July 12, 1981; Adam Clymer, "Right Wing Seeks a Shift by Reagan," *New York Times*, September 6, 1981, 20.
34. "Bush Lauds Christians' Role," *New York Times*, June 14, 1982; Baptist Press, "Bush Endorses Religious Right," *Southern Baptist Advocate*, August/September 1982, 4.
35. Howell Raines, "Reagan Endorses Voluntary Prayer," *New York Times*, May 7, 1982; Jerry Falwell, Direct Mail, February 29, 1984, "Moral Majority—School Prayer, Feb. / March 1984" folder, People for the American Way, Washington, D.C.
36. Ronald S. Godwin, "Symbols Wear Thin," *Moral Majority Report*, August 1982, 2; Charles Austin, "Religious Right Growing Impatient with Reagan," *New York Times*, August 16, 1982; Ronald Reagan, *Abortion and the Conscience of a Nation* (Nashville: Thomas Nelson, 1984); McKeegan, *Abortion Politics*, 66; Smith, *Faith and the Presidency*, 593; Jerry Falwell, Moral Majority direct mail, September 2, 1986, folder 4, MOR 1–5, Liberty University Archives, Lynchburg, VA.
37. Jerry Falwell, "A Bystander—How Not to Be One," *Christian Life*, October 1983, 24.
38. McKeegan, *Abortion Politics*, 97; Jerry Falwell, *Moral Majority Report*, July 1984, 1.
39. Ellen M. Rosenberg, *The Southern Baptists: A Subculture in Transition* (Knoxville: University of Tennessee Press, 1989), 183.
40. John Rees, "The Religious Right's Dr. Tim LaHaye," *Review of the News*, August 8, 1984, 36–37.
41. Smith, *Faith and the Presidency*, 337.
42. Jerry Falwell, Direct Mail, May 16, 1985, "Moral Majority—'Star Wars' letter, 5/3/85" folder, PFAW.
43. Jerry Falwell, Direct Mail, August 1985, "Moral Majority—MM / National Issue Survey, 8/85" folder, PFAW.
44. Jerry Falwell, "A Hero's Story," *Liberty Report*, May 1988, 3–4; Jerry Falwell, Moral Majority Direct Mail, June 1988, "Moral Majority—Fundraising Iran / Contra 1988" folder, PFAW.
45. "INF Treaty Will Leave Europe Defenseless," *Liberty Report*, June 1988, 27.
46. E.J. Dionne, Jr., "Voters Delay Republican Hopes of Dominance in Post-Reagan Era," *New York Times*, November 10, 1988.
47. Martin Mawyer, "Strength, Savvy of the New Right Scares Liberals," *Moral Majority Report*, November 1984.
48. Dale Buss, *Family Man: The Biography of Dr. James Dobson* (Wheaton, IL: Tyndale House Publishers, 2005), 88, 154–155, 170.
49. John Dillin, "US Conservatives on the March: Religious Right Optimistic," *Christian Science Monitor*, March 19, 1986.

Chapter 9

Ronald Reagan and the Republican Party: Responses to Realignment

Robert Mason

The results of the 1980 elections encouraged high hopes among Republicans that their party's long period of minority status was at last reaching a close. This minority status dated back to the Great Depression and the New Deal; on the campaign trail Ronald Reagan invoked positive recollections of Franklin D. Roosevelt, in part to develop the theme that his goal was to overturn finally the Democratic coalition that first emerged under Roosevelt and then to replace it with a similarly durable Republican alternative—to achieve an electoral realignment in his party's favor.[1] During the many decades since the party's Depression-era decline, Democratic shortcomings had sometimes helped Republicans to achieve electoral success, notably for the presidency. But data on party identification showed that consistently more Americans saw themselves as Democratic rather than Republican supporters, and Republicans only secured control of Congress for two years after the 1946 elections and for another two years after the 1952 elections. It was this lengthy record of electoral failure that Republicans hoped to transcend. The belief in the possibility of a realignment helped to inform the political ideas and initiatives of Republicans during the Reagan era. When Reagan made a campaign appearance at Ohio State University in 1984, a sign in the crowd captured the mood of the moment. "You are witnessing the great realignment," it read.[2]

Reagan's leadership of the Republican Party during the 1980s was responsive to the promise of realignment. He had a longtime interest in boosting the Republican Party's fortunes through the recruitment of conservative voters who still identified with the Democratic Party, an interest rooted in his own transition from Democratic to Republican affiliation. Unlike Franklin Roosevelt and Richard Nixon before him—who also as president identified a realigning opportunity for their party—he did not dedicate himself to the construction of coalition-building strategies, however. Reagan did not immerse himself in the detail of electoral politics or of party-related matters. His contribution to his party's cause instead assumed a more neutral emphasis; he lent support to its candidates without charting a particular course that it should take. Though not without qualification, this support amounted to a particularly generous and energetic program on behalf of his party's candidates, identifying Reagan as dedicated to the duties of party leadership to an extent that was unusually great by comparison with other modern presidents. His popularity helped the party, as did his successful contribution to the dissemination of the message that the party's approach to economics—previously often seen as responsive to an elite—offered more promise of renewed and increased prosperity to many ordinary Americans than did the policies of the Democrats. The difference that Reagan made as a result of his political activity was significant but his impact was in some respects limited, especially because it was not at all straightforward to share his personal popularity with the party at large. Beyond Reagan, within the administration there was some imaginative engagement with the party's electoral prospects, especially in connection with the new problem of the "gender gap." The success of these efforts did not match the larger success of Reagan's work for the party, and this gender gap proved to be largely resistant to such initiatives.

However, despite its significance, Reagan's contribution was not enough for some Republicans. There were frustrations among movement conservatives and congressional Republicans that Reagan did not do more to revitalize the party according to their respective designs. These frustrations led to activities that aimed more proactively to build the party's coalition, but that actually undermined Republican efforts to maximize the benefits of the Reagan legacy. Such disappointments with Reagan reflected a misinterpretation of the political opportunity that Republicans encountered in the 1980s. Although this period of opportunity provided party gains, it began primarily with disillusionment with the Democrats, rather than any notable pattern of pro-Republican conversion.

The background to the confidence at the start of the 1980s in the party's future chiefly involved the travails of the Democratic Party and of liberalism. In the late 1970s there were certainly many signs—encouraging to the Republicans—of a turn away from liberalism. Opinion polls reported a mood of increasing skepticism toward government activism. One polling organization, for example, found in 1973 that about a third of respondents agreed "the best government is the government that governs least," but in 1981 that this proportion had risen to three in five. There was a conservative trend, too, at the end of the 1970s, in attitudes on social issues, including drugs, abortion, and the Equal Rights Amendment. This trend was of a rather glacial nature, however, by comparison with the pronounced transformation of ideas about foreign policy. While in 1973 only about one in five Americans viewed the Soviet Union in a highly negative way, by the start of 1980 this proportion had increased to more than three in five.[3] Disappointments with the Carter administration encouraged a new willingness to turn to the Republicans. A National Republican Congressional Committee poll in June 1980 found that voters now had more confidence in Republicans than in

Democrats in tackling a host of foreign and domestic issues, with the lonely exception of unemployment, where the Democratic advantage endured.[4] The results encouraged Rep. Guy Vander Jagt of Michigan, the committee's chair, to conclude, "For the first time since the 1930s, the Republican label is not baggage."[5]

Republican efforts as well as Democratic failings helped to craft the climate of realignment. The late 1970s was also a remarkable period of institutional revitalization and organizational innovation on the Republican side, which equipped the party to reap as effectively as possible the benefits of disillusionment with the Democrats. Under William E. Brock, III, as national chair between 1977 and 1981, the Republican National Committee undertook a variety of initiatives to provide the party with electoral advantage, including programs to train candidates and to equip them with the financial and professional resources they needed to win office.[6] Beyond the party, the many organizations of the "New Right" generated grassroots support for conservative causes, often assuming a populist edge in doing so. Its leaders believed in their capacity to activate a conservative majority, especially within blue-collar and religious constituencies, which were often beyond the reach of the Republican mainstream.[7] Their activity was not, however, straightforwardly in the Republican cause but instead embraced a bipartisan approach, prepared to support conservative Democrats and to oppose nonconservative Republicans. A belief in the party's shortcomings as a majority-mobilizing vehicle often informed New Right activism. Exemplifying such skepticism about the Republican Party, in 1977, John T. "Terry" Dolan of the National Conservative Political Action Committee (NCPAC) described it "a fraud," offering the characterization that it was "a social club where rich people go to pick their noses."[8]

The nature of the 1980 election results then boosted the belief among Republicans that an opportunity for party growth had arrived. The comfortable margin of Reagan's victory was a surprise because of the widespread view beforehand that the election was "too close to call."[9] The party's breakthrough in the Senate—also unexpected—was particularly crucial in fostering the realignment belief. It encouraged the perception that this was a party success, and not just a repudiation of Carter. That the victory was a rather unexpected one further boosted this mood. In fact, the recapture of the Senate was less decisive and less meaningful than at first it seemed. Not only were sparsely populated states important among the gains that Republicans made, but the overall margin of victory was narrow and a relatively small shift between the parties would have brought a Democratic win instead.[10] By contrast with the popular belief in a Republican breakthrough, academic analysts tended to be much more cautious about the meaning of the 1980 results. They usually interpreted them as a vote against the Carter administration's failings rather than any positive endorsement of conservatism. According to such a perspective, these results did not signal the arrival of an electoral realignment, but they perhaps offered Republicans the chance to consolidate such gains on a more lasting basis. Political scientist Austin

Ranney, for example, argued that the Republicans now encountered "a great opportunity to become again the nation's majority party"—largely the product of dissatisfaction with the Carter administration. What was crucial, according to Ranney, was the nature of the Republican response to this opportunity under Reagan as president.[11]

The political scientists were right to be cautious. There was no Republican realignment during the 1980s, though the party made gains. In terms of party identification data, two surges toward the party took place, one at the start of Reagan's first term and the second at the time of his reelection, in total reducing the Democrats' advantage of party identification by about a half. But an advantage nevertheless persisted.[12] Political analysis by administration aides showed that insiders shared the sense that the apparent opportunity for realignment was proving to be an illusion. Although in the early Reagan years Richard Wirthlin, the administration's key pollster, said that a "creeping realignment" was in progress, he later defined the Republicans as a "parity party," rather than the majority, suggesting that the Republicans' 1980s breakthrough was not to outperform their Democratic rivals but to reach a position of even competition.[13] Lee Atwater went further than Wirthlin by questioning the significance of parties to electoral politics, suggesting skepticism about the feasibility of a realignment similar to that of the New Deal era. Instead of one party rising as the other declined in popularity, Americans were drifting away from affiliation with either of the parties, he thought. Echoing views widespread among political scientists, Atwater observed in 1986, "We are going through a period of political dealignment and I expect this process of dealignment to continue for the indefinite future." He linked the phenomenon with "the transition to the communication age," thus agreeing with analysts who linked the decline of party with the rise of television.[14]

Scholarly understandings of dealignment often blamed candidates as well as the news media for the decline of parties in electoral politics in favor of "candidate-centered politics." On the whole, however, Reagan took no such steps toward dealignment; a desire for realignment through the Republican Party's revitalization characterized his actions instead. He was a loyal contributor to his party's cause. Widely identifying Reagan as a key strength for the party, Republican politicians commonly looked to the president for assistance in the task of party revitalization. Reagan worked hard to share his popularity with the party at large. The energy that he devoted to his party's needs as well as to his own candidacy identified him as unusual among recent presidents. An enthusiastic fund-raiser and campaigner for the party's candidates, he nevertheless remained aloof from the development of electoral strategy, relying on managers and aides to deal not only with its detail but also with its larger design.[15] In some respects, this party leadership took a neutral approach, meaning that Reagan was unusual both in the extent of his work for his party and in its nature; other recent presidents tended to do less for the party but nevertheless had a vision for its future in mind when undertaking the duties of party leadership.[16] John

Patrick Diggins notes that Reagan was "less party-oriented than traditional Republicans, such as Richard Nixon, less concerned with factions within the GOP than with his own personal convictions," and in speeches he reached out to Democratic as well as Republican supporters.[17] Such an extra-partisan posture was an asset in campaigns for what remained the minority party. This work for the party's cause was notable in 1980, when Republicans adopted an unusually party-focused, as opposed to candidate-centered, campaign strategy, and this party strategy informed Reagan's presidential quest. It was, political scientist Charles O. Jones observed, "perhaps the most party-oriented campaign in recent decades," in which Reagan emphasized Republican unity and helped other Republican candidates. A similarly party-focused endeavor was often, if not always, evident in later campaigns.[18] During the 1986 midterm campaign, in response to the White House political office's advice of wide-ranging partisan endeavor, Reagan traveled 24,800 miles in visiting twenty-two states and making fifty-four appearances.[19] Finally, in 1988 Reagan undertook campaign activities that amounted to what Rollins praised as "the greatest baton-pass in the history of American politics," involving support for Bush tailored to the presidential campaign's strategic needs, assistance for other Republican candidates, and fund-raising for the party at large.[20]

These efforts were not always welcome. Wary of voters' association of the administration with recession in 1982, some Republican candidates rejected the offer of presidential assistance in that year's midterm contests.[21] Nor were they always advantageous to a candidate's cause. In the South, a common Republican strategy in seeking a congressional breakthrough involved a stress on a candidate's connection with Reagan. The Democrats' counterstrategy frequently promoted their candidate's local roots against their opponent as a Washington-linked outsider. The counterstrategy was often successful. In a 1981 special House election in Mississippi, for example, Wayne Dowdy, the Democrat, neutralized Republican Liles Williams's focus on Reagan by stressing local issues and an anti-Washington message, though not by attacking the popular president; Dowdy won, even though Thad Cochran and then Jon Hinson had held the district for the Republicans since 1972.[22]

Reagan's work for the party did not lack qualification. He was unwilling to campaign against any congressional Democrat who supported his 1981 economic package. A potential justification for such unpartisan activity was the hope that disaffected Democratic officeholders might change party in numbers large enough to achieve a Republican breakthrough.[23] Along these lines, Representative Eugene Atkinson, whose Pennsylvania district was a blue-collar, labor stronghold, joined the Republicans in October 1981, a conversion that Reagan hailed as "[sending] a loud and clear message to Americans that our party, the Republican Party, stands for the working men and women of this country."[24] The move was not a good one for Atkinson, who suffered defeat the following year. It failed to act as a precedent for many other Democratic politicians; a push for converts after the 1984 reelection victory secured about a hundred state and local officials.[25]

The impact of "Operation Open Door," a similar effort in 1985 to persuade voters registered as Democrats to change to the Republicans, was also relatively insignificant. According to national chair Frank Fahrenkopf, Jr., the project achieved its hundred-day goal to win a hundred thousand new Republicans in Florida, Louisiana, North Carolina, and Pennsylvania, but among these voters identified as interested in changing party only about fifty-four thousand had completed the necessary paperwork.[26] "Operation Open Door" was by no means a unique example of the Reagan era's party-building activities. Although a period of relative inactivity followed Brock's departure as national chair in 1981, under Fahrenkopf, from 1983, the national committee established new projects to improve the party's grass-roots infrastructure. It took time for the Democrats to emulate the Republican National Committee's example and Republicans thus maintained the organizational advantage that Brock created.[27] Because candidate quality emerges as an important variable in most studies of congressional contests during this period, such work helped to maximize Republican chances in open-seat campaigns.[28]

Operation Open Door sought to answer the leading Republican charge against Reagan's party efforts, which related to the 1984 campaign. In 1984, mindful of the party's minority status, the Reagan campaign team developed a strategy that made no effort to persuade the president's non-Republican supporters to join the party. As Richard Darman put it, "we used the term 'Republican'... only before Republican audiences in small rooms."[29] Political aide Edward J. Rollins later explained the strategy by noting that the campaign's target voters were Democrats, "who in a lot of cases wanted the checks-and-balances system and did not want a Republican Congress just because they wanted a Republican President." Rollins nevertheless argued that a maximized Reagan vote was likely to benefit other Republican candidates.[30] Staffers also noted that there was a registration drive during the campaign, intended to persuade Reagan supporters to formalize their affiliation with the party at large; they claimed that this effort secured four million new registrants across the country, thus overshadowing the subsequent Operation Open Door.[31] When the party made few gains in the House of Representatives, however, minority leader Representative Robert Michel of Illinois blamed Reagan, who "really never, in my opinion, joined that issue of what it really means to have the numbers in the House."[32] It was not only the reelection campaign's above-party approach that blurred the connection between Reagan and the Republican Party, however. In recognition of Reagan's popularity, some Democratic incumbents emphasized their own connection with the president and support for his agenda.[33] Frustrated with what he saw as a similar tendency among some opposition candidates in 1986, Reagan noted that campaigning against them was "like punching a pillow."[34] But the 1984 reelection strategy facilitated such a Democratic emphasis, because it inescapably yet enthusiastically celebrated the achievements of the previous four years. It was open to a congressional incumbent, barely less than the White House incumbent, to harness the electoral benefits of this context.[35] Indeed, political scientist Ellis Sandoz interpreted the Reagan campaign as a call for an endorsement of the incumbents' record, powerful in mobilizing support for Reagan, but much more beneficial to reelection-seeking Democrats than for nonincumbent Republican candidates. "Reagan's coattails were prodigiously long from this angle, extending to virtually all incumbents who sought reelection to Congress," Sandoz observed.[36]

Still, administration officials argued that Reagan's popularity and his work for the party improved Republican prospects at the polls.[37] Analyses by political scientists lend support to such claims. One study, for example, suggests that Reagan's personal popularity was worth three percentage points in the growth of the party's identifiers during the 1980s.[38] According to another, in the 1988 presidential election, the popularity of Reagan and his administration's record benefited Bush, perhaps to a critically significant extent.[39] The danger of such a personalized rationale for party support was its likely instability, however.[40] Still another quantitative study, one of the 1986 House results, provides evidence of this danger. Reagan's popularity was a significant factor in voter behavior, the study suggests, but disapproval of his performance as president apparently acted as a stronger motivation for voters than approval.[41] More fundamentally, party support rooted in a president's popularity was unlikely to outlive the administration's tenure; it did not operate as the foundation of an electoral realignment.

An understanding of Reagan's contribution to the Republican Party that considers only his work for its candidates and attempts to share his popularity with the party at large is inadequate, however. Despite the neutrality of his party efforts and his aloofness from factional conflict as president, Reagan successfully contributed to the promotion of a new climate of conservatism through his emphasis on the rhetoric of freedom, his optimistic promotion of antistatism's merits, and his return to anticommunist toughness as a route to better superpower relations. Since the arrival of the Democrats as the nation's majority party in the 1930s, Republicans had often responded to New Deal liberalism's enduring strength either with defensive accommodation or with reactionary opposition, and they struggled to develop a positive alternative.[42] "Of a sudden, the GOP has become a party of ideas," remarked Senator Daniel Patrick Moynihan, Democrat of New York, in 1980.[43] Conservatism's new liveliness partly reflected the problems of liberalism and the Democratic Party; Walter F. Mondale, Carter's vice president and the 1984 presidential nominee, subsequently said, "I sensed late in my public career that we were running out of new ideas."[44] Among Republicans and conservatives, it was by no means Reagan alone who contributed to this development, but he played an important role in popularizing this new conservatism. In his celebratory study of Reagan, Dinesh D'Souza, who worked in the Reagan White House, writes that he "redefined the message of the Republican Party to make it appealing to a majority of middle- and working class Americans."[45] According to D'Souza, though he did not achieve a realignment of party identification, Reagan secured "an ideological realignment" because "[h]e shifted the political center by changing the terms of debate."[46] Less celebratory works offer Reagan praise along these lines; Jules Tygiel, for example, claims that Reagan "established a new-moribund political conservatism as a viable, if not dominant, American ideology."[47] This revitalization of conservatism in public policy notably involved economic matters; "Reaganomics" represented an influential shift of approach to policy in this area. The extent to which the impact of Reaganomics was a positive one remains the subject of controversy, but it was certainly with much more electoral success that Republican politicians now promoted their credentials as better custodians of the economy than their Democratic rivals. With Reagan leading the way, Republicans labeled their programs as enhancing the economic prospects of ordinary Americans, and many voters agreed with this characterization.[48] In the longer term—less tangible, but real nonetheless—Reagan's legacy for the Republican Party was significant, too. By the start of the twenty-first century, the party contained many who considered Ronald Reagan as their political inspiration and exemplar.[49]

These achievements were not adequately substantial for some of those conservatives who had been most enthusiastic about Reagan's candidacy and party leadership, however. Believing that a coalition between economic and social conservatives was the most promising route to a Republican majority, they saw Reagan as the ideal politician to consolidate such a coalition. In this way, Reagan's party leadership involved an idea about realignment, even if he did not see his goal exactly in this way. In his 1975 book *The Making of a New Majority Party*, *National Review* publisher William A. Rusher advanced such an argument, though he advocated the creation of an independent conservative party because he did not expect Republicans to embrace the arrival of social conservatives. Like other conservatives, Rusher identified Reagan as the ideally charismatic politician to engineer such a union. Reagan, however, soon made clear his rejection of a third-party route to conservative dominance in favor of "a new and revitalized second party, raising a banner of no pale pastels, but bold colors which make it unmistakably clear where we stand on all of the issues troubling the people," as he put it in a 1975 speech to conservatives.[50] As these comments suggest, the conservative confidence in Reagan was not a matter of wishful thinking but a reflection of his pronouncements of support for fusion between economic and social conservatives; it was a goal with which he had been associated since the 1960s.[51] New Right leaders claimed—inaccurately—that their movement's activism accounted for Reagan's 1980 victory and consequently demanded that the administration address its agenda.[52] The administration's record often disappointed these leaders as inadequately conservative. "The question when Reagan was elected was whether he was going to be closer to Eisenhower as a caretaker or to Roosevelt as a revolutionary," commented Terry Dolan, NCPAC chair, in 1984. "He's been generally closer to Eisenhower, preserving a status quo established by previous liberal administrations."[53] A 1983 survey of conservative leaders reported that almost two-thirds did not consider his agenda a conservative one, but moderate or even liberal.[54]

A White House advocate of such views was Morton C. Blackwell, an aide during the first term responsible for liaison with conservative groups. Blackwell argued in favor of the electoral importance of "moral issues"—of conservative positions on abortion, drugs, homosexuality, and the family.[55] He also claimed that the party's fortunes at the polls depended on the extent and enthusiasm of activism in its support, therefore arguing that the administration should take action to energize conservatism.[56] Such arguments, which acknowledged that many conservative concerns lacked popularity among the electorate as a whole, were common among those who argued in favor of a right-wing route to a majority. New Right leader Paul M. Weyrich claimed, too, that inattention to moral issues was likely to depress turnout among those otherwise likely to support Reagan and the Republican Party.[57]

Blackwell was out of step with some of the administration's more influential figures. A more conventional view acknowledged the electoral utility of support among cultural traditionalists, but it also understood the potential danger among the larger electorate of excessively close association with their ideas. In his analysis of the 1984 presidential landslide, outgoing White House chief of staff James A. Baker, III—whose political pragmatism infuriated conservatives—insisted that its impressive proportions did not indicate the Republican coalition's strength. Instead, Baker concluded, the strength of Reagan's popularity hid the coalition's essential fragility because the interests of its various elements were diverse and even, at times, mutually contradictory. The concerns of "yuppies"—the quintessentially 1980s term for young, urban professionals—were very different from those of evangelical Christians, notably. "Opposition to abortion, for instance, is not an issue that is popular among most yuppies—particularly among yuppie women," Baker pointed out.[58] Toward the end of the Reagan years, a Gallup poll, which sought to develop a typology of the contemporary electorate, lent weight to the perspective that this coalition was fragile. It reported that the Republicans' core supporters were "Enterprisers," 16 percent of voters, and "Moralists," 14 percent. The former were wealthy, well-educated whites with economically conservative yet socially moderate attitudes. The latter were middle-income people, often southerners and in many cases born-again Christians, who were strongly conservative on social issues and foreign policy, but generally favored programmatic spending. To win, a Republican presidential candidate needed to add other groups to form a majority coalition, but to maintain the core vote of Enterprisers and Moralists was challenging enough.[59]

As Baker noted, it was Ronald Reagan's achievement that the coalition secured cohesion during the 1980s. Conservative critics were often reluctant to attack Reagan publicly for what they identified as the administration's shortcomings, exculpating Reagan and blaming aides instead.[60] This reluctance demonstrated Reagan's leadership strength; Reagan, for example, offered a degree of support, unsuccessfully, in 1982 to a constitutional amendment to ban abortion, and he remained a passionate advocate of pro-life arguments. He appointed antiabortion people to key positions and his administration's spending cuts included family-planning programs among their targets.[61] Such initiatives balanced Reagan's personal opposition to abortion with an awareness that more Americans were in favor of abortion rights than against.[62] In response to political pressures—and in recognition of the measures' greater popularity than that of pro-life initiatives—Reagan offered similar support to a constitutional amendment to permit prayer in schools, while administration officials defended against legal challenge state laws that established moments of contemplative silence as an alternative to formal prayer. The amendments' defeat was not politically problematic beyond the frustrations of the complaints of social conservatism's promoters; Reagan, who sometimes employed biblical allusions when speaking on a host of issues, was still able to present himself to voters as the defender of social conservatism against a powerful, secularist liberalism.[63] Especially important in this regard was Reagan's pledge to reshape the federal judiciary and his actions toward this goal. During campaigns he emphasized his intention to nominate judges with a conservative interpretation of the Constitution, and administration aides investigated potential nominees with unprecedented attention to their legal beliefs in order to implement this goal.[64] Such actions were not enough for his conservative critics, but in many cases they were enough for socially conservative voters. In 1984 Reagan won four in five born-again Christians, and in 1988 Bush secured the votes of a similar proportion of white evangelicals and fundamentalists. During the Reagan years their Republican allegiance increased on a scale unequaled by other groups.[65]

While conservatives saw the surge of support for the party among the "Moralist" constituency as a development that was both ideologically congenial and promising in electoral terms, some moderates saw the party's coalition in different terms. In early 1982 Senator Robert W. Packwood of Oregon employed the belief in an opportunity for an electoral opportunity in ways quite different from conservatives. Chair of the National Republican Senatorial Committee, Packwood blamed Reagan for the loss of a historic opportunity for party revitalization. He attacked Reagan's "idealized concept of America" for its failure to recognize the nation's diversity and consequently for an inattention to groups whose electoral support the party needed to achieve lasting gains. "You cannot write [women who work for wages] off and the blacks off and the Hispanics off and the Jews off and assume you're going to build a party on white Anglo-Saxon males over 40," Packwood said. "There aren't enough of us left."[66] (Packwood did not acknowledge the greater willingness than before of Jewish Americans to support the Republican Party.)[67] The comments enraged fellow Republicans, and Packwood—whose moderate politics had already made him a target of the New Right—soon lost his position of being in charge of the campaign committee.[68]

In identifying the appearance of a "gender gap" as problematic for the party, Packwood echoed the comments of pollster Louis Harris, who claimed in 1981 that "for President Reagan and the Republicans, the single most formidable obstacle to their becoming a majority party in the 1980s is the vote of women."[69] In fact, Packwood underestimated the seriousness of the administration's engagement with the gender gap, though he more accurately perceived the insubstantial nature of the steps that leading Republicans took to heal the gap. Still, the problem did not receive as much attention as it deserved. The gender gap's emergence in the 1980 contest between Reagan and President Jimmy Carter involved a significant difference between men's and women's voting behavior; an exit poll suggested that this gap was as great as nine percentage points, with Reagan securing a vote of 56 percent among men but only 47 percent among women. Such a difference was a new development in recent electoral history, and it reflected contrasting evaluations of Reagan and the Republican Party, whose solutions to the period's economic and international difficulties appealed more to men than women. Men were more likely than women to view Reagan's Cold War and welfare policy positively, and the administration's record in office continued to inspire such conflicting evaluations.[70] Responses to the administration's economic record similarly suggested that the Reagan-era Republican Party's conservatism enjoyed more confidence among men than women, because of distinctive approaches to political judgments. Women, who tended to view the economic outlook with more pessimism than men, were more likely to make a political decision according to their evaluation of the administration's overall economic performance, while men were more likely to do so according to their own bread-and-butter situation.[71] The gender gap was not, by contrast, the result of the Republican Party's movement toward antifeminism, dramatized by the 1980 national convention's omission of a platform commitment to the Equal Rights Amendment. This was a common belief, especially because feminist activists popularized the concept of the gender gap and promoted this interpretation in order to encourage Republican attention to their agenda. In fact, conservative views on the amendment were no more common among women than men, and women were no more likely to choose a candidate on these grounds.[72]

Administration officials created thoughtful analyses of the gender gap, rightly concluding that men and women viewed Reagan and his policies differently and that there was no straightforward way to heal the gap. They offered some bold policy ideas that included a more compassionate understanding of welfare and a more supportive attitude toward the needs of women in the workplace.[73] There was a competing belief that incorrect perceptions of the administration's goals and achievements were a key problem, however, and that better communication with women was an adequate response.[74] On the whole, the administration looked for more simple solutions. Perhaps its most imaginative initiative was the creation of a White House Coordinating Council on Women, following the advice of Elizabeth Dole, in charge of the public liaison office. Designed to identify opportunities for government action to help women, the council lost momentum on Dole's departure from the White House to become transportation secretary in early 1983. Tanya Melich, a Republican activist who worked against antifeminism within the party, called the council "a campaign tool, not a commitment to further policies for women."[75] Other initiatives similarly reflected campaign imperatives that encouraged symbolism and not substance. By stressing his support for workplace equality, Reagan included an appeal to those women likely to be sympathetic to his economic agenda in his State of the Union addresses between 1982 and 1984. He did not mention this commitment in post-reelection State of the Union addresses, however.[76] Appointments similarly showed sensitivity to the election cycle; the proportion of women nominees to Senate-confirmed subcabinet positions reached a high of one in four in 1984, a proportion that markedly dropped in 1985.[77]

Despite the insubstantial nature of the administration approach to the gender gap, the results of the 1984 election suggested that its problem among women was in decline. Better communication and amended perceptions seemed to have made a difference. During 1983 and 1984 both the Republican Party and the Reagan campaign ran advertising targeted at women. Campaign operatives attributed part of Reagan's recovery among women to the measured nature of his response to the Soviet Union's destruction of a South Korean civilian airplane in September 1983, which modified the "trigger-happy" image that had partly contributed to the gender gap's emergence in 1980.[78] Although Geraldine Ferraro was the Democrats' vice-presidential nominee, her party downplayed efforts to mobilize women in the belief both that this support was safe and that such efforts might alienate men.[79] The Republicans still enjoyed less success among women than men. In achieving a landslide victory over Mondale, Reagan won a majority among women; that this was a smaller majority than that among men was a relatively inconsequential aspect of his larger success. But in 1984 the votes of women accounted for a number of Democratic victories, including the Senate contests in Illinois, Massachusetts, and Michigan, and the Vermont gubernatorial election.[80] The results of the 1988 presidential election then provided further evidence that Republican attention to the gender gap was inadequate, suggestive of its superficiality. An exit poll gave George H.W. Bush a 50–49 percent edge among women over Michael Dukakis, but it reported that 57 percent of men favored him over his Democratic rival.[81] The result was similar to the Reagan–Carter gender gap of 1980. During the 1990s, the gender gap became a yet more visible difference between support for the Democratic and Republican parties.[82]

The gender gap became significant during the Reagan era not because the Republican Party lost support among women but because it made gains among men without scoring similar gains among women. The phenomenon involved the greater mobilization of new support for the party among men, especially white men in the South, as opposed to women.[83] This perspective suggests that the failure to tackle the reasons for women's disaffection with the Republican Party in a substantial rather than a symbolic way made sense for any larger strategy to achieve party growth. The party's new appeal to men helped it to achieve a long-desired breakthrough toward what Wirthlin described as "parity" status.

A similar obstacle hindered efforts to achieve new support among minority groups that Packwood mentioned. The Republican Party's conservatism was incompatible with their effective cultivation, while it was successful in garnering other support. Of their support among African Americans, administration expectations were low. In 1982 White House staffer Dan J. Smith recommended a strategy not to win African American support but simply "to convince black voters that Republicans do not so threaten their vital interests that blacks must turnout [sic] in record numbers to vote against us."[84] Two years later the Reagan campaign's target was just 10 percent, about the level achieved by the Republican in every presidential contest since Barry Goldwater in 1964. When a campaign poll suggested that support among African Americans was at 16 percent, pollster Richard Wirthlin found the result "surprising."[85] In fact, a 1980 project run by the national committee to promote better communications with black voters in five U.S. Senate races offered promising results; in Oklahoma, for example, more than four in ten African Americans voted for Don Nickles, not so significantly smaller than his 53.5-percent share of the electorate at large.[86] But the momentum of these RNC efforts did not survive Brock's departure in 1981.[87]

The Reagan administration's record on race reinforced the belief that the Republican Party did not take these problems seriously. Reagan articulated a color-blind philosophy that encouraged the perception, whether fair or not, that he did not appreciate the existence of inequalities and intolerance.[88] Reagan's lack of confidence in federal power made him uncomfortable with much action to protect civil rights. It led him to oppose the Internal Revenue Service's denial of tax exemptions to Bob Jones University, a Christian institution that forbade interracial dating and marriage, for example, later insisting that he did not realize that the case involved civil rights and revising his position to emphasize questions of the service's regulatory powers as problematic.[89] He also favored scaling back the Voting Rights Act's reach on its renewal until significant sentiment in Congress encouraged him to endorse it.[90] Even leading Republicans within the African American community signaled dissatisfaction with the record, especially involving policies on affirmative action and minority business.[91] In fact, policies of minority preference remained unchanged, a reflection of political concerns, among other factors.[92] But the Reagan administration's conservatism meant that it did not embrace an agenda of activism on race. "The President is unlikely to make significant inroads into the Black community without abandoning his strategic commitment to federalism, further budget cuts and merit-based employment practices," wrote Elizabeth Dole in early 1982.[93]

In noting the difficulty that Republicans faced in constructing a policy agenda that appealed to a larger number of African Americans, Dole argued that symbolism was not enough to fashion such an appeal. Efforts to win African Americans were indeed largely limited to such symbols as appointments, an unsatisfactory approach especially in contrast to the Democrats' egalitarian commitment.[94] The party's critics believed that one factor that limited its policy options was a desire to exploit the electoral benefits of racism—to win the votes of whites opposed to progress on race.[95] George H.W. Bush's 1988 presidential campaign earned particular controversy for its apparent use of racialized appeals—alluding to race-related controversies with coded language that did not explicitly mention race—to build white support.[96] Closely associated with this strategy, Lee Atwater, who became RNC chair after running the Bush campaign, nevertheless said that the party's level of African American support needed to reach 20 percent "if we want to become a majority party."[97] Based on the party's 1980s record, such aspirations sounded hollow.

There was more serious attention among Republicans to Latino Americans, a demographic group of great diversity, growing in political importance. They sometimes identified the family-oriented conservatism, associated with some Latinos, as a way to overcome the Democrats' appeal as the party of minorities and of the less socioeconomically privileged. In south Texas, the 1984 Republican message to Latino Democrats was that their party's nomination of Mondale represented its capture by "far-out, kookie, left-wing Democrats," for example.[98] On the whole, however, the administration strategy in cultivating Latino voters did not differ much from the African American approach of symbolism, involving connections with Latino groups (although it proved difficult to persuade senior administration officials to make appearances before such groups) and appointments.[99] A particularly notable example was Reagan's appointment of Lauro F. Cavazos as education secretary, the first Latino cabinet member, in 1988; this was, according to former political aide Lyn Nofziger, "a political favor to George Bush."[100] Using Hispanic Americans as a category, exit polling reported that more than one in three among them voted for Reagan in 1980 and 1984 but that this proportion dropped back to three in ten in 1988.[101]

Despite his anger with the White House after the 1984 elections, minority leader Robert Michel did not display enough dedication to the achievement of a Republican majority in the House to satisfy some of his colleagues there. The apparent prospect of an electoral realignment to the party's benefit kindled a desire within the Republican contingent to assume a more aggressive posture toward the Democratic majority. So did an increase in partisanship among Democrats, who were less willing than before to share legislative influence with members of the opposition party. Such opportunities for productive cooperation had previously discouraged any efforts in the House to work for a majority, as did the judgment of most legislators that as individuals already with electoral success they had little to gain from work of this kind. Over time the result of these incentives had been a lack of interest among House Republicans in tackling the problem of the party's minority status. "There are more rewards for being a good minority legislator than there are for trying to become a majority legislator," Representative Newt Gingrich of Georgia later observed.[102]

Gingrich was especially aware of obstacles to a House quest for a majority, because he was foremost among a congressional group challenging the logic that discouraged work in pursuit of this goal. It was not a group that worked in cooperation with a larger, administration-orchestrated plan for party growth, however. Instead, frustrations with White House progress toward a realignment helped to inform their activities. Gingrich criticized the administration's party-building efforts as inadequately aggressive; in his view they did not create a bold enough line of distinction between Republicans and Democrats. When the 1982 recession arrived, he privately scolded chief of staff James Baker on the grounds that the administration's "lack of effective leadership on behalf of the Reagan program has allowed us to take fundamental public support and lose it in the trivia of daily headlines." Poor communication with the public and poor coordination with congressional Republicans were problematic, he told Baker.[103] Gingrich later found fault with the 1984 campaign because "Reagan should have prepared for [his second term in] office by forcing a polarization of the country...[by] running against liberals and radicals."[104] There were similar criticisms of the 1986 campaign, which "was not run as a national partisan campaign, highlighting the philosophical differences between Republicans and Democrats," instead relying on "the same feel good, empty rhetoric that dominated the 1984 race," according to Representative Vin Weber of Minnesota.[105]

The determination with which Gingrich tackled the party's minority problem caused White House speechwriter Anthony Dolan to note that he "may have enough energy and talent to elect a Republican House by himself."[106] Gingrich worked with other House Republicans in forming the Conservative Opportunity Society (COS) in 1983, and he later assumed control of GOPAC, an organization established in 1979 to raise funds toward the goal of a majority, which under his leadership boosted its already considerable efforts to prepare good Republican candidates for office.[107] As his criticisms of White House activities suggested, Gingrich believed in the importance of political confrontation as a way to dramatize differences between the parties; after the passage of the 1981 economic package he advocated an emphasis on the Republicans as "the low interest rate, low inflation, high take-home pay and high jobs creation party" and the Democrats as "the high interest rate, high inflation, low take-home pay and low jobs creation party."[108] Gingrich later credited Richard Nixon with advice that helped to inspire COS's creation; Nixon advised Gingrich, "If you really want to become the majority, you have to fill the place with ideas."[109] But COS was usually unsuccessful in informing its attacks on the Democratic majority with policy substance. The group first won attention for its use of "special order" speeches—exploiting the House's C-SPAN broadcasts, which began in 1979—criticizing the Democratic leadership. Its attention later shifted to the discussion of legislative detail, but concerns among alleged ethics violations caused Gingrich to lead a clamor in 1987 and 1988 for an investigation of Representative James Wright of Texas, the House speaker. Thus, COS retained its reputation for attack rhetoric rather than policy substance.[110] In 1990, Vin Weber, one of the organization's key figures, commented that while COS "encouraged greater activism among House Republicans," it devoted excessive attention to "wedge issues against the Democrats, without also creating magnet issues that would attract the public." Thus, COS was seen "as primarily negative and confrontational," Weber concluded.[111]

The Republican Party's development during the Bush and Clinton years suggested that Ronald Reagan had enjoyed notable success in maintaining its unity, important in securing electoral success. Conflict between economic and social conservatives escalated, and factionalism led to Patrick J. Buchanan's debilitating if unsuccessful primary challenge to George H.W. Bush in 1992.[112] Moreover, Bush was unable to emulate Reagan in persuading congressional Republicans to support tax increases considered necessary by the White House. Instead, his proposal ignited a ferocious response from Gingrich and others on Capitol Hill, sure that such initiatives dashed Republican chances for electoral gain.[113] The arrival of such profound conflicts provided evidence of the party's success under Reagan in containing and minimizing differences.

Among the 1980s Republican responses to the prospect of electoral realignment, Gingrich's ideas about the pursuit of a majority secured most influence and prominence during the 1990s. The transformation of the House Republican attitude toward the goal of party gain was significant; at the start of the 1980s most emphasized a conciliatory approach toward the Democratic majority, preferring compromise to confrontation. By the start of the 1990s, COS's "bomb-throwing" strategies were achieving dominance in the House, and they led to Gingrich's capture of the leadership and to the 1994 breakthrough. The "Contract with America" sought to balance a positive vision for conservatism with negative attacks on the Democrats. But the 104th Congress did not manage to recapture Reagan's sunny, optimistic brand of Republicanism, instead garnering a reputation for negativity and attack. Even while the Republican Party now benefited from the 1980s' legacy of "parity" status, it thus proved difficult for it to maintain the popularity achieved during the Reagan years and to move decisively toward national majority status.

Notes

For support of the research that informs this chapter, I am grateful to the Arts and Humanities Research Council, the Carnegie Trust for the Universities of Scotland, and the John W. Kluge Center at the Library of Congress.

1. William E. Leuchtenburg, *In the Shadow of FDR: From Harry Truman to Ronald Reagan* (Ithaca, NY: Cornell University Press, 1983), 209–227.
2. Richard Brookhiser, *Outside Story: How Democrats and Republicans Reelected Reagan* (Garden City, NY: Doubleday, 1986), 286.
3. William G. Mayer, *The Changing American Mind: How and Why American Public Opinion Changed between 1960 and 1988* (Ann Arbor: University of Michigan Press, 1992), 19–85.
4. Market Opinion Research, "U.S. Nat ional Study: Statistical Summary," June 1980, and National Republican Congressional Committee news release, July 7,

1980, "Republican Convention," box 28, ERAmerica Records, Manuscript Division, Library of Congress, Washington, D.C.
5. Michael J. Malbin, "The Republican Revival," *Fortune*, August 25, 1980, 85.
6. Philip A. Klinkner, *The Losing Parties: Out-Party National Committees, 1956–1993* (New Haven: Yale University Press, 1994), 133–154.
7. Jerome L. Himmelstein, *To the Right: The Transformation of American Conservatism* (Berkeley: University of California Press, 1990), 80–94.
8. David W. Reinhard, *The Republican Right since 1945* (Lexington: University Press of Kentucky, 1983), 246.
9. William Schneider, "The November 4 Vote for President: What Did It Mean?" in Austin Ranney, ed., *The American Elections of 1980* (Washington, D.C.: American Enterprise Institute for Public Policy Research, 1981), 212–227.
10. William A. Rusher, *The Rise of the Right* (New York: William Morrow, 1984), 305–308; Norman J. Ornstein, "Assessing Reagan's First Year," in Ornstein, ed., *President and Congress: Assessing Reagan's First Year* (Washington, D.C.: American Enterprise Institute for Public Policy Research, 1982), 91–92; Roger H. Davidson and Walter J. Oleszek, "Changing the Guard in the U.S. Senate," *Legislative Studies Quarterly* 9 (1984): 638.
11. Austin Ranney, "The Carter Administration," in Ranney, ed., *American Elections of 1980*, 2.
12. Paul Allen Beck, "Incomplete Realignment: The Reagan Legacy for Parties and Elections," in Charles O. Jones, ed., *The Reagan Legacy: Promise and Performance* (Chatham, NJ: Chatham House, 1988), 161–163.
13. Kevin P. Phillips, *Post-Conservative America: People, Politics and Ideology in a Time of Crisis* (1982; New York: Vintage, 1983), 220; Hedrick Smith, "Congress: Will There Be Realignment?" in Paul Duke, ed., *Beyond Reagan: The Politics of Upheaval* (New York: Warner, 1986), 162.
14. A. James Reichley, *The Life of the Parties: A History of American Political Parties* (New York: Free Press, 1992), 379–380.
15. James W. Davis, *The President as Party Leader* (New York: Praeger, 1992), 12; Laurence I. Barrett, *Gambling with History: Reagan in the White House* (1983; New York: Penguin, 1984), 34; Lou Cannon, *President Reagan: The Role of a Lifetime* (New York: Simon & Schuster, 1991), 42–47, 504, 535.
16. Sean J. Savage, *Roosevelt, the Party Leader, 1932–1945* (Lexington: University Press of Kentucky, 1991); *Truman and the Democratic Party* (Lexington: University Press of Kentucky, 1997); *JFK, LBJ, and the Democratic Party* (Albany: State University of New York Press, 2004); Cornelius Cotter, "Eisenhower as Party Leader," *Political Science Quarterly* 98 (1983), 255–283; Robert Mason, "'I Was Going to Build a New Republican Party and a New Majority': Richard Nixon as Party Leader, 1969–73," *Journal of American Studies* 39 (2005): 463–483.
17. John Patrick Diggins, *Ronald Reagan: Fate, Freedom, and the Making of History* (New York: Norton, 2007), 308.
18. Charles O. Jones, "The New, New Senate," in Ellis Sandoz and Cecil V. Crabb, Jr., eds., *A Tide of Discontent: The 1980 Elections and Their Meaning* (Washington, D.C.: Congressional Quarterly Press, 1981), 109.
19. Memo, Mitch Daniels to Donald T. Regan, June 19, 1986, folder 3, box 192, Donald T. Regan Papers, Manuscript Division, Library of Congress; Jane Mayer and Doyle McManus, *Landslide: The Unmaking of the President, 1984–1988* (1988; Glasgow, UK: Fontana, 1989), 404.

20. Memo, Frank J. Donatelli to Kenneth M. Duberstein, November 7, 1988, "1988 Political Campaign (1)," box 3, series I, Kenneth M. Duberstein Files (Office of the Chief of Staff), Ronald Reagan Presidential Library, Simi Valley, California.
21. Albert R. Hunt, "National Politics and the 1982 Campaign," in Thomas E. Mann and Norman J. Ornstein, eds., *The American Elections of 1982* (Washington, D.C.: American Enterprise Institute for Public Policy Research, 1983), 39.
22. James M. Glaser, *Race, Campaign Politics, and the Realignment in the South* (New Haven: Yale University Press, 1996), 46–52, 130–137.
23. Hedley Donovan, "'We Can Have and Should Have Some Loosening of Interest Rates,'" *Fortune*, September 21, 1981, 70–71.
24. Hunt, "National Politics," 1.
25. Jack Germond and Jules Witcover, "Low-Level Converts Best Bet For GOP," *Orlando Sentinel*, June 15, 1985, A19.
26. "GOP Voter Drive Falls Short," Allentown, PA, *Morning Call*, August 23, 1985, A6.
27. Sidney M. Milkis, *The Presidents and the Parties: The Transformation of the American Party System Since the New Deal* (New York: Oxford University Press, 1993), 274; Klinkner, *Losing Parties*, 158–178.
28. See, e.g., Gary C. Jacobson, "Strategic Politicians and the Dynamics of U.S. House Elections, 1946–86," *American Political Science Review* 83 (1989): 773–793; David Ian Lublin, "Quality, Not Quantity: Strategic Politicians in U.S. Senate Elections, 1952–1990," *Journal of Politics* 56 (1994): 228–241.
29. Jonathan Moore, ed., *Campaign for President: The Managers Look at '84* (Dover, Mass.: Auburn House, 1986), 226–227.
30. Ibid., 225–226.
31. Unsigned, "Talking Points: Organizational Efforts," October 24, 1984, "Political Affairs 8/84–1/85 (1 of 4)," box 10, series I, James A. Baker, III, Files, Ronald Reagan Presidential Library.
32. Ellis Sandoz, "The Silent Majority Finds Its Voice," in Sandoz and Cecil V. Crabb, Jr., eds., *Election 84: Landslide without a Mandate?* (New York: Mentor, 1985), 5.
33. Moore, ed., *Campaign for President*, 228.
34. Kiron K. Skinner, Annelise Anderson, and Martin Anderson, eds., *Reagan: A Life in Letters* (New York: Free Press, 2003), 568.
35. Gary C. Jacobson, "Congress: Politics after a Landslide without Coattails," in Michael Nelson, ed., *The Elections of 1984* (Washington, D.C.: CQ Press, 1985), 221–222.
36. Sandoz, "Silent Majority Finds Its Voice," 5.
37. See, e.g., Donald T. Regan, handwritten notes, November 2, 1986, folder 2, box 193, Regan Papers.
38. William Mishler, Marilyn Hoskin, and Roy E. Fitzgerald, "Hunting the Snark: Or Searching for Evidence of that Widely Touted but Highly Elusive Resurgence of Public Support for Conservative Parties in Britain, Canada, and the United States," in Barry Cooper, Allan Kornberg, and William Mishler, eds., *The Resurgence of Conservatism in Anglo-American Democracies* (Durham, NC: Duke University Press, 1988), 85–86.
39. Abramowitz and Segal, "Beyond Willie Horton and the Pledge of Allegiance" and Paul J. Quirk, "The Election," in Michael Nelson, ed., *The Elections of 1988* (Washington, D.C.: CQ Press, 1989), 85.

40. Warren E. Miller, "A New Context for Presidential Politics: The Reagan Legacy," *Political Behavior* 9 (1987): 91–113.
41. Gary C. Jacobson and Samuel Kernell, "National Forces in the 1986 U.S. House Elections," *Legislative Studies Quarterly* 15 (1990): 74–80.
42. Robert Mason, *Minority: The U.S. Electorate and the Republican Party from Hoover to Reagan* (forthcoming).
43. Robert M. Collins, *Transforming America: Politics and Culture in the Reagan Years* (New York: Columbia University Press, 2007), 59.
44. Steven M. Gillon, *The Democrats' Dilemma: Walter F. Mondale and the Liberal Legacy* (New York: Columbia University Press, 1992), 304.
45. Dinesh D'Souza, Ronald *Reagan: How an Ordinary Man Became an Extraordinary Leader* (1997; New York: Touchstone, 1999), 73.
46. Ibid., 254.
47. Jules Tygiel, *Ronald Reagan and the Triumph of American Conservatism* (New York: Longman, 2004), ix. See also, e.g., Lewis L. Gould, *Grand Old Party: A History of the Republicans* (New York: Random House, 2003), 394–435; and Andrew E. Busch, *Reagan's Victory: The Presidential Election of 1980 and the Rise of the Right* (Lawrence: University Press of Kansas, 2005), 178–181.
48. Collins, *Transforming America*, 59–91; Mark A. Smith, *The Right Talk: How Conservatives Transformed the Great Society into the Economic Society* (Princeton: Princeton University Press, 2007), 123–202.
49. Charles Mahtesian, "Reagan as Majority Maker," *National Journal*, June 12, 2004, 1857; John M. Broder, "In Search of Reagan," *New York Times*, January 20, 2008, D1.
50. William A. Rusher, *The Making of the New Majority Party* (New York: Sheed and Ward, 1975); Robert Mason, *Richard Nixon and the Quest for a New Majority* (Chapel Hill: University of North Carolina Press, 2004), 215–226 (quotation, 218).
51. Tygiel, *Ronald Reagan and the Triumph of American Conservatism*, 202–204.
52. Jeffrey L. Brudney and Gary W. Copeland, "Evangelicals as a Political Force: Reagan and the 1980 Religious Vote," *Social Science Quarterly* 65 (1984): 1072–1079; Jerome L. Himmelstein and James A. McRae, Jr., "Social Conservatism, New Republicans, and the 1980 Election," *Public Opinion Quarterly* 48 (1984): 592–605.
53. "What Conservatives Think of Ronald Reagan: A Symposium," *Policy Review*, Winter 1984, 12–19 (quotation, 15).
54. "Whither, Conservatives? A Survey of Conservative Leaders," *Conservative Digest*, October 1983, 7–11.
55. Memo, Morton C. Blackwell to Elizabeth H. Dole, December 2, 1981, "Religion," OA 4537, series I, Elizabeth H. Dole Files, Ronald Reagan Presidential Library.
56. Letter, Morton C. Blackwell to Richard C. Wirthlin, August 12, 1982, "Polling Data 1982 [1 of 3]," OA 6391, series I, Dole Files.
57. Paul M. Weyrich, "Beware, Reagan's Vulnerable," *New York Times*, January 26, 1984.
58. A. James Reichley, *The Life of the Parties: A History of American Political Parties* (New York: Free Press, 1992), 379; Diggins, *Ronald Reagan*, 166, 172.
59. Harry Straight, "Nation's Voters Going to Pieces: Old Political Labels Lose Meaning," *Orlando Sentinel*, January 10, 1988, A1; Norman Ornstein,

Andrew Kohut, and Larry McCarthy, *The People, the Press & Politics: The Times Mirror Study of the American Electorate* (Reading, MA: Addison-Wesley, 1988).
60. "What Conservatives Think of Ronald Reagan."
61. Donald T. Critchlow, "Mobilizing Women: The 'Social' Issues," in W. Elliot Brownlee and Hugh Davis Graham, eds., *The Reagan Presidency: Pragmatic Conservatism and Its Legacies* (Lawrence: University Press of Kansas, 2003), 302–312.
62. Peggy Noonan, *What I Saw At the Revolution: A Political Life in the Reagan Era* (1990; New York: Ivy, 1991), 164–165; James T. Patterson, *Restless Giant: The United States from Watergate to Bush v. Gore* (New York: Oxford University Press, 2005), 177.
63. Bruce J. Dierenfield, "'A Nation under God': Ronald Reagan and the Crusade for School Prayer," in Eric J. Schmertz, Natalie Datlof, and Alexej Ugrinsky, eds., *Ronald Reagan's America* (Westport, CT: Greenwood, 1997), 235–261.
64. David M. O'Brien, "The Reagan Judges: His Most Enduring Legacy?" in Charles O. Jones, ed., *The Reagan Legacy: Promise and Performance* (Chatham, NJ: Chatham House, 1988), 60–101.
65. Jerome L. Himmelstein, *To the Right: The Transformation of American Conservatism* (Berkeley: University of California Press, 1990), 122–123, 203.
66. "Reagan's Concept of America Hurts Party, Packwood Says," *New York Times*, March 2, 1982.
67. Alan M. Fisher, "The Jewish Vote in 1982: A Good Look, A Good Predictor," *Jewish Social Studies* 47 (1985): 281–294; Milton Himmelfarb, "Another Look at the Jewish Vote," *Commentary*, December 1985, 39–44.
68. Linda Greenhouse, "Robert William Packwood: Apparent Loser Emerges Triumphant," *New York Times*, May 9, 1986, D4; Gillian Peele, *Revival and Reaction: The Right in Contemporary America* (Oxford: Clarendon Press, 1984), 138.
69. Tanya Melich, *The Republican War against Women: An Insider's Report from Behind the Lines*, updated ed. (New York: Bantam, 1998), 184.
70. Martin Gilens, "Gender and Support for Reagan: A Comprehensive Model of Presidential Approval," *American Journal of Political Science* 32 (1988): 19–49.
71. Carole Kennedy Chaney, R. Michael Alvarez, and Jonathan Nagler, "Explaining the Gender Gap in U.S. Presidential Elections, 1980–1992," *Political Research Quarterly* 51 (1998): 311–339.
72. Jane J. Mansbridge, "Myth and Reality: The ERA and the Gender Gap in the 1980 Election," *Public Opinion Quarterly* 49 (1985): 164–178.
73. See, e.g., memo, Ann Dore McLaughlin to Donald T. Regan, November 5, 1982, folder 4, box 58, Regan Papers; memo, Elizabeth H. Dole to Ronald Reagan, November 13, 1982, "Women—Gender Gap [2 of 2]," OA 6393, series I, Dole Files; memo, Faith Ryan Whittlesey to James A. Baker, III, and Michael Deaver, May 24, 1983, "W.H. Staff Memoranda—Public Liaison [2 of 2]," box 6, series I, Baker Files; Rachel Flick, "What Do Women Want? The Three Reasons for Ronald Reagan's Gender Gap," *Policy Review*, Winter 1984, 80–82.
74. Adam Clymer, "Warning on 'Gender Gap' From the White House," *New York Times*, December 3, 1982, A26.

75. Melich, *Republican War against Women*, 187–188 (quotation, 188).
76. Kira Sanbonmatsu, *Democrats, Republicans, and the Politics of Women's Place* (Ann Arbor: University of Michigan Press, 2002), 137.
77. Janet M. Martin, "An Examination of Executive Branch Appointments in the Reagan Administration by Background and Gender," *Western Political Quarterly* 44 (1991): 178–180.
78. Xandra Kayden and Eddie Mahe, Jr., *The Party Goes On: The Persistence of the Two-Party System in America* (New York: Basic, 1985), 173.
79. Joan Walsh, "How Reagan Bridged the Gender Gap," *In These Times*, November 21–December 4, 1984, 6.
80. Scott Keeter, "Public Opinion in 1984," in Gerald M. Pomper, Ross K. Baker, Charles E. Jacob, Scott Keeter, Wilson Carey McWilliams, and Henry A. Plotkin, *The Election of 1984: Reports and Interpretations* (Chatham, NJ: Chatham House, 1985), 101.
81. Jean Bethke Elshtain, "Issues and Themes in the 1988 Campaign," in Michael Nelson, ed., *The Elections of 1988* (Washington, D.C.: CQ Press, 1989), 116.
82. Karen M. Kaufmann and John R. Petrocik, "The Changing Politics of American Men: Understanding the Sources of the Gender Gap," *American Journal of Political Science* 43 (1999): 864–887.
83. Barbara Norrander, "The Evolution of the Gender Gap," *Public Opinion Quarterly* 63 (1999): 566–576.
84. Letter, Dan J. Smith to Michael K. Deaver, August 4, 1982, "Miscellaneous Memo/Corres. '82 (July thru Dec.) (7)," OA 7621, Michael K. Deaver Files, Ronald Reagan Presidential Library.
85. Memo, Richard B. Wirthlin to James A. Baker, III, Michael K. Deaver, Edward J. Rollins, and Stuart Spencer, September 27, 1984, "Political Affairs 8/84–1/85 (3 of 4)," box 10, series I, Baker Files.
86. Pearl T. Robinson, "Whither the Future of Blacks in the Republican Party?" *Political Science Quarterly* 97 (1982): 207–231.
87. Adam Clymer, "Republicans Worry about Eroding Black Support," *New York Times*, April 14, 1982, A20.
88. Jeremy D. Mayer, "Reagan and Race," in Kyle Longley, Jeremy D. Mayer, Michael Schaller, and John W. Sloan, *Deconstructing Reagan: Conservative Mythology and America's Fortieth President* (Armonk, NY: M. E. Sharpe, 2007), 70–89.
89. Cannon, *President Reagan*, 519–525.
90. Dan T. Carter, *From George Wallace to Newt Gingrich: Race in the Conservative Counterrevolution, 1963–1994* (Baton Rouge: Louisiana State University Press, 1996), 58.
91. Memo, Melvin L. Bradley to James A. Baker, III, February 14, 1982, "Public Liaison (2 of 2)," box 10, series I, Baker Files.
92. Hugh Davis Graham, "Civil Rights Policy," in W. Elliot Brownlee and Graham, eds., *The Reagan Presidency: Pragmatic Conservatism and Its Legacies* (Lawrence: University Press of Kansas, 2003), 283–290.
93. Memo draft, Elizabeth H. Dole to James A. Baker, III, January 30, 1982, "Black Strategy 1982 (1 of 4)," box 5, series I, Dole Files.
94. Memo, Jim Cicconi to Elizabeth H. Dole, Edward J. Rollins, Lee Atwater, and Red Caveney, April 7, 1982, "Blacks: Jan–June 1982 (2 of 5)," box 6, series I, Dole Files.

95. Monte Piliawsky, "The 1984 Election's Message to Black Americans: Challenges, Choices and Prospects." *Freedomways* 25, 1 (first quarter, 1985): 18–27.
96. Thomas Byrne Edsall with Mary D. Edsall, *Chain Reaction: The Impact of Race, Rights, and Taxes on American Politics* (New York: Norton, 1991), 221–225.
97. Louis Bolce, Gerald De Maio, and Douglas Muzzio, "Blacks and the Republican Party: The 20 Percent Solution," *Political Science Quarterly* 107 (1992), 63.
98. Report, sent by Lee Atwater to Margaret Tutwiler, September 8, 1984, "Political Affairs 8/84–1/85 (3 of 4)," box 10, Baker Files.
99. Memo, Michael Deaver to Outreach Strategy Group," June 6, 1983, "Daily Status Reports BS and DB to MKD [2 of 2]," OA 8546, Deaver Files; memo, Elizabeth H. Dole to Edwin Meese, III, James A. Baker, III, and Michael Deaver, May 29, 1982, "Hispanics Jan-June 1982 [1 of 5]," OA 5455, series I, Dole Files.
100. Lyn Nofziger, *Nofziger* (Washington, D.C.: Regnery Gateway, 1992), 245.
101. The proportions were 36 percent in 1980 (in the three-way race involving Carter, Reagan, and the third-party liberal Republican candidate Representative John B. Anderson), 37 percent in 1984, and 30 percent in 1988. Gerald M. Pomper, "The Presidential Election," in Gerald M. Pomper et al., *The Election of 1988: Reports and Interpretations* (Chatham, NJ: Chatham House, 1989), 71.; Quirk, "Election," 82.
102. William F. Connelly, Jr. and John J. Pitney, Jr., *Congress' Permanent Minority? Republicans in the U.S. House* (Lanham, MD: Rowman & Littlefield, 1994), 5–8, 24–26, 154–157 (quotation, 5).
103. Letter, Newt Gingrich to James A. Baker, III, February 25, 1982, folder 7, box 34, William A. Rusher Papers, Manuscript Division, Library of Congress.
104. Nina J. Easton, *Gang of Five: Leaders at the Center of the Conservative Crusade* (New York: Simon and Schuster, 2000), 159.
105. Milkis, *Presidents and the Parties*, 279.
106. Memo, Anthony R. Dolan to Paul Laxalt, July 25, 1984, folder 7, box 26, Rusher Papers.
107. Douglas L. Koopman, *Hostile Takeover: The House Republican Party, 1980–1995* (Lanham, MD: Rowman & Littlefield, 1996), 51; Lee Edwards, *The Conservative Revolution: The Movement That Remade America* (New York: Free Press, 1999), 283.
108. Newt Gingrich, "Republican Strategy for the Fall of 1981," undated, folder 2, box 133, Regan Papers.
109. Newt Gingrich, *Lessons Learned the Hard Way: A Personal Report* (New York: HarperCollins, 1998), 170.
110. Julian E. Zelizer, *On Capitol Hill: The Struggle to Reform Congress and Its Consequences, 1848–2000* (Cambridge, UK: Cambridge University Press, 2004), 212–215; Connelly and Pitney, *Congress' Permanent Minority?* 27–28, 84–86.
111. Adam Meyerson, "Wedges and Magnets: Vin Weber on Conservative Opportunities," *Policy Review*, Spring 1990, 38.
112. Gillian Peele, "American Political Parties and the Bush Presidency," in Dilys M. Hill and Phil Williams, eds., *The Bush Presidency: Triumphs and Adversities* (New York: St. Martin's Press, 1994), 63–83.
113. Milkis, *President and the Parties*, 292–294.

Part III

Legacies

Chapter 10

The Baptist and the Messiah: Ronald Reagan and Margaret Thatcher

Dominic Sandbrook

On February 6, 1994 the Republican National Committee held a lavish gala dinner to celebrate the eighty-third birthday of Ronald Reagan. It was a warm, cheerful evening of bonhomie and backslapping, and the guests applauded vigorously at the effusive tribute of Reagan's guest of honor:

> Sir, you strode into our midst at a time when America needed you most. This great country had been through a period of national malaise bereft of any sense of moral direction. Through it all, throughout eight of the fastest moving years in memory, you were unflappable and unyielding.
>
> With that Irish twinkle and that easy homespun style, which never changed, you brought a new assurance to America. You were not only America's President—important as that is—you were a great leader. In a time of average men, you stood taller than anyone else.

Moments later Reagan, who was in excellent spirits, rose to thank his audience. "I can't tell you how thrilled Nancy and I am to be with you here tonight to celebrate the forty-fourth anniversary of my thirty-ninth birthday," he began with a smile. Then he turned to thank his principal guest:

> Before I get started here, I want to thank my dear friend, Margaret Thatcher, for being part of yet another important milestone in my life and for those very kind words. As most of you know, Margaret and I go back quite a way. We met at a time before she became Prime Minister and I became President. From the moment we met, we discovered that we shared quite similar views of government and freedom. Margaret ended our first meeting by telling me, "We must stand together," and that's exactly what we've done in the years since—as friends and as political allies.
>
> Margaret Thatcher is one of the giants of our century. For me, she has been a staunch ally, my political soulmate, a great visionary and a dear, dear friend.[1]

Margaret Thatcher and Ronald Reagan dominated the English-speaking world during the 1980s. One was the daughter of a stern Methodist grocer from a sleepy market town in the English Midlands; the other was the son of a bankrupt store manager from a quiet rural community in the American Midwest. Yet despite their unprepossessing origins, Thatcher and Reagan successfully stormed the barricades of government in Britain and the United States, won election after election, and set their stamp on an entire decade. Entirely different in experience and temperament, they nevertheless constituted a formidable partnership and always saw themselves as a double act, working to haul their respective countries out of the pit of economic decline and to present a united front against Soviet Communism.

They had first met in 1975, shortly after Thatcher's surprising victory in the Conservative leadership election. Reagan was already planning a bid for the Republican presidential nomination in 1976. Given what was to follow, Thatcher was surprisingly little known in her own country, let alone the United States. A relatively obscure cabinet minister for four years, standing out from her colleagues only by virtue of her femininity and her reputation as the "milk snatcher" who had overseen radical cuts at the Department of Education, she had only recently deposed the incumbent Conservative party leader Edward Heath in a rebellion predicted by very few political insiders. Yet even at this early stage, after only a couple of hours of conversation, the two struck up an immediate rapport. "I knew that I was talking to someone who instinctively felt and thought as I did," Thatcher wrote afterward, "not just about policies but about a philosophy of government, a view of human nature, all the high ideals and values which lie—or ought to lie—beneath any politician's ambition to lead his country."[2] Reagan, too, felt that he had found a political soul mate. "We found ourselves in great agreement," he later told an interviewer. "She was extremely well informed, but she was firm, decisive, and she had targets in mind of where we should be going. I was just greatly impressed."[3]

In January 1981, Reagan took the oath of office as the fortieth president of the United States. Margaret Thatcher was already well ahead of him; despite having been written off by most British political commentators, she had been elevated to the premiership in May 1979 after a crippling winter of strikes had brought down the Labour government. She was ecstatic at the thought of seeing her American friend again, and delighted that she would be his first foreign visitor. One of her aides described her behavior as the day of the visit approached as "intolerable": she was, he grumbled, "on a complete high" and "tremendously worked up about seeing Reagan." But when she finally arrived in the United States, at the end of February 1981, her reception lived up to all her expectations. Washington greeted her, according to one correspondent, as "a heroine of pan-Atlantic conservatism...a kind of Baptist to Reagan's Messiah." The administration had arranged dinners and parties, long meetings with the president, and even the award of an honorary doctorate from Georgetown University. The visit was an undiluted triumph, and as Thatcher left, she told Reagan: "Your problems are our problems, and when you look for friends, we will be there."[4] Not even during World War II had the ideological and emotional bond between the president and the prime minister been so strong. Indeed, the warmth of the relationship actually embarrassed some observers. How did the trip go, one British politician asked the foreign secretary, the patrician Lord Carrington. "Oh, very well indeed," he replied mournfully. "She liked the Reagan people very much. They're so vulgar."[5]

As early as Reagan's first weeks in office, therefore, the two leaders already shared a strong sense of common endeavor that was to endure, barely tarnished by such minor squabbles as the Grenada controversy, throughout their period in office, and beyond. From their collaboration in the Falklands War to their mutual contempt for social democracy and their public determination to defeat Soviet Communism, Thatcher and Reagan were perceived by admirers and critics alike as a double act: one famous British antinuclear poster of the early 1980s even showed them as Rhett Butler and Scarlett O'Hara in a parody of *Gone with the Wind*, the tagline reading: "She promised to follow him to the end of the earth. He promised to organise it!"[6] And of course the two consciously played up their sense of partnership. In March 1985, with both in their second terms after winning thumping reelection landslides, Thatcher returned to Washington for a dinner marking the two hundredth anniversary of Anglo-American diplomatic relations. "The menu underscored the conviviality of the visit," reported *Time*: "poached salmon 'Nancy,' followed by filet of veal 'special relationship' and raspberry mousse 'Margaret.'" In his toast, Reagan paid tribute to the famous alliances between Churchill and Roosevelt and Macmillan and Kennedy, and then said: "I'd like to add two more names to that list: Thatcher and Reagan." In her reply, meanwhile, Thatcher told the guests that she was often asked what the special relationship really meant. "It is special," she said simply. "It just is. And that's that."[7]

And yet there was, after all, much more to it than that. For despite Reagan's invocation of the Churchill–Roosevelt and Macmillan–Kennedy partnerships, the relationship between the Californian president and his Lincolnshire counterpart had no genuine precedent. In both the earlier cases, the relationship was much more ambiguous than is often acknowledged; indeed, in both cases the relationship was partly a literary fiction, constructed after the president's untimely death by his self-consciously nostalgic British ally. Between Churchill and Roosevelt, for example, there existed a surprising degree of tension over such issues as the future of the British Empire, the direction of war strategy, and relations with the Soviet Union, while Kennedy and Macmillan came close to falling out over the question of an independent British nuclear deterrent. But the crucial point is that in both cases, the relationship was essentially a diplomatic one. Their shared attachment to democratic freedom and hatred of Nazism apart, Churchill and Roosevelt had surprisingly little in common ideologically. And while, like their predecessors, Kennedy and Macmillan represented parties on different wings of the political spectrum, they also came from utterly different political generations and therefore had strikingly little in common, as even the briefest comparison of their rhetoric and achievements would indicate.

The Thatcher–Reagan relationship was very different. Domestic issues were just as important as international ones: during Thatcher's first months in office, Reagan's advisors closely followed the course of her economic revolution, while in January 1980 the chairman of the Republican National Committee Bill Brock took the extraordinary step of showing two of her 1979 party political broadcasts as part of the Republican response to President Carter's State of the Union address.[8] Yet while Reagan might invoke the model of the wartime Grand Alliance, this close ideological alliance was simply without precedent in Anglo-American history. What made it even more unusual was the fact that historically, the stronger transatlantic relationship was that between the Democrats and the Labour Party, not that between the Republicans and the Conservatives. Although the Labour left long nursed a tradition of bitter anti-Americanism, senior party figures in the 1950s and 1960s, such as Harold Wilson, Tony Crosland, and Dennis Healey, consciously looked to the United States, and specifically to the Kennedy administration, for inspiration: indeed, Wilson publicly compared himself both to Kennedy and later to Lyndon Johnson.[9]

But while Labour officials were keen to borrow advertising and electoral techniques from the Democrats, the Conservatives rarely showed much interest in exchanging ideas from the Republicans, and before Thatcher became leader in 1975, the Conservative Party could hardly be described as pro-American at all. Despite their attachment to the anti-Communist alliance, many senior Tories made little secret of their distaste for the brashness, materialism, and vulgar populism of American political culture. It is striking to note that neither Edward Heath nor Enoch Powell, the two dominant figures of Conservative politics in the 1960s and 1970s, had much affection for the United States, and during Heath's premiership the special relationship was generally considered to have sunk to its lowest ebb in living memory. It had already taken a substantial battering during the mid-to-late 1960s, when Wilson and Johnson had fallen out over British nonparticipation in the Vietnam War, the devaluation of the pound, and the British retreat from East of Suez, and despite the fact that Heath and Richard Nixon were both nominally conservatives, relations between the two were little warmer than glacial. Since Britain's economic and military power was so palpably in decline, most American politicians had generally lost interest in the relationship by the mid-1970s: it is notable, for example, that Henry Kissinger mentions Britain astonishingly rarely in his memoirs of the period, that Jimmy Carter made little effort to rekindle the relationship after taking office in 1977, and that Carter and Thatcher got on extraordinarily badly during the year-and-a-half that they coincided in office.

Unlike the earlier relationships to which Reagan paid tribute in 1985, therefore, his special relationship with Margaret Thatcher was primarily based upon personal and ideological comradeship rather than diplomatic necessity: indeed, during the Falklands War of 1982, his ambassador to the United Nations, Jeane Kirkpatrick, privately complained that he allowed his affection for Thatcher's Britain to outweigh more important geopolitical considerations.[10] What made this ideological camaraderie all the stronger, of course, was the fact that both Reagan and Thatcher saw themselves as political outsiders who had risen to the top over the opposition of the old-fashioned elites who controlled their respective parties. Thatcher's identity as an outsider is well known: not only was she a lone woman in a Cabinet filled with men, but she had been brought up in a provincial, lower-middle-class Methodist family, was rarely thought of as a potential leader before she unexpectedly toppled Heath in 1975, and spent much of her time in office surrounded by Heath's former allies and acolytes, many of whom looked down on her socially, disliked her abrasive style, and had serious doubts about her political agenda. But Reagan, too, was an outsider of sorts, a Western governor who had spent his entire political life outside the nation's capital and had risen to power by fiercely attacking the established elites. As his biographer Lou Cannon noted, Reagan's closest allies were almost all Californians with virtually no experience of Washington, and when he took the oath of office in January 1981, he had none of the "alliances and friendships normally forged by politicians as they scramble up the career ladder." Both Reagan and Thatcher, Cannon thought, "seemed less lonely in international affairs because of the other."[11]

Not only were both Reagan and Thatcher political outsiders, they were in many ways extremely unlikely candidates to lead their respective countries. Just ten years before Reagan's election, in fact, it would have seemed highly implausible that California's governor and Britain's education secretary, both of whom occupied positions well to the right of the political center, would one day dominate the Atlantic world. Admirers of the pair, as well as political scientists keen to emphasize the profound demographic and economic forces that drove them into office, often present their triumphs as a saga of inevitability, making it impossible to imagine a world in which they would not have won election after election. Yet both Reagan and Thatcher owed large debts to contingency and circumstance, and both endured periods when they were widely written off. When Reagan launched his campaign for the Republican nomination in 1980, for instance, he already had two failures (in 1968 and 1976) to his name. The second in particular had been an excellent opportunity to win the nomination against a ponderous, unelected president, and Reagan's failure—which was partly self-inflicted after wild talk of budget cuts badly damaged him in New Hampshire—could easily be seen as proof that he was too extreme to be elected. Like Thatcher, he was lucky at the crucial moments: lucky that Watergate slashed through the upper echelons of the Republican establishment; lucky that Gerald Ford lost the 1976 election to Carter; lucky too that Carter's own presidency was consumed by the Iranian revolution and hostage crisis. Even days before the 1980 election, his victory was far from assured; had the American hostages in Teheran been released, Carter might well have sneaked home, and Reagan's name would have long since joined those of Dewey, Taft, and Goldwater in the ranks of Republican failures.

If anything, Thatcher's success was even more implausible. The first woman to lead a British political party, she had been elected in 1975 not because of her own self-evident virtues but simply because angry Tory MPs wanted to punish their leader Edward Heath. Most wanted simply to pave the way for a third candidate and were astonished when she actually won the leadership, and her place was not truly secure until after victory in the Falklands War, toward the end of her first term.[12] Like Reagan, she owed her success to the sheer pressure of events as much as to her own strengths and abilities. Perhaps above all, both of them owed a great deal to the extraordinary economic turmoil of the late 1970s, which effectively ripped apart the premises of Keynesian demand management that had underpinned the appeal of the Democratic and Labour parties. Yet even given the horrendous economic conditions of the time, Thatcher could easily have lost her first general election as Tory leader if James Callaghan, her avuncular Labour opponent, had gone to the country in October 1978, as many of his advisors urged. Had he done so, Callaghan might well have won; if so, comments Thatcher's biographer, "the experiment of her leadership would almost certainly have been finished." Even after her victory in 1979 her position remained extremely insecure: without the Winter of Discontent she might have been a mere footnote in history, but without the Falklands War she might well have become a byword for prime ministerial disaster.[13]

Emphasizing the role of contingency in the success of both Reagan and Thatcher does not mean denying that powerful, subterranean historical forces—the rise of the suburbs, the decline of heavy industry, the growth of populist individualism, and so on—were at work throughout the 1970s and 1980s. But it is worth noting that they were so successful at the polls not merely because they were accomplished and compelling communicators, or because their message clearly resonated with millions of voters, but also because they faced center–left opponents struggling to come to terms with the challenges of the late 1970s. In both Britain and the United States—and across the industrialized world more generally—the optimistic assumptions of Keynesian social democracy had been seriously eroded by energy crises, soaring inflation, and industrial decline. In the academy, Princeton's liberal economist Alan Blinder later reflected, there had been an astonishing "intellectual turnabout," such that "by about 1980, it was hard to find an American academic macroeconomist under the age of 40 who professed to be a Keynesian."[14] As Paul Volcker, President Carter's hawkish chairman of the Federal Reserve, explained to an interviewer,

> We are all Keynesians now—in terms of the way we look at things. National income statistics are a Keynesian view of the world, and the language of economists tends to be Keynesian. But if you mean by Keynesian that we've got to pump up the economy, that all these relationships are pretty clear and simple, that this gives us a tool for eternal prosperity if we do it right, that's all bullshit.[15]

Even in Britain, where Keynesianism was more deeply entrenched, the tide was turning. Addressing the Labour faithful in 1976 for the first time as prime minister, James Callaghan admitted: "We used to think that you could spend your way out of a recession and increase employment by cutting taxes and boosting government spending." But those days, he went on, were gone: "I tell you in all candour that that option no longer exists, and in so far as it ever did exist, it only worked on each occasion since the war by injecting a bigger dose of inflation into the economy, followed by a higher level of unemployment as the next step."[16]

The success of Reagan and Thatcher in the 1980s, so often presented merely as the inevitable triumph of the right, actually makes little sense without taking into account this ordeal of the old center–left. From the conservatives' perspective, it was astonishing good luck that on both sides of the Atlantic they faced social democratic parties exhausted and damaged by the tribulations of office during the late 1970s. Of course there was an element of contingency in this; as already noted, both Reagan and Thatcher, like so many successful political leaders, were extremely fortunate in their opponents. A popular and enthusiastic Edward Kennedy, untainted by Chappaquiddick and the collapse of his marriage, would undoubtedly have posed Reagan a more serious challenge than either Carter in 1980 or Mondale in 1984, not least because Kennedy was the only American politician who could match Reagan for sheer star quality. Similarly, it is hard to imagine a less effective Labour leader than Michael Foot (except, perhaps, for Tony Benn): had Dennis Healey tried a little harder to smooth over the divisions after the 1979 election, it is plausible that he would have been elected leader, obviating the need for an Social Democratic Party (SDP) breakaway and presenting Thatcher with tough, patriotic, battle-hardened opposition in the early 1980s.

But there was more to this than contingency. It was not mere coincidence that both center–left parties became badly and bitterly divided in the late 1970s and 1980s, and neither was it a coincidence both Reagan and Thatcher saw their opponents' momentum dissipated by third-party distractions of John Anderson and, in Britain, the SDP. While Keynesianism seemed tired and threadbare, treated as yesterday's news by commentators impatient for new ideas, right-wing ideas—notably monetarism and supply-side economics—had become unexpectedly exciting, even glamorous. As early as the fall of 1977 a *Newsweek* cover story predicted an era of "pragmatic new conservatism," while the radical journalist Andrew Kopkind noted that same season that it was "already a cliché of columnar journalism in Washington, that the political vectors of the country all run right."[17] "We're still struggling to give birth to a popular movement that can fight for social and economic justice," one Massachusetts activist admitted in 1979. "We don't have one…At the moment, most of the choices are being defined by the Right."[18]

But on both sides of the Atlantic, the experience of managing the transition to a post-Keynesian order proved enormously divisive, especially on the left, where the turn of the tide was the cue for an outpouring of internecine rage. The ordeal of Britain's Labour Party, severely weakened by internal faction-fighting that pitted defiant grassroots activists and disaffected backbenchers against exhausted ministers, is well-known: after losing the 1979 election, the party did not regain power for another eighteen years. But Reagan's Democratic opponents fared little better. In this context, Jimmy Carter's nomination in 1976 was actually an early sign of the weakness of the old Democratic apparatus as well as of the impending collapse of old-fashioned social democratic liberalism. And like his British counterparts, Carter found it almost impossible to hold together a party whose basic political and economic assumptions had been badly damaged by the onset of inflation. Many liberal activists were horrified by Carter's insistence on strict anti-inflation austerity measures, particularly after he appointed Paul Volcker to run the Federal Reserve, and union leaders, who had never really liked him anyway, turned against him within a matter of months. As early as December 1978 Edward Kennedy publicly humiliated him at a disastrous Democratic midterm convention, and Carter himself always blamed Kennedy's primary campaign against him for his defeat in the 1980 presidential election.[19]

What all this suggests is that although the electoral successes of Reagan and Thatcher are often discussed in the context of the supposedly inevitable rise of the New Right, the decisive political phenomenon of the period was not so much the rise of the right but the collapse of the center–left, which had staked all its chips on Keynesian management and abandoned itself to fratricidal bloodletting when the gamble failed to pay off. Indeed, what is really striking about the politics of the late 1970s and early 1980s is that in terms of public opinion, the New Right made astonishingly little headway. The American presidential election of 1980, for instance, is often presented as an ideological realignment or a watershed in national political attitudes. Yet exit polls reveal that instead of voting to endorse Ronald Reagan, most Americans were motivated by the desire to remove the hapless and horrendously unpopular Jimmy Carter. In his comprehensive analysis of the result, Andrew Busch notes that voters chose Reagan not because they admired his platform, but simply because they wanted change, and because, unlike the well-meaning but woolly Carter, he projected an impression of strong leadership. Yet they were not particularly enthusiastic about their new president: no candidate had ever won the highest office with such weak approval ratings, and a glance at Reagan's job approval ratings during his time in office rather explodes the notion that he was a particularly popular leader. Although Reagan's approval rating twice reached 68 percent, in May 1981 and May 1986, this was hardly something to brag about: Eisenhower had reached 79 percent, Johnson 80 percent, Ford 74 percent, and even the despised Carter 75 percent. For much of his first term, in fact, Reagan's rating skulked in the low forties, and in January 1983 no less than 56 percent of those asked expressed disapproval of his record.[20]

Thatcher's popularity, meanwhile, was even more fragile. Like the presidential election that brought Reagan to power, the general election of 1979 was ultimately a referendum on the performance of the Callaghan government, which had been fatally damaged by the strikes of the Winter of Discontent. Thatcher herself was still not popular; indeed, she won despite being much less personally popular than her amiable opponent, "Sunny Jim" Callaghan. And such was the economic and social turmoil of the early 1980s—due in part, but not solely, to her rigorous economic austerity—that her ratings fell much lower than those of her American friend. By the end of 1981, with unemployment reaching a record three million, her approval rating was down to a mere 25 percent, the lowest for any prime minister since records began. The government's rating, meanwhile, was even worse: a pitiful 18 percent of those asked said they approved of its record. And although Thatcher's ratings were rescued by economic recovery and the Falklands War, they were never particularly healthy, largely because she remained such a confrontational and controversial figure. Throughout her time in office, in fact, support for the Conservatives never went above 50 percent, a staggering statistic, given that this was supposedly a conservative decade.[21]

In this respect, therefore, Anglo-American politics in the 1980s present us with a paradox. Despite the enormous success of the New Right at the electoral level—thanks not least to the weakness and divisions of its adversaries—its ideas clearly struggled to make much headway among the public at large. For all the talk of an American realignment in 1980, liberal values remained strikingly resilient: again, polls consistently found strong public support for Social Security, Medicare, and government spending in general, while support for affirmative action actually went up during the Reagan years.[22] Neither was there any great right turn in public attitudes in Britain. In 1987, the year of Thatcher's third successive victory, Gallup found that just 13 percent shared her view that the poor were responsible for their own condition—a proportion that had actually fallen from 35 percent ten years earlier! A year later, another poll found that only 43 percent of Britons wanted to live in a "capitalist society in which private interests and free enterprise are most important"; by contrast, 49 percent wanted to inhabit "a mainly socialist society."[23]

Yet the resilience of the social democratic consensus explains why, despite their success as election winners, both Reagan and Thatcher were, judged by their own standards, relative failures in government. Both had more in common with the controversial conservative disappointments who preceded them than they cared to admit: while Reagan, like Richard Nixon, could be accused of running from the right and governing from the center, Thatcher, like Edward Heath, issued ferocious statements about rolling back the state before doing no such thing. In Reagan's case the pattern was already clear in California between 1967 and 1975, and his governorship offered an uncannily accurate preview of what was to follow. In Sacramento, as later, Reagan coasted into office against an exhausted opponent battered by events beyond his control; in Sacramento, he benefited from facing a divided and directionless opposition; in Sacramento, he came up against a vaguely centrist ideological consensus that proved more resilient than conservatives had predicted; in Sacramento, above all, he built an unexpected reputation as a slightly semi-detached but popular and effective administrator, a pragmatist whose record of compromise rarely matched his red-blooded rhetoric. Time and again Reagan opted for practical politics rather than ideological purity, whether it be in raising taxes during his first term, pumping record amounts of money into education, signing a pioneering abortion bill in 1967, or delighting environmentalists with his decision to block the trans-Sierra highway. "A lot of people, including me, thought he would be very ideological," remarked George Deukmejian, then a state senator and later governor. "We learned quickly that he was very practical."[24] For his biographer Lou Cannon, the key to Reagan was that he was "simultaneously conservative and pragmatic"; the historian Alonzo Hamby even calls him "a slightly right of center accommodationist."[25]

Reagan's record in California stands as a rebuke to both admirers and critics who see him as a political innocent who cared more about ideological dogma than practical administration. The New Right activists of the late 1970s who pictured him as one of their own, or who fantasized that he had been converted to the joys of supply-side economics would have done better to look closely at his record. Within months of the new administration taking office, David Stockman, an acute if self-serving observer of Reagan's flirtation with supply-side, admitted that nobody in the administration "understands what's going on with these numbers," and concluded that Reagan was just another "consensus politician," with "no blueprint for radical governance."[26] It was an exaggeration, perhaps, but it contained more than a grain of truth. From the perspective of Reagan's more extreme supporters, he *did* look like just another consensus politician, failing to trim the size of the federal bureaucracy, failing to roll back the advance of the state, failing to balance the budget, failing to outlaw abortion across the nation, and failing to stem the tide of so-called permissiveness that had overtaken national life since the 1960s. And what Reagan's admirers often forget, in fact, is that during the last two years of his presidency the pages of conservative publications such as the *Wall Street Journal, National Review,* and the *American Spectator* were full of laments for missed opportunities, tactical blunders, and roads not taken. "I feel like we're back to 1977," Norman Podhoretz told the readers of *Commentary* in August 1988.[27]

But this, of course, was precisely what made Reagan so popular. Had he followed the advice of the most fanatical supply-siders or the most zealous leaders of the religious right, he would surely have forfeited the support of the great majority of the American people, whose values, as we have seen, were planted firmly in the center ground. As in California, he proved himself not only a great communicator but a great compromiser, able to work effectively with congressional opponents and also to reach out to independent voters who would have been repelled by administrative radicalism. From the perspective of many voters, therefore, it was Reagan the pragmatist who reflected the aspirations and values of Middle America, not the "extremists" and "special interests" who supposedly controlled the Democratic Party.

Despite her famous appetite for confrontation, the same might be said, albeit rather more cautiously, of Margaret Thatcher. Like Reagan, she was simultaneously conservative and pragmatic, effectively dumping extreme monetarism after her first couple of years in office. Even when dealing with her infamous "enemies within" she practiced the art of the possible, ducking an early fight with the miners so that she could gather her forces for the great struggle of 1984, and horrifying diehard Ulster Unionists by signing the Anglo-Irish agreement the following year. Like Reagan, she took care to stake her claim to the practical center ground, arguing—not without reason in some cases—that it was the likes of Foot, Benn, and Kinnock who were the extremists. And like Reagan, she knew that in a society where social democratic values died hard, right-wing radicalism must have its limits.

During the first years of Thatcher's government, for instance, she was besieged by think-tank reports calling for the privatization of the National Health Service (NHS), but she always drew back. When a Central Policy Review Staff report floating ideas for education vouchers, the privatization of higher education, and the replacement of the NHS by a part-privatized insurance system was leaked to the press in September 1982, her response was to promise that the NHS would never be sold off, and even to brag that "we are spending 5 per cent more in real terms in the Health Service than Labour"—hardly the behavior of a die-hard radical.[28] Indeed, despite Thatcher's uncompromising reputation, it is striking that once in office, she rapidly parted company with her most zealous advisors: the radical systems analyst John Hoskyns, for example, was initially appointed to run her Number Ten Policy Unit, but walked out in the autumn of 1981 complaining that she had been "absorbed" by the bureaucracy. Rather like some British David Stockman, Hoskyns felt that he was "knocking his head against a wall," suggesting that in Whitehall, as in Washington, administrative inertia, conservatism, and consensus were more powerful than the New Right ideologues had imagined.[29] It was hardly surprising, then, that like Reagan, Thatcher failed to roll back the state or to reverse the social and cultural changes that had transformed family life. "For all her boasts on one side, and the howls of 'Tory cuts' on the other," writes her most authoritative biographer, "she actually failed to curb public spending significantly, failed to prune or privatise the welfare state [and] failed to change most of the British public's fundamental attitudes."[30]

What this does not mean, of course, is that Reagan and Thatcher were insignificant or inconsequential political actors. For one thing, even though their apparent electoral invincibility—particularly in Thatcher's case—partly depended on the weakness of the opposition, the perception that they were winners, and that their ideas had carried the day, made an enormous impact on their opponents. The British historian Mark Garnett even suggests, with a keen sense of irony, that Labour might have won the 1992 general election if they had held fast to their social democratic principles instead of attempting, admittedly rather half-heartedly at first, to imitate their opponents; and this, of course is what, in the American context, endless liberal Democratic commentators and academics have been arguing for years.[31] But it never happened: indeed, there is a good case that Reagan and Thatcher won their greatest victories by converting not their friends but their opponents to the joys of neoliberal populism.

This was not, however, simply a case of slavish imitation. The Democratic Party, for example, was already moving to the right well before Reagan became president: as we have seen, Carter's nomination in 1976 partly reflected the disintegration of the liberal faction, while in 1980 the Democratic-controlled Joint Economic Committee came out in favor of supply-side economics. In the early 1980s, meanwhile, so-called Atari Democrats such as Bill Bradley and Paul Tsongas argued for a new liberalism that heavily emphasized technology, business, and wealth creation. But it was the foundation of the Democratic Leadership Council in 1985, set up in deliberate response to Reagan's crushing landslide a few months before, that really marked the turning point. From its inception, the group disavowed the social-democratic economic populism that had carried Walter Mondale to defeat, arguing instead for "market-based" solutions to welfare and unemployment. By 1992, when the DLC alumnus Bill Clinton coasted to the presidential nomination, the group's emphasis on the interests of business, free-market economics, and close attention to the Southern vote was well on the way to becoming Democratic orthodoxy.[32]

While the rightward journey of Britain's Labour Party was slower and more turbulent, reflecting the greater resilience of social democratic traditions in British politics, it followed roughly the same course. By the late 1980s Neil Kinnock had already begun to discard unpopular left-wing policies, notably unilateral disarmament, and by 1992 the two parties were probably ideologically closer than at any point in living memory. And when Labour finally regained office in 1997, it did so under a prime minister who had publicly stated his admiration for Margaret Thatcher, and a Chancellor who had promised to stick to the Conservatives' spending plans for his first three years. Gordon Brown, wrote the right-of-center commentator Simon Jenkins with only slight exaggeration, was "Thatcherism's most coveted St Paul, a convert and soldier of the faith."[33] And of course both Blair and Brown drew inspiration from events across the Atlantic, where Clinton had already famously declared that the "era of big government is over." Even before he took office, he had made the key decision to reject major public investment in favor of paying off the Reagan deficit, deeply disappointing his liberal economic adviser and fellow Rhodes scholar Robert Reich, who now found himself pushed to the sidelines of the administration.[34] And while Clinton privately chafed against the constraints of presidential leadership in the age of bond markets, outsourcing, and globalization, he proved strikingly willing to ditch long-cherished liberal programs in the name of the new order—not least by signing the landmark welfare reform bill in 1996.[35]

In a strange way, therefore, there is a case that the conservative revolution reached its high point not in the 1980s but in the decade that followed. It was in the 1990s, after all, that neoliberalism, profiting from a protracted economic boom and the disorientation of the left after the collapse of the Soviet bloc, cemented its place at the heart of Anglo-American politics; indeed, it was the 1990s that saw some of the most audacious attacks on the old social democratic state—the privatization of Britain's railways, for example, or Clinton's dismantling of "welfare as we know it." Yet while the parallels between Reagan's heirs and Thatcher's legatees are powerful and convincing, there was one enormous difference. In purely partisan, electoral terms, rather than ideological ones, Reagan's impact was far more impressive, for the quarter-century following his election was a golden age for the Republican Party. Between 1980 and 2004 they won five out of seven presidential elections, captured the balance of power in the Supreme Court, turned the South into a conservative heartland at every level, and enjoyed unprecedented influence on Capitol Hill, especially after the record-breaking landslide of 1994. It was hardly surprising that by the early twenty-first century, no Republican would have dreamed to question Reagan's heroic status, for since his elevation to the presidency, their party—thanks of course to deep structural changes from the rise of the suburban Sunbelt to the decline of the old industrial North—had never had it so good.

Thatcher's legacy, however, was very different. The force of her ideas is beyond dispute: Jenkins, an admirer turned skeptic, remarks that Thatcherism became "the ruling consensus" of British politics after 1990, casting the leaders of both parties as "convinced disciples, going even where their mistress had feared to tread."[36] For her party, however, the years after her departure were far from golden. Although John Major managed to drag the party to one last election victory in 1992, all thereafter was dust and desolation. After the humiliating devaluation of the pound and flight from the European exchange rate mechanism in 1992, the Conservatives lost three successive general elections, all by heavy margins. One leader after another—Major, William Hague, Ian Duncan Smith, Michael Howard, David Cameron—struggled to rebuild their fortunes, but they never managed even a consistent lead in the opinion polls. As late as the summer of 2007, seventeen years after Thatcher's departure, they found themselves commanding the support of no more than a third of the electorate, while paradoxically, Thatcher herself remained at the center of British political life, openly courted and praised by the new Labour prime minister.

Why did Reagan and Thatcher have such different electoral legacies? The obvious answer lies not in the leaders themselves, but in the entirely different contexts in which they operated. If John Hinckley's marksmanship had been rather more accurate, there is surely little doubt that the "Reagan revolution" would have continued anyway. After all, Reagan was in many respects building on Jimmy Carter's economic policy (for instance in the battle against inflation), and in any case, the forces that drove the Republican Party forward would have yielded results at some point, even without their most articulate champion. But those demographic and social forces, notably the utter transformation of the South since World War II, simply had no parallel in Britain, where there was no comparable migration of people or capital, no regional realignment, and not a even cultural reawakening to compare with the rise of the religious right. Reagan, in other words, had been swimming with the tide; Thatcher, in large part, had been swimming against it.

This also explains why the two leaders occupy such different places in the recent histories of their respective countries. Reagan's death in June 2004 was the cue for national mourning on a scale not seen since Eisenhower's demise in 1969. More than a hundred thousand people filed past the former governor's coffin at his presidential library in California, while on the day of the funeral itself, every American military base in the world fired a twenty-one-gun salute in Reagan's honor, church bells across the nation tolled forty times, and several states held a minute's silence. Democrats joined Republicans in paying tribute to Reagan's legacy; black joined white in the crowds and the queues. Three years later, Gallup found that only Abraham Lincoln matched Reagan's standing as "the greatest United States president," while millions of viewers of the Discovery Channel's series voted Reagan "the greatest American" ahead of Lincoln, Martin Luther King, and George Washington.[37]

Thatcher, by contrast, remained an enormously divisive public figure, endlessly lampooned in left-wing newspapers, her final departure anxiously anticipated by BBC executives who knew that their coverage, whether adulatory or critical, was bound to alienate part of the audience.[38] Like Reagan, she was widely acknowledged as the progenitor of the modern political order. Yet while Reagan was fondly remembered for his emollient style, aw-shucks patriotism, and all-round amiability, Thatcher was remembered more for her thirst for confrontation, her abrasive rhetoric, and supposed hatred of compromise. A tentative conclusion, therefore, might be that Reagan was more fondly remembered simply because his task had been much easier. He had inherited the reins of power in the country that was already moving sharply to the right, had faced remarkably weak opposition, and had often pulled his punches at the moment of decision. Margaret Thatcher, on the other hand, had taken power in a country with a much stronger social democratic tradition. To achieve her aims, she had fought long and deeply controversial public battles with public servants, trade unionists, and even many of her own colleagues, while searing events like the miners' strike had left scars that would not heal for decades. Unlike Reagan, she had fought against the winds of history, rather than allowed herself to be carried by them. "Thatcher was a truly revolutionary leader," notes Jenkins. "She was dissatisfied by what she saw around her and set herself to change it utterly... Unlike most radicals who end by running before the wind of events... Thatcher headed straight into oncoming gales." The same might have been true of Reagan in the 1960s, but it was not true of Reagan, or of American life, in the late 1970s and 1980s. That explains why Reagan became so widely loved, and why he is more likely to become a venerated national hero. But it also suggests that of the two, Thatcher was the more courageous, and the greater figure. She was not Reagan's John the Baptist; he was hers.[39]

Notes

I would like to thank Professor Michael Heale for his comments on an earlier draft of this piece, which were as acute and thoughtful as ever.

1. The transcript of Thatcher's speech is online at her foundation's website: http://www.margaretthatcher.org/speeches/displaydocument.asp?docid=108327?. The text of Reagan's speech is at http://odur.let.rug.nl/~usa/P/rr40/speeches/gala_speech.htm.
2. Margaret Thatcher, *The Downing Street Years* (London: Harper Collins, 1993), 157.
3. Hugo Young, *One of Us: A Biography of Margaret Thatcher* (London: Macmillan, 1989), 250.
4. John Campbell, *Margaret Thatcher: Volume Two: The Iron Lady* (London: Jonathan Cape, 2003), 263–264.
5. Young, *One of Us*, 252.
6. The poster can be viewed online at the Peace Museum website, www.vredesmuseum.nl/t_vision/paneel13.html.
7. *Time*, March 4, 1985.
8. Geoffrey Smith, *Reagan and Thatcher* (London, 1991), 19–21; Stephen F. Hayward, *The Age of Reagan: The Fall of the Old Liberal Order, 1964–1980* (New York: Prima Lifestyles, 2001), 533–534.
9. See Dominic Sandbrook, *White Heat: A History of Britain in the Swinging Sixties* (London: Little, Brown, 2006), 114–116.
10. Smith, *Reagan and Thatcher*, 81–82.
11. Lou Cannon, *President Reagan: The Role of a Lifetime* (New York: Public Affairs, 2000), 45, 408.
12. John Campbell, *Margaret Thatcher: Volume One: The Grocer's Daughter* (London: Pimlico, 2001), 306–311.
13. Ibid., 414.
14. Alan S. Blinder, "The Rise and Fall of Keynesian Economics," *The Economic Record*, December 1988, 278.
15. Robert M. Collins, *More: The Politics of Economic Growth in Postwar America* (Oxford: Oxford University Press, 2000), 181–182.
16. *The Times* (London), September 29, 1976.
17. *Newsweek*, November 7, 1977; *New Times*, September 30, 1977.
18. David S. Broder, *Changing of the Guard: Power and Leadership in America* (London: Viking Press, 1981), 158–159.
19. See Theodore H. White, *America in Search of Itself: The Making of the President 1965–1980* (New York: Harper & Row, 1982), 417.
20. Andrew E. Busch, *Reagan's Victory: The Presidential Election of 1980 and the Rise of the Right* (Lawrence, Kan.: University Press of Kansas, 2005), 129, 135. Historical approval ratings are online at http://www.ropercenter.uconn.edu/data_access/data/presidential_approval.html.
21. Campbell, *Margaret Thatcher: Volume Two*, 123–125.
22. Thomas Ferguson and Joel Rogers, *Right Turn: The Decline of the Democrats and the Future of American Politics* (New York: Hill & Wang, 1986), 15–17; James T. Patterson, *Restless Giant: The United States from Watergate to Bush v. Gore* (Oxford: University of Oxford Press, 2004), 65–67, 85.
23. Mark Garnett, *From Anger to Apathy: The British Experience since 1975* (London: Jonathan Cape, 2007), 243.

24. Lou Cannon, *Governor Reagan: His Rise to Power* (New York: Public Affairs, 2003), 197.
25. Ibid., 186; Alonzo L. Hamby, *Liberalism and its Challengers: From FDR to Reagan* (New York: Oxford University Press, 1985), 350.
26. *Washington Post*, November 12, 1981; David A. Stockman, *The Triumph of Politics: Why the Reagan Revolution Failed* (New York, 1986), 9.
27. *Wall Street Journal*, August 17, 1988; and see John Ehrman, *The Eighties: America in the Age of Reagan* (New Haven: Yale University Press, 2005), 149–150.
28. Campbell, *Margaret Thatcher: Volume Two*, 171–172.
29. John Ranelagh, *Thatcher's People* (London: HarperCollins, 1991), 241.
30. Campbell, *Margaret Thatcher: Volume Two*, 800.
31. Garnett, *From Anger to Apathy*, 248–255.
32. See Collins, *More*, 188–189; Godfrey Hodgson, *The World Turned Right Side Up: A History of the Conservative Ascendancy in America* (New York: Houghton Mifflin, 1996), 206–209; Kenneth S. Baer, *Reinventing Democrats: The Politics of Liberalism from Reagan to Clinton* (Lawrence, Kan.: University Press of Kansas, 2000).
33. Simon Jenkins, *Thatcher & Sons: A Revolution in Three Acts* (London: Allen Lane, 2006), 272.
34. See Robert B. Reich, *Locked in the Cabinet* (New York: Random House, 1997); George Stephanopoulos, *All Too Human: A Political Education* (New York: Little, Brown & Co., 1999).
35. See Ron Haskins, *Work over Welfare: The Inside Story of the 1996 Welfare Reform Law* (Washington, DC: Brookings Institution Press, 2006).
36. Jenkins, *Thatcher & Sons*, 1–2.
37. *USA Today*/Gallup poll, February 9–11, 2007, http://www.pollingreport.com/wh-hstry.htm. On *The Greatest American*, see *New York Times*, July 7, 2005.
38. See *The Times* (London), August 8, 2006.
39. Jenkins, *Thatcher & Sons*, 1.

Chapter 11

Transforming the Presidency: The Administration of Ronald Reagan

Joel D. Aberbach

Introduction

Ronald Reagan's presidency is justly noted for its administrative style and practices. One prominent scholar, Terry Moe, even described Reagan, in an essay published after Reagan's first term, as likely "the most administratively influential president of the modern period."[1] While Richard Nixon developed what came to be known as the "administrative presidency,"[2] it was Reagan, utilizing some tools not available to Nixon and unencumbered by Nixon's numerous mistakes, who brought this approach to fruition. His mark is seen today in the way George W. Bush has staffed and organized his administration, and in its policy implementation practices.

This chapter examines the ways the Reagan presidency was staffed and administered, with emphasis on the nature of its relationship with the permanent government (the bureaucracy). It looks at the techniques the administration employed, utilizing both secondary sources and survey data gathered when Reagan was president, and evaluates the Reagan administration's immediate influence and its long-term impact on the ways presidents operate in the American system. My goals are to examine the context in which the Reagan administration's administrative tactics were developed, to analyze the significance of Reagan's administration in legitimating a particular model of the presidency, to look at the administration's impact on the presidencies that have come after it, and to consider issues arising from the strategy followed by the Reagan presidency.

My fundamental argument is that the Reagan administration was vitally important in pushing forward an interpretation of presidential supremacy that, by fits and starts, is transforming the underlying constitutional order in the United States. Executive supremacy grew, marked by substantially increased control over the bureaucracy and the use of the regulatory process and other administrative mechanisms to alter and sometimes to override legislation that the president disliked. Underlying this approach is a political theory resting on the notion that presidential elections are a kind of plebiscite, yielding a mandate that legitimizes presidential supremacy. These notions conflict with traditional ideas about presidential power in a separation of powers system. Reagan's administration provided a model for his successors, most especially George W. Bush, of how to increase presidential influence, while problems such as the Iran–Contra scandal and the gradual exhaustion of the administration also demonstrated the weaknesses of his approach.

Presidential Power

Richard Neustadt's classic book on *Presidential Power* was initially published in 1960. The title of this elegant treatise might lead one to expect an analysis of a commanding figure. But Neustadt argues strongly that presidents cannot command because they must function in a system of "separated institutions *sharing* powers."[3] This complex system gives substantial power to numerous actors—members of the House and Senate, bureaucrats, and others—who have their own bases of support and generally act to protect their own interests and those of their constituencies. Given this situation, presidents must use persuasion. As Neustadt argues:

> When one man shares authority with another, but does not gain or lose his job upon the other's whim, his willingness to act upon the urging of the other turns on whether he conceives the action right for him. The essence of a President's persuasive task is to convince such men that what the White House wants of them is what they ought to do for their sake and on their authority.[4]

Presidents, according to Neustadt, are most effective when they do what the system demands, that is, bargain with others using the many resources at their disposal. The wise president uses command infrequently because the conditions for successful command are rarely met, and the costs can be considerable. Compromise is the coin of the realm by necessity. Loyalty cannot be assumed, so the president is well advised to guard his power prospects, serve as his own key intelligence officer, and even his own staff director.[5] The word "ideology" does not appear in the index; a whole chapter is devoted to "The Power to Persuade."

One key task of the president is to teach the public realism. This is essential because so much is uncontrollable, both politically and in the wider world sphere. A major presidential goal should be to bring public expectations into line with what can reasonably be achieved. Absent this, the president is likely to be perceived as a failure, with his public prestige and professional reputation in shambles and his bargaining position greatly diminished.

Neustadt's president is no goody two-shoes. At his best (they have all been male so far, but hope springs eternal), he is a tough bargainer and a shrewd judge of others' strengths and weaknesses. He plays the game hard when the situation demands it, though he is basically rule-abiding. He implicitly recognizes, even if often grudgingly, the truth of Charles O. Jones's statement: "[S]ome believe that the president is the presidency, the presidency is the government, and ours is a presidential system...They will be proven wrong."[6]

Terry Moe's analysis starts with an assumption similar to Neustadt's; the U.S. system puts severe limits on the president. "The president is embedded in a much larger network of political institutions that seriously limit what he can do. Above all the constitutional system guarantees that the president and Congress will be locked in institutional struggle, particularly over issues bearing on their relative powers."[7] However, according to Moe, the system is out of equilibrium. The president is the one nationally elected officer of the government. He is by far the country's most visible political leader, and, with growing force generated by changes in the environment (such as the rise of media-generated public expectations for performance), the nation holds him primarily responsible for government policy and performance. His reelection and ultimately his place in history are at stake. Because of the design of the system, however, he cannot easily make the government do what he wants; in fact, he is often frustrated by the incongruity between what he wants and what he can get. In Moe's terminology, there is a marked "incongruence among structures, incentives, and resources."[8] Systems do not remain in this state for long. Or, in the case of the U.S. presidency, Moe says: "If presidents are dissatisfied with the institutional arrangements they inherit, then they will initiate changes to the extent that they have the resources to do so."[9]

What a dissatisfied president does to the presidency, according to Moe, is politicize and centralize. He favors "responsive competence" over "neutral competence."[10] He draws authority into the center (the institutional presidency in the White House), uses the power of appointment to fill the government to the maximum extent possible with people who are loyal to him or to his ideas, increases the number and strategically picks the locations for positions that are occupied by appointees, and generally does whatever he can to get his way.

As I noted in an essay that contrasted the two presidencies represented by the treatments of Neustadt ("the first presidency") and Moe ("the second presidency"):

> The two presidencies described in the literature have quite different implications for the way the institution is organized and for the nature of the relationship between the president and the bureaucracy. While the first president holds his interests tightly—he is the best judge of his own power prospects and, in the end, is well advised to be his own chief of staff—the second is surrounded by a set of like-minded advisers who pursue his interests. The first president expects to bargain with his cabinet and subcabinet appointees (who represent a variety of interests). The second expects a tightly knit team. The first president casts a wary eye on the bureaucracy but is, despite sometimes difficult struggles, resigned to its pursuit of interests that are often different from his own. The second president takes on the bureaucracy and insists that it serve his

interests and does what he wants it to do. Where the first president aims to live with what Richard Hofstadter has called "a harmonious system of mutual frustration," the second president will not accept frustration. He expects to get his way with Congress and the bureaucracy. If he cannot get Congress to go along, he expects the bureaucracy to do his bidding and structures his administration with this in mind.[11]

The fact that the president is the single nationally elected figure in American government is particularly important in the Moe conception as a justification for the way the president behaves. The incongruence between structures, incentives, and resources not only stimulates the "dynamics of institutional change" that Moe writes about, but the president, as the "only politician" with "an electoral incentive to pursue some broader notion of the public interest, even if restricted to the interests of the coalition that supports him,"[12] has special legitimacy. The presidential election gives him a mandate that no other figure has. The authority flowing from the mandate, in this view, legitimates what the president does to take command.

The Nixon Administration

The initial period of Richard Nixon's administration was quite conventional. Nixon, who had been elected with less than 44 percent of the popular vote, started with a fairly classic conception of his role as president and of the way to run a presidential administration. Most of the cabinet he appointed was not close to him personally and, as Richard Nathan notes, they were not close to him "even politically."[13] Nixon went so far as to allow his cabinet members to select members of the subcabinet. He set to work developing a legislative program and sought congressional approval for his proposals. All in all, he did little out of the ordinary, and seemed poised to serve in ways that any reader of Neustadt would have found fairly unremarkable.

But Nixon was soon frustrated. He believed that he was being sabotaged by the career bureaucracy and by many of his own appointees. He found the Congress, controlled by the opposition, an irritating impediment. He wanted control, and he demanded personal loyalty. Gradually, he evolved an approach to governing that Nathan labels the "administrative presidency" strategy.[14] It called for a set of cumulatively radical changes in the means of governance.

The strategy had four key elements:

1. Personnel shifts—placing trusted lieutenants in top agency posts. Initially, Nixon built up the White House staff, but this approach failed because of difficulty in controlling the government from the center. He then began a process of placing "little known Nixon loyalists" in the agencies.[15] The idea was to have people who were totally dependent on Nixon in key posts so as to ensure adherence to White House requests and wishes. (As John Ehrlichman is reported to have said of the appointees: "When we say

jump, they will only ask how high?")[16] These officials were carefully instructed in ways, many of them overtly illegal, to remove recalcitrant civil servants and gain control of the career bureaucracy.
2. Budget impoundments and reductions—Nixon refused to spend money that had been duly appropriated by Congress on programs he wanted to cut or eliminate.
3. Reorganization—used in attempts to abolish or subvert governmental activities the Nixon administration did not favor.
4. Regulation writing—regulations were written to achieve the goals of the administration, rather than goals reasonably attributed to the legislation itself.

Most of the elements of this strategy had been used before by other administrations. What made the Nixon administration special was the scope and depth of its use of each element as well as the fact that all were used in an evolving, conscious strategy to aggressively circumvent legislative and other restraints and to gain complete control of a bureaucracy that the administration believed was more committed to its own (often Democratic-initiated) programs than to President Nixon's priorities.

Nixon won the 1972 election by an overwhelming margin (giving him more claim than he had from 1968 to an electoral mandate), but his administration soon collapsed in the Watergate scandal. The Watergate hearings publicized evidence of a sorry history of abuse of power, including such internal publications as the "Malek Manual" that instructed political appointees in illegal and marginally legal ways to inhibit and remove career officials.[17] The Congress reasserted its authority in a variety of ways, including passage of the Congressional Budget and Impoundment Control Act of 1974 and the War Powers Resolution. Democrats won the 1974 midterm election overwhelmingly, producing a large and feisty majority in Congress that seemed an indicator that the Nixonian approach to the presidency and to presidential power (both in its legal and illegal aspects) would be buried for a very long time, if not forever.

And, overall, this proved true in the Ford and Carter administrations that were much more modest in their conduct and in their notions about the presidency. But things changed quickly with the Reagan administration, one that set about boldly using a modified administrative presidency strategy that was tailored to Reagan's political strengths, to changed political circumstances, and to lessons learned from the failures of the Nixon administration.

The Reagan Administration

Reagan had several advantages over Nixon and he used them well, especially in the initial years of his presidency. At the risk of leaving some important elements out, let me list just a few: first, he won his initial election clearly and relatively decisively, a big advantage over Nixon's situation in 1968. Second, where Nixon's politics were a bit murky, Reagan was clearly a conservative who did not mask his basic ideological position. He could claim a "mandate" from the voters without sounding hollow. Third, Reagan brought a Republican Senate in with him. While the senatorial elections could be explained away as idiosyncratic, they were widely interpreted in Washington as evidence that Reagan's election represented a fundamental shift in the nature of American politics. The Republican Senate represented a huge advantage for Reagan in appointments requiring Senate confirmation. Fourth, the Civil Service Reform Act of 1978, passed during the Carter administration, gave an opportunistic and assertive presidential administration authority to manipulate the civil service in ways that were illegal when Nixon was president. Fifth, the Carter administration pioneered the use of the reconciliation provisions of the 1974 Congressional Budget Act (passed in reaction to Nixon's high-handed use of budget impoundments) to cut spending. Reagan's advisors noticed this and used it to great effect in their initial attack on existing programs they did not like. Sixth, in the years since Nixon's presidency, the number and financial support of conservative think tanks had grown in Washington and around the country, giving the incoming Reagan administration a reservoir of identified talent to appoint to key positions and depth in preparing its agenda.[18] Seventh, as Nathan notes with regard to cabinet making, but the point applies to other areas, "many of the key planners of the Reagan presidency "had learned the ropes under Nixon."[19] They had experienced his failures, thought hard about how to do things "better" this time, and overall had a reservoir of talent and experience that Nixon had lacked: some people had been there, others had been in think tanks, and less than ten years had passed since 1974.

Perhaps no area exemplifies the Reagan administration's approach to administration and the administrative presidency strategy better than personnel. Where Nixon had begun his administration with a cabinet of notables who were given wide latitude to select subcabinet members of their choice and with an inconsistent brand of conservatism that has fostered substantial debate about his political direction,[20] the Reagan administration started with a very different approach to staffing the administration and with a quite clear direction. The emphasis was on loyalty to Reagan's ideas as well as to the man. As Bert Rockman notes:

> More than any recent Presidency, the Reagan administration not only had clear goals but also had a clear strategic concept. It knew what it wanted. It also knew who it wanted to help it...More than any other administration...many individuals who composed this one were loyal to the ideas for which Ronald Reagan stood. Much of this zealotry was summed up in the now famous slogan "Let Reagan be Reagan." It is hard to imagine a similar catch phrase being conjured up for any other American President.[21]

Reagan's planning began in November 1979, a year before the election, with Edwin Meese commissioning Pendleton James, who had worked for the Nixon administration, to put together a personnel operation. It has been characterized as "tighter than any other" previously undertaken.[22] Cabinet members had to agree to White House selection of their subordinates. The aim was that loyalty to the president and his views was to dominate the "tugs of Congress, interest groups, and the bureaucracy."[23] James Pfiffner, like Rockman, emphasizes that the screening undertaken would not have worked as well in previous administrations because Reagan's clearly defined ideology set him apart form earlier presidents "who had much broader sets of values."[24]

Cabinet nominees were consulted, but passing muster with a formidable array of Reagan associates (Lyn Nofziger, Fred Fielding, Martin Anderson (domestic) or Richard Allen (national security), and the triad of James Baker, Michael Deaver, and Edwin Meese) was essential before appointees were selected.[25] Selections of cabinet offices were made in consultation with a group of Reagan friends and close associates known as his "kitchen cabinet,"[26] and those selected had to go through an indoctrination course developed by Meese.[27] The net result was an administration whose appointees were like-minded to a remarkable degree for an American government. Unlike the Neustadt model, where appointees often are chosen to represent the views of a variety of outside interests to the administration, Reagan's administration was designed to consist of people who would represent the president's views in their dealings with the career bureaucracy and with constituency groups that might be wary of or opposed to the goals of the administration. Richard Nathan quotes Reagan on the night of the election as saying that his intention was to bring about "a new structuring of the presidential cabinet that will make cabinet officers the managers of the national administration—not captives of the bureaucracy or special interest they are supposed to direct."[28] A March 1981 *National Journal* analysis quoted by Nathan was even more succinct about what the administration had in mind: "the role of Cabinet officers and senior appointed officials is to function as loyal lieutenants dedicated to the pursuit of presidential objectives."[29]

Not surprisingly, there was some grumbling on the right that not all appointees were sufficiently Reaganite. Becky Norton Dunlop, writing in a 1987 volume edited by Robert Rector of the Heritage Foundation and Michael Sanera who had been a Reagan appointee to the Office of Personnel Management, complained that some appointments were meant to heal fissures in the Republican Party, some slipped through because of influence with figures outside the process, some people the personnel selection people wanted refused to serve, and some simply represented mistakes made in judging the true colors of those selected.[30]

While there is surely truth in this assessment, data gathered for a set of interview studies I did with Bert Rockman show the tremendous success of the Reagan process. (The Nixon administration data were gathered in 1970, before the onset of the administrative presidency push. The Reagan data were collected in 1986–1987, a time when the administration's early zeal had already faded with time and scandal.) A total of 65 percent of Nixon's appointees were Republicans, but that percentage rose to 97 for the Reagan administration. And the figures are, in a sense, even more impressive for the appointees below the very top (PAS, or Passed with the Advice of the Senate) category. Only 59 percent of Nixon's appointees were Republicans, while 98 percent of Reagan's were Republicans. (Incidentally, there were no Democrats in the Reagan sample, but a quarter of the Nixon appointees regularly voted Democratic.) More tellingly, measures of political ideology showed that the Reagan appointees were not only more overwhelmingly Republican, they were much more conservative than Nixon's appointees. Only 19 percent of Nixon's appointees opposed an active role for government in the economy, whereas 74 percent of Reagan administration appointees held similar views—with most of the rest in the middle category on the measure.[31] In short, grumbling by some aside, the Reagan administration was remarkably effective in getting conservative Republican appointees into key positions.

In addition to success in getting the sorts of political executives it wanted in place, the Reagan administration was tremendously successful in its efforts to manipulate the civil service system. I'll say a bit about Reductions in Force (RIFs) later, but the administration also used the provisions of the 1978 Civil Service Reform Act to great effect in getting the kind of career people it wanted into key positions in targeted positions and agencies. The 1978 act changed the system from one of rank-in-the-position to one of rank-in-the-person (creating the Senior Executive Service, commonly known as the SES). This allowed the administration to locate those civil servants who shared its views and move them into the very top career positions in the agencies (defined as the top career positions in units whose incumbents report to political appointees), and the administration used this opportunity very effectively. Where Nixon's top civil servants had been about three to one Democratic in their party affiliations, the Reagan administration actually had slightly more Republicans than Democrats among its top civil servants, with those slightly below the top two to one Democratic.

Further, the administration was particularly effective in the social service agencies that were its main targets. While the SES career bureaucracy was strongly Democratic in these agencies, the Reagan administration managed to put almost all the Republicans into the top positions (67 percent), with the other (slightly lower positions in the hierarchy) positions only 12 percent Republican and 77 percent Democratic.[32] In short, the administration made spectacular use of this available tool, something that the data in figure 11.1 show was not used by the less committed Bush I administration.

Moreover, the Reagan administration managed to close the career bureaucracy off from the policymaking process to a quite substantial degree. Top civil servants in general reported significantly less frequent contacts with Congress, interest groups, and the public at large in the Reagan administration than they reported in the Nixon administration.[33] The frequency of contacts also went down with their own department heads and with heads of other departments. Not surprisingly, top career civil servants' self-perceptions of influence in the policy process also went down considerably.[34]

1986–87

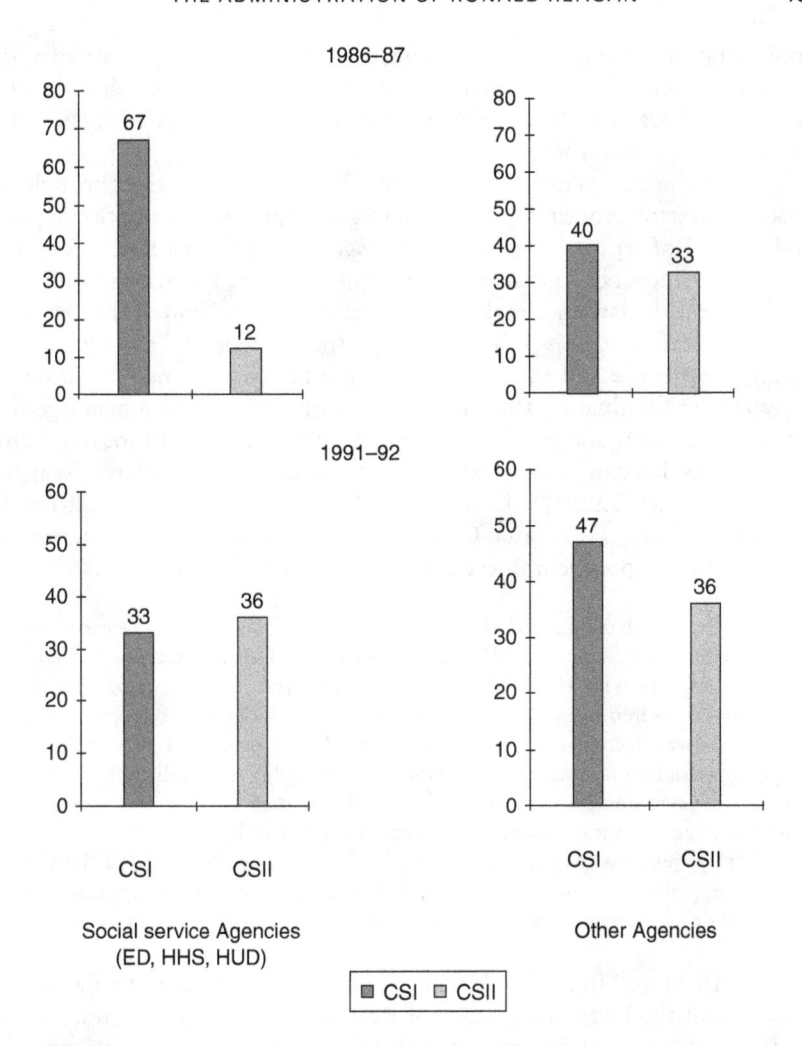

[Chart: Social service Agencies (ED, HHS, HUD) — CSI: 67, CSII: 12]

[Chart: Other Agencies — CSI: 40, CSII: 33]

1991–92

[Chart: Social service Agencies (ED, HHS, HUD) — CSI: 33, CSII: 36]

[Chart: Other Agencies — CSI: 47, CSII: 36]

Figure 11.1 Percentage Republican, senior civil servants, by agency type, job status, and year.

Source: Adapted from Joel D. Aberbach and Bert A. Rockman, *In the Web of Politics* (Washington: Brookings Institution Press, 2000), 108.

Note: CSI, Career civil servants who occupy the top rungs in their administrative units and report to political appointees; CSII, career Senior Executive Service members who report to other civil servants, not political appointees.

In short, the data suggest that, to a considerable extent, the Reagan administration managed to cut top career civil servants out of the action and thereby gain a significant level of control over the bureau chiefs and other such civil servants who Neustadt, in *Presidential Power*, cites as major players in the American system. Neustadt argues that these top bureaucratic actors have four "masters" in the American system (Congress, clients, staff, and themselves) in addition to the President.[35] Under Reagan, even in 1986–1987 when the survey data cited in the last paragraph were collected and the administration was not nearly as strong as it was in its first year or two, the presidency retained an unusually high level of control over its top civil servants, and was clearly still able to restrain their contacts with the other four masters Neustadt wrote about.

The administration did not stop with efforts to gain control through the personnel system. Another tool it used to great effect was regulation writing (and control of regulation writing). As Rector and Sanera note: "The real content and impact of legislation is determined by the regulations formulated to implement the law and by the bureaucratic interpretation of those regulations. Academically, this ability to shape the content of broad legislation through regulation and administrative action has been termed *bureaucratic discretion*."[36] Eliminating this "bureaucratic discretion" was a major goal of the administration and it moved firmly and assertively to do so. According to Cornelius Kerwin, whose book on rulemaking is a standard, Reagan's Executive Order 12291, which followed earlier less extensive efforts by Presidents Nixon, Ford, and Carter, was "arguably the most significant incursion by any president into the core process of rulemaking"[37]:

> This order mandated a regulatory impact analysis for all rules whose estimated effect on the economy was $100 million or more. This amounts to full cost-benefit analysis with the additional feature that the proponents of any new rule were required to demonstrate a net gain to society prior to its promulgation...It was accompanied by a set of regulatory principles that exhorted agencies to adopt nonregulatory options for accomplishing public policy objectives whenever possible and to use the least intrusive and burdensome regulatory devises when government intervention was the only realistic alternative.
>
> [And] President Reagan did not stop with Executive Order 12291. During the course of his presidency he signed numerous other executive orders requiring the development of specific types of information during rulemaking.[38]

Kenneth Mayer, in his book on executive orders and presidential power, agrees about the huge significance of Reagan's executive order, noting that it was meant "to wrest control over federal regulatory activity from executive branch agencies," and that it "spurred a 'minor revolution' in constitutional theories of presidential authority over administration."[39] As Mayer notes: "One reason Reagan took the executive order route is that Congress would have refused to voluntarily grant such a measure of control, and attempts to seek legislative reform of regulatory institutions failed throughout the Reagan presidency."[40] The order "cite[d] no specific statutory or constitutional provision as the basis for the president's authority to issue it...[I]t relies on a unitary picture of presidential picture of presidential authority to manage and control the activities of all executive branch officials and agencies (at least insofar as permitted by statute)."[41] In brief, Executive Order 12291 was a major push forward in the assertion, at the expense of Congress and the agencies, of presidential power in rulemaking.

The Reagan administration used other tools as well as part of its "administrative presidency" strategy. Nathan cites a variety of them. First, spending projects from the Carter administration that the administration did not want to pursue were put on "hold" and many were cancelled through "rescissions," somewhat ironically a mechanism formalized by the 1974 Budget Impoundment and Control Act. The administration also used the "reconciliation" device in the Budget Act to make significant cuts to programs it did not like. Second, the Reagan administration pursued both "removal of existing regulations and the relaxation of their enforcement...as an important instrument of policy redirection."[42] Third, Reductions in Force (RIFs) were used to terminate career employees, reduce others in grade, and discourage program staff in programs that it did not favor (e.g., the Economic Development Administration).

As Nathan points out, an especially noteworthy element of the Reagan administration's approach was its use of both legislative and administrative tactics.[43] It had advantages not enjoyed by the Nixon administration, both in the form of a Senate majority for six years and some statutes that could be used effectively to pursue goals that Nixon felt could only be achieved through purely administrative means. The question remains whether the Reagan approach was ultimately successful and what its implications have been for both the presidency and American democracy.

Impact

Writing in 1983, Nathan, concluded that "regardless of what the Reagan administration will face in the future, it has already left a distinct imprint on the federal establishment."[44] There can be little doubt that what he wrote was right at that time, and in important ways continues to be right. What I will do in this section is look briefly at some successes and failures of the administration's approach and the ways in which it influenced future administrations. The concluding section will consider some of the broader issues arising from the strategy followed by the Reagan presidency.

First, it is important to emphasize that the Nixon experience and the difficult presidencies of Ford and especially Carter had raised serious questions about the presidential office itself—Nixon through his illegal behavior and his successors through the great difficulties of handling the office in a period of great congressional assertiveness. When Reagan left office, there were certainly many doubts about him and about his policies and approach, but few about the viability of the presidential office. He had gotten through two terms and had a significant impact on both the office and the country.

Second, Reagan had added a measure of legitimacy to the administrative presidency strategy, refining it and also bringing it somewhat more in line with tradition by, where feasible and convenient, using dual administrative and legislative tactics. Nathan sees this as a key Reagan innovation,[45] made possible in large part by changes in the congressional budget process and by Republican control of the Senate.

Third, Reagan had demonstrated once again the dangers of the administrative presidency approach, and illustrated its limits. His appointees at the

Environmental Protection Agency (EPA), for example, while fully behaving with the zealousness his appointments strategy sought, also got themselves into such trouble that one (Ann Gorsuch) had to resign and another (Rita LaVelle) went to prison, to be replaced by more moderate types (such as William D. Ruckelshaus) "representing a striking departure from the earlier appointments."[46] Ruckelshaus was even given "permission to appoint his own senior staff at EPA."[47] Gorsuch, as Richard Nathan indicates, had "cut the budget and staff of her agency and relaxed the enforcement of federal regulations to prevent and reduce air and water pollution; she also changed some of the regulations themselves."[48] Her successor followed a much more moderate course, particularly in the period through the 1984 election.[49]

There were many other areas where the administration's assertive approach was more successful. However, in at least some of those cases, as Jeffrey K. Stine points out with respect to policy on natural resources,

> the administration's efforts rarely effected long-term change, primarily because of the White House's essential political strategy. Rather than using a legislative approach, Reagan relied on "administrative fiat"—reorganizing federal agencies; significantly reducing or reallocating money and personnel; altering, withdrawing, or weakening the enforcement of federal regulations; and placing like-minded loyalists in key positions within the federal bureaucracy. As Resources for the Future analyst Paul R. Portney observed: "There is a price to pay for inattention to legislative change...subsequent administrations can more easily reverse policies through administrative action alone." "Fundamental change," Portney added, "is much more likely if an administration takes the time to work closely with Congress in redirecting policy," something that the Reagan administration consistently avoided.[50]

As noted earlier, the Reagan administration did not necessarily confine itself to an administrative strategy in situations where it could combine that with more lasting alternatives, but Stine is surely right that changes are likely to last longer when given a legislative seal. The core of an administrative strategy is that it enables the president to sidestep other actors and institutions when it suits his purposes. A weakness is that the next president can easily undo what his or her predecessor did using similar administrative techniques. There are seemingly big benefits to following the administrative strategy: speed and short-term certainty are obtained and delay and compromise avoided. The cost is that what's been accomplished can fairly easily be undone. In the world portrayed by Moe, where few attempts have been made to teach constituents "realism" and a system out of equilibrium puts overwhelming pressures on presidents to achieve immediately, the choice of an administrative strategy in most cases seems clear and just about irresistible. In Neustadt's world that choice is likely to provoke telling resistance from other actors in the system. While the resistance may fail, it can be costly in undermining presidential legitimacy and, as the EPA case demonstrates, lead to great embarrassment for the administration (and sometimes policy reversals).

Fourth, Reagan demonstrated the truth behind Neustadt's notion that presidents cannot fully rely on their subordinates. Reagan's "distance from detail," or, less kindly put, laziness, made his strategy of relying on zealous subordinates a necessity,[51] but also left him vulnerable to their worst failings. His somewhat pathetic pleas of ignorance in the Iran–Contra case and ultimate assumption of responsibility probably saved him,[52] even if also exposing him and his office to terrible ridicule. (Iran–Contra also led productively to a house cleaning in the president's office and further moderation of the administration's policies and approach, a trend that had started earlier.) As David Gergen noted, Reagan was "a president whose extensive delegation of authority and inattention to important details made him more dependent upon the quality of the people around him than is wise. In one instance, he paid dearly because he chose the wrong people."[53] Many, however, would argue that the country paid dearly in a lot of other areas that had the wrong people in charge but did not get quite the attention ultimately paid to the Iran–Contra scandal.

Presidents who Followed

Reagan finished his term on a high note, his popularity restored amidst foreign policy triumphs, and he left office on a wave of nostalgia for his presidency. While in retrospect, especially in light of Iran–Contra, many might have been uneasy with Moe's glowing 1985 assessment of his administrative style (and with Nathan's very positive 1983 assessment), I think it fair to say that the underlying approach to the presidency that the Reagan administration practiced emerged strengthened from his eight years in office. The approach was rescued from the utter illegitimacy of the Nixon presidency, and especially the first year or two of Reagan's term stand as a working model that some others might think a success worthy of refinement and emulation.

Reagan's two immediate successors, George H.W. Bush (Bush I) and Bill Clinton, were each more restrained in their approach to the presidency, certainly in the area of appointments policy and in their approaches to the career civil service. However, both employed some of the tools of the administrative presidency quite assertively. Bush I, for example, based his Council on Competitiveness on Reagan's Executive Order 12291 and used "signing statements" to make clear his intention not to enforce parts of statutes he had signed that he regarded as having "no binding legal force" because of his interpretation of the Constitution.[54] And as I wrote in an earlier piece on the Clinton administration that analyzed his use of elements of the administrative presidency strategy: "Particularly after the Republicans took control of Congress in 1995, the Clinton administration worked assiduously to use the administrative levels at its command [such as executive orders and regulation writing] to get its way on policy."[55]

But the clear administrative heir of Ronald Reagan has been George W. Bush (Bush II). His appointments process, while somewhat less White-House-centered than Reagan's, was in most cases steadfast in making loyalty to Bush and his agenda and a willingness to carry out White House directives a paramount concern, especially in subcabinet level selections. Very assertive use of executive orders, of the rulemaking process, of recess appointments, and of information control (including threats to fire civil servants who passed data on program cost projections to Congress), as well as claims (disavowed at times when they became public) of the president's right as commander-in-chief to ignore anti-torture laws and treaties if he judges that necessary to protect national security, are among the tools that the Bush II administration has used, even after it had control of both houses of the Congress.[56] And in the area of executive privilege (one compromised by Reagan's need to turn over documents in the aftermath of Iran–Contra), Bush's behavior has shown that he "wanted to not only revitalize executive privilege but also expand the scope of that power substantially."[57]

Bush II, in summary, has certainly used the tools of the administrative presidency quite effectively, expanding presidential power in several ways. Further, he did this in a period where he had a quite disciplined Republican congressional majority for much of the time (the exception being the year and a half between Senator Jeffords' defection and the 2002 election and then, starting in 2007, with Democrats in control of both houses of the Congress), so split party control or some type, as was the case in both the Nixon and Reagan administrations, is not the driving force here. The final results cannot be fully assessed while the Bush II administration is still in office. However, it seems clear that the administration has fallen victim to the effects of its appointments strategy—Who can forget: "Brownie, you're doing a heck of a job"?[58]—and to a set of policies that, far from teaching the public realism, have left the country badly in debt, mired in a war of dubious origins that has gone poorly and has lost public support, negatively exposed in policies such as those on torture that are intimately tied to a presidential approach that puts the president and his administrative authority above the law, and beset by the effects of passionate internal divisions fed by perceptions that the administration acts illegitimately to impose its will.

The practices of the Bush II administration—though not necessarily the policies—owe much to its predecessors, especially to Nixon but even more to Reagan, though it has added its own emphases and innovations. Its political and administrative significance are now coming into clearer and clearer focus:

> The George W. Bush administration is an important milestone in evolving notions of governance and policy that are increasingly identified with the Republican Party in the United States...Bush has married a rising theory of presidential power that received its impetus in the Nixon administration, and was more successfully implemented in the Reagan administration, to a set of policy ideas developed by American neoconservatives. The future of both aspects of Bush's approach may be in question, but their import is not in doubt.[59]

In brief, the administrative fingerprints of the Reagan presidency are all over the Bush II administration, though the caution often displayed by Reagan in practice, despite his frequently reckless rhetoric, is much less in evidence.

Some Concluding Comments

It is hard to argue with Moe's basic contention that presidents are sorely tempted to centralize and politicize administration—though Rudalevige and Lewis argue that the two are substitutes rather than complements[60]—and that many do so. It is equally hard to argue with Neustadt and Jones (and it appears Moe himself[61]) that this approach contradicts the basic model of the American political system.

A dilemma for the American system is that tensions between the desires of many presidents for control—more and more manifest in recent developments that are loosely categorized under the rubric of the "administrative presidency," and less and less tied to the justification of a presidential mandate, namely, Bush's controversial win in the disputed 2000 election and his subsequent behavior—and the underlying features of the system will not go away. The American system is built on the assumption that interests, and the institutions that were designed to represent different interests, will clash. Indeed this is regarded as highly desirable, at least in terms of the system's design,[62] so tension in and of itself is hardly the problem. The system, however, is also built on the assumption that compromise will be the result of this tension, not domination by one institution (command). It is a dilemma that has not been worked out, and it is now one tinged with partisan overtones,[63] but there is little doubt that the Reagan presidency gave one side of the debate a greater degree of legitimacy and laid a foundation for what—often with disastrous results—has followed.

Notes

This is a slightly revised version of a paper originally prepared for delivery at the Conference on the United States in the 1980s: *The Reagan Years*, Rothermere American Institute, University of Oxford, November 10–12, 2005, and first published in Peter Bursens and Peter Thijssen, eds., *Zoon politikon. Tussen effectiviteit en legimiteit* (Brugge: Vanden Broele, 2006), 211–230. Reprinted with permission of Vanden Broele.

1. Terry M. Moe, "The Politicized Presidency." In John E. Chubb and Paul E. Peterson, eds., *The New Direction in American Politics* (Washington: Brookings, 1985), 235–271.
2. See Richard P. Nathan, *The Administrative Presidency* (New York: Wiley, 1983); and *The Plot that Failed: Nixon and the Administrative Presidency* (New York: Wiley, 1975).
3. Richard E. Neustadt, *Presidential Power* (New York: Signet, 1964), 42, emphasis in original.
4. Ibid., 43.
5. Ibid., 149.

6. Charles O. Jones, *The Presidency in a Separated System*, second ed. (Washington, D.C.: Brookings, 2005), 359.
7. Moe, "The Politicized Presidency," 240.
8. Ibid., 237.
9. Ibid., 238.
10. Ibid., 239.
11. Joel D. Aberbach, "The State of the Contemporary Presidency: Or, is Bush II Actually Ronald Reagan's Heir?" in Colin Campbell and Bert A. Rockman, eds., *The George W. Bush Presidency: Appraisals and Prospects* (Washington, D.C.: CQ Press, 2004), 46–72, 47.
12. Moe, "The Politicized Presidency," 238.
13. Nathan, *The Administrative Presidency*, 8.
14. Ibid.; Nathan, *The Plot that Failed*.
15. Nathan, *The Plot that Failed*, 74.
16. Ibid., 81.
17. Senate Select Committee on Presidential Campaign Activities, Book 19, *Executive Session Hearings on Watergate and Related Activities: Use of Incumbency—Responsiveness Program*, 93 Cong. 2 sess. 1974.
18. For example, see Charles L. Heatherly, ed., *Mandate for Leadership: Policy Management in a Conservative Administration* (Washington, D.C.: Heritage Foundation, 1981).
19. Nathan, *The Administrative Presidency*, 89.
20. For example, see John C. Whitaker, "Nixon's Domestic Policy: Both Liberal and Bold in Retrospect," *Presidential Studies Quarterly*, 1996, 26(1): 131–153.
21. Bert A. Rockman, "The Style and Organization of the Reagan Presidency." In Charles O. Jones, ed., *The Reagan Legacy* (Chatham, NJ: Chatham House Press, 1988), 3–29, 24.
22. James P. Pfiffner, "Nine Enemies and One Ingrate: Political Appointments during Presidential Transitions." In G. Calvin Mackenzie., ed., *The In-and-Outers* (Baltimore: Johns Hopkins University Press, 1987), 60–76, 72.
23. Ibid., 72.
24. Ibid., 73.
25. Jones, *Presidency in a Separated System*, 113.
26. James P. Pfiffner, *The Strategic Presidency* (Lawrence, KS: University of Kansas Press, 1996), 61.
27. Jones, *Presidency in a Separated System*, 113.
28. Nathan, *The Administrative Presidency*, 72; the quotation was drawn from a *New York Times* story.
29. Ibid.
30. Robert Rector and Michael Sanera, eds., *Steering the Elephant* (New York: Universe Books, 1987), 146–147.
31. Joel D. Aberbach and Bert A. Rockman, *In the Web of Politics: Three Decades of the U.S. Federal Executive* (Washington: Brookings Institution Press, 2000), 104, 110.
32. Ibid., 108.
33. Ibid., 116.
34. Ibid., 117.
35. Neustadt, *Presidential Power*, 47.
36. Rector and Sanera, *Steering the Elephant*, 332.
37. Cornelius M. Kerwin, *Rulemaking: How Government Agencies Write Law and Make Policy*, third ed. (Washington, D.C.: CQ Press, 2003), 61.

38. Ibid., 61–62.
39. Kenneth R. Mayer, *With the Stroke of a Pen* (Princeton: Princeton University Press, 2001), 6, quoting Lawrence Lessig and Cass R. Sunstein.
40. Ibid., 128.
41. Ibid.
42. Nathan, *The Administrative Presidency*, 77.
43. Ibid., 81.
44. Ibid.
45. Ibid.
46. Jeffrey K. Stine, "Natural Resources and Environmental Policy." In W. Elliot Brownlee and Hugh Davis Graham, eds., *The Reagan Presidency* (Lawrence: University of Kansas Press, 2003), 233–256, 242.
47. Ibid., 243.
48. Nathan, *The Administrative Presidency*, 78.
49. Stine, "Natural Forces and Environmental Policy," 245.
50. Ibid., 233–234.
51. Bert A. Rockman, "The Style and Organization of the Reagan Presidency." In Jones, ed., *The Reagan Legacy*, 3–29, 9.
52. David M. Abshire, *Saving the Reagan Presidency* (College Station: Texas A & M Press, 2005), 89, 114, 119–121, 135–136, 194–196.
53. David Gergen, *Eyewitness to Power* (New York: Simon & Schuster, 2000), 198.
54. Quoted in Charles Tiefer, *The Semi-Sovereign Presidency: The Bush Administration's Strategy for Governing without Congress* (Boulder, CO: Westview Press, 1994), 3.
55. Joel D. Aberbach, "A Reinvented Government, or the Same Old Government?" In Colin Campbell and Bert A. Rockman, eds., *The Clinton Legacy* (New York: Seven Bridges Press, 2000), 118–139, 129.
56. Joel D. Aberbach, "The Political Significance of the George W. Bush Administration." *Social Policy and Administration*, Vol. 39, No. 2 (2005): 130–149.
57. Mark J. Rozell, *Executive Privilege: Presidential Power, Secrecy, and Accountability*, second ed. (Lawrence, KS: University of Kansas Press, 2002), 147.
58. White House Office of the Press Secretary, "President Arrives in Alabama, Briefed on Hurricane Katrina," September 2, 2005, accessed October 15, 2005.
59. Aberbach, "The Political Significance," 144.
60. Andrew Rudalevige and David E. Lewis, "Parsing the Politicized Presidency: Centralization and Politicization as Presidential Strategies for Bureaucratic Behavior," paper presented at the 2005 Annual Meeting of the American Political Science Association, Washington D.C., September 1–4, 2005.
61. Moe, "The Politicized Presidency," 240, 243.
62. Alexander Hamilton, John Jay, and James Madison, *The Federalist Papers* (New York: Random House: The Modern Library, 1937), especially nos. 10 and 51.
63. See, e.g., the analysis of data for both governmental elites and the general public in Joel D. Aberbach, "The Executive Branch in Red and Blue." In *The Annenberg Democracy Project, A Republic Divided* (New York: Oxford University Press, 2007), 157–193.

Chapter 12

The Road to Mount Rushmore: The Conservative Commemoration Crusade for Ronald Reagan

Niels Bjerre-Poulsen

> *Reagan belongs on Mount Rushmore, and he'll be there, after the carpers die off.*
>
> William F. Buckley Jr.

The struggle over the political legacy of Ronald Reagan is as intense now as it was when he left the White House in 1989. In fact, two different, though clearly related, struggles are taking place. One mostly takes place in academic circles and concerns Reagan's rightful place in the annals of American history. The other takes place in the political arena and concerns his place in the public imagination and the American heritage.[1]

A central element in the latter struggle is what most aptly can be described as a conservative commemoration crusade for Ronald Reagan—an attempt to institutionalize a particular historical memory of him, as well as to canonize him as *the* role model for future American presidents. Both the academic discussion and the political struggle evolve around the question of whether Reagan was what presidential scholars would characterize as a "great president."[2]

Among the critical issues in the academic assessment of Reagan's presidency are his role in the ending of the Cold War, the extent to which he reinvigorated the executive, and the social and political impact of the alleged "Reagan revolution."

Conservative activists clearly find that a lot is at stake in the struggle over the Reagan legacy. Not only do many Americans generally regard the president as a powerful symbol of the political system: some presidents are even seen as the embodiment of the *zeitgeist*, or as catalysts for an entire era. Reagan is one of them.[3] To movement conservatives, he is the key character in a narrative where conservative ascendancy is the central theme in the nation's recent history.

My concern in the following is not to assess whether Reagan did in fact play a transformative role, but to analyze the political attempts from within the conservative movement to shape the public memory of Reagan according to this idea.

This commemorative crusade for Reagan serves present needs within the conservative movement, but it is also fueled by a clear sense that he has been vastly underrated in most academic assessments.[4] One such assessment is the presidential ranking that the late historian Arthur M. Schlesinger, Jr. conducted for the *New York Times Magazine* in 1996.[5]

When Schlesinger, Jr. asked thirty-two historians and political scientists to rank the American presidents, Ronald Reagan landed in the bottom half of the "average" category. Seven rated him as "near great," eleven saw him as average, nine thought he was "below average," and four categorized him as a "failure."[6]

To many conservatives, the result only confirmed long held suspicions of a liberal bias in the academic evaluation of presidents. They would argue that Schlesinger's survey reflected the dominant role of liberals at the nation's major universities and the extent to which it had allowed them to set the terms of political discourse. Liberals had allegedly created a dominant narrative, where Franklin Roosevelt was the greatest president of the twentieth century. In this narrative, the ability to use the federal government to further develop social reforms had become the primary measure of presidential success.[7]

Reagan's low rating in the Schlesinger survey did not remain unchallenged for long. Claiming that the former study had fallen along "predictable ideological lines," the Intercollegiate Studies Institute (ISI)—America's oldest conservative youth organization—soon conducted its own survey among what it described as a more "politically balanced" group of scholars.[8] Here, Ronald Reagan had moved from the "Low Average" category to the "Near Great" category.[9]

In 2000, The Federalist Society and the *Wall Street Journal* likewise joined forces in order to challenge Schlesinger's survey.[10] Notably, however, their ranking of presidents was remarkably similar to Schlesinger's, except in the case of Reagan. As in the ISI survey, he had been elevated from Low Average to the Near Great category, where he joined Jefferson, Jackson, Eisenhower, Theodore Roosevelt, and Franklin D. Roosevelt (who, for his part, had been moved one step down the ladder from the "Great" category).

A standard lament among conservative commentators is that liberal scholars are either unable or unwilling to recognize Reagan's greatness as president. In his book *Ronald Reagan: How an Ordinary Man Became an Extraordinary Leader* (1997), Dinesh D'Souza presents the argument in a chapter entitled "Why Reagan Gets No Respect."[11]

D'Souza readily admits that he himself, like many fellow conservatives, found it hard to appreciate Reagan's leadership qualities while working for him in the White House: "Like many other Americans, I liked Reagan as a person, but like many other conservatives, I worried that he lacked the intellectual temperament and administrative skills to give new direction to the country."[12] It is worth noting that D'Souza did not join the Reagan administration until 1987. Apparently, the previous six years of Reagan in office had not allayed his worries.

According to D'Souza, it was only much later he fully realized that Reagan's greatness defied common intellectual standards. Reagan was "a visionary—a conceptualizer who was able to see the world differently from the way it was."[13] He was guided by "moral imagination" and a "providential understanding of destiny—both his own and that of his country."[14] Following D'Souza's logic, Reagan was a great president, not in spite of his intellectual deficiencies, but because of them. Like Lincoln, he "approached evil with a pure childlike simplicity that sophisticated people take pride in having outgrown." His apparent closed-mindedness was merely a reflection of "a Churchillian tenacity about his moral and political beliefs."[15] According to D'Souza, then, Reagan's success should compel us to rethink common criteria for presidential greatness.[16]

The notion that intellectuals—and nonconservative intellectuals in particular—are generally unable or unwilling to appreciate Reagan's greatness has also been forwarded by the president's former speechwriter Peggy Noonan:

> Ronald Reagan's old foes, the political and ideological left, retain a certain control of the words and ways by which stories are told. They run the academy, the media; they control many of the means by which the young—that nice, strong 20-year-old boy walking down the street, that thoughtful girl making some money by yanking the levers of the coffee machine at Starbucks—will receive and understand history. But the academy and the media may not in time tell Mr. Reagan's story straight; and if they do not tell the truth it will be for the simple reason that they cannot see it. They have been trained in a point of view. It's hard to break out of your training.[17]

Noonan's implicit assumption is that any reservations about the Reagan presidency on the part of ordinary Americans—people who are neither in academia or the media—can be attributed to a distortion of the historical record. However, Reagan remained a polarizing figure while in office, and throughout most of his eight years as president, his approval ratings were lower than those of his predecessors.[18] In 1985, presidential scholar George C. Edwards could conclude that Reagan polarized the polity "along partisan, racial, and sexual lines."[19] Yet, it was a common perception in the media throughout most of his time in office that he was in step with public opinion.[20]

Part of the explanation for this seeming paradox is that Reagan himself was a lot more popular than were his policies. In polls specifically asking for approval of the president as a person, his scores were twenty-five–thirty points higher than his job approval ratings.[21] A majority of Americans appreciated his personal charm as well as his extraordinary ability to combine charisma with an everyman quality. To some extent, he probably remained personally popular by seeming detached from some of the policies of his own administration.[22]

The last year of Ronald Reagan's presidency was marked by his stunning foreign policy success with the signing of the INF treaty in December 1987, but it was also tainted by the congressional investigations into the Iran–Contra scandal. By the time he left the White House, it was far from self-evident that he would go down in history as a great or near-great president, and his popularity actually declined in the years after his departure.

Many Americans were concerned about the national debt and still angry about the Iran–Contra scandal. George H.W. Bush saw the advantages of distancing himself from his predecessor by setting the goal of making "kinder the face of the Nation."[23] By 1992, Reagan's popularity had dropped from 63 percent to 48 percent in a *New York Times* poll. Interestingly, his predecessor, Jimmy Carter who had left office with an approval rating of only 34 percent, had increased his to 50 percent in the same poll.[24]

However, in the following years, Reagan's standing improved significantly. A common reverence for past presidents is an important part of the nation's symbolic code and accounted for some of this improvement. So did the announcement that the former president had been diagnosed with Alzheimer's disease. More importantly, however, the United States entered a long economic boom in the 1990s, and the huge budget deficits of the previous decade turned out to be of little consequence. Furthermore, the Cold War really was over. By 2002, as much as 73 percent of those asked in a Gallup poll thought that Reagan had been a good president.[25] Many remembered a man who has restored national pride and reinvigorated the presidency. Such sentiments emboldened conservative activists whose aim was to secure a place for Reagan as the greatest president of the twentieth century.

In most current conservative narratives, Reagan was an unrelenting champion of conservative principles, who headed a revolution, both in foreign and domestic policy. However, many movement conservatives viewed him differently while he was in office. A poll taken among 350 conservative leaders in October 1983 found that 63 percent of them were "disappointed" with his leadership.[26] The same feeling prevailed in a survey published in the Heritage Foundation's journal *Policy Review* in October 2003: out of twelve leading conservative activists and intellectuals asked to evaluate Reagan's presidency, nine expressed disappointment.[27] Iran–Contra also compelled many conservatives to distance themselves from Reagan. Congressman Newt Gingrich declared that the president would "never again be the Reagan that he was before he blew it. He is not going to regain our trust and our faith so easily."[28]

Such sentiments are rarely expressed by present-day conservatives looking back at the 1980s. It is worth pondering why Reagan has now been granted such a unique position in the conservative pantheon. Beyond a genuine interest in giving him what most conservatives see as his rightful place in the nation's history, just what is at stake for the conservative movement itself?

First of all, Reagan helped convince many skeptics within the movement that they could constitute the political mainstream, and not forever be relegated to the role as "remnants" in a mass society dominated by liberal values. He became the face of majoritarian conservatism. With him as the leading figure, conservatives were able to offer an upbeat message that had always escaped them before. Conservatism was no longer "the thankless persuasion."[29]

Reagan and the people around him managed to take over many liberal premises, including liberalism's optimistic view of human nature, in order to present what George F. Will once called "Conservatism without tears."[30] Alternative welfare measures gave the impression that conservatism mostly differed from liberalism in its choice of methods. That it merely applied different means to the same end.

With Reagan's activist politics, conservatism no longer appeared as a reactive force, but as an innovative one, and the president himself was the perfect embodiment of this new style. Unlike Barry Goldwater and other predecessors, he was able to use a vernacular that is normally the domain of liberal politicians. He projected the ebullience of Franklin D. Roosevelt himself, just as he skillfully employed his rhetorical techniques in his attack on the New Deal order.

Reagan embodied the promise of partisan realignment. The concept of "Reagan democrats" testified to this, as did his landslide reelection in 1984. Ironically, however, Reagan's campaign for reelection also affirmed the limited scope of his conservative "revolution." The "Morning in America" theme clearly signaled that he had no intention of spending his political capital on any major assault on the welfare state. As Marc Landy and Sidney Milkis have noted, "Reagan's second term was a study in anticlimax. Not a single important act of retrenchment was even proposed, let alone enacted."[31]

How do conservatives attempt to preserve Reagan as an asset for their movement? First of all, they bypass the academic historians and explore other ways of institutionalizing the historical memory of him. The Reagan commemoration crusade has taken a variety of forms. Since 2003, a growing number of governors around the country have recognized Reagan's birthday, February 6, as "Ronald Reagan Day." In 2007, forty-two of them did so. Likewise, a string of proposals have been introduced in Congress attempting to name things after the former president or get his image on either the ten-dollar bill or the twenty-dollar bill.[32]

A leading force in this commemoration crusade is "the Ronald Reagan Legacy Project." It was launched in 1997 by Grover C. Norquist and has since been run by his organization Americans for Tax Reform. Norquist was and is an influential figure within the Republican Party. Among other things, he coauthored the 1994 *Contract with America*, just as he served on the Republican Platform Committees in 1988, 1992, and 1996. During George W. Bush's first tenure in the White House, Norquist gained status as an important conservative gatekeeper, and his weekly strategy sessions drew large crowds of lawmakers and lobbyists.

Members on the Advisory Board of the Ronald Reagan Legacy project have included prominent conservatives such as John Ashcroft, Tom Delay, Dick Armey, Newt Gingrich, Jeane Kirkpatrick, Chuck Hagel, Mitch McConnell, and George W. Bush's chief strategist, Karl Rove.[33]

From the outset, Norquist's organization attempted to give the memory of Reagan a very tangible form in monuments and the naming of public buildings and facilities. One of the explicit goals was to place a major monument in each of the 50 states, and something named after the late president in each of the country's 3,054 counties.

The Legacy Project experienced an early success in 1998, when Congress was persuaded to rename Washington National Airport as Ronald Reagan National Airport. The symbolism was evident: New York had John F. Kennedy International Airport. Now the nation's capital had an airport named after the man who fired eleven thousand striking air-traffic controllers. That same year, Washington, D.C.'s largest federal office building (apart from the Pentagon) was likewise named after Reagan—the president who in his first inaugural address had declared that the federal government wasn't the solution, but the problem.[34]

In his book *Abraham Lincoln and the Forge of National Memory* (2000), historian Barry Schwartz has argued that "commemoration transforms historical facts...into objects of attachment by defining their meaning and explaining how people should feel about them."[35] The people behind the Reagan Legacy Project have clearly understood that this process requires an active agent. Making someone—even an American president—an object of commemoration requires active promotion. They firmly believe that the proliferation of memorials would in and of itself help establish Reagan as a towering historical figure for future generations. As Michael Kamburoeski, former executive director of the Reagan Legacy Project, has explained: "We want to create a tangible legacy so that 30 or 40 years from now, someone who may never have heard of Reagan will be forced to ask himself, 'Who was this man to have so many things named after him?'"[36]

Not all conservatives agree with this goal. Some have pointed to the irony in honoring a president who declared that his goal was to shrink the federal government by spending billions of dollars from the taxpayers on federal building projects and the like. In 2001, conservative commentator George Will described the Reagan commemoration crusade as "the spirit of Leninism and Saddam Husseinism, and all other countries in which the maximum leader smears his image all over the place in his name."[37]

Such criticism, however, has not deterred Grover Norquist and his associates. The two most ambitious projects have been to place a Reagan monument on the Mall in Washington, D.C. and promoting the idea of adding Reagan's face to Mount Rushmore in South Dakota. As for the latter, conservatives have occasionally called for such action since 1988. A legislative proposal was first introduced in the House in 1999, and a new proposal was introduced in July 2004.[38] However, the idea has never garnered much support. Some opponents have argued along technological lines—the fear of destroying the existing monument. Others have simply argued that the very idea of adding something to an existing work of art is bad, regardless of whom or what you add. So far, such arguments have stopped legislative proposals, but they haven't stopped conservative calls to "put Reagan on the Rock."[39]

Mount Rushmore was always a long shot, but for several years, the people behind the Reagan Legacy Project were much more optimistic about the prospects for a Reagan memorial on the Mall in Washington, D.C. The successful renaming of the Washington National Airport encouraged them to press on.[40] In 2001, Representative James V. Hansen (Rep.-UT) introduced a bill that would authorize a memorial, but despite support from Speaker Dennis Hastert and other prominent Republicans, the obstacles were significant.[41]

The National Mall is administered by three federal commissions, among them the National Capital Planning Commission. In 2000, all three committees had rejected the idea of a Reagan monument. Furthermore, Congress has previously agreed on a twenty-five-year "cooling off period" before a potential honoree can even be considered for a monument. This so-called Commemorative Works Act was signed by none other than President Reagan in 1986.

However, such obstacles did not deter Representative Hansen. His "Ronald Reagan Memorial Act of 2001" (HR452) proposed to override the three panels and disregard the cooling-off period. The major arguments for doing this were allegedly the urgency due to Reagan's illness from Alzheimer's disease and fear that the former president might otherwise be forgotten.[42] In other words, Hon. Hansen's argument for *not* waiting until after Ronald Reagan had passed away was that the former president was seriously ill, just as his argument for not letting the project stand the test of time apparently was that it might not stand the test of time.

Among those testifying in favor of HR452 was Grover Norquist, who saw no problem in ignoring the twenty-five-year rule, since no one was likely to change their minds about the values and policies that Reagan represented anyhow (ironically, also the best possible argument for not making an exception to the rule). Reagan, Norquist argued, was an exceptional case that should force Congress to bend the rules. He supported this view by playing the strongest conservative trump card: the Churchill analogy:

> Reagan was a Churchillian figure in that he stood up against the traditional establishment view of what was happening and he said, "Guys, you have it wrong," just as Churchill did. And history has made it very clear that Churchill was right about the nature of National Socialism in Germany and history has shown that Ronald Reagan was right about the nature of the Soviet Union and the Socialist government there.[43]

Finally, Norquist added that a memorial would provide Congress with an opportunity to "recognize the will of the people who elected [Reagan] overwhelmingly twice to the Presidency," and that it would "pay tribute to our armed forces."[44]

The latter argument may have reflected an awareness of a basic problem involved in placing a Reagan monument on the Mall. The monuments here do not merely pay tribute to great men in the nation's past. They are supposed to symbolize central ideas and concepts in America's civil religion. Thus, the Lincoln Memorial symbolizes equality and the preservation of the Union. The FDR memorialized on the Mall is the president who in the midst of economic despair told the American people that the only thing they had to fear was "fear itself." He is not primarily the father of the liberal New Deal order, but rather the incurable optimist who restored the nation's hope and self-confidence amidst economic depression and global conflict. That is why a monument honoring him could gather bipartisan support, even in the polarized political climate of the mid-1990s.[45]

The Mall is not a place where one would celebrate the political triumph of American conservatism. It is a place, where a consensus on the symbolic meanings of the memorial projects has evolved over decades. The four presidential monuments now present on the Mall were all constructed many years after these great presidents had passed away. Work on the Washington memorial began in 1848. Work on the Lincoln Memorial began in 1912. Thomas Jefferson had to wait more than a hundred years: his memorial was authorized in 1934. The Roosevelt Memorial opened fifty-two years after his death—that is, in 1997.

The attempt to place a monument for a recent president on the Mall is not unprecedented, though. When Theodore Roosevelt died in 1919, a group of very well-sponsored Republicans formed Roosevelt Memorial Association and began its efforts to do just that. In 1925, Congress even authorized them to present a budget for a Roosevelt memorial between the Washington monument and the Potomac.[46]

However, the enterprise soon encountered resistance. Some felt that it was too early, and that the grass should be given "time to grow on his grave before we pile up the marvel."[47] Others felt that the Roosevelt Memorial Association was attempting to manufacture a historical reputation that had no foundation in the historical record. TR's leadership qualities and political achievements notwithstanding, his presidency had not been a transformative one.[48] The parallels to the debate on Reagan's legacy are evident.

Despite the pleas of Grover Norquist and others, the plans for a Reagan memorial on the Mall suffered a major blow when the Bush administration urged Congress to respect the original version of the 1986 Commemorative Works Act.[49] In the following years, conservatives in Congress attempted to maintain the possibility of an exception to the law by blocking an amendment that included a ban on future memorials, monuments, and interpretive centers on the Mall. However, such legislation was eventually passed in November 2003, thus ending the dreams of a Reagan memorial there in the immediate future.[50]

Occasionally, the effort to secure a prominent place for Reagan in the national pantheon involves open competition with leading liberal icons. The

Reagan Legacy Project explicitly mentions John F. Kennedy as a major rival. The interest group has created a standard "Letter of Support" that people can print out and send to elected officials. One of the statements in the letter is "His (Reagan's) legacy is more powerful than John F. Kennedy's who has been honored with more than 600 dedications in America."[51]

However, it is not John F. Kennedy but Franklin D. Roosevelt who conservative activists see as the main competitor as "greatest president of the twentieth century." Replacing the president who thought that government should be used to secure all Americans freedom from want, with the president, who declared that government wasn't the solution, but the problem, would be an attractive symbolic victory.

Part of the struggle with FDR's legacy has (literally) been in the small change department. In 2003, Republican representative Mark Souder, along with eighty-nine cosponsors, proposed to let Reagan replace FDR on the dime. Some found this ironic, since FDR was the hero of Reagan's youth and in many ways a role model for him as president, albeit in style rather than in content. However, that merely made the idea all the more appealing to conservatives. To them Reagan's own story of conversion to conservatism personalized a larger shift in society—a shift to the right among a majority of Americans.

Souder's proposal ran into a major obstacle when Nancy Reagan objected. In a statement, the former First Lady declared:

> I do not support this proposal and I am certain that Ronnie would not. When our country chooses to honor a great president such as Franklin Roosevelt by placing his likeness on our currency, it would be wrong to remove him and replace him with another. It is my hope that the proposed legislation will be withdrawn.[52]

As a compromise, Souder and his cosponsors proposed to keep FDR on half of the dimes. The Republican Congressman told the press that "a couple of guys, maybe ten or so, said they wanted to knock FDR off the dime. But most guys aren't spoiling for a fight on Reagan versus FDR, and I don't think the Democrats really want that either."[53] Despite this gesture, no further action was taken on the proposal.

Sir Winston Churchill is perhaps the only person more revered than Reagan among American conservatives. Hence, it is hardly surprising that another element in the ongoing attempt to secure Reagan's legacy as the greatest American leader of the twentieth century has been to pair him with this statesman, who, in the words of Thomas Sowell, not only saved his own country, but civilization.[54]

Comparisons of Churchill and Reagan usually establish a dichotomy between, on the one hand, these two staunch defenders of principle and, on the other hand, the appeasing "Chamberlains." For conservatives, Reagan's story, like Churchill's, is one of ridicule and ultimate vindication. As Rod D. Martin wrote in his Reagan obituary on the home page of the National

Association of Evangelicals: "It was fashionable for a time to consider Ronald Reagan a warmonger and a fool. Perhaps this is the best indicator of his Churchillian stature; for like Reagan, Churchill was so maligned, and like Churchill, Reagan saved the world."[55] Law professor Steven G. Calabresi—a cofounder of the Federalist Society—has argued that "Mr. Reagan was...one of the greatest foreign policy geniuses to occupy the presidency. Indeed, he is on par with Winston Churchill in this regard."[56] Dinesh D'Souza concurs: "In the cold war, Reagan turned out to be our Churchill; it was his vision and leadership that led us to victory."[57]

However, pairing Reagan with Churchill goes beyond mere historical analogies. It provides a direct connection to Victorian notions of "great figures, great events, great ideas"—notions that leading neoconservatives such as Gertrude Himmelfarb, Irving Kristol, and their son William Kristol have made the cornerstones of their vision for America.[58] Writing in *The New Republic* shortly after 9/11, Himmelfarb points to Churchill as role model: "Among other things that we are rediscovering in the past is the idea of greatness—great individuals, great causes, great civilizations. It is no accident that Churchill has re-emerged now, at a time when the West is again under assault."[59] The notion of Reagan as Churchill's political and intellectual heir is the central theme in Spencer Warren's article "Reagan and Churchill; Closer Than You Might Think," published on the home page of the conservative Claremont Institute:

> Reagan's recently published extensive writings on foreign and national security affairs mirror the wisdom and understanding found in the eight published volumes of Churchill's speeches. As a result, we now know Reagan was the most thoughtful, knowledgeable figure in this field to occupy the White House (along with Theodore Roosevelt).[60]

Steven F. Hayward of the American Enterprise Institute takes the argument a step further. In his book *Greatness; Reagan, Churchill & the Making of Extraordinary Leaders* (2005), he portrays Reagan as Churchill's political heir and only equal.[61] Hayward goes to great lengths to demonstrate that the two, despite very different upbringings, actually lived "parallel lives" ("In a startling similarity, they both dug fishponds of nearly identical dimensions at their country homes").[62]

Vindication is a major theme in the book: "one marker of great statesmen is that they are usually controversial during their time, and remain so in historical reckoning."[63] "Why," asks Hayward, "were Churchill and Reagan virtually alone among their contemporaries in their particular insights and resolves?"[64] Reading on, one gets a clear sense that the primary purpose of Hayward's book is not to answer the question, but simply to validate the underlying assumption that they were indeed the two towering figures in the twentieth century—both endowed with the ability to "ben[d] history to their will."[65]

Pairing Churchill with Reagan entails obvious problems. Among them is the close association of the former with the leading icon of American liberalism, Franklin Delano Roosevelt. The predominant conservative response to this problem is simply to ignore FDR. When he is mentioned, it is often simply to take the blame for concessions given to Stalin at the Yalta conference, while Churchill gets a free pass. The conservative *Insight Magazine* could tell their readers in 1999 that "Roosevelt, Not Churchill, Appeased Stalin in WWII."[66] In *The Weekly Standard,* President George W. Bush's former speech-writer David Frum struck the same chord while arguing for Churchill as the "Man of the Century":

> A morally alert assessment of the men of our century has to take the terrible events of our century into account. And measured against those events, FDR has to be found wanting. Of the three great killers of this century, one (Mao) was aided by Communist sympathizers within the Roosevelt administration, who tilted American policy in his favor in 1944–45. Another (Stalin) benefited from Roosevelt's almost willful naiveté about the Soviet Union. Roosevelt apparently believed that if only he granted Stalin enough concessions—from control of Poland to the repatriation of Soviet prisoners of war—he could somehow avert a postwar confrontation. Instead Roosevelt's concessions cost millions of lives and sullied the history of the United States—and the confrontation came anyway.[67]

The commemoration crusade has not merely been concerned with Reagan's place in history. It also attempts to prescribe a conservative standard for future political leaders.[68] Among the memorial projects with this aim is a proposal to rename Sixteenth Street NW, leading to the White House, as Ronald Reagan Boulevard.[69] According to Grover Norquist,

> The Symbolism of Ronald Reagan Boulevard leading to the White House is quite powerful. Ronald Reagan was the greatest president of the 20th century, and it's only fitting that his name be on a street heading towards the White House. This dedication makes a clear statement that any Presidential hopeful must follow in the path of Ronald Reagan if he or she wishes to be successful.[70]

The people behind the "Ronald Reagan Legacy Project" evidently have a clear sense of the prescriptive part of commemoration and the use of projecting a specific image of the presidency itself into the future. Grover Norquist has been very explicit about this: "Conservatives have been reticent to promote their heroes, and liberals have been aggressive. If you want to contend for the future, you have to contend for the public understanding of the past."[71]

However, turning the Reagan years into a "usable past" for future conservatives requires a very selective reading of the era. Few would deny a general political shift to the right, but it is much harder to argue that Reagan's leadership was defined by ideological coherence. Libertarians and fiscal conservatives will have to forget that Reagan, after his huge initial tax cuts in 1981, raised taxes several times in the following years.

They also need to forget about record-breaking budget deficits (unless they believe that they were actually "strategic deficits," intended to eat at the welfare state from below—or that Democratic control of Congress made them unavoidable), the $165 billion bailout of Social Security, the fact that Reagan abandoned promises to dismantle the Department of Energy, the Department of Education, affirmative action, and other controversial programs. Likewise, they will have to forget that entitlement programs such as Medicare and Medicaid more than doubled on Reagan's watch, just as federal spending increased as a proportion of national output.[72]

Social conservatives will have to forget that with the possible exception of appointments to the federal judiciary, Reagan's support for their views on issues such as abortion and school prayer never went beyond lip service.[73] In fact, one might argue that a reconstructed narrative of the Reagan years is more helpful to the Religious Right now than Reagan himself ever was while in office.

Neoconservatives, for their part, need to forget about less "Churchillian" aspects of Reagan's foreign policy, such as the decision to pull the remaining American troops out of Lebanon after a suicide bomb had killed 241 American marines in Beirut in 1983, or the 1986 trading of arms for hostages with Iran.[74]

Finally, conservatives, who like to present Reagan as the president who restored "moral clarity" in American foreign policy by calling the Soviet Union an "Evil Empire," need to forget that Reagan's finest contribution to the ending the Cold War was ultimately his pragmatism. It was amidst stern warnings from many of his fellow conservatives that he struck a deal with Mikhail Gorbachev when the chance occurred. A deal that led to the signing of the INF treaty in December, 1987. A deal that ultimately contributed to the end of the Cold War.[75]

Many conservatives reacted to the INF treaty with outrage back then. Commentator George Will concluded that "December 8 will be remembered as the day the Cold War was lost."[76] Some conservative activists even found a need to organize an "Anti-Appeasement Alliance." Howard Phillips, chairman of the Conservative Caucus, declared that the president was "a very weak man with a strong wife and a strong staff." Reagan, he contended, had become "a useful idiot for Soviet propaganda."[77] This weak appeaser has all but disappeared from the conservative discourse on the Reagan years. Only "America's Churchill," whose stand on principle brought down "the evil empire," remains.

The conservative commemoration crusade for Ronald Reagan reached a new high in June 2004 with the state funeral of the former president. In the following years, however, the calls for monuments and other tributes quieted down.[78] One could point to a number of practical and political reasons for this, including, of course, the Democratic takeover of Congress after the midterm elections in November 2006. Perhaps it also mattered that the Reagan legacy proved to be a mixed blessing for an administration under siege and a Republican Party in disarray.

By 2007, George W. Bush had lost his status as "Reagan's son," and the Reagan legacy was used to hit his administration from both sides.[79] Movement conservatives would argue that the president had failed by betraying Reaganite principles of limited government, while moderates would argue that he had failed by ignoring Reagan's example of reaching out to political opponents.[80]

The Reagan legacy was also a mixed blessing for others in the Republican Party. By 2007, a Republican candidate who did not invoke Ronald Reagan and present himself as a Reaganite had indeed become a rarity. Appropriately, Ronald Reagan Presidential Library in Simi Valley provided the setting when ten presidential hopefuls of the party gathered for their first debate on May 3, 2007, and as one might expect, all of them attempted to present themselves as the true heirs of Reagan.

However, many movement conservatives were unmoved, particularly by the frontrunners, McCain, Giuliani, and Romney. They shouted "betrayal," conveniently forgetting that they had shouted the same thing after Reagan two decades earlier. In 1988, conservative fundraiser Richard Viguerie asked "What Reagan Revolution?" and warned fellow conservatives that "to oppose Ronald Reagan can be dangerous, but to help him can be fatal."[81] By 2007, this sense of betrayal was seemingly forgotten. Viguerie had now created a "Reagan test" of true conservatism that all presidential candidates of the GOP had to pass in order to get the support of movement conservatives.[82]

Conservative activists would like to use the memory of Reagan to place conservatism as the triumphant ideology of the twentieth century and the conservative movement right at the center of the nation's political culture. They would also like to use it to prescribe a conservative path to success for future leaders of the nation. However, these goals may not be compatible for the time being. While Reagan might have become a popular conservative, little indicates that he was popular *because* he was conservative. It is by no means a given that he can serve as a cultural icon and a conservative lodestar at the same time.

Furthermore, while the reputational entrepreneurs of the conservative movement might attempt to embody the memory of Ronald Reagan at public sites and symbolic structures, they will not be able to control how these places of commemoration will eventually be read by future generations. The images and associations that presidents and other important public figures evoke are bound to be contested as the political winds change. This is well illustrated by the existing presidential monuments on the National Mall. Jefferson, Lincoln, and FDR were all strongly partisan figures in their time, and the planning and construction of their memorials were often subject to fierce partisan disputes. One may argue that for all of them, transforming the American party system was an essential part of their road to presidential greatness.[83] Yet, their legacies have transcended partisanship. With the passage of time, most people have forgotten about the ideological struggles that these presidents were involved in. Interviews made among those visiting their monuments today reveal that very few people even know which parties they belonged to.[84]

The same thing would most likely happen to public commemorations of Reagan—not least given the fact that many Americans seemed to like him *despite* the policies of his administration. His popularity has grown as the memory of him has become depoliticized. This is the basic dilemma of the conservative commemoration crusaders: the more successful they are in promoting Reagan as a cultural icon, the less he will be able to serve as political role model. A Ronald Reagan on the National Mall or on Mount Rushmore would not be a symbol of triumphant conservatism but a symbol of national pride and optimism. He would most of all be perceived as the true heir of Franklin D. Roosevelt and his conception of political psychology.

Notes

1. Historian Michael Kammen reminds us of the difference between history and heritage. He describes heritage as a manifestation of selective memory—a particular reading of the past, which is often given a material form (monuments and sites) or a ritual form (commemorations). Michael Kammen, "History is Our Heritage: The Past in Contemporary American Culture." In Michael Kammen, *In the Past Lane; Historical Perspectives on American Culture* (New York: Oxford University Press, 1997), 213–225.
2. See Marc Landy and Sidney M. Milkis, *Presidential Greatness* (Lawrence: University of Kansas Press, 2000). Landy and Milkis' concept of presidential "greatness" entails more than competence, charisma, and statesmanship. They define the great presidents as "conservative revolutionaries," who had "the opportunity and capacity to engage the nation in a struggle for its constitutional soul" (198).
3. For a recent scholarly work that grants President Reagan the role as metonymy for an era, see Gil Troy, *Morning in America: How Ronald Reagan Invented the 1980s* (Princeton: Princeton University Press, 2005).
4. Conservative attempts to remedy this include Martin Anderson, *Revolution: The Reagan Legacy* (Stanford: Hoover Institution Press, 1990 [1988]); William F. Buckley, Jr., *Ronald Reagan: An American Hero* (London: DK Publishing, 2001); Dinesh D'Souza, *Ronald Reagan: How an Ordinary Man Became an Extraordinary Leader* (New York: Simon & Schuster, 1997); Steven F. Hayward, *The Age of Reagan, 1964–1980: The Fall of the Old Liberal Order* (Roseville: Prima Lifestyles, 2001); Peggy Noonan, *When Character was King: A Story of Ronald Reagan* (New York: Penguin, 2002); Peter Robinson, *How Ronald Reagan Changed My Life* (New York: Regan Books, 2004); Peter Schweizer, *Reagan's War* (New York: Anchor Books, 2002); and Peter Wallison, *Ronald Reagan: The Power of Conviction and the Success of His Presidency* (Boulder: Westview Press, 2004).
5. Arthur M. Schlesinger, Jr., "The Ultimate Approval Rating," *New York Times Magazine* (December 15, 1996), 46–51.
6. Ibid.
7. See Alvin S. Felzenberg, "'There You Go Again': Liberal Historians and the *New York Times* Deny Ronald Reagan His Due," Policy Review (March–April, 1997).
8. See James Piereson, "Historians and the Reagan Legacy," The *Weekly Standard*, 3 (3) (September 29, 1997): 22–24.
9. The partisan pattern in the ISI survey was evident in most reassessments: among the Republican presidents, Nixon had moved from "Failure" to "Below

Average" and Eisenhower had moved from "High Average" to "Near Great." Among the Democrats, both Bill Clinton and Jimmy Carter were moved from "Low Average" to "Failure," Woodrow Wilson was moved from "Near Great" to "Low Average." Lyndon B. Johnson was moved from "High Average" to "Failure," while Kennedy was moved from "High Average" to "Below Average." The results of the survey are summarized in Meena Bose, "Presidential Ratings: Lessons and Liabilities," *White House Studies*, Winter 2003.

10. James Lindgren, "Rating the Presidents of the United States, 1789–2000," The Federalist Society and The *Wall Street Journal*, November 16, 2000 (http://www.fed-soc.org/pdf/pres-survey.PDF). The Federalist Society for Law and Public Policy Studies is a conservative association that functions as a legal network for law students and members of the legal profession.
11. D'Souza, *Ronald Reagan*.
12. Ibid., 22.
13. Ibid., 28.
14. Ibid.
15. Ibid., 29.
16. Ibid., 227–228.
17. Peggy Noonan, "Why We Talk About Reagan," *Wall Street Journal* (February 8, 2002), A18.
18. See Michael Schudson, "Ronald Reagan Misremembered." In David Middleton and Derek Edwards, eds., *Collective Remembering* (London: Sage, 1990), 120–138. It is true, however, that Reagan left the White House with higher approval ratings (68 percent) than when he entered it. The only other president since FDR who has done that is Bill Clinton.
19. George C. Edwards, "Comparing Chief Executives," *Public Opinion* (June–July, 1985), 54.
20. Schudson, "Ronald Reagan Misremembered."
21. Ibid., 111 ff.
22. Troy, *Morning in America*, 13, 82–83.
23. "Inaugural Address of George Bush," January 20, 1989. The Avalon Project at Yale Law School, http://www.yale.edu/lawweb/avalon/presiden/inaug/bush.htm.
24. Quoted from Robert Dallek, *Hail to the Chief* (New York: Oxford University Press, 2001), 82.
25. Frank Newport, Jeffrey M. Jones, and Lydia Saad, "Ronald Reagan From the People's Perspective: A Gallup Poll Review," *The Gallup Poll*, June 7, 2004, http://www.galluppoll.com/content/?CI=11887.
26. Quoted from Troy, *Morning in America*, 158.
27. Adam Meyerson, Editorial, *Policy Review*, July and August, 1997, http://www.hoover.org/publications/policyreview/3573507.html.
28. Quoted from Troy, *Morning in America*, 250.
29. The expression is taken from the title of Clinton Rossiter's book *Conservatism in America: The Thankless Persuasion* (New York: Alfred A. Knopf, 1962).
30. George Will, "Is It Safe to Be a Liberal Again?" *The Washington Post* (May 5, 1998), C07.
31. Landy and Milkis, *Presidential Greatness*, 224.
32. Among them are a 2004 proposal by Republican Representative Dana Rohrabacher that would place him on the twenty-dollar bill. "Reagan the

new face of the $10 bill?" *CNNMoney*, June 11, 2004, http://money.cnn.com/2004/06/08/news/economy/reagan_hamilton/index.htm.
33. In 1999, the members of the Board of Advisors were: Grover G. Norquist, chairman; Martin Anderson, senior fellow, Hoover Institution; Conrad M. Black, chairman, Telegraph Group Limited; The Honorable Morton C. Blackwell, committeeman, Republican National Committee; Ward Connerly, chairman, American Civil Rights Coalition; Edwin Feulner, president, The Heritage Foundation; The Honorable Jim Geringer, governor of Wyoming; The Honorable Frank Keating , governor of Oklahoma; The Honorable Jack Kemp, co-director, Empower America; Ambassador Jeane J. Kirkpatrick, senior fellow, American Enterprise Institute; Rabbi Daniel Lapin, president, Toward Tradition; The Honorable Michael Leavitt, governor of Utah; The Honorable Jim Nicholson, chairman, Republican National Committee; The Honorable Marc Racicot, governor of Montana; Phyllis Schlafly, president, Eagle Forum; The Honorable Richard B. Stone, former U.S. senator (D-Florida); Paul Weyrich, president, Free Congress Foundation. *The Ronald Reagan Legacy Project*, "The Reagan Legacy Project announces Board of Advisors," February 4, 1999, http://www.conservativenews.org/Politics/archive/199902/POL19990204a.html.
34. "In this present crisis, government is not the solution to our problem; government is the problem." Ronald Reagan, First Inaugural Address, January 20, 1981, http://www.reaganfoundation.org/reagan/speeches/first.asp. Among the Ronald Reagan Legacy Project's other successful efforts is legislation that recognizes February 6 as "Ronald Reagan Day."
35. Barry Schwartz, *Abraham Lincoln and the Forge of National Memory* (Chicago: University of Chicago Press, 2000), 12.
36. Quoted from Michael Mechanic, "Sugarcoating Reagan," *Mother Jones*, March 1, 2001, http://www.motherjones.com/news/feature/2001/03/reagan_DUP2.html.
37. Interview on MSNBC, May 23, 2001. Quoted from "Honoring the Memory: 'Trivializing' Ronald Reagan," Center for American Progress, June 10, 2004, http://www.americanprogress.org/issues/2004/06/b88803.html.
38. H.R. 4980, http://thomas.loc.gov/cgi-bin/query/D?c108:1:./temp/ ~mdb-sns4x0P::.
39. "Put Reagan on Rushmore" (editorial), *Human Events,* July 4, 2006.
40. See Nicholas Confessore, "Reagan Unremembered; Teflon," *The New Republic* (April 30, 2001), 18–20.
41. "Hearing on H.R. 107, H.R. 400, and H.R. 452 before the Subcommittee on National Parks, Recreation, and Public Lands of the Committee on Resources, U.S. House of Representatives, One Hundred Seventh Congress, First Session (March 8, 2001), Serial No. 107–2," http://commdocs.house.gov/committees/resources/hii71123.000/hii71123_0.HTM.
42. Statement by Hon. James V. Hansen, ibid., 19–20.
43. Statement by Grover Norquist at "Hearing on H.R. 107, H.R. 400, and H.R. 452," 60.
44. Ibid., 61, 63.
45. J. Jennings Moss, "Reverence for FDR Crosses Spectrum—Franklin Delano Roosevelt," *Insight on the News*, May 15, 1995, http://findarticles.com/p/articles/mi_m1571/is_n19_v11/ai_16951818.

46. Merrill D. Peterson, *The Jefferson Image in the American Mind* (New York: Oxford University Press, 1960).
47. John Burroughs quoted from Alan Havig, "Presidential Images, History, and Homage: Memorializing Theodore Roosevelt, 1919–1967," *American Quarterly*, Vol. 30 , No. 4 (Autumn 1978): 514–532.
48. The efforts to create a Roosevelt memorial also clashed with the rivaling efforts to create a memorial for Thomas Jefferson—a struggle that the supporters of a Jefferson memorial won in 1926. There is an ironic twist to the story: in October 1931, Analostan Island in the Potomac was renamed "Roosevelt Island." The following year, however, Republican president Herbert Hoover was solidly defeated by another Roosevelt—Franklin Delano. As one of his last actions in office, he changed the name of the Island to "Theodore Roosevelt Island" to avoid any confusion with the incoming president. The entire political struggle is well described in Havig, "Presidential Images."
49. Jim Abrams, "Too Soon for Reagan memorial on the Mall," *Chicago Sun-Times*, March 9, 2001, http://findarticles.com/p/articles/mi_qn4155/is_20010309/ai_n13893516/print.
50. Monte Reel, "Preservation Law Puts Leash on Mall Projects," *The Washington Post*, November 20, 2003, P. DZ10.
51. "Letter of Support to Send to Elected Officials," Ronald Reagan Legacy Project.
52. Quoted from Jim Geraghty, "A Dime Worth a Difference," *National Review Online*, December 10, 2003, http://www.nationalreview.com/geraghty/geraghty200312100838.asp.
53. Ibid.
54. "It is enough of a claim to historic greatness for a man to have saved his own country. Churchill may have saved civilization." Quoted from the home page of the Churchill Centre, http://www.winstonchurchill.org/i4a/pages/index.cfm?pageid=817. Admiration for Churchill is actually a bipartisan enthusiasm in America. After all, it was upon President Kennedy's initiative that the British statesman became an honorary citizen of the United States. However, conservative Republicans have clearly taken Churchill-worship to a higher level, just as they have excelled in the strategic use of Churchill-quotations.
55. Rod D. Martin, "Remembering Ronald Reagan," National Association of Evangelicals, http://www.nae.net/index.cfm?FUSEACTION=editor.page&pageID=36&IDcategory=1. Another example of this use of historical analogy is Spencer Warren, "Reagan and Churchill; Closer Than You Might Think," The Claremont Institute, October 6, 2004, http://www.claremont.org/writings/041005warren.html.
56. Steven G. Calabresi, "Reagan Belongs on Kings Row; Why Envious Professors Won't Give the Gipper his Due," *Opinion Journal*, December 4, 2000, http://www.opinionjournal.com/hail/under.html?id=65000721.
57. D'Souza, *Ronald Reagan*, 197.
58. The quote is from Gertrude Himmelfarb's essay, "Of Heroes, Villains and Valets." In *On Looking into the Abyss: Untimely Thoughts on Culture and Society* (New York: Alfred A. Knopf, 1995), 38.
59. Gertrude Himmelfarb, "*The Roar*," *The New Republic*, Vol. 225 , No. 22 (November 26, 2001): 26.

60. Warren, "Reagan and Churchill."
61. Steven F. Hayward, *Greatness; Reagan, Churchill & the Making of Extraordinary Leaders* (New York: Crown Forum, 2005). Hayward is, at least indirectly, linked to the ongoing conservative Reagan commemoration crusade. According to him, the idea to turn the Reagan–Churchill comparison into a book came from former Reagan advisor Martin Anderson, who also serves on the Advisory Board of "Ronald Reagan Legacy Project." Hayward's attempt to link Reagan to Churchill is also evident in the tentative title of his forthcoming book, *The Age of Reagan: Lion at the Gate, 1980–1989* ("The Last Lion" was the label that William Manchester gave Churchill in his multivolume biography of the British statesman).
62. Ibid., 27.
63. Ibid.
64. Ibid., 167.
65. Ibid., 168.
66. *Insight on the News*, "Roosevelt, Not Churchill, Appeased Stalin in WWII," December 13, 1999, http://www.insightmag.com/.
67. David Frum, "What Makes a Man of the Century?" *The Weekly Standard* (January 10, 2000), Vol. 5, No. 16.
68. See Grover G. Norquist, Michael Reagan, Phil Gramm, Ralph Reed, Elliott Abrams, Gary L. Bauer, Frank Keating, Trent Lott, Christopher Cox, David Beasley, James C. Miller, Richard K. Armey, David McIntosh, and Jean Kirkpatrick, "*Reagan Betrayed*," *Policy Review*, Issue 84 (July/August 1997). The notion of constructing the memory of the nation's past presidents to serve present political needs is by no means new. For examples, see Merrill D. Peterson, *Lincoln in American Memory* (New York: Oxford University Press, 1994); Merril D. Peterson, *The Jefferson Image in the American Mind* (New York: Oxford University Press, 1960); and Barry Schwartz, *Abraham Lincoln and the Forge of National Memory* (Chicago: The University of Chicago Press, 2000).
69. H.R. 352 was introduced by Henry Bonilla (Rep.-TX) on July 28 and referred to the House Committee on Government Reform, http://thomas.loc.gov/cgi-bin/bdquery/z?d109:HR03525:@@@X.
70. "Ronald Reagan Blvd. Leads to the White House," Ronald Reagan Legacy Project News, August 4, 2005, http://www.reaganlegacy.org/pressreleases/pdf/080405pr-Reagan,%20DC.pdf.
71. Quoted from Gloria Borger, "In Search of Mount Reagan," *U.S. News & World Report*, Vol. 123, No. 23 (December 15, 1997): 35.
72. Arthur Schlesinger, Jr., "He Knew How to Lead People," *Newsweek*, Vol. 143, Issue 24 (June 14, 2004): 44. See also Karl Zinsmeister, "Summing Up the Reagan Era," The *Wilson Quarterly* (Winter, 1990): 110 ff; and James T. Patterson, *Restless Giant; The United States from Watergate to Bush v. Gore* (Oxford: Oxford University Press, 2005), 162–170.
73. Hugh Heclo, "Ronald Reagan and the American Public Philosophy," in W. Elliot Brownlee & Hugh Davis Graham, *The Reagan Presidency; Pragmatic Conservatism and Its Legacies* (Lawrence: University Press of Kansas, 2003), 17 ff., and Joshua Green, "Reagan's Liberal Legacy; What the new literature on the Gipper won't tell you". *Washington Monthly*, January/February, 2003 (http://www.washingtonmonthly.com/features/2001/0301.green.html).

74. One might think that the latter is particularly difficult to ignore, since the 1986 Iran–Contra scandal played such a central role during Reagan's last years in office. Nevertheless, the Reagan Presidential Library has chosen to simply avoid any mentioning of the scandal in its exhibits. For a discussion of the role of presidential libraries as places of worship in the nation's civil religion, see Benjamin Hufbauer, *Presidential Temples; How Memorials and Libraries Shape Public Memory* (Lawrence: University Press of Kansas, 2005).
75. See John Lewis Gaddis, *The United States and the End of the Cold War: Implications, Reconsiderations, Provocations* (Oxford: Oxford University Press, 1994). One might of course argue that it was Reagan's conservative credentials that made it possible for him to overcome resistance at home and secure support for the treaty in the U.S. Senate.
76. Quoted from Richard Reeves, *President Reagan; The Triumph of Imagination* (New York: Simon & Schuster, 2005), 446.
77. Quoted from Jacob V. Lamar, Jr., "An Offer They Can Refuse," *Time*, December 14, 1987, http://www.time.com/time/printout/0,8816,966229,00.html.
78. However, such activities have not died out. In September of 2006, Congress decided to find a space for a statue of Reagan in the U.S. Capitol building, by using a little-noticed law from 2000 to replace a statue of fellow Californian Thomas Starr King—a Lincoln ally during the Civil War. See Jesse McKinley, "Reagan Wins Another Vote, To a Place in Congress," *The New York Times* (September 5, 2006).
79. Bill Keller, "The Radical Presidency of George W. Bush; Reagan's Son," *The New York Times Magazine*, January 26, 2003, http://select.nytimes.com/search/restricted/article?res=F00616FF39540C758EDDA80894DB404482.
80. For conservative stories of betrayal, see Bruce Bartlett, *Impostor: How George W. Bush Bankrupted America and Betrayed the Reagan Legacy* (New York: Doubleday, 2006); and Michael D. Tanner, *Leviathan on the Right: How Big-Government Conservatism Brought Down the Republican Revolution* (Washington, D.C.: Cato Institute, 2007).
81. Richard Viguerie, "What Reagan Revolution?" *The Washington Post* (August 21, 1988): C2.
82. "Viguerie Says Leading GOP Candidates Fail the 'Reagan Test,'" press release, May 3, 2007, www.ConservativesBetrayed.com.
83. See Landy and Milkis, *Presidential Greatness*, 8–11.
84. "A Move for a Reagan Monument," *CBS News*, September 23, 2000, http://www.cbsnews.com/stories/2000/09/23/national/main235881.shtml.

Chapter 13

Toward a Historiography of Reagan and the 1980s: Why Have We Done Such A Lousy Job?

Gil Troy

> *If you can write a nation's stories, you needn't worry about who makes its laws,*
> Dr. George Gerbner, University of Pennsylvania

I finished writing my book *Morning in America: How Ronald Reagan Invented the 1980s* in the spring of 2004.[1] I received the copyedited manuscript back in June 2004, giving me my last chance to make substantive changes to the text. Fortunately, my deadline was mid-June, one week after Ronald Reagan's death.

This coincidence allowed me to rewrite the introduction, acknowledging a dramatic tonal shift in the conversation about Ronald Reagan. I first wrote an introduction with academics' contempt for Reagan in mind. The subtext of my words offered a defiant statement, insisting: "Yes, I can write a balanced work about Ronald Reagan without being a rightwing Neanderthal—and more scholars should undertake such efforts." The new and ultimately final introduction sought to reconcile the contempt most academics have for Ronald Reagan with the effusive eulogizing of June 2004, wherein even the *New York Times*' front page article compared Reagan to Dwight Eisenhower, John Kennedy, and Franklin D. Roosevelt.[2]

Studying Ronald Reagan is not for the faint-hearted—or the untenured. Reagan scholarship suffers from two overlapping afflictions, characteristic of today's academic and popular cultures. The intense partisanship emanating from both Washington, D.C. and the academy makes it difficult to assess Reagan calmly, soberly. All too many discussions need to be run through the increasingly tiresome "red" or "blue" litmus test to determine whether one is a Reagan friend playing to conservative red America or a Reagan foe playing to liberal blue America. Reagan's centrality in launching the rise of modern conservatism keeps passions stoked about him, both pro and con.

Paradoxically, President George W. Bush's contentious time in office hardened some assessments of Reagan, with critics blaming Reagan for starting it all. However, some Bush critics softened on Reagan. Forgetting their anger in the 1980s, they partially rehabilitated Reagan to contrast him to their current target, the second President Bush. At the same time, conservatives frustrated with Bush's shortcomings became even more nostalgic for Reagan.

The second affliction has to do with the superficiality beclouding so many discussions of politics, in the media and in too many classrooms. Reagan's death and Gerald R. Ford's death two-and-a-half years later unleashed a cascade of adulatory adjectives describing the two presidents' respective personalities. But simply declaring Reagan "optimistic" or Ford "decent" does not explain how the president interacts with his surroundings or shapes the times. Moreover, in both cases, the funeral coverage precluded any serious criticism of the two presidents, making it harder for historians to do their jobs. As I said of a different ruler when I played Marc Antony in sixth-grade, we should come neither to bury Reagan nor to praise him. Our goal as historians should be to understand Ronald Reagan, his impact and his times.

The partisanship and superficiality fed what I call the Reagan "yuck factor" among scholars or what Professor Alan Brinkley more elegantly termed "the problem of American conservatism."[3] Given the tremendously high percentage of historians who are liberals, and given how many of those who lived through Reagan's time detested conservatives, most veteran historians simply would not consider spending significant time with Reagan. Furthermore, the great expectations surrounding Edmund Morris's disappointing work *Dutch*[4] (1999)—and the millions of dollars Random House invested—inhibited other scholars and publishers from pursuing a project, except in the conservative think-tank world. The next generation of scholars, who grew up in the Reagan era, found it safer to study "conservatism," Republicans, or Reaganite suburbia than to risk being besmirched by studies of Reagan himself.[5] Only now are we starting to see the too-long delayed flow of dissertations and monographs.

As a result, nearly thirty years after Ronald Reagan's election, twenty years after his retirement, Reagan scholarship does not measure up to scholarship regarding other presidencies. Comparing where Franklin Roosevelt historiography was three decades after Roosevelt's inauguration, or doing the same for John F. Kennedy, paints a sobering picture. By 1962, both James MacGregor Burns and Arthur M. Schlesinger had written majestic, multivolume works that remain the gold standards for Roosevelt and New Deal scholarship.[6] Similarly, by 1990, Kennedy scholarship was already in a third phase. The eulogies that hailed Kennedy and Camelot combined with the pathographies that exposed him were now yielding illuminating syntheses that actually analyzed him and his presidency. Moreover, the sheer volume of books on Kennedy offered a rich and dense mother lode of tidbits and interpretations.

Surprisingly simplistic stereotypes of Ronald Reagan defined the scholarship in the first two decades after Reagan's inauguration. For starters, many scholars viewed him as an "amiable dunce," gleefully quoting the Democratic Wise Man Clark Clifford, or as a "Mr. Magoo," in the biting phrase of the historian Garry Wills.[7] These approaches deployed entertaining riffs about Reagan's various gaffes to reinforce a political condemnation of his policies.

The first wave of insider memoirs seemed to confirm scholars' contempt. The most influential—and popular—"serve and tell" books had Reagan's second-term chief of staff Donald Regan revealing the president's reliance on an astrologer for scheduling, and had Reagan's budget-cutting wunderkind David Stockman describing a passive, uncurious, presidential simpleton swayed by Pentagon cartoons posing a choice between a vigorous, GI-Joe-type defense and a wimpy Woody Allen–David Stockman budget-cutting approach.[8] This caricature was so ubiquitous that in a University Press of Kansas anthology of modern Reagan scholarship edited by W. Elliott Brownlee and Hugh Davis Graham, Professor James Patterson felt compelled to insist that Reagan was *not* a moron.[9] Few historiographical controversies about national leaders need to start from such a basic level.

Other critics sidestepped the question of Reagan's intelligence to condemn him as rigid and doctrinaire, a reverse Robin Hood. This impression too was rooted in the Reagan wars of the 1980s. During the hard fought 1984 reelection campaign against Walter Mondale, one Republican National Committee official listed the many different attacks Mondale had launched against the president. Quoting Mondale's claim from March 24, 1984, that "I've been very careful in this campaign to keep this impersonal and deal with the facts," Michael Bayer proceeded to catalogue all of Mondale's insults, which included words and phrases such as:

> figurehead...cruel, unfair...cheerleader...remote...like Pac Man... Cuttlefish...out of touch...not in charge...unwilling to learn... Unaware... reckless...Arrogant...all happy talk, no straight talk...all television, no vision...shallowness...bad judgment...entirely negative...pass the buck... candidate of the wealthy "yuppies"...government of the rich, by the rich, for the rich...cynicism...atrocious abdication of leadership...all blue skies, no blue print...shallowness...lack of follow-through...Khomeinis of the American society...Policies that are cold as ice...double-dealer...bigotry and ignorance...sheer meanness.[10]

This cranky list is contradictory. Consider the attacks on Reagan as a "figurehead...cheerleader...remote...out of touch...not in charge... unwilling to learn... Unaware...reckless...all television, no vision." These suggest Reagan was clueless and passive. Yet accusations that he was "cruel, unfair...arrogant," creating a "government of the rich, by the rich, for the rich" together with the "Khomeinis of the American society," all suggest Reagan was actively, effectively mean.

Few people are both foolish and evil. It is possible, but it requires quite a combination of attributes. In 1984—and again in 2004—Democrats had trouble convincing the American people that the President of the United States was both soft-headed and hard-hearted.

Reagan's defenders were equally unsubtle—and contradictory. A list of some pro-Reagan book titles shows why many neutral observers felt that partisans simply reversed polarities to produce their particular works. Reagan's supporters published books remembering *When Character Was King*, hailing *The Power of Conviction and the Success of His Presidency*, appreciating *How Ronald Reagan Changed My Life*, and, my personal favorite, simply linking *God and Ronald Reagan*.[11]

Often the arguments were also dissatisfying. In Dinesh D'Souza's book describing *How an Ordinary Man Became an Extraordinary Leader* (1997), D'Souza proclaimed when assessing Reagan's first-term defiance of the Soviet Union: "no other Western leader since Churchill had so unapologetically asserted the moral superiority of the West." Yet fifty pages later, D'Souza justified "Reagan's apparent change of stance toward the Soviet Union in his second term" by quoting Winston Churchill's assessment of Edmund Burke's apparent inconsistency in detesting the French Revolution while defending the American Revolution. Churchill wrote: "A statesman in contact with the moving current of events and anxious to keep the ship on an even keel and steer a steady course may lean all his weight now on one side and now on the other."[12] In other words, Reagan was Churchillian when he was resolute and equally Churcillian when he compromised.

Many of the less partisan scholars threw up their hands in frustration, declaring Ronald Reagan an "enigma"—a word I banned in my McGill University honors history seminar on Reagan and the 1980s. In his long-delayed and partially fictionalized meditation on Reagan, *Dutch*, Edmund Morris wrote after unparalleled access to Reagan's files and friends: "Dutch remained a mystery to me, and worse still...an apparent airhead."[13] This admission seemed more revealing about Morris than about Reagan. Morris had gone on a futile search for Reagan's inner essence, forgetting that the important questions about a president center on what he accomplished not who he really was. In the process, this biographer had been defeated by his subject.

Many of those who accepted the interpretation of Reagan as some sort of uniquely inaccessible and indecipherable human being enjoyed retelling the story first told by Reagan's adopted son Michael Reagan. While serving as governor of California, the elder Reagan helped officiate at the younger Reagan's graduation. As the son approached the father on the podium, the governor extended his hand and said: "My name is Ronald Reagan, What's yours?"[14] Decades earlier, the great journalist William Allen White said of William McKinley: "Living thirty years in politics, McKinley became galvanized with a certain coating of publicity. He lost his private life and his private view. He walked among men a bronze statue, for thirty years determinedly looking for his pedestal."[15] So too with Reagan. While Michael Reagan's anecdote appeared to reflect disconnectedness, it may simply have been a reflection of the automatic reflexes of an overexposed public man, whose years as a celebrity included three decades in the Hollywood limelight before being immersed in the political fishbowl.

These four perspectives on Reagan as the dummy, the Ayatollah, the superhero, and the enigma have mired too much Reagan scholarship in the political muck of the 1980s, which has added resonance—and edge—today. Moreover, Reagan's historical stock plummeted during the administration of his vice president and successor, George H.W. Bush. Lacking what he dismissively called that "vision thing," Bush charmed reporters by rejecting Reagan's ways. A "National Ethics Week" contrasted the Bush administration's vows of rectitude with the ethical cesspool reporters believed they found in the Reagan administration. From the start, Bush posed as an engaged chief executive who was too busy to nap during the day as Reagan had. Flaunting his overbooked schedule and "hyper" style suggested that George Bush would not be the delegator-in-chief that Reagan had been. "I am less interested in image than in getting things done," Bush would say, as he jabbed his predecessor, sometimes subtly, sometimes obviously.[16]

Early in Bush's tenure, a Knight-Ridder article noted how Bush staffers "hoping to make their man look good at Reagan's expense...point out how hard Bush works, how knowledgeable he is on the issues and how much he hates being managed by the staff." Richard Nixon read the article and warned Bush's chief of staff John Sununu that the staff must be more circumspect. Bush actually called Reagan and apologized.[17]

Ironically, Reagan's reputation improved thanks to a Democrat, Bill Clinton. The boom of the 1990s softened criticism of Reagan for being materialistic and superficial as the Democratic Party also positioned itself as the party of "peace and prosperity." The government's surge in revenues and the economy's astronomical growth made the Reagan deficit, one of his greatest apparent failures, shrink in importance. Clinton had a hard time taking credit for the economic good times without sharing credit with the man who presided over its beginning, Ronald Reagan. Economists disagree regarding how much credit presidents deserve for any boom, including this one. But if any president deserved credit for what some simply recognized as the baby-boom boom, both Reagan and Clinton did.

Beyond economics, both Clinton's conservatism and his libertinism redeemed Reagan. When Clinton declared in 1996 that the "era of big government" was over, then proved his claim with an election-year welfare reform, the young Democrat flattered his older Republican predecessor by imitating him. In 1998, when Bill Clinton's dalliance with a White House intern caused a lengthy scandal, many Americans yearned for Reagan's old-fashioned prudish formality. Reagan often groused about the explicit sex scenes blighting Hollywood movies. Reagan also had such a strong sense of 1950s-style propriety he never took off his suit jacket in the Oval Office.

Reagan's personal affliction during the Clinton era also created a criticism-free zone around the ailing president as a beloved national icon. In 1994, Reagan wrote a farewell letter to the American people, acknowledging his Alzheimer's disease. As Reagan lost his memory, Americans' memories of him softened. By 2003, when CBS planned to broadcast a mini-series critical of the Reagans during the November sweeps months, the network crossed an increasingly sensitive trip wire. Not only was Reagan's historical stock soaring, but his wife Nancy was enjoying an extreme image makeover as she handled her husband's decline with a grace few Americans had perceived in the 1980s.

The continuing partisan clashes, Reagan's fluctuating historical reputation for ahistorical reasons, and the psychobiographical sideshows trying to unpack Reagan's psyche rather than assess his accomplishments stunted the growth of Reagan studies. As a result, the first wave of defining works about Reagan and the 1980s still dominate much of the discussion, especially Lou Cannon's *President Reagan: The Role of a Lifetime* (1991), Haynes Johnson's *Sleepwalking through History* (1991), and Robert Dallek's *Ronald Reagan: The Politics of Symbolism* (1984).[18] Two were reprinted in 2000, one in 2003, illustrating the continuing fascination with Reagan along with the failure of new perspectives rooted in the new material now available at the Reagan Presidential Library to command attention.

Although scholars have not surmounted all these obstacles to a thoughtful discussion about Ronald Reagan, the last few years have triggered something of a Reagan revival. The strongest voice in this turnaround has been Ronald Reagan's. The Ronald Reagan Presidential Library in Simi Valley, California, has reintroduced Reagan, often to his advantage. The Reagan emerging from his presidential papers is far more intelligent, ideological, interested, and eloquent than the oft-caricatured goof-off manipulated by his handlers.

The speechwriting files are particularly impressive. In those papers, Ronald Reagan shines through as the national preacher with a deft editorial hand. Indeed, his speechwriters wrote the first drafts, but Reagan often penned the best lines. Again and again, in his distinctive small scrawl, Reagan trimmed the staffers' long, complex sentences into pithy, understandable lines while replacing their abstract statements with punchy facts and memorable anecdotes.

Many Americans have been able to rediscover this hands-on, thoughtful Reagan through publication of his speeches, letters, and diaries. *Reagan in His Own Hand* (2001) and *Reagan: A Life in Letters* (2003), collections of speeches and correspondences by Kiron K. Skinner, Annelise Anderson, and Martin Anderson, reinforce what the documents at the Reagan Library prove—Reagan was an articulate, idea-driven ideologue, and after twenty years of governing he was more politician than actor.[19] Moreover, the recently published Reagan diaries, so ably edited by Douglas Brinkley, capture a more engaged and engaging private and public personality than many perceived at the time.[20]

Brownlee and Graham's 2003 anthology *The Reagan Presidency: Pragmatic Conservatism and its Legacies* published papers from a conference held at the Ronald Reagan Presidential Library that mined newly released records. Indeed, the Library captures Reagan in the act of being a "pragmatic conservative" again and again. Along those lines, the historian Alonzo Hamby, deemed Reagan an "incrementalist" in his authoritative work

Liberalism and its Challengers: From F.D.R. to Bush (1992). The journalist Frances FitzGerald called Reagan a "supple" politician and an "American Everyman" in *Way Out There in the Blue* (2000).[21] Hamby characterized Reagan's conservatism as surprisingly populist, flexible, and successful, reflecting Reagan's "own shrewd sense of the politically possible and a fundamental uncertainty in his own mind about how far to the right he wanted to go."[22]

Ultimately, Reagan was too much the populist crowd-pleaser to be the revolutionary—and too aware of his limited mandate to run too far ahead of public opinion. For all the liberal laments about Reagan's extremism, for all the conservative cries to "Let Reagan be Reagan"—in many ways when he was trimming, compromising, playing to the center, Ronald Reagan *was* being Ronald Reagan. To an old Hollywood lawyer friend familiar with his marathon negotiations both as president of the Screen Actors' Guild and as a contract player in the days of the big studio moguls, Reagan wrote: "You know, those people who thought being an actor was no proper training for this job were way off base. Everyday I find myself thankful for those long days at the negotiating table with Harry Cohen, Freeman, the brothers Warner et al."[23] In 1983, The Reagan White House released a detailed document "Ten Myths That Miss the Mark"—denying that the Reagan administration was hostile to the poor, to blacks, to women, to environmentalists, to education.[24] In short, addicted to polls, trying to remain popular, the Reagan administration embraced the key revolutions of the last few decades Reaganism supposedly sought to repel.

Just as Ronald Reagan shaped America, the political realities of modern America shaped the Reagan administration. America's majoritarian instincts, its system's gravitational pulls toward the center and toward compromise, triumphed. And rather than being the fire-breathing conservative critics feared, Reagan emerged as a more mainstream type of leader, one who played to the center—and revitalized it. As early as February 1981, conservatives denounced Reagan's "consensus politics," demanding "confrontational politics." A year later, forty-five Conservative Political Conference participants signed an eight-page statement blasting the administration as filled with moderates still addicted to government spending, lukewarm on "the President's 'new federalism,'" and too conciliatory and Kissingeresque on foreign policy. In October 1983, 63 percent of three hundred fifty conservative leaders polled declared themselves "Disappointed" with Reagan as president.

Conservatives were most outraged that Reagan slighted "the social agenda." Reagan's designation of Sandra Day O'Connor as his first Supreme Court appointee in July 1981 infuriated conservatives, who doubted her commitment to eradicating abortion. "Reagan Choice for Court Decried by Conservatives but Acclaimed by Liberals," the *Washington Post* proclaimed.[25]

At the end of the day, in many ways Reagan stayed within the New Deal–Great Society governing status quo, fine-tuning it more than destroying it. As a result, intentionally or not, he ended up legitimizing rather than repudiating much of the legacy of the 1960s and 1970s. Reagan's reign was one of reconciliation more than it was one of revolution. In culture as in politics, in society as in government, it was an era of restoration.

Exhausted by the political tumult of the 1960s, and dispirited by the social chaos of the 1970s, Americans wanted to restore order, to resurrect the assurances of yesteryear. Reagan, with his traditionalist rhetoric, promised a return to the old regime, the old ways. Yet, as England's Charles II discovered during his seventeenth-century Restoration, the world had fundamentally changed. New ideas cannot be purged. The new leader was too pragmatic, too political, too accommodating to engage in a futile attempt to turn back the clock. As a result, Reagan led the country "Back to the Future," as the popular movie series of the 1980s suggested.

These historians' mostly political judgments need to be supplemented by cultural judgments too. Ronald Reagan's experiences and Americans' experiences in the 1980s cannot easily be separated, nor should they be. Not since the days of Franklin Roosevelt had one president so dominated a decade. Presidential historians have underestimated the cultural impact a president can have, especially in the modern age. The administrations of first Reagan, and most recently Bill Clinton, suggest that the time has come to assess a president's cultural legacy as well as his political achievements.

Much more than most presidents, Reagan came to office with a specific cultural agenda—he wanted a cultural revolution, or at least a restoration. An old-fashioned Midwesterner, Reagan loved the flag, hated abortion, and squirmed when watching movies with sex scenes and vulgar language. He and many of his supporters feared that America's anything goes culture was undermining the country's moral fiber. This search for cultural renaissance shaped the Reagan narrative. "The American electorate seeks from its national leadership this sense of shared values, this reaffirmation of traditional American beliefs," Reagan proclaimed in 1983. "They do not want a President who's a broker of parochial concerns; they do not want a definition of national purpose, a vision of the future."[26]

A number of recent works have recognized the Reagan Revolution's powerful cultural resonance. James Patterson's *Restless Giant: The United States from Watergate to Bush v. Gore* (2005) combines politics and culture in describing Reagan's "politics of values" and showing how Reagan's vision of the United States "as a great and exceptional nation—continued after 1984 to appeal to millions of Americans and to help him survive serious bungling in his second term."[27] John Ehrman's *The Eighties: America in the Age of Reagan* (2005) states that "Understanding the United States during the 1980s begins with understanding Ronald Reagan."[28] Robert M. Collins in *Transforming America: Politics and Culture during the Reagan Years* (2007) notes that paradoxically during the 1980s, "politics moved right just as culture moved left."[29] Collins pays particular attention to the "subterranean forces" transforming Reagan's America such as "the revolution in information technology, especially in computers, the increasing globalization of the national economy; and the dramatic restructuring of the corporate system, which led not only to monumental financial scandals but also the emergence of reinvigorated, leaner and more competitive business enterprise."[30]

As President Reagan pursued his cultural agenda—albeit halfheartedly—Culture Wars broke out from coast to coast. Liberals sought to expand their gains from the 1960s and 1970s. Conservatives felt confident enough to counterattack. The forces of right and left clashed repeatedly on abortion, busing, school prayer, the literary canon, school textbooks, museum exhibits, suitable nomenclature for women, blacks, gays. The ensuing debate roused millions. Some ended up alienated and entrenched themselves on the far left or the far right, nurturing their anger and a mirror-image, embittering sense of victimization.

Nevertheless, even as the debate became polarized in newspapers and on campuses, most Americans embraced a contradictory consensus in the center. The changes occurred more gradually and more reasonably than the Chicken Littles of the Left or the Right sometimes hoped and sometimes feared. Following the president's own mixed messages, the age of Reagan became an age of conservative libertinism, as a majority of Americans disliked abortion but wanted the option in an emergency—studies suggested that 56 percent considered abortion "murder," and 68 percent believed it defied "God's will," yet 67 percent supported a woman's right to choose, and, each year, as many as 3 percent of all American women had abortions. Similarly, most Americans condemned divorce, drug use, and promiscuity in principle, but many often succumbed to temptation in practice. As values of the 1960s and 1980s merged, individualism trumped moralism. Most Americans were more willing to indulge impulses than submit to authority, to live for the moment rather than be constrained by tradition.

This was not an age of neo-Victorianism, however, with everyone hypocritically indulging behind closed doors while parading around in tuxedos and puffy dresses. Americans wore their libertinism on their sleeves, even as many agreed with the conservative critique. It was libertinism, meaning indulgent behaviors, rather than libertarianism, because many who indulged nevertheless believed in the value of standards. By at least accepting standards, this "constructive hypocrisy," as William Bennett called it, was better than the more consistent nihilism many media leaders seemed to champion.[31] Still, the result was a culture of confusion, a culture of moral crusading and vulgar displays, a culture that placed sex and violence increasingly in the public square, whether you liked it or not.

Not surprisingly, by broadening the scope of their analyses beyond government, scholars appreciate Reagan's impact even more. Patterson calls Reagan "consequential."[32] Ehrman calls him a "Transformational President." In *Morning in America*, which organizes the story of Reagan's presidency in a year-by-year manner, with each chapter corresponding to a year in the 1980s, I mischievously call Reagan the "greatest president since FDR"—using the *Time*'s Person-of-the-Year standard of the individual who has made the greatest impact for good or ill.[33]

Reagan demonstrated that politics was more than a power game and a question of resource allocation. Reagan treated politics as a clash of ideas, symbols, values, and cultures. Richard Reeves, in a 2005 volume, was surprised to discover just how much respect he had for Reagan and Reaganism, noting that "No other President became a noun in that way." Reagan, Reeves argued, saw "the world in terms of ideas," and was able to implement some of the concepts he imagined could change the world.[34]

For all his notoriety as an anti-intellectual, Reagan understood the anthropological dimensions of politics in ways that only the most sophisticated of scholars were starting to grasp in the 1980s. In *Affairs of Party,* her 1983 work examining Northern Democrats' political culture before the Civil War, the historian Jean Baker gave politics a Reaganesque description as a "symbolic demonstration of the way Americans led their public lives" and "a series of community rituals embodying national values."[35] Reagan instinctively understood that to shape modern America he had to dominate American culture in its broadest terms, "not simply" referring to "the arts" but "to the ways a society makes meaning," as Yale's David Greenberg describes it in *Nixon's Shadow: The History of an Image* (2003).[36] Reagan's ambition targeted what Professors Meg Jacobs and Julian Zelizer would call in 2003 the "ideologies, languages, and symbols" that "shaped all political actors" in his time.[37]

Reagan made many of these ideas and symbols politically powerful by weaving them into a broader narrative. "If you can write a nation's stories, you needn't worry about who makes its laws," said Dr. George Gerbner, of the University of Pennsylvania's Annenberg School for Communication.[38] Reagan understood how to transcend the various fiascos that occurred on his watch. "Successful leaders do not necessarily do more than other leaders," the Yale political scientist Stephen Skowronek writes in *The Politics Presidents Make* (1993); "successful leaders control the political definition of their actions, the terms in which their places in history are understood."[39] Reagan's cultural renaissance, his renewal of American confidence, became central ingredients in his recipe for success.

John Patrick Diggins' interpretation of Reagan in his sweeping, stimulating, 2007 volume hinges on viewing Reagan in the broadest possible terms. *Ronald Reagan: Fate, Freedom and the Making of History* views Reagan as an Emersonian liberal, celebrating the self against authority and seeking to save modern liberalism from its blind spots regarding big government at home and Communist totalitarianism abroad.[40] Diggins' achievement lies not only in portraying Reagan as a philosopher–activist who proved that individuals can shape history, but in locating Reagan's mission in the broader sweep of American political and intellectual history.

Thanks to all these studies, by 2008, the Princeton historian Sean Wilentz was also surprised to find himself endorsing the growing consensus. Wilentz acknowledged his disdain for Reagan for decades and his public profile as a liberal. Nevertheless, he called Ronald Reagan "the single most important political figure" of "The Age of Reagan," from 1974 to 2008.[41]

In fact, contrary to the stereotype, the 1980s emerges as a decade of fascinating intellectual ferment, not just shop-till-you-drop indulgence. Reaganism triggered a necessary debate about the nature of the welfare state. Underlying these questions were philosophical issues surrounding the government's proper dimensions, the obligation of the fortunate to the needy, and ultimately, Americans' commitment to each other. "After all," the Democratic Speaker of the House Tip O'Neill noted, "The Constitution begins with the words, 'We, the people.' It does not begin, 'I, the individual.'"[42] Conservatives often bested liberals in the bookstores. Milton and Rose Friedman's *Free to Choose* (1980) celebrated Reagan-style laissez-faire economics.[43] Charles Murray's *Losing Ground: American Social Policy, 1950–1980* (1984) mourned the failure of the Great Society.[44] And Allan Bloom's surprise best seller *The Closing of the American Mind* (1987) denounced the epidemic of sensuality and superficiality among his students—and throughout society.[45] In return, liberals dominated the op-ed pages, with essays "Exploding Some Myths about Social Programs" in the *Los Angeles Times* or arguing in *Harper's* how Ronald Reagan was "Making the World Safe for Plutocracy."[46] Even as the political balance wavered, Democrats and liberals tended to be on the defensive intellectually and ideologically.

In Washington, D.C., these sweeping philosophical, historical, economic, and ideological debates often became mired in political horse-trading and posturing. But in a bipolar, personality-driven media universe both these transcendent and petty concerns became concentrated in a clash of the titans. Especially early on, much of this complicated, multidimensional debate over a nearly trillion-dollar budget with tens of thousands of individual entries played out as a legendary struggle between the president of the United States Ronald Reagan and the speaker of the House Tip O'Neill.

Despite all the progress made in recent years, we still need some great big books on Reagan and his times. Recent historians have laid the groundwork and begun to catch up after a lamentably slow start; we still need someone to offer that grand synthesis. Ronald Reagan needs his Arthur Schlesinger; or, to think of it differently, Lou Cannon's authoritative biography needs to be updated and put in more interpretive and lyrical terms. We need a majestic, accessible, scholarly, sweeping, ultimately approving but not mindlessly reverential entry into the Reagan biographical sweepstakes to command attention and make the battle lines clearer. Many of us from the incrementalist school are pulling Reagan scholarship back from the partisan brink, arguing in essence, "he wasn't a moron, but we won't call him a genius." We give him his due—and acknowledge his strengths—while also remembering his weaknesses, which makes for a more accurate picture but will not galvanize an argument as Arthur Schlesinger's *Age of Jackson* (1945) did in the 1940s about Andrew Jackson, or Schlesinger's *The Coming of the New Deal* (1958) did about Franklin Roosevelt a decade and a half later.[47] Steven Hayward is trying to achieve that kind of monumental stage-setting with *The Age of Reagan* (2001). However, with a projected result of three huge volumes, and with an approach that is admittedly "hard on liberals," the book may be too heavy—and politically too heavy-handed—to succeed.[48]

The Reagan period also needs a thorough, thoughtful, definitive, foreign policy analysis, along the lines of what Robert Dallek did for Franklin Roosevelt.[49] Paul Lettow has reappraised and made central Reagan's "antinuclearism," as he calls it; Peter Schweizer has reappraised and made central Reagan's anticommunist "crusade"—if we are still allowed to use that word in polite company.[50] Both Lettow and Schweizer, like FitzGerald in *Way Out There in the Blue*, follow one thread in the foreign policy tapestry, when we need to see an entire, comprehensive work of art.

The question of Reagan's role in ending the Cold War remains unresolved. In the post–Cold War historiographical tug-of-war, partisans often prefer to lionize "Gorby" and discount "Ronnie," or vice versa. Mikhail Gorbachev certainly helped trigger the Soviet reformation and ultimately Communism's collapse. But Gorbachev was the product of the internal rot of the Soviet system, not its cause. He emerged because the Soviet system had become technologically backward and economically dysfunctional, as well as politically oppressive. Looking back, Gorbachev's foreign affairs adviser Anatoly Chernyaev would realize that what the reformers called "the Brezhnev period [of] stagnation" in the 1970s was misnamed; it was in fact "the gradual dying of our society."[51]

Ronald Reagan deserves more credit than many historians have given him for responding to Gorbachev effectively. In the waning days of his administration, beset by the Iran–Contra scandal, plagued by doubts from the left and the right, Ronald Reagan struck just the right balance with Gorbachev. Reagan was resolute enough not to be underestimated—and flexible enough to encourage Gorbachev's revolution; Reagan was also resolute enough to defy his worried advisers—and flexible enough to embrace the new-style Soviet leader. As always, Reagan was more surefooted with Russia than the Middle East, in an arena of long-term interest to him rather than a quagmire imposed on him. The formidable Anatoly Dobrynin, the veteran Soviet ambassador to the United States, acknowledged that Reagan's surprising suppleness sustained both *perestroika* (restructuring) and *glasnost* (openness), Gorbachev's domestic and international reformations. "If Reagan had stuck to his hard-line policies in 1985 and 1986," Dobrynin said, "Gorbachev would have been accused by the rest of the Politburo of giving everything away to a fellow who does not want to negotiate. We would have been forced to tighten our belts and spend even more on defence."[52] Reagan's greatness here—along with Gorbachev's—renewed the faith of Princeton's Fred Greenstein and many others—in the unfashionable notion that individuals shape history.[53]

The Reagan period also needs an authoritative economic history. Here, too, the continuing debates during the Bill Clinton and George W. Bush eras about tax cuts, small government, and conservatism suggest we will have to wait a while to avoid tendentious discussions. However, complex questions have not been adequately answered, including:

- Just who (or what) killed the great inflation—was it Ronald Reagan, Jimmy Carter, or Paul Volcker?

- Just who (or what) caused the Great Prosperity—was it the Reagan boom, the great technology boom, or maybe the baby-boom boom (actually the baby-boom-growing-up-and-starting-to-earn boom)?
- And how about this perennial political hot potato that demands more precise analysis—who were the winners and who were the losers of the great prosperity? Does the growing gap between CEOs and workers reflect a more stratified society, a more burdened middle and lower class, or did the poor *not* get poorer and somehow even benefit as the rich became so much richer?

All too often, it seems that these difficult questions have been approached as theological issues and not intellectual puzzles. In most of the scholarship you are far more likely to learn about the scholar's beliefs today than the economic realities of yesterday.

Here, too, a balanced perspective will improve Reagan's standing. Despite the massive federal deficits, the Great Inflation ended. And after a sharp but relatively short recession, the economic miracle of the 1980s and 1990s began. Many economists attributed the low inflation rate to the very tight monetary policy of the Federal Reserve Chairman Paul Volcker, a Carter appointee. Volcker graciously shared credit with Reagan, saluting him for staring down the PATCO union when air traffic controllers struck in summer 1981, and, more generally, for not interfering with the Federal Reserve inflation-cutting strategy. Here, Reagan's instincts and ideology meshed. Reagan, like Volcker, believed the "Supply Side" doctrine that inflation could be controlled by adjusting the money supply—and he knew that Volcker was the money supply manager. Thus, in the crude accounting of the presidential credit sweepstakes, Reagan not Carter—the man who appointed Volcker—earned the bragging rights for the economic boom.

Finally, there are a host of smaller but no less important studies regarding the politics, culture, society, economy of the 1980s, about the functioning of the presidency, the federal bureaucracy, the Congress, the parties, the states. Colleagues are beginning to tackle these issues, much more work needs to be done.

When Mr. Reagan came to town, Americans happily left the 1970s behind, trying to bury the traumas of Watergate, Vietnam, the energy crisis, stagflation—that unprecedented economic knockout punch of high inflation and high unemployment—and the Iranian hostage crisis. Americans feared that the end of the American Century had arrived nearly a quarter of a century prematurely. The Soviets seemed to be on the march with America languishing. Few Americans in the 1970s would have predicted the great bull market of the 1980s, the resurgence of American confidence and patriotism, the end of the Cold War, or the collapse of the Soviet Union within a matter of years. By the end of the 1980s, many Americans did feel restored, and Ronald Reagan had earned bragging rights for many of these successes.

And yet, the restoration may have been more symbolic than actual. Serious social crises remained unsolved. The Reagan boom did not eliminate poverty, racism, crime, family breakdown, urban deterioration, and a mass epidemic of individual psychic distress. Many Americans continued to fear the future. Japan and West Germany threatened to eclipse the United States economically—fears that proved groundless within a few years. And despite Reagan's many odes to national unity, millions felt alienated—and only further marginalized by all the morning-in-America celebrations.

The restoration of the 1980s can be compared to the era's urban gentrification projects. Slick, gleaming, high-tech towers of glass and steel often replaced decaying slums—but the problems were relocated, not solved. Amid so many dizzying developments, it was hard to determine which changes were real, and which were cosmetic.

In dominating this decade, Ronald Reagan was the star of this restoration. Politically and culturally he defined the times. The individualism he celebrated as a national achievement tended to individuate and separate most, even as it spurred some to great achievements that benefited the nation. Ideologically, Reagan's conservatism reoriented Americans away from big government, triggering a nationwide argument about government's role, capitalism's advantages, morality's relevance, and individual charity's limitations. Tactically, Reagan set new standards in media management and mastery, conquering the brave new media world. Culturally, he reconciled the 1960s' ideals with 1980s' ambitions. He and his "revolution" did not repudiate all the social, political, and cultural trends he denounced. Reagan himself was the first divorced president, perhaps the first president to host a gay couple overnight in the Executive Mansion when his wife's interior decorator slept over, and the father of a quarrelling clan whose members did drugs, "shacked up," and married multiple times. Despite his rhetoric, Reagan helped Americans adapt to the 1960s' and 1970s' great changes, integrating them into their lives.

The tensions that generated the great 1960s rebellions had not disappeared. Feeling alienated and powerless to shape big government or get traction in American society, most Americans wallowed in their anonymity. In turn, the anonymity and social estrangement diluted Americans' feelings of civic attachment and moral commitment. A 1986 Harris Poll found that 60 percent of Americans believed "what I think doesn't count much anymore"; 82 percent admitted they would act on a friend's stock tip—even if it constituted illegal insider training.[54] "Is it possible that we could become citizens again and together seek the common good in the post-industrial, postmodern age?" the sociologist Robert Bellah and his colleagues wondered in their surprise bestseller *Habits of the Heart* (1985).[55] "Freedom is a moral accomplishment," the British theologian Jonathan Sacks would write in *The Politics of Hope* in 1997, showing that the problem outlasted the 1980s and transcended Reagan's America. "It needs strong families, cohesive institutions, habits of civility and law-abidingness, and a widely diffused sense of fellow-feeling...When moral language breaks down—as it has broken down—much else is at risk, including freedom itself."[56]

Reagan's traditional celebrations of morality and citizenship charmed Americans. Yet for all the talk, Reagan's combination of nonconfrontational affability and feel-good libertinism did not stop the social and moral decay. In establishing a public plane where the radical individualism and indulgent libertinism of the left and the right could meet happily, he further undermined America's "moral language" and institutions.

Perhaps Reagan's greatest asset—and his greatest gift to Americans—was his optimism. His faith in America and in the future was contagious, and a welcome corrective to the traumatic Nixon years, the drifting Ford years, the despairing Carter years. His can-do optimism, his sense of America as a shining "city set upon a hill," tapped into one of the nation's most enduring character traits. Americans wanted an Era of Good Feelings, and they got it. Ironically, even as Reagan seemed to be repudiating the greatest legacies of Franklin D. Roosevelt, John F. Kennedy, and Lyndon B. Johnson, Reagan's have-your-cake-and-eat-it-too politics echoed theirs. Like Reagan, Roosevelt, Kennedy, and Johnson all sought to conjure up a democratic Eden painlessly, with no trade-offs. Neither the great conservative president of the 1980s nor the great liberal presidents who preceded him really demanded that Americans solve social problems through individual or collective sacrifice.

Paradoxically, Ronald Reagan's odes to an older, simpler, more idealistic, more community-oriented America helped spawn a new, sprawling, often selfish, deeply individualistic society. In reinvigorating American capitalism, Reagan helped unleash the American id. Many of the forces that triggered the boom to which Reagan claimed bragging rights were social solvents. Consumerism, materialism, individualism, entrepreneurship, the antigovernment backlash, the information age, capitalism itself, the end of the Cold War, all helped dissolve traditional ties and certainly fostered an American hedonism. But all these centrifugal forces made Ronald Reagan's centripetal force—his celebrity, his patriotism, his communal vision for modern America, in short his narrative—all the more important, then and now.

So, yes, we have done a lousy job as historians—but we are improving. Reagan scholarship may not be where Kennedy or Roosevelt scholarship was after a similar amount of time elapsed following those presidencies. The gap reflects the excitement and political inspiration the New Deal and the New Frontier generated, especially among academics. But Reagan scholarship, especially after the last few years, does compare most favorably to Truman, Eisenhower, and Lyndon Johnson scholarship. In 1970, twenty-five years after he became president, Harry Truman, still alive, was more often considered a prickly failure rather than a Plain Speakin' savant; Merle Miller's bestselling *Plain Speaking* was four years from publication.[57] In 1982, thirty years after his election, Eisenhower was also considered to be clueless; Fred Greenstein's *The Hidden-Hand Presidency* (1982) had just been published.[58] In 1993 Lyndon Johnson's reputation was still in the Vietnam-defined, Napalm-poisoned dumps; Robert Dallek's *Flawed Giant* was five years from publication.[59] Moreover, it would be another half-decade or so before the likes of George McGovern would "discover greatness" in Lyndon Johnson, arguing that Vietnam should not eclipse Johnson's domestic record and broader aspirations.[60]

All this raises the question, as we watch a new crop of graduate students approach the field, just whose magnum opus in formation is going to help us Get Right With Reagan, and prove our collective abilities to transcend the political and intellectual biases of the 1980s—and of today.

Notes

1. Gil Troy, *Morning in America: How Ronald Regan Invented the 1980s* (Princeton, NJ: Princeton University Press, 2005).
2. *New York Times*, June 6, 2004, A1.
3. Alan Brinkley, "The Problem of American Conservatism," *The American Historical Review* 99 (1994): 409.
4. Edmund Morris, *Dutch: A Memoir of Ronald Reagan* (New York: Random House, 1999).
5. Mary C. Brennan, *Turning Right in the Sixties: The Conservative Capture of the GOP* (Chapel Hill: University of North Carolina Press, 1995); Lisa McGirr, *Suburban Warriors: The Origins of the New American Right* (Princeton, NJ: Princeton University Press, 2001); Jonathan Schoenwald, *A Time for Choosing: The Rise of Modern American Conservatism* (New York: Oxford University Press, 2001).
6. James MacGregor Burns, *Roosevelt: The Lion and the Fox, 1882–1940* (New York: Harcourt, Brace, 1956); *Roosevelt: The Soldier of Freedom, 1940–1945* (New York: Harcourt Brace Jovanovich, 1970); Arthur M. Schlesinger, *The Crisis of the Old Order, 1919–1933* (Boston: Houghton Mifflin, 1957); *The Coming of the New Deal, 1933–1935* (Boston: Houghton Mifflin, 1958); *The Politics of Upheaval: 1935–1936* (Boston: Houghton Mifflin, 1960).
7. Clark Clifford, *Counsel to the President: A Memoir* (New York: Random House, 1991), 644; Gary Wills, "Mr. Magoo Remembers: An American Life. by Ronald Reagan," *New York Review of Books*, December 20, 1990, 29.
8. David Alan Stockman, *The Triumph of Politics: How the Reagan Revolution Failed* (New York: Harper & Row, 1986), 291; Donald T. Regan, *For the Record: From Wall Street to Washington* (San Diego: Harcourt Brace Jovanovich, 1988).
9. W. Elliot Brownlee and Hugh Davis Graham, eds., *The Reagan Presidency: Pragmatic Conservatism & Its Legacies* (Lawrence, KS: University Press of Kansas, 2003), 356.
10. "Mondale the Mean," Republican National Committee, in Michael J. Bayer to Maureen Reagan, October 15, 1984, Series I, Memorandum File, Subseries C, 1984–January 1985, James A. Baker III MSS, Ronald Reagan Presidential Library, Simi Valley, CA.
11. Peggy Noonan, *When Character was King: A Story of Ronald Reagan* (New York: Viking, 2001); Peter J. Wallison, *Ronald Reagan: The Power of Conviction and the Success of His Presidency* (Boulder, CO: Westview Press, 2004); Peter Robinson, *How Ronald Reagan Changed My Life* (New York: Regan Books, 2003); Paul Kengor, *God and Ronald Reagan: A Spiritual Life* (New York: Regan Books of HarperCollins, 2004). See also Martin Anderson, *Revolution* (San Diego: Harcourt Brace Jovanovich, 1988); Dinesh D'Souza, *Ronald Reagan: How an Ordinary Man Became an Extraordinary Leader* (New York: Free Press, 1997).

12. D'Souza, *Ronald Reagan*, 136, 185–186.
13. Morris, *Dutch*, 579.
14. Michael Reagan, *On the Outside Looking In* (New York: Zebra Books, 1988), 96.
15. William Allen White, *Masks in a Pageant* (New York: The MacMillan company, 1928), 155.
16. *U.S. News & World Report*, June 26, 1989, 27.
17. Owen Ullman quoted in *Chicago Sun-Times*, April 2, 1989, 45. See also *Washington Post*, April 11, 1989, A17.
18. Lou Cannon, *President Reagan: The Role of a Lifetime* (New York: Simon & Schuster 1991, 2000); Haynes Johnson, *Sleepwalking through History: America in the Reagan Years* (New York: Norton, 1991, 2003); Robert Dallek, *Ronald Reagan: The Politics of Symbolism* (Cambridge, MA: Harvard University Press, 1984, 2000).
19. Ronald Reagan, *Reagan in His Own Hand: The Writings of Ronald Reagan that Reveal His Revolutionary Vision for America*, ed. Kiron K. Skinner, Annelise Anderson, and Martin Anderson (New York: Free Press, 2001); Ronald Reagan, *Reagan: A Life in Letters*, ed. Kiron K. Skinner, Annelise Anderson, and Martin Anderson (New York: Free Press, 2003).
20. Ronald Reagan, *The Reagan Diaries*, ed., Douglas Brinkley (New York: HarperCollins, 2007).
21. Alonzo L. Hamby, *Liberalism and its Challengers: From F.D.R. to Bush*, second ed. (New York: Oxford University Press, 1992); Frances FitzGerald, *Way Out There in the Blue: Reagan, Star Wars, and the End of the Cold War* (New York: Simon & Schuster, 2000).
22. Hamby, *Liberalism and its Challengers*, 385–386.
23. Ronald Reagan to Laurence W. Beilenson, August 1, 1986, in Reagan, *Reagan: A Life in Letters*, 428.
24. "Ten Myths that Miss The Mark," Issue Alert, March 2, 1983, 118188PD, Box 11, FG 001, Ronald Regan Library, Simi Valley, California.
25. *Washington Post*, July 8, 1981, A2.
26. Ronald Reagan, "Remarks at a Dinner Marking the 10th Anniversary of the Heritage Foundation," October 8, 1983, in Public Papers of the Presidents, John T. Woolley and Gerhard Peters, *The American Presidency Project* (online). Santa Barbara, CA: University of California (hosted), Gerhard Peters (database). Available from World Wide Web: http://www.presidency.ucsb.edu/ws/?pid=40580.
27. James T. Patterson, *Restless Giant: The United States from Watergate to Bush v. Gore* (New York: Oxford University Press, 2005), 191–192.
28. John Ehrman, *The Eighties: America in the Age of Reagan* (New Haven: Yale University Press, 2005), 9.
29. Robert M. Collins, *Transforming America: Politics and Culture during the Reagan Years* (New York: Columbia University Press, 2007), 5.
30. Ibid., 4.
31. *Chicago Tribune*, October 30, 1995, 11.
32. Patterson, *Restless Giant*, 191.
33. Troy, *Morning in America*, 347.
34. Richard Reeves, *President Reagan: The Triumph of Imagination* (New York: Simon & Schuster, 2005), xvi, xii.

35. Jean H. Baker, *Affairs of Party: The Political Culture of Northern Democrats in the Mid-Nineteenth Century* (Ithaca: Cornell University Press, 1983), 262.
36. David Greenberg, *Nixon's Shadow: The History of an Image* (New York: W.W. Norton, 2003), xii.
37. Meg Jacobs and Julian E. Zelizer, "The Democratic Experiment: New Directions in American Political History." In *The Democratic Experiment: New Directions in American Political History*, ed., Meg Jacobs, William J. Novak, and Julian E. Zelizer (Princeton, NJ: Princeton University Press, 2003), 7.
38. Edward Feulner, Jr., "Shaping America's Values Debate," September 15, 1992, A Heritage Foundation Symposium, *Heritage Lecture #428*, http://www.heritage.org/Research/Religion/HL428.cfm.
39. Stephen Skowronek, *The Politics Presidents Make: Leadership from John Adams to George Bush* (Cambridge, MA: Belknap Press, 1993), 17.
40. John Patrick Diggins, *Ronald Reagan: Fate, Freedom and the Making of History* (New York: W.W. Norton & Co., 2007).
41. Sean Wilentz, *The Age of Reagan: A History, 1974–2008* (New York, HarperCollins, 2008), 1.
42. Tip O'Neill with William Novak, *Man of the House: the Life and Political Memoirs of Speaker Tip O'Neill* (New York: Random House, 1987), 348.
43. Milton and Rose Friedman, *Free to Choose: A Personal Statement* (New York: Harcourt Brace Jovanovich, 1980).
44. Charles Murray, *Losing Ground: American Social Policy, 1950–1980* (New York: Basic Books, 1984).
45. Allan Bloom, *The Closing of the American Mind: How Higher Education has Failed Democracy and Impoverished the Souls of Today's Students* (New York: Simon and Schuster, 1987).
46. Vernon Jordan, "Exploding Some Myths about Social Programs," *Los Angeles Times*, February 16, 1981, 2: 9; Walter Karp, "Making the World Safe for Plutocracy," *Harper's*, October 1981, 30–36.
47. Arthur M. Schlesinger, *Age of Jackson* (Boston: Little, Brown and Company, 1945); *The Coming of the New Deal* (Norwalk, CT: Easton Press, 1958).
48. Steven F. Hayward, *The Age of Reagan: The Fall of the Old Liberal Order, 1964–1980* (Roseville, CA: Forum, 2001), viii.
49. Robert Dallek, *The Roosevelt Diplomacy and World War II* (New York: Holt, Rinehart and Winston, 1970).
50. Paul Vorbeck Lettow, *Ronald Reagan and His Quest to Abolish Nuclear Weapons* (New York: Random House, 2005); Peter Schweizer, *Reagan's War: the Epic Story of His Forty Year Struggle and Final Triumph over Communism* (New York: Doubleday, 2002).
51. Beth A. Fischer, "Reagan and the Soviets: Winning the Cold War?" In W. Elliot Brownlee and Hugh Davis Graham, eds., *The Reagan Presidency: Pragmatic Conservatism & Its Legacies* (Lawrence, KS: University Press of Kansas, 2003), 124.
52. Fred Greenstein, "Reagan's Style of Politics and Governing," History News Network, http://hnn.us/roundup/entries/5590.html
53. See Fred Greenstein, *The Presidential Difference: Style and Character in the Oval Office from FDR to Bill Clinton* (New York: The Free Press, 2000).
54. Louis Harris, *Inside America* (New York: Vintage Books, 1987), 33, 35, 109.

55. Robert N. Bellah, Richard Madsen, William M. Sullivan, Ann Swidler, and Steven M. Tipton, *Habits of the Heart: Individualism and Commitment in American Life* (Berkeley: University of California Press, 1985, 1996), 271.
56. Jonathan Saks, *The Politics of Hope* (London: Jonathan Cape, 1997), 39.
57. Merle Miller, *Plain Speaking: An Oral Biography of Harry S. Truman* (London: Gollancz, 1974).
58. Fred I. Greenstein, *The Hidden-Hand Presidency: Eisenhower as Leader* (Baltimore, MD: Johns Hopkins University Press, 1982, 1994).
59. Robert Dallek, *Flawed Giant: Lyndon Johnson and His Times, 1961–1973* (New York: Oxford University Press, 1998).
60. George McGovern, "Discovering Greatness in Lyndon Johnson," *New York Times*, December 5, 1999.

Epilogue

Ronald Reagan and the Historians

M.J. Heale

For many years academic historians, many of them liberal Democrats, gave Ronald Reagan a bad press. In a survey of historians taken between 1988 and 1990 some 62 percent rated him as either below average as a president or even a failure.[1] Representative of this assessment was the history published by Michael Schaller in 1992, which argued that Reagan's appeal was "based on his easy charm, not his talent or accomplishment."[2] While Schaller admired Reagan's communication skills, he described a president who was barely in charge of his administration, he emphasized the scandals associated with it, and questioned whether Reagan deserved much credit for ending the Cold War. Reagan emerged as sort of sincere Wizard of Oz, an illusionist who believed in his illusions: "Reagan succeeded, as few actors or politicians have, in persuading Americans to suspend their disbelief. It was an era when saying something made it so, when, as in a daydream, anything seemed possible."[3] Leading journalists too offered less than admiring analyses. In what remains the best biography of Reagan, Lou Cannon presented him as a man with considerable gifts but also serious limitations, a supremely self-confident president who was able to set a direction for his administration but whose lack of curiosity and his failure to analyze issues in depth meant that he was somewhat at the mercy of his staff.[4] Haynes Johnson offered a president who failed to address the real problems of the country, one who was "sleepwalking through history."[5]

Yet as the twenty-first century replaced the twentieth a spectacular reevaluation of the Reagan presidency occurred, both among academic historians and among serious journalists. (This academic reappraisal paralleled Reagan's growing popularity with the wider public. Reagan's approval rating as president, as measured by Gallup, had been 57 percent in November 1988; in June 1992 it was down to 50 percent, but in February 1999 it reached a stunning 71 percent, and was confirmed at the same figure in June 2006.[6]) Reagan always had his partisan admirers, of course, but now more detached scholars began to find much to praise. Some have been advancing Reagan to the front ranks of American presidents, placing him alongside such greats as

Franklin Roosevelt and Abraham Lincoln. Yet this reappraisal has not convinced everyone. Several of the essays in this volume are clearly bemused by this phenomenon and offer something of a corrective to it. Reagan's political skills can be admired, as these authors note, but they question how far his performance as president and his legacy can be regarded as positive. Unlike some of the earliest assessments, for the most part they show real respect for the president, but they are not disposed to endorse the enthusiastic judgments that have recently surfaced in Reagan historiography.

There were several influences that contributed to Reagan's rising status. One was the publication of many of his writings, initially radio addresses that he had composed himself in the 1970s and later other documents from his presidency, which revealed an intelligent man engaged with public issues. Second, a historiographical reappraisal of American conservatism generally had been underway, as scholars were obliged to explain the political success of Republicanism in the late twentieth century, so that conservatism was seen increasingly as a mainstream movement and its prophets worthy of respect. And third, Reagan's performance in the White House came to be compared favorably with those of his successors. Reagan never compromised the dignity of the White House, unlike Bill Clinton. And his reluctance to use military force and his rapprochement with the Soviet Union can seem examples of wisdom when contrasted with the foreign policy of George W. Bush. Even the veteran dean of American conservatism William F. Buckley thought in 2007 that Reagan would have shown prudence over Iraq and would have "shunned a commitment of the kind we are now engaged in."[7] Thus Reagan's stature has grown in retrospect.

One major reappraisal that showed heightened respect for Ronald Reagan was the 2003 volume edited by W. Elliot Brownlee and Hugh Davis Graham.[8] It is clear that several of the essays in this were influenced by the publication of Reagan's radio addresses of the 1970s, with their display of an informed political intelligence and a committed agenda. The agenda, however, was not a brittle one. Conservative he might have been, attached in particular to a limited range of ideas, such as lowering taxation and confronting the Soviets from a position of strength, but Reagan was a politician too, flexible and prepared to compromise. For him, half a loaf was better than none. While other writers, such as Cannon, had discussed Reagan's pragmatic temperament, it was primarily this collection that promoted the image of the Reagan presidency as one of "pragmatic conservatism."[9] Gareth Davies, for example, drew attention to "the sheer evangelical, right-wing radicalism" of Reagan's initial welfare proposals, as well as his willingness to negotiate and compromise in order to make "modest advances toward his agenda." This made him "a pragmatic ideologue," willing to enter the log-rolling political territory that doctrinaire right-wingers would have scorned.[10] Other scholars have adopted this characterization, which resolved some of the contradictions in understanding Reagan. In one of the best accounts of the 1980s, Robert M. Collins used the term "Pragmatic Ideologue" in the title of one of his chapters.[11] In the context of the aggressive conservatism of the George W. Bush era, associated as it is with unwavering neoconservative convictions, the pragmatism of the Reagan White House has become more apparent.

Yet more positive ratings of Reagan and his presidency in the scholarly literature followed in the wake of the Brownlee and Graham study. Gil Troy in 2005 again presented Reagan as the conservative as pragmatist, the easy-going ideologue who reassured rather than alarmed. Possessed of a remarkable performing instinct, Reagan brilliantly stage-managed and to a degree dominated the political scene, lifting the country from the malaise of the Carter era. He thus saved the presidency from irrelevance and nudged the national tone in a conservative direction, bringing about a "Reaganized" America to which Bill Clinton would be obliged to accommodate. John Ehrman's book of the same year presented the Reagan era as one of constructive conservatism. Reagan was "a man of conservative instincts, but above all a practical politician, one who knew the importance of concentrating on a few priorities and who had an instinct for when to take a deal."[12] His administration promoted a highly competitive economy and ensured that most Americans benefited as Reagan deftly presided over an era of transition from post–World War II liberalism toward the technologically driven information age of Bill Clinton. Another 2005 study, by experienced presidential chronicler Richard Reeves, insisted that Reagan was in fact a hardworking president, in charge of his own administration, able to resist the advice of his aides and tell his wife to back off, and spending a lot of time telephoning members of Congress to secure their support for administration bills. Reeves documented in valuable detail his thesis that Reagan ran his own administration and that he was not easily manipulated. Reagan's "imagination" nudged the country in new directions, promoting conservatism at home and forging an unlikely rapport with Mikhail Gorbachev.[13]

Two years later came a pair of books that elevated Reagan yet further. Robert M. Collins's volume continued to burnish the Reagan image. Reagan had his limitations, but he was a figure of intelligence and judgment, a distinctive blend of ideologue and pragmatist, and possessed of an optimism that allowed him to be bold and often to defy the conventional wisdom. His economic policies, especially supply-side economics, worked better than his critics prophesied, and the restructuring of the economy enabled the United States to become an economic powerhouse in the 1990s. Overall, Collins concluded, Reagan's legacy was a positive one, helping to engineer a long economic recovery, bringing the Cold War to a conclusion on the West's terms, and slowing the growth of the federal government. He allowed Reagan his own epitaph: "All in all, not bad, not bad at all."[14] Even more striking was John Patrick Diggins' *Ronald Reagan*, which was less enthusiastic than Collins on Reagan's domestic record, but argued that he achieved true greatness in his foreign policy. Diggins was concerned to elucidate Reagan's moral philosophy, and he made a fascinating case for the "Emersonian" cast of Reagan's mind, with his belief in the divinely inspired goodness of human beings. In this Reagan was an unusual conservative, convinced—like many liberals—that human desires needed to be unleashed rather than constrained. This optimistic belief in human nature was inseparable from his conviction that people could make a difference. Such an outlook increasingly distanced him from his more conservative advisers and propelled him into his determined negotiations with the Soviet Union. Reagan failed in many of his domestic objectives, government remaining hopelessly big, but on a larger stage "American ideals did for others what they could not do for us."[15] Confident in himself and in human goodness, Reagan put faith in personal contact, persistent negotiation and the fostering of goodwill. Diggins praised him for "defying destiny and taking control of events."[16] Others who might have been president in the 1980s, so it is implied, trapped in Cold War verities, very likely would not have achieved the extraordinary goal of ending the Cold War peacefully.

If Ronald Reagan can be credited with ending the Cold War he can hardly be denied a place of honor in the presidential pantheon, but recent scholars have found more to praise in his record than his foreign policy. They have reached a near consensus on some of the claims made for the Reagan presidency; on others there is debate. Reagan's partisans have hailed a "Reagan Revolution," and while most academic discussions have stopped short of characterizing the era as a "revolution," they do generally agree that it represented at least a "turning-point," for good or for ill. Both conservative and liberal authors have generally agreed that there was a turn to the right, as Reagan helped to rehabilitate conservatism and even to make palatable the kind of right-wing ideas that had fated Barry Goldwater to defeat in the presidential election of 1964.

Reagan's success in moving American political culture away from the "New Deal Order" or the "consensus liberalism" of the middle decades of the twentieth century has meant that he has been frequently been compared to Franklin D. Roosevelt. Reagan's assault on big government has sometimes been seen as an attack on Roosevelt's New Deal, though Reagan himself tended to be irritated with such suggestions: "I'm trying to undo the 'Great Society.' It was LBJ's war on poverty that led us to our present mess."[17] Richard Neustadt, the preeminent scholar on the presidency, noted several comparisons with Roosevelt, not only in temperament, but also the degree to which some of Reagan's political stances and policies were arguably prompted by Roosevelt.[18] Revisionist historians do not necessarily rank Reagan alongside Roosevelt—Alonzo Hamby contended in a chapter entitled "The Roosevelt of the Right" that he is better bracketed with the somewhat less effective Eisenhower—but Gil Troy for one confidently argued that "Ronald Reagan was the greatest American president since Franklin D. Roosevelt—using the *Time* man-of-the-year standard of 'the person who most affected the news and our lives, for good or for ill.'"[19]

Whether or not he can be ranked with Roosevelt, Reagan entered the White House at a time when presidential authority was at a low ebb, and almost all commentators have agreed that Reagan renewed faith in the presidency as an institution. A much greater claim made for Reagan, and the most difficult to assess, is that he revived the national spirit after the celebrated "malaise" of the late 1970s. Robert Collins suggested that what Reagan termed "the recovery of our morale" may have been his "greatest, or at least the most fundamental" triumph, one that underpinned other successes.[20] While several authors have made claims of this sort, their evidence has tended to be thin. If Reagan did achieve a revival of American self-confidence, it is not clear that it went very deep or lasted very long. By the time of the 1992 presidential campaign the spirit seems largely to have evaporated, to judge from the degree to which the insurgent presidential candidacy of Ross Perot was able to exploit popular unease with the nation's course.

What is susceptible to a degree of measurement is the electoral performance of Reagan's Republican party, and some have seen its successes since the 1980s as evidence of a measure of realignment, of the Republican party displacing the Democratic party as the normal party of government. Reagan, Reeves argued, "remoulded and revitalized" the Republican party and made it "the dominant party in the country."[21] Perhaps. While it might be conceded that Ronald Reagan helped to make conservatism respectable, it is not clear that this has translated into giving the Republican party clear majority status. For one thing the rightward move in the political mainstream is reflected in part in the repositioning of the Democratic Party toward the center in order to avert electoral losses. Another difficulty with the view that Reagan revitalized the Republican Party is that there were more Democrats in Congress after the 1988 elections than after the 1980 elections. Reagan's remarkable personal popularity was not enough to build a decisive Republican political ascendancy across the political system. This is the reason presidential historian Alonzo Hamby ultimately drew back from ranking him alongside Roosevelt, because he failed to bring about a significant political realignment or a "broadly-based ideological revolution."[22]

There is now wide agreement on several of the claims made about the Reagan legacy—rehabilitating conservatism, turning the country in a new, rightward direction, restoring faith in the presidency, reviving American self-respect, and contributing critically to the ending of the Cold War. That Reagan deserves greater honor than that accorded by some of the first assessments is now established. But the essays in this volume suggest that there should be limits to the degree to which the Reagan presidency should be celebrated. They serve as something of a corrective to the tendency in recent years to push Reagan toward the top of the presidential league table.

One irony is that so much attention has been paid to the Reagan presidency at a time when many political scientists have tended to play down the role of the president in the American political system. Over the last generation analysts of the American political process have tended to emphasize its multicentred or atomistic nature, the clashes between the executive and legislative branches, the importance of Congress rather than the White House in formulating significant public policies, the apparently increasing roles of the bureaucracy and the judiciary in determining policy, and the impact of lobbies and single-interest groups. Such terms as "the new American political system," "the new institutionalism," "split-level government," and "post-electoral politics" have been applied to a political process in which the presidency is only one institution among many competing for power.

It could be said that the American polity has stumbled back toward the government of "checks and balances" envisioned by the Founding Fathers. One reason for this fragmentation has been the weakening of the party system. Voters have become "dealigned." Many of them do not vote the straight party line in election after election. A large number simply do not go to the polls, some vote one way in presidential elections and another way in state and congressional elections, some switch their votes from one election to the next. Presidential—and other—candidates no longer rely greatly on party machinery to mobilize support, but rather raise huge sums themselves to buy time on television to project themselves directly to the voters. Among other things, the atrophy of the old party machinery has worked to the advantage of charismatic candidates such as Ronald Reagan and Bill Clinton.

Almost everyone has acknowledged Reagan's extraordinary powers as a performer. Authors have waxed eloquent on Reagan's capacity to embody American traits or myths or to serve as the "American Everyman." Dan Rather in this volume discusses Reagan's capacity to personify America, the sense, in Lou Cannon's phrase, "that America was inside of him." This gave him a "fundamental" and "innate" understanding of his country, and allowed him to connect with his fellow Americans, or at least many of them. As Godfrey Hodgson puts it, "Reagan was exactly the President many Americans wanted; a President who could restore what has always been one of the sovereign American virtues, self-belief." On this analysis, not only was Reagan a consummate performer, but he also possessed a rare ability to divine what Americans wanted. What is less clear is how far these talents, and Reagan's capacity to embody the national zeitgeist, should be seen in a positive or negative light.

On the one hand, it can be argued that these are valuable attributes in the presidency, perhaps essential in the contemporary and fragmented political system, where the president serves as a symbol of unity and the ubiquity of the camera puts a premium on the capacity to communicate. Such qualities, it has often been suggested, enabled Reagan to provide a kind of mood music that allowed Americans to feel better about themselves.[23] Indeed, this was one of Reagan's avowed objectives. He once remarked to the American Bar Association: "One of my dreams is to help Americans rise above pessimism by renewing their belief in themselves,"[24] and he told Godfrey Hodgson of his ambition to help bring about a "spiritual revival" in America. It can also be argued that Reagan's unusual rapport with the public changed expectations of how a president should perform, that a principal duty is to catch the public mood and to offer rhetorical leadership, a duty that his immediate successor was unable to execute satisfactorily. Since Reagan a substantial literature has arisen on the "public presidency" and the functions of presidential rhetoric.[25]

While an ability to engage with and influence the public mood can be a powerful tool of leadership, some scholars have been uneasy about the presidential use of rhetoric and symbolism, especially when deployed by Ronald Reagan. It has been argued that he tended to substitute image for substance, that he made the presidency a branch of show business and in so doing distracted attention from serious issues. Michael Schaller, for example, argued that the "trivialization of political discourse was another legacy of the Reagan years."[26] Even authors who suggested that on balance the positive outweighed the negative in the Reagan years tended to concede that his style served to blank out a dark side of American life. Reagan's inveterate optimism, suggested Collins, shielded him from confrontation with some of the unwelcome realities of his time, such as rising economic inequality or AIDS.[27]

Authors who argued that Reagan's greatest qualities were his capacity to personify American myths and his ability to communicate were often raising questions about his legacy. These attributes were essentially personal, and go a long way toward explaining his popularity and such successes as Reagan can claim for his administration. As Godfrey Hodgson points out, Reagan possessed a "strangely original but effective personality," one that, among other things, allowed him "to articulate the deep undertows of national emotion." But personal qualities are not readily transferable. Dan Rather suggests that Reagan "changed our understanding of what a president is and should be," but a president who tries to model himself on Reagan has a hard and perhaps impossible act to follow. Some of the essays in this volume turn on Reagan's unique personality, as well as the values that were intimately linked to it.

Several authors here suggest the ambiguous or brittle nature of the Reagan legacy. Gil Troy talks about "the Reagan Revolution's powerful cultural resonance," though, as Stephen Tuck shows, the resonance had its limits. Tuck points out that it was African American artists who were reorientating national popular culture, and even if the conservatism in national politics put the national civil rights groups on the defensive, they continued to fight, sometimes successfully on particular issues, and there was extensive civil-rights-related activity at grassroots level. The era was not wholly defined by Ronald Reagan.

And even granted the resonance of Reaganism, whether it was a mostly beneficial force can be questioned. As Gil Troy notes, at the end of the 1980s many Americans may have believed that American strength and pride had been "restored," but the restoration was "more imaginary than real," evocative of the gleaming urban gentrification projects of the era that hid rather than solved serious social problems. Many of the forces that Reagan encouraged, while promoting a long economic boom, were also social solvents, so that Reaganism "helped spawn a new, sprawling, often selfish, deeply individualistic society." In this perspective, the function of rhetoric was to camouflage such unappealing tendencies. Niels Bjerre-Poulsen too is intrigued by the mythology surrounding Reagan, in his case by the way in which conservatives have tried to use it to establish hegemony over national memory, to replace Franklin Roosevelt with Reagan as the twentieth-century icon. Part of the drive behind this commemorative crusade, he finds, was rooted in conservative frustration with the belittling image of Reagan found in the academic literature. The complex irony of this determined memorializing endeavor is that it requires conservatives to overlook several untoward aspects of the Reagan record, to forget that several of them were excoriating Reagan by the end of his presidency, and that Americans in any case are more likely to remember Reagan as a symbol of national pride rather than as the font of conservatism. As he points out, Reagan may have become a popular conservative, but there is little evidence that his popularity was owed to his conservatism.

Other contributors to this volume too imply that Reagan's record may not bear too close an inspection if conservatives want to iconize him. Iwan Morgan discusses the incoherence of Reaganomics, as the administration tacked in different directions in different years, sometimes undoing what had been done before. The economic growth of the 1980s, he argues, was owed less to Reagan's vaunted "supply-side" experiment than to a particular mix of monetary and fiscal policies. President Clinton later secured greater economic success by reversing Reaganomics while George W. Bush's attempt to resurrect Reagan's economic policies has had worrying consequences. In short, even during Reagan's presidency Reaganomics did not work as intended, and has stored up long-term problems for the American economy. Dominic Sandbrook emphasizes the role of contingency in Reagan's rise, which owed more to chance than to a rising conservative tide, and moreover he failed to secure many of his stated objectives. Only in retrospect has the Reagan era become a conservative golden age.

Reagan may have campaigned against big government, but, as Peter Bourne's essay implies, in transforming the drug problem from a public health issue to one of law and order, his drug policy served to enhance the law enforcement structures of federal and state governments. Joel Aberbach adds the perspective of a political scientist, and argues that the "administrative presidency" that Reagan developed, furthering his priorities through his appointing power and through rewriting regulations, can be readily undone by his successors. George W. Bush may have used Reagan as a model, though his lack of Reagan's personal qualities may help to explain the difficulties he ran into during his second term with Congress and the courts, not to mention with public opinion. Robert Mason too emphasizes the limited nature of the Reagan legacy. He shows that even a popular and politically highly skilled president could not make much of a difference to the long-term strength of his party, could not bring about the political realignment he yearned for. With Reagan's departure conflict and factionalism among Republicans mounted again, and the popularity that his sunny optimism had imparted to the party was eroded.

Reagan's personal qualities may not be transferable, but his popularity has risen rather than diminished with time. If Reagan's sunny image has tended to eclipse the dark side of the 1980s, these essays do indicate how it did affect the course of American politics. The Republican Party may not have benefited from a major electoral realignment, but it and the larger political environment in which it operated did change. Some of the significant changes, these essays suggest, came during or after the Reagan presidency. Thus, as Dominic Sandbrook emphasizes, Reagan was elected in the first place not because a right-wing revival was sweeping all before it, but because the opposition was discredited and divided. The upsurge in support for Reaganism came later. Reagan is remembered more fondly by his countrymen than his soul mate Margaret Thatcher is by hers because in the United States alone sociodemographic and cultural forces toward the end of the twentieth century served to strengthen the political right. Bjerre-Poulsen points out that Reagan vitally contributed to this process, helping to convince many conservative activists that they could become the mainstream. Daniel Williams examines Reagan's relationship with a key constituency on the right. He shows that while Reagan did not provide the Christian right with much in terms of substance, his approbation did serve to energize it, opening the way for its advancement into the Republican Party in the late 1980s and 1990s. (Peter Bourne notes that in his drugs policy Reagan did reach beyond symbolic gestures to this constituency.) Previous studies have discussed Reagan's appeal to other segments of the new right-wing formation. Earl and Merle Black, for example, concluded that the realignment of southern white voters in the 1980s was largely attributable to the Reagan presidency, and "made possible the Republicans' congressional breakthrough in the 1990s."[28] Thus if Reagan failed to secure the kind of electoral realignment he dreamed of, he did nonetheless help to move the Republican party to the right, in the process pulling the hapless Democrats toward the center.

Lou Cannon presciently observed: "Politically, Reaganism was a time bomb with a delayed fuse."[29] The real Republican breakthrough did not come until 1994, with the party's historic electoral victories in both houses of Congress, and opinions differ on how far the Reagan era contributed to this outcome. The party's belated success, after all, owed something to events in the 1990s. Yet, as already indicated, some of the essays in this volume reinforce certain earlier studies in suggesting that Reagan paved the way for it. The drive by Newt Gingrich to make the Republicans the majority party in the House, as Mason shows, owed something to his frustrations with the unaggressive party-building efforts of the Reagan administration. Further, as other scholars have pointed out, the Reaganites had introduced radical notions of Social Security and pension reform, and while their failure to effect these disappointed right-wing groups they also incited them to new drives, and this neoconservative mobilization had some impact on the 1994 midterm elections, on the centrist policies of the Clinton administration, on the welfare reform of 1996, and on George W. Bush's plans for changing the pension system.[30] Reagan, then, helped to make right-wing ideas respectable and to put them on the national agenda, and his transformation into an icon served to invigorate the conservative elements in the Republican party.

The success of Reagan in energizing conservative and Christian right activists, despite his failure to deliver many of their objectives at the time, is again testimony to his remarkable personality. As Hodgson argues, it was less his championing of specific policies as his ability to articulate and to personify a profound aversion to contemporary liberalism, a liberalism that seemed to betray an elite disdain for traditional America, which drew many Americans to him. His personality was one of the weapons he deployed in seeking to overcome the fragmented nature of the polity that he inherited. Some of these essays help to explain how he adapted to that political system in which party organization on its own could no longer impose much coherence. Reagan's personal popularity often exceeded his approval rating, and he could use it to try to bend other branches of government to his will. He may not always have been successful in this, but his television performances before the nation were often designed to mobilize popular pressure on the Democratic majority in the House of Representatives. In his remarkable first year in particular, when his popularity was boosted by his feisty response to an assassination attempt and his flinty reaction to the strike by the air traffic controllers, Congress was wary of crossing him.

Aberbach too explores the Reagan answer to divided government. The administrative presidency was a way of by-passing an uncooperative Congress. Previous studies have examined Reagan's attempt to further his political priorities by appointing conservatives to office, especially in the judiciary but also in executive agencies. Aberbach shows that loyalty to Reagan and his ideas was a major consideration in appointments throughout the government, and also finds that senior civil servants tended to play a diminished role in policy-formation. Rulemaking also became an active concern, serving to reduce the autonomy of executive agencies and enhance control from the White House. Reflections of these administrative techniques can also be found in Peter Bourne's essay. In those parts of the bureaucracy dealing with drugs, appointees had to be ideologically right and they drew up regulations in accordance with the moral perspective of the Christian right. Reagan's amiable persona, perhaps, allowed him to place right-wingers through the executive and judicial branches of government who often did not share his disarming charm. Where a strong party system had once helped administrations overcome the constitutional checks and balances laid down by the Founding Fathers, Ronald Reagan relied on his charisma, his power of appointment, and the White House's control over bureaucratic rulemaking.

Reagan's distinctive personality and convictions were perhaps even more important in foreign than domestic affairs, and arguably explain why the former was the scene of his greatest triumph. While fault has been found, for example, with Reagan's policies toward Latin America, not to mention the huge embarrassment of the Iran–Contra affair, his rise in recent historiography owes much to the credit he has been accorded for his part in bringing about a peaceful conclusion to the Cold War. Essays in this volume corroborate that judgment. Presidents have greater opportunity to pursue their own agendas in foreign policy, where Congress and the courts, and perhaps interest groups too, are less obtrusive. The weaknesses in the Soviet system and the fortuitous succession of Mikhail Gorbachev to the Soviet premiership, of course, were essential ingredients in the historic events of the late 1980s, but so too was Ronald Reagan. Political decisions by political leaders, as Jack Matlock says, were critical in the dynamics that produced the end of the Cold War, and part of this, as Simon Head argues, was Reagan's fervent belief in his ability to make a personal breakthrough. Matlock reports Reagan's keen attention to learning about the psychology of the Soviet leaders; Head underlines his vindication over such experts as Henry Kissinger who ridiculed the idea that a president could personally overcome the ideological divide with the Soviets. As their essays show, it was the particular characteristics possessed by Ronald Reagan, his immunity to Cold War conventional wisdom, his optimism in the future, his vision of a nuclear-free world, his confidence in communication and in his own ability to persuade and to negotiate, and, not least, his capacity to carry most of his people with him that made possible his historic engagement with the Soviet leadership. Any other American politician who might have been elected president in the 1980s arguably could not have carried off such a coup.

Reagan's high rating in recent public opinion polls probably owes more to his reputation for restoring American prestige in the world and his part in ending the Cold War than to an informed understanding of his domestic record. Neither Reagan's seductive personality nor his administrative presidency was readily transferable to his successors. Historians and political scientists have paid homage to his "legacy," though it may be questioned how resilient it is. Reagan's role in ending the Cold War certainly deserves respectful examination, although, as he was the first to insist, he did not bear sole responsibility. Reagan perhaps slowed the long-term growth of government—after he had increased federal spending to pay for his defence build-up—and helped create those conditions that allowed Bill Clinton in 1996 to say that "the era of big government is over."[31] Yet his strongest presidential admirer George W. Bush has been perceived as resurrecting a form of "big government conservatism." Reagan helped inaugurate an era of low taxes, though, as Morgan shows, his example proved an inadequate fiscal model for his successors. Hodgson emphasizes Reagan's personal, indeed "unique," qualities, but personal qualities fade or die with the person. It may be that Reagan's example has served to make personality even more central to the American way of conducting politics. He revived and embodied a populistic streak in American politics, conveying a sense that he was one of the people, an "everyman," poised against a distrusted political establishment. This was part of his legacy. Other presidential candidates, from Bill Clinton to George W. Bush, have not been shy about parading their folksy credentials, although whether personality should be so central to the American political process is open to question.

Reagan could claim honorable legacies, but it is not clear that he provided Americans with a long-term model of governance. Perhaps he did something to restore American morale, but this appears to have dissipated very quickly during the one-term presidency of his successor. During the presidential campaign of 1992, there were times when the candidates of the two major parties trailed a third-party candidate able to exploit the public's lack of confidence in their political representatives. In April 1995, when another highly personable president occupied the White House, 74 percent of Americans declared themselves "dissatisfied with the way things are going in this country."[32] Perhaps the rosy remembrance of Reagan means that no successor can match up, that his fabled optimism has indirectly spawned a kind of public pessimism that magnifies rather than hides the weaknesses in the American system of politics.

Notes

1. Robert K. Murray and Tim H. Blessing, *Greatness in the White House: Rating the Presidents,* second ed. (University Park: Penn State University Press, 1994), 79–91.
2. Michael Schaller, *Reckoning with Reagan: America and its President in the 1980s* (New York: Oxford University Press, 1992), 58.
3. Ibid., 181.
4. Lou Cannon, *President Reagan: The Role of a Lifetime* (New York: Public Affairs, 2000 [slightly updated edition of 1991 book]).
5. Haynes Johnson, *Sleepwalking through History: America in the Reagan Years* (New York: Norton, 1991).
6. Gallup Brain, http://brain.gallup.com/content.
7. Quoted in Johann Hari, "Ship of Fools," *Independent* (London), July 13, 2007, *Extra*, 4–5.
8. W. Elliot Brownlee and Hugh Davis Graham, eds., *The Reagan Presidency: Pragmatic Conservatism and its Legacies* (Lawrence: University of Kansas Press, 2003).
9. The term had been used before. In a 1990 collection of essays, Dilys M. Hill and Phil Williams wrote: "Reagan was a pragmatic conservative, a President who combined strong conviction with a profound realisation of the need for compromise and flexibility." Dilys M. Hill, Raymond A. Moore, and Phil Williams, eds., *The Reagan Presidency: An Incomplete Revolution?* (Basingstoke: Macmillan, 1990), 9.
10. Brownlee and Graham, *Reagan Presidency,* 225.
11. Robert M. Collins, *Transforming America: Politics and Culture during the Reagan Years* (New York: Columbia University Press, 2007), chapter 2.
12. John Ehrman, *The Eighties: America in the Age of Reagan* (New Haven: Yale University Press, 2005), 206.
13. Richard Reeves, *President Reagan: The Triumph of Imagination* (New York: Simon & Schuster, 2005).
14. Collins, *Transforming America,* 236, 255.
15. John Patrick Diggins, *Ronald Reagan: Fate, Freedom, and the Making of History* (New York: Norton, 2007), 397.
16. Ibid., 13, 430.
17. Diary entry, January 28, 1982, in *Ronald Reagan, An American Life: The Autobiography* (New York: Simon and Schuster, 1990), 316.
18. Richard Neustadt, *Presidential Power and the Modern Presidents: The Politics of Leadership from Roosevelt to Reagan* (New York: Free Press, 1990), 273.

19. Gil Troy, *Morning in America: How Ronald Regan Invented the 1980s* (Princeton, NJ: Princeton University Press, 2005), 5.
20. Collins, *Transforming America*, 237.
21. Reeves, *President Reagan*, 475, 477.
22. Alonzo L. Hamby, *Liberalism and its Challengers: F.D.R. to Bush*, second ed. (New York: Oxford University Press, 1992), 385, 388.
23. For example, see Cannon, *President Reagan*, 746; Collins, *Transforming America*, 237.
24. John K. White, "The Reagan Persona and the American Value Consensus." In Richard S. Conley, ed., *Reassessing the Reagan Presidency* (Lanham MD: University Press of America, 2003), 43.
25. For example, see Jeffrey K. Tulis, *The Rhetorical Presidency* (Princeton: Princeton University Press, 1987); Gary L. Gregg, *The Presidential Republic: Executive Representation and Deliberative Democracy* (Lanham MD: Rowman and Littlefield, 1997).
26. Schaller, *Reckoning*, 181.
27. Collins, *Transforming America*, 133.
28. Brownlee and Graham, *Reagan Presidency*, 13n.
29. Cannon, *President Reagan*, 756.
30. Brownlee and Graham, *Reagan Presidency*.
31. M.J. Heale, *Twentieth-Century America: Politics and Power in the United States, 1900–2000* (London: Arnold, 2004), 214.
32. Derek Bok, *The State of the Nation: Government and the Quest for a Better Society* (Cambridge MA: Harvard University Press, 1996), 1.

Index

abortion, 135, 136, 141–42, 143, 159–60, 237
Adolescent Family Life Act, 143–44
African American protest under Reagan, 119–33
  civil rights movement, 121
  employment discrimination, 126–28
  female leadership in, 123
  gay liberation, 131–32
  grassroots protest, 123
  hip hop as manifestation of, 119–22
  historiography of, 121
  residential discrimination, 129–30
  South African apartheid, 123–25
AIDS epidemic, 131–32
Anderson, John, 181
Anderson, Martin, 102–103, 140
Andropov, Yuri, 61–62, 63, 84, 85, 87
Anti-Ballistic-Missile Treaty (ABM) of 1972, 59, 87
Arrington, Richard, 127
Atkinson, Eugene, 155
Atwater, Lee, 154, 164

Baker, Howard, 20, 141
Baker, James, 107, 108, 165
Bambaataa, Afrika, 121
Bauer, Gary, 142, 146
Bennett, William F., 237
Blackwell, Morton, 159
Blair, Tony, 186
Blinder, Alan, 112
Boone, Pat, 137
Bradley, Bill, 186
Brezhnev, Leonid, 59, 61, 63, 66–67, 83, 84
Brinkley, Alan, 230

Brock, William E., III, 153
Brooks, Genevieve, 129–30
Brown, Archie, 65
Brown, Edmund G. ("Pat"), 29
Brown, Gordon, 186
Brownlee, W. Elliott, 9, 250
Buckley, William F., Jr., 22, 209, 250
budget deficit, federal, 102, 104, 107, 113
Bush, George H.W., 6, 67, 94, 113, 164, 166
  attitude to religious right, 142, 145
  distances himself from Reagan, 212, 233
Bush, George W., 2, 8, 94
  impact of presidency on Reagan historiography, 230
  as Reagan disciple, 19–21, 102, 113, 191, 203–204, 220–21

Calabresi, Steven G., 218
Cannon, Lou, 23–24, 234, 239, 249
Carlucci, Frank, 73
Carter, Jimmy, 1, 4–5, 182
  anticipates Reagan policies, 187
  Cold War policies of, 59, 63, 66–67
  drugs policies of, 44, 47
  economic policies of, 103
  religious right and, 137
  See also under elections, 1976 and 1980
Carter, Rosalynn, 49
Casey, William, 86
Cazavos, Lauro, 164
Chernenko, Konstantin, 61, 63, 84
Chernyaev, Anatoly, 69, 240
Chuck D., 121, 122

Churchill, Winston, 215, 217–18
civil rights
   Reagan and affirmative action, 127–28, 163
   See also African American protest
Civil Service Reform Act (1978), 198
Clark, William, 89
Clinton, Bill, 2, 20, 128, 186
   Reagan legacy and, 27, 112, 186, 203, 233
cocaine, 51–52
Cold War, 1, 2
   1984 as turning point in U.S. policy, 88, 96
   Daniloff espionage controversy, 69
   deployment of INF missiles, 60, 61–62
   "evil empire" speech (Reagan), 88
   Geneva summits (1985), 64, 65–68
   historiography of, 240, 252
   idea of U.S. "victory," 71, 73, 75–76, 96–97
   impact of Gorbachev, 65
   Korean airliner shot down, 61, 85
   Moscow summit (1988), 73
   political issue in 1980, 4, 59, 152
   Reagan arms buildup (1981–83), 84
   Reagan's approach to, 57–99, 138
   religious right and, 144, 145
   Reykjavik summit, 69–70, 90–94
   Strategic Defense Initiative, 61, 70, 82, 85–96 *passim*
Collins, Robert, 102, 250, 253
Committee on the Present Danger, 83
Congress
   and Reagan Revolution, 7, 8
   and Reaganomics, 104
   and War on Drugs, 54
   See also under particular elections
Congressional Black Caucus, 123, 124, 125
conservatism, 119, 153
   in 1990s, 186
   Conservative Political Action conference (1974), 37
   in federal bureaucracy, 197–98
   historiography of, 230
   intellectual vitality by late 1970s, 181, 196
   political fortunes of, since 1980, 2–3, 8, 39, 152, 157, 158, 235
   See also Thatcher, Margaret; *See also under particular policy areas and individuals*
Conservative Opportunity Society, 165–66
Conyers, John, 123
Coolidge, Calvin, 1
"crack" cocaine problem, 52
Crowe, William, 93

Daniloff, Nicholas, 69
Darman, Richard, 156
Davies, Gareth, 250
de Gaulle, Charles, 25
de Havilland, Olivia, 35
de Klerk, F.W., 125
Deaver, Michael, 24
Deficit Reduction Act of 1984, 107
Dellums, Ron, 123, 125
Democratic Leadership Council, 186
Democratic Party, 54, 110, 120, 144, 151–66 *passim*, 182, 253
Deukmejian, George, 184
Diggins, John Patrick, 155, 238, 251–52
Dobrynin, Anatoly, 63–64, 85, 87, 240
Dobson, James, 146
Dolan, John T., 153, 158
Dole, Elizabeth, 161
Dole, Robert, 128
Dowdy, Wayne, 155
drug abuse policy
   during 1970s, 41, 43–44
   race and, 53–54
   under Reagan, 41–56
D'Souza, Dinesh, 157–58, 210
Duberstein, Kenneth, 20

Eagleburger, Lawrence, 86
Economic Recovery Tax Act (ERTA), 106
economy
   centrality to Reagan agenda, 101, 102–103
   collapse of Keynesianism, 180
   exchange rates, 110–111
   the "great expansion" post-1980, 101, 112

INDEX

income distribution under Reagan, 108–109
   performance in 1970s, 3, 101
   political issue in 1980, 4
   Program for Economic Recovery (1981), 103
   recession of 1981–83, 103
   savings rate under Reagan, 109–10
   trade performance under Reagan, 110–11
   See also budget deficit, federal; inflation; interest rates; monetary policy; productivity, economic; taxation policy; unemployment
Edwards, George C., 211
Ehrman, John, 251
Eisenhower, Dwight D., 1, 8
elections
   1966, 29
   1972, 195
   1976, 176
   1980, 2–7, 14n16, 59, 139–40, 153, 155, 160, 179–80, 182
   1982, 8
   1984, 3, 36, 62, 64, 88, 105, 144–45, 156–57, 160, 162, 165, 231
   1986, 8, 157
   1988, 64, 120, 145, 164
   1992, 166, 186
   1994, 2
   2008, 2, 221
   "critical elections" theory, 39
energy crisis of 1970s, 4
environmental policy under Reagan, 201–202

Fahrenkopf, Frank, Jr., 156
Falwell, Jerry, 135–46 *passim*
Family Research Council, 146
Ferraro, Geraldine, 162
Fischer, Beth, 84–85
Fitzgerald, Frances, 96
Flynn, Errol, 35
Ford, Betty, 136
Ford, Gerald R., 1, 5, 6, 136, 230
Fort Apache: The Bronx, 130
Free South Africa Movement, 123
Friedman, Milton, 239

gay rights, 131–32, 136
gender gap, 160–62
Gerald, Gil, 132
Gergen, David, 203
Gingrich, Newt, 2, 164, 165, 166, 212
Giuliani, Rudolph, 48
Goldwater, Barry, 30, 252
GOPAC, 165
government
   growth of, 2–3, 185
   "permanent campaign" and, 27
   popular attitudes to, 5, 152
   Reagan and, 7, 21, 45, 46, 101, 130
Gorbachev, Mikhail, 1, 57, 63, 67–76, 84–97 *passim*, 240
   elected Soviet general secretary, 65
   proposes elimination of nuclear weapons, 68
   United Nations speech (1988), 74
   visits U.S. in 1987, 72
Gordievsky, Oleg, 77n11
Gorsuch, Ann Buford, 202
Graham, Billy, 135, 138
Graham, Hugh Davis, 9, 250
Grandmaster Flash, 119
Great Society, 7, 119, 252
Greenspan, Alan, 112
Greider, William, 107
Gromyko, Andrei, 61, 64, 71, 85

Haig, Alexander, 77n13, 85, 89
Hamby, Alonzo, 234–35
Harding, Warren, 1
Heath, Edward, 176, 178, 179
Heston, Charlton, 35
Himmelfarb, Gertrude, 218
Hispanic voters, 164
Hodgson, Godfrey, 254
Hofstadter, Richard, 194
Hooks, Benjamin, 121
Hutchinson, Earl Ofari, 132

Ice, T., 122
Ice Cube, 131
incarceration rates, under Reagan, 53, 122
inflation
   under Carter, 4, 101, 103
   under Reagan, 104–105
interest groups, 199
interest rates, 104

Intermediate-Range Nuclear Forces
  negotiations (INF), 61, 67–68
INF treaty (1987), 71–73
Iran-Contra scandal, 8, 70, 145, 203, 204, 212
Iranian hostage crisis, 4, 20, 30, 93

Jackson, Henry "Scoop," 83
Jackson, Rev. Jesse, 120
Jacob, John, 128
James, Pendleton, 196–97
Jenkins, Philip, 4
Johnson, Lyndon B., 1, 5, 8, *See also* Great Society
Jones, Charles O., 155, 193

Kamburoeski, Michael, 214
Kennedy, D. James, 141
Kennedy, Edward M. ("Ted"), 8, 182
Kennedy, John F., 1, 83, 230
King, Martin Luther, Jr., 120, 124
Kinnock, Neil, 186
Kissinger, Henry, 90, 95
Kirkpatrick, Jeane, 179
Klein, Joe, 27
Koop, C. Everett, 142
Kvitsinsky, Yuly, 61

Laffer, Arthur, 107
LaHay, Tim, 144–45
Landy, Marc, 3
Leffler, Melvyn, 96, 97
Leland, Mickey, 126
Ligachev, Yegor, 71, 73–74
Lincoln, Abraham, 188
Lindsay, Lawrence, 101
Luce, Henry, 22
Lutuli, Albert J., 124

MacDonald, Ian, 52–53
Mandela, Nelson, 126
marijuana, 56n11
  as central focus of War on Drugs, 45, 49
  NAS report on (1982), 50
Matlock, Jack
  briefs Reagan on Gorbachev "Theses," 72–73
McAteer, Ed, 140
McCain, John, 21, 28n3

McKinley, William, 232
Mecklenburg, Marjory, 142
media and Reagan, *See* Reagan, and media
Meese, Edwin, III, 46, 47, 53, 146, 196–97
Michel, Robert, 156, 164
Milkis, Sidney, 3
Moe, Terry, 192, 193–94, 202
Mondale, Walter, 6, 105, 157, 186, 231
monetary policy, 103, 105, 181
  "supply-side" economics, 107–108, 113
Moore, Stephen, 101–102
Moral Majority, *See* Falwell, Jerry
Morris, Edmund, 232
Moyers, Bill, 6–7
Moynihan, Daniel Patrick, 157

Nathan, Richard P., 196, 197
National Association for the Advancement of Colored People (NAACP), 121
National Association of Religious Broadcasters, 142
National Urban League, 128
Neustadt, Richard, 192, 199, 202, 203
Nitze, Paul, 61, 83–84, 86
Nixon, Richard M., 1, 3, 4, 5, 8, 14n14, 59, 83, 165, 233
  administrative approach of, 194–95, 197, 198
  drugs policies of, 41
Nofziger, Lyn, 164
Noonan, Peggy, 211
Norquist, Grover, 213–14, 219
North, Oliver, 145
nuclear weapons
  proliferation of, 58

O'Connor, Sandra Day, 142, 235
O'Neill, Thomas P. ("Tip"), 7, 54, 239

Packwood, Robert, 160
Patterson, James T., 9, 231, 236
  on the 1970s, 3
  on 1980 election, 6
Perle, Richard, 83, 86
Perot, H. Ross, 46, 253
Pierce, Charles, 120

Podhoretz, Norman, 184
Poindexter, John, 70
poverty, under Reagan, 108, 121
presidency
   Reagan's impact on, 26–27, 191–205
   regulatory reform, 200
presidential greatness, assessing, 3, 209–23
Presidential Power (Neustadt), 192
prison, *See* incarceration rates
productivity, economic
   under Reagan, 105, 106
Public Enemy, 121
Putin, Vladimir, 94

Ransby, Barbara, 126
Raspberry, William, 129
Reagan, Maureen, 36
Reagan, Michael, 232
Reagan, Nancy, 89, 234
   and War on Drugs, 49–50
Reagan, Ronald
   in 1980, 5–7, 35, 139–40, 179–80
   1982 London speech on Soviet decline, 94–95
   1983 letter to Andropov, 85, 89–90
   1984 speech on U.S.-Soviet relations, 62, 64, 85
   as actor in politics, 25, 29, 31
   apartheid and, 124–25
   Cold War policies of, 57–99
   as consensus politician, 184, 235
   as conviction politician, 8, 24, 35–37, 45, 94–95, 144, 159–60, 211, 234
   cultural agenda of, 236, 242
   death of, 188
   economic credo of, 106–107
   and FDR, 7, 39, 151, 252
   as "the Gipper," 33
   GOP and, 151–66
   as "great communicator," 23, 95
   gubernatorial record, 184
   hatred of nuclear weapons, 68, 89–91
   historical reputation of, 1–9, 13n5, 19, 39, 57, 184, 209–22, 229–44, 249–60
   inattention to detail, 81, 86
   innovative approach to administration, 191–205
   and media, 20, 21, 24–25, 26
   minority voters, 163
   Moscow visit (1988), 73
   political exit of, 22, 31, 37–38
   pre-presidential career, 22–23, 29, 33–37, 138, 179
   Reaganomics, legacy of, 112–14
   religious beliefs of, 36, 138, 141
   rhetorical power of, 25–26, 31, 33–34, 234
   Supreme Court nominations of, 142
   Thatcher, and, 175–88
   view of Gorbachev, 65–66, 67
   War on Drugs, 41–55
   work-ethic of, 30–31
   See also particular policy areas and administration staffers
Reagan Presidency, The (Brownlee and Graham), 9
Reed, Ralph, 146
Reeves, Richard, 20–21, 238
Regan, Donald, 108, 231
Reich, Robert, 186
religion
   evangelical voters in 1980, 5–6
   prayer in schools, 143, 160
   Reagan and, 36, 135–46
Republican Party, 137, 144, 146, 253
   1980 gains, 7
   black voters and, 163–64
   political fortunes since 1980, 2, 8, 187, 257
   under Reagan, 151–66
Roberts, Paul Craig, 107–108
Robertson, Pat, 145
Robinson, Randall, 124
Rockman, Bert, 196
Rollins, Edward, 156
Ronald Reagan Legacy Project, 213–14, 219
Roosevelt, Franklin D., 1, 7, 219, 230, 252
Roosevelt, Theodore, 216
Ruckelshaus, William D., 202
Rusher, William, 158

Sakharov, Andrei, 93
Schaller, Michael, 255
Schlesinger, Arthur M., Jr., 210
Schweiker, Richard, 143

Scowcroft, Brent, 81
Shevardnadze, Eduard, 65, 73, 76, 93
Shultz, George, 61, 62, 64, 65, 71, 76, 85–94 *passim*
    on Reagan's nuclear abolitionism, 90
Skowronek, Stephen, 238
Smith, William French, 46
Souder, Mark, 217
South Africa, apartheid in, 123–25
Southern Baptist Convention, 140
Soviet Union
    impact of defense spending on, 58, 63, 71
    invades Afghanistan, 59
    "Star Wars," *See* Strategic Defense Initiative
Stein, Herbert, 106
Stockman, David, 46, 106–107, 184, 185, 231
Strategic Arms Limitation Treaty ("SALT"), 59, 83
Strategic Arms Limitation Treaty II ("SALT II"), 59, 87, 138–39
Strategic Arms Reduction Talks ("START"), 61, 72, 93–94
Strategic Defense Initiative ("SDI"), 61, 68, 70, 82, 85–96 *passim*
Strategic Offensive Reduction Treaty (2002), 94
Sugarhill Gang, 119
Sununu, John, 233
"supply-side" economics, *See under* monetary policy

Tax Reform Act of 1986, 108
taxation policy under Reagan, 103, 108
Thatcher, Margaret, 71, 90, 93
    appraises Reagan's contribution, 175
    as conviction politician, 176
    domestic reforms of, 178
    limited popularity of, 183
    meetings with Reagan, 175, 176–77
    Reagan on, 175
Thomas, Clarence, 128
Tobin, James, 102
Troy, Gil, 251
Tsongas, Paul, 186
Ture, Norman, 108
Turner, Carlton, 46, 47, 50, 52
Tutu, Desmond, 124

unemployment
    under Carter, 4, 101
    under Reagan, 103–104, 105–106
Union of Soviet Socialist Republics (USSR), *See* Soviet Union
United States Attorneys Office
    politicization under Reagan, 48

Vance, Cyrus, 84
Vander Jagt, Guy, 153
Viguerie, Richard, 146, 221
Volcker, Paul, 11, 103, 105, 181, 182, 241

War on Drugs, *See* drug abuse policy
Watt, James, 142
Weber, Vin, 165–66
Weinberger, Caspar, 73, 86, 87, 91
West, Cornel, 120
Weyrich, Paul, 142, 146, 159
Wilentz, Sean, 238
Will, George F., 213, 220
Williams, Juan, 124
Wills, Garry, 34
Wirthlin, Richard, 154
women's rights, 139
Wright, James, 165

Yakovlev, Alexander, 74
Yellen, Janet, 112
"yuppies," 159

Printed in the USA
CPSIA information can be obtained
at www.ICGtesting.com
CBHW030829121224
18870CB00003B/6